Spirituality in Practice

Spirituality in Practice

Dr. Akbar Husain
Professor, Department of Psychology
Aligarh Muslim University, Aligarh

Dr. Ruchi Singh
Department of Psychology
Aligarh Muslim University, Aligarh

The Readers Paradise
New Delhi - 110002

Spirituality in Practice
by Akbar Husain & Ruchi Singh

First Edition in India, 2022

ISBN - 978-93-85958-17-5

Published by
The Readers Paradise
103, 4787/23, Ansari Road, Daryaganj,
New Delhi - 110002
011-23246222, 9811197091, 9312220441
thereadersparadisesales@gmail.com

Price Rs. 895.00

Pages : 258 | Paper - 80gsm | Size - 5.5x8.5

Type Setting by
Sanya Computers

Printed in India
Balaji Offset

About the Authors

Dr. Akbar Husain is a Professor in the Department of Psychology, and the Dean, Faculty of Social Sciences, Aligarh Muslim University, Aligarh. He received his Ph.D. Degree in Psychology from the Aligarh Muslim University, Aligarh (INDIA) in 1981. He was awarded D.Litt. degree in Psychology in 2015 for his work on Explorations and Applications of Spirituality in Psychology. He has over thirty eight years of teaching and research experience. He has successfully supervised 10 M. Phil. dissertations and 30 Ph.D. theses at the Aligarh Muslim University, Aligarh. He has authored, co-authored and edited 35 books, and contributed 240 research papers, theoretical articles and book chapters in National and International Journals and Books. Prof. Husain has attended and presented papers, gave Invited Talk/Lecture and Keynote Addresses in the several National and International Conferences and Seminars. He was Editor of the Journal of the Indian Academy of Applied Psychology (2002-2005) and Journal of Educational Research, University of Malaya (2009). Prof. Husain is also reviewer of various National and International Journals of Psychology. He has standardized numerous psychological tests and completed four research projects. He is a Life Member Annual Member of Various National and International Associations. Prof. Husain has visited several contries for attending conferences and teaching assignments. In recent years he has been involved in conducting the researches on various topics such as spiritual values/virtues, spiritual practices, spiritual experiences, spiritual fitness, spiritual personality, spiritual support, spiritual distress, etc. related to the area of Spiritual Psychology. In addition to this his current areas of research are: Health Psychology, Counseling Psychology, and Positive Psychology.

E-mails: profakbar6@gmail.com, a.husain.py@amu.ac.in

Dr. Ruchi Singh is a UGC Post Doctoral Fellow in the Department of Psychology, Aligarh Muslim University, Aligarh. She received her Ph.D. Degree in Psychology from the Aligarh Muslim University, Aligarh (INDIA) in 2016. Her field of specialization is Spiritual Psychology. She has published a number of theoretical and empirical articles in refereed journals of Psychology. Besides she has standardized few psychological tests. She has also attended and presented papers in National and International Conferences/Seminars of Psychology.

Email: ruchisinghamu1989@gmail.com

'Haif, khuda beech mein aa gaya / varna maine toh asraar tasawwuf ka jaan liya tha' —'Alack, god came from nowhere/ otherwise, I was close to understanding the mysteries of spirituality.'

Yaas Yagana Changezi

"Talk to me not of god/I need no fabrication / Let me look for divinity among humans/ To me, this is god; this is spirituality/ For, I know that god is a monomania and spirituality is multidimensional/ Then, why should I embrace the former at the cost of the latter…?

Pablo Neruda

My spirituality came from God.
Spirituality is greater than any school of thought.
Nothing is more purifying on earth than spirituality.
Spirituality is present from birth to death.

Akbar Husain

Spirituality is the essence of human life.
Only spirituality converts a living being into a transcendental human being.

Ruchi Singh

Contents

Preface

Everything in existence is surrounded by spirituality. Human beings with limited knowledge should try to know his nature. Hinduism is guided and practiced by own philosophy. A human being can know and experience him through different facets of human nature. This book is an attempt towards understanding the aspects of human spirituality.

Spirituality and Yoga has been accepted as the treasurers of Indic civilization. These have been practiced by people who followed religious/spiritual beliefs in the uniform treatment of people belonging to different faiths, and belief that there is a single God. The common goal of both practices is the realization of Self and God-consciousness. Spirituality and Yoga are the exercises to approach inner seeking and the internal state of mind about which we are unaware. These exercises are important for becoming spiritual and to take on mystical and devotional paths in Hindu tradition through learning and knowledge.

Human spirituality realises the presence of God through various levels of God-consciousness. It is God who has put 'i-consciousness' in us. Human spirituality had always been towards nurturing nature and worshiping God. This is a greater truth towards ultimate realization. Spiritual practices enable us to proceed to the Divine and awaken our divine consciousness. God is worshipped for this and other worldly achievements. Spirituality maintains the natural law of harmony and peace. Spirituality is the universal life force which develops the wisdom of the third eye. Spirituality transcends the ego-bound senses of perception and action represented by individual. It cultivates energy, strength, intellect and spiritual progress.

Religious practices associated with spirituality occupy a high place in the Hindu tradition. If they are properly understood and practised then it can lead to harmony even in diverse groups. Spiritual practices assured the fullest development and satisfaction. It has proved that spiritual practices such as prayer, meditation, reading scriptures and yoga if they pursued with devotion are efficacious. These are potent to develop super-consciousness and leads higher levels of perfection till an individual reaches the ultimate goal. The goal of all spiritual practice is the rediscovery of true identity with Reality. Through pracising spirituality one can realises the identity of the *Jivatman* and *Paramatman*. Moreover, spiritual practices raises human cognitive psyche -mind, intellect, and consciousness; all of which are interwoven in the fabric of Creation.

An alternative approach to defining spirituality is suggested in this book as a natural phenomenon that is most centrally practicing and experiential in nature. This approach may be termed as analytical but is based on acronym which is manifested in cognitive, personality, and behavioral expressions. The practising aspects of religion-based spirituality itself can be conceptualized as consisting of experiences that have certain phenomenological qualities involving modifications in the operations of self and relative to normal modes of functioning which have an impact on thought, behavior, lifestyle, and personality.

This book contains ten chapters which cover the following aspects of spirituality: **Adhyatmikta, What is Spirituality?**, **Spirituality: A Right Path to Knowledge and Practice, Holistic Spirituality**, **Practising Aspects of Spirituality in Hinduism**, **Spirituality within Yoga**, **Ruhaniat**, **Spirituality at**

the Workplace, Spiritual Resources as the means for Healthy Living, and Spiritual Practices for the Inner Transformation. Spirituality helps in developing intuitive and imaginative power, and these imply seeking and delving deep into the Self. Spiritual practices are the beginning of a long journey into the mind and beyond when learning is initiated each day. Various forms of practical spiritualities such as "world-oriented," "Hindu-oriented," "people-oriented" "God-oriented," "nature-oriented" and "holistic" have been dicussed in this book.

Akbar Husain

Ruchi Singh

Chapter One

ADHYATMIKTA

"The Sanskrit equivalent word of spirituality is *Adhyatmikta*, which is obtained by combining the prefix *adhi* with the word *atman* (or self). It denotes subjectivity *(atmanam adhikrtya)* as well as *atmano visayakam jnanam* or the transcendental knowledge pertaining to the Self" (Dwivedi, 2015, p. 32).

Adhyatmikta is invaluable treasure of Indian culture, literature and language, music, dance, Hindu scriptures and sculpture. "Spirituality has been valued in the Indian culture from time immemorial, and it is no surprise that many innovations in the field of spirituality is originated in India" (Bhawuk, 2011, p. 25). "Hinduism attached so much importance to spirituality that it had made it the ultimate goal of life and attempted to visualize spirituality in all walks of life" (Dwivedi, 2015, p. 27).

Today, majority of us suffer from spiritual ailments which could be diagnosed as spiritual problems. This is because people became disconnected from the welfare of the humanity. Common perception is that religious people are more or less spiritual. Nowadays the most formidable challenge is how to maintain the spiritual life.

Adhyatmikta realizes the existence of God and follows the unity principle. *Adhyatmikta* is transcendent and transformative in nature. It is a process of personal transformation. In *Adhyatmikta* we study about the spiritual states of the person. In India we don't have contest between religious dogma and spirituality. Both believers and non-believers may have attitude towards spirituality. *Adhyatmikta* strengthen the spirit. Spiritual exercise like meditation helps to cope with spiritually lethargic boredom. *Adhyatmikta* is our spiritual nature made of *Atman, Dharma, Havan/homa, Yama, Atman-gyan, Tantra, Moksha, Indriyas, Karma, Tapas* and *Ananda.*

Atman (Soul)

We all accept that a living being is called 'living' when he possesses that conscious principle, known as '*Atman*'. In other words, until the atomic soul, energy of the eternally existing, blissful, knowledgeable Supreme Lord, remains in the body, it is identified as a person. By the existence of that principle, 'I' remains and by the absence of that principle, 'I' do not remain; that is my nature (means, I am a soul).

We differ in outer appearances, but within us is the soul which connects all. *Atman* is a part of God and is one of the highest levels of spiritual state. Meditation helps us to see the connectedness between soul and God. When the soul puts on an outer form of a human body, it is still a soul within and this soul is the same essence as our self.

Atman is connected with every part of the body. There is no doubt that we cannot see the soul. The soul is not visible to our physical eyes. We could see with our spiritual eye in meditation we would then recognize the consciousness within us. Meditation is the process of awareness where we realize our self as soul. Meditation is the process of realizing our inner connectedness. The soul (*Atman*) is eternal, it never born and never dies but only changes the human body after death. Death is only of the human body not of the soul because it is birth less and death less as well. As Lord Krishna says in the Bhagavad-Gita.....

na jayate mriyate va kadachin

nayam bhutva bhavita va na bhuyah

ajo nityah shashvato 'yam purano

na hanyate hanyamane uharire

(Bhagavad Gita, chapter 2,Verse 20)

The soul never takes birth and never dies at any of the time. Nor it comes into existence again when the new body is created. The soul is unborn, eternal, imperishable, and primeval and is undying. It is never destroyed even when the human body is destroyed (Dwivedi, 2015, p. 27). In the Bhagavad Gita, Lord Krishna also says in Chapter-2, verse 22 that- As one wears new garments after giving up old ones, in the same way, the soul giving up the old material bodies and accepts new ones (Dwivedi, 2015, p. 27).

According to the Bhagwad Gita, living entities are not part of the Supreme, but a part of His energy. We, the souls, are the servants of Krishna, eternally. In the seventh chapter of the Gita, Krishna explains that soul is a part of his potency. This means soul is servitor of Super-soul.

Dharma (Duty in life)

Adhyatmikta and *Dharma* are part and parcel of a Hindu's life. The concept of *Dharma* is normally considered as the righteous way of life. But it has a very wide range of meanings and the interpretation of *dharma* changes with a person's age, gender, class, conditions (contexts) and occupations etc, with a variety of meanings. *Dharma* is considered as duty in life without complaint to the common man. *Dharma* is the way of life which is accepted by the society and when it followed properly by the man it brings peace and prosperity to all of the society, this is the meaning of *dharma* to a knowledgeable person and *dharma* is the divine law which governs all of the human affairs to a devout Hindu. It is the established and accepted code of conduct of righteousness and good behaviour.

According to Anandamurti (2012), one who follows *dharma* should cultivate ten characteristics of *dharma* within the self. The first characteristic of *dharma* is *dharti* (patience). In the spiritual context, if one expects immediate results after starting the practice of *Tantra* that would not be realistic. Therefore, be patient. So the first characteristic of *dharma* is *dharti*. The second characteristic of *dharma* is *kshama* (forgiveness). Each and every action produces an opposite and equal reaction provided the unchanged three relative factors. But because of transformation from one state to another state, these three factors often change. Suppose someone has started doing some mischief by hitting you: certainly this action will have a reaction. For you, when time comes to take revenge, you do not express any reaction yourself. In this way, the continuity of the chain has been broken down by you. The point, at which the cycle of action and reaction stops because of your initiative, is known as forgiveness. The third aspect of *dharma* is *damah* (control). *Damah* is the state of achieving control over internal enemies - that is, debasing propensities like uncontrolled mind and desires. All the decisions in the life of a person should be taken by stable mind unaffected by emotions of attachment, fear and other worldly sensational cravings. The fourth is *asteya* literally means not to steal anything physically or mentally exhibited by the attributes like integrity and honesty. The person should believe in taking the ownership of the things only earned by him/her own self. The fifth characteristic of *dharma* is *shaucha* (cleaning) and this is of two types: external and internal. External cleanliness is that of body, clothes and surroundings. Internal cleanliness refers to the cleaning of mind and heart. The sixth feature of *dharma* is *indriya nigraha* (control over sensory organs). There are ten *indriyas* (sensory organs) five sensory (eyes, ear, nose, skin & tongue) and five motor (vocal cord, hands, legs, anus & genital). In the *dharmic* life the control over the sensory and motor organs is considered imperative. So, in the spiritual context one will have to exercise control of these organs. The seventh characteristic of *dharma* is *dhi* (benevolent intellect). If human intellect is not channelized well then it may becomes destructive; it exploits and corrupts society and, even it may become a demonic force. *Dhi* means intellect that helps to regenerate the society, which is beneficial not only for human beings but for all beings as well. The eighth characteristic of *dharma* is *vidya* (internal assimilation of external objectivities). It can be of two types: *vidya* and *avidya. Avidya* is mainly concerned with external life whereas *vidya* is concerned with internal life. On the one hand, *avidya* helps us to develop in the physical context; on the other hand, *vidya*, helps us to strive in attaining the liberation. So, both *vidya* and *avidya* will help human beings to achieve success in the physical and spiritual world. The ninth characteristic of *dharma* is *satyam* (truth). It is to be observed in our individual and collective lives. The tenth and final characteristic of *Dharma* is *akrodha* (non-anger). In the present day context, it is a very subtle propensity. We should not be guided by *krodha* or anger. It is very dangerous for the self and surrounding as well. One may show anger to stop unholy or anti-social activities done by sinful people in the society. That is known as "sentient anger".

Thus *dharma* is what maintains and supports life and universe. In Hinduism Dharmic duties of a Hindu follower are categorized into seven categories known as *Sapta Dharma.*

1) *Nitya dharma* consists of the duties conduct by a person in his daily life honestly and sincerely. According to Manusmriti there are five paths of dharma that are applicable to all of the human beings irrespective of their gender, social classes or caste (*varna*) and stage of life in their daily life, also known as '*samanya dharma*' or '*sadharana dharma*': *Ahimsa, Satya, Asteya, Soucha, Indriya-nigraha.* (Rao, 2012, p. 36). *Ahimsa,*

Satya and *Asteya* are three paths of *Yamas* (first step of the Raj Yoga of Patanjali).

2) *Sva dharma* means what is appropriate or right for an individual. There is a code of conduct for every person that is more appropriate for him or her. That is his *sva dharma*, may be translated as profession or vocation. It enables a person to develop a mode of conduct of his own, it also enables a person to develop his skills/ talent capacities to the fullest extent professionally- talent in sports, arts and music, etc. *Sva dharma* should not come into conflict with the other *dharma* followed by Muslims and Christians etc. *Sva dharma* determines the proper duties of specific groups according to their degree of participation in the *varna* and *asrama* system.

3) *Varna dharma* means class and *dharma* means duties, so *varna dharma* literally means the duties of the particular class. Hindu society consists of four *varnas*- *Brahman, Ksatriyas, Vaisyas and Sudras,* and each *varna* can be divided into a number of *jatis* or castes. Hindus not only divide the society into four classes but also assign particular social function to each class. That specific social function assigned to a *varna* (class) is called by *varna dharma* of that class.

Although the duties of these four *varnas* are not explicitly mentioned in the hymn of the *purusasukta*, but that's imagery which correlates each *varna* with a separate social body part, is used in the Manusmrti for the separation of the functions among the various class of human beings. The *Brahman* take the lead as a 'head' of the social body supply the organizing principles of intelligence that direct the activities of the other three members of the social body. They are priestly scholar- teachers whose duty is to perform sacrifices and to teach and recite religious/spiritual literature (*vedas*). The *Ksatriyas* as the "arms" of the social body exercise their military and physical power as kings and warriors to protect people and country from internal contention as well as external attacks. The *Vaisyas* as the "legs" of the social body, their duty is to sustain the power of the society through their activities in agriculture and commerce. The "*Sudras*" as the "feet" of the social body' serve the other three higher *varnas*.

But as the time is being changed and people become literate and open-minded the system of *varna* is abused because of creating disaffection among people is, in fact misunderstood. The fact that *varna* system is based on action and quality not on birth. At the time of Rig Veda the *varnas* were established therefore *varna* was based on action and quality (*karma* and *guna*). In ancient India the examples of *jatyutkarsa* and *jatyapakarsa* indicate that birth factor did not determine the *varna* of a person. Yajnavalkya mentioned that if a person born in the Brahman family and take up the profession of the other *varna*, then his *varna* or *jati* will change accordingly. According to the *Dharmashastra* if one does not follow the professions related to their *varnas* will desist to be of the *varna* of their birth.

"According to Swami Vivekananda, it was all Brahmins in the beginning of the Vedic civilisation and Brahmins divided themselves into four classes to do the four types of the social functions like spiritual, intellectual, administration, business and physical work. Because to bring perfection in every division, these four divisions are necessary for every human society" (Jitatmananda, 2007, p.46).

4) *Ashrama dharma:* As it has earlier stated that the meaning and interpretation of the *dharma* change's with a person's age, gender, class and occupations etc. In Hinduism, human life is divided into four stages (*ashramas*) as:

A: *Brahmacharyashrama*: It is believed that this is the first stage of life, also known as a student life age range between 8 and 20 + years. The stage of *brahmacharyashrama* refers to the traditional period when a boy would go to the home of his teacher (*acharya*, *guru*) to learn the Vedas. In fact it is the stage of life of learning or the quest for knowledge. This first stage of life remains before a person gets married. The student who learn the *veda* known as *Brahmacarin. Brahmacarin* means one who is 'celibate', being that to remain celibate is to control sexual energy and to be unpolluted by sex, can be sublimated for a religious purpose, usually understood as the retention of semen. This stage would last between nine and as many as thirty-six years, According to Manu, during this period of time the *brahmacarin* would learn all or a number of the Vedas, and after completing this stage student would undergo a ritual of homecoming and he would soon become married and entered into the householder's life. During this stage of life a student also learn about the duties and responsibilities of the each of the four stages (*asharmas*) of life.

B: *Grihasthashrama:* The second stage of life is known as *grihasthashrama* (family life). It begins after a person gets married and during this stage a true Hindu devotee is dedicated to his/ her domestic affairs, lives with their family and earns honestly their living. During this stage of life a female plays her *stree dharma* and a male plays the *purusha dharma*. *Grihasthashrama* is considered more important as compared to the other three *ashramas* because it only is the stage of life in which a man complete two (*kama* and *artha*) of the four *purusharthas (dharma, artha, kama, moksha*) because in the remaining three *ashramas* there is no any system to perform these two purusharthas (*artha* and *kama*). Besides this he also pursue his responsibilities for family and society according to *Dharma*, so he also perform the aim of life (*purusharthas*). By achieving three *purusharthas* of life, he also prepares himself for achieving the ultimate aim of life that is *Moksha*. This stage is also considered important for the social service point of view. After fulfilling his domestic responsibilities one should return his remaining money to the society again for helping the needy people in the society who live in the other three *ashramas* of life.

Here *brahmacharya dharma* is different from the *grihasta dharma* as well as in the *grihasta dharma, stree dharma* is different from *purusha dharma* in meaning and interpretation.

C: *Vanaprasthashrama:* This is the third stage of life in which a person renounces all of the worldly pleasures and retreat into the forest to devote him to rituals. This stage of life begins when a person is wrinkled and sees his grandchildren then he should retire from all of his household duties and go to the forest to live an ascetic life. The main aim of the *vanaprasthashrama* is to prepare onself for the next *ashrama* that is *sanyasashrama*. In this stage of life a person tries to live without worldly attachments, pleasures and family ties and spend his time in the spiritual practices and social services.

D: *Sanyasashrama:* According to Hinduism, this is the fourth and final stage of the human life in which a person renounce his family ties and also the world completely and lives an ascetic life and spends time in utter devotion (*bhakti*), *japa*, worship, meditation, sings of psalms, hymns and *bhajans*, in order to realize the God, because the ultimate goal is to achieve *moksha* by only realizing the God.

5) *Nimitta Dharma:* *Nimittya* means occasional. In Hinduism, *nimittya dharma* are performed only on the specific occasions which occur at regular intervals: performing rituals, *puja, vrata, diksha*, fasting and pilgrimage, birth or death cermonies etc.

6) *Apad dharma*: The term '*Apad*' may be translated as emergency. *Apad dharmas* are performed when a person cannot perform his regular (*nimittya*) *dharma* under certain testing circumstances as- killing an animal or even a person for the purpose of self defence, a doctor can assure a dying person that he will recover soon and will live long and also by telling falsehood to a murderer save a life. It is believed that when by telling a falsehood one save a life or try to stop any thing that is wrong or that's results will be surely wrong, so at that situation a falsehood is better than hundreds of truths.

7) *Yuga dharma*: *Yuga* means a particular period of time so *yuga* dharma literally means the dharma (duties) of a particular period of time and keep changes from period to period *(yuga* to *yuga*) for example, many orthodox rituals that were followed in the earlier period (*yuga*) are no longer followed in the current period of time (*yuga*). *Dharmic* activities of a *yuga* are different from the *dharmic* activities of the another *yuga*.

Havan (Homa)

The ritual of Havan dates back to thousands of years, also known as homa/havan-yagya. This is an age-old Hindu ritual in which offerings of *ghee* (clarified butter), googol, sugar and other *saamaagri* (exotic herbs) are offered into the sacred fire to the accompaniment of Sanskrit mantras. *Homa/havan* is done by making offerings of the chips of wood sprinkled with clarified butter, exotic herbs, coconut, lotus seeds, fruits, flowers, sandal chips and more in the sacrificial fire of *Havan Kund*. It can be done by doing daily worship of the deities and offering the *panchopchar* (five-fold rituals) consists of offerings to the deity *gandha* (sandal wood paste), *dhup* (frankincense), *deep* (a lit lamp), *pushpa* (flowers), and *naivedya* (holy sacraments). So it relates to performing '*Agnihotra*' and offering of '*havis*' to the

God through havan-yagya. It is believed that it purify the environment around. It is also believed that *havan* built a protective shield and dispelled negative energies around the house where this ritual is performed. *Havan* can be organized at home, temple or office. As *havan* is a vedic ritual of Hinduism but was adopted in ancient times by *Buddhism* and *Jainism* also. According to Husain, Beg, and Dwivedi (2013) it has been given such an important place that it has been described as one of the five daily obligations (*Dev Yajna*) of Hinduism.

Saxena, Gupta, and Pandya (2007) conducted an experiment to study the impact of *yagya* on indoor microbial environments. They found reduction in the colony counts of all micro-flora and further that the reduction in the microbe level was significant even on the 2nd and 3rd day after *Yagya*, and continued even up-till seven days after *Yagya.*

Bansal, Kaur, Gupta, Kumar, and Kaur (2015) conducted a study to see "Is there any scientific basis of *Hawan* to be used in Epilepsy-Prevention/Cure? In their study they found that the routine of performing *Hawan* might keep the threshold value of the therapeutic components in the body and help in preventing epilepsy.

Yama (self-restraint)

Yama (self-restraint) is the first path of *raja yoga* and foundational to all yogic thoughts. *Yama* is absolutely necessary for developing a positive personality. It is about the development of positive personality traits that will transform the human nature into a divine nature and annihilate negative qualities and cravings. About the absolute necessity of *yamas* and *niyamas,* Sri Aurobindo (1971) has stated in the *Synthesis of Yoga* that "It (Raja yoga) does not start with *Asana* and *Pranayama*, but insists first on a moral purification of the mentality. This preliminary is of supreme importance; without it the course of the rest of the *Raja yoga* is likely to be troubled, marred and full of unexpected mental, moral and physical perils. This moral purification is divided in the established system under two heads, five *Yamas* and five *Niyamas*. The first are the rules of moral self-control in conduct such as truth-speaking, abstinence from injury and killing, from theft, etc.; but in reality these must be regarded as merely certain main indications of the general need of moral self-control and purity. *Yama* is, more largely, any self-discipline by which the *rajasic* egoism and its passions and desires in the human being are conquered and quieted into perfect cessation. The object is to create a moral calm, a void of the passions, and so prepare for the death of egoism in the *rajasic* human being. The *Niyamas* are equally a discipline of the mind by regular practice of which the highest is meditation on the divine being, and their object is to create a *sattvic* calm, purity and preparation for concentration upon which the secure pursuance of the rest of the *yoga* can be founded" (p. 539).

In *Yoga-Sutra,* self-restraints (*Yamas*) and self-observances (*niyamas*) have been described as the first two limbs of yoga. Surendranath Dasgupta explains the purpose of enlistment of *yamas.* "The purpose of *Yoga* meditation is to steady the mind on the gradually advancing stages of thoughts towards liberation, so that vicious tendencies may gradually be more and more weakened and at last disappear altogether. But before the mind can be fit for this lofty meditation, it is necessary that it should be purged of ordinary impurities. Thus, the intending *Yogin* should practice absolute non-injury to all living beings (*ahimsa*), absolute and strict truthfulness (*satya*), non-stealing (*asteya*), absolute sexual restraint (*brahmacarya*), and the acceptance of nothing but that which is absolute necessary (*aparigraha*)" (Dasgupta, 1922/

1991, p. 270). Dasgupta (1953/2006) has further stated these things in his introduction to the third volume of *the Cultural Heritage of India.* According to Haridas Bhattacharyya (1953/2006) "the *Yoga-Sutra* agrees with Buddhism and Jainism that men's minds are constantly swayed by thoughts of expanding the self at the cost of others. Thoughts of injury, deceit, unlawful gain sex, and greed toss the soul from object to object and keep up the stream of thought and activity. It is very necessary for the *Yogin* to control these wild propensities of the mind by cultivating the habits of non-injury (*ahimsa*), truthfulness (*satya*), non-stealing (*asteya*), continence (*brahmacarya*), and non-acceptance of gifts (*aparigraha*)" (p. 86).

(A)*Ahimsa* literally means non-violence abstinence from injury, abstinence from malice towards all of the living creatures of this universe at all time and in all ways. It also came to mean kindness towards all of the living creatures (human beings, animals, trees, insects and even the forests also). In Hinduism, it is believed that everyone born as an animal, so one should respect all of the living creatures. Nath (1983) "Inspired by a spirit of universal love, Hindus believe in praying for the well-being of all of the living beings. His prayer is:

Sarve bhavantu sukhinah

Sarve santu niraamayaah!

Sarve bhadraani pashyantu

Maa kashchid dukha bhaaga bhavet!

May one and all be happy and in comfort, may one and all be happy and in good health, may one and all do well and be happy, may one and all be blissfully free from anxiety, want and suffering" (pp. 185-186).

According to Swami Vivekananda "the highest truth is this: God is present in all human beings. They are his multiple forms… the first of all worships is the worship of those around us… he also serves God who serves all other beings" (Jaisingh, 2007, p. 152).

(B) *Satya* means truthfulness. The philosophic meaning pursuing the truthful path and search the 'ultimate truth' is also a part of *nitya dharma*. In this context in Upanishad it has been said that:

"asato ma sadgamaya!

tamasoma jyotir gamaya !!

mrityormaamritam gamaya !

Om shanti shanti shanti !!"

Brihadaranyaka Upanishads (1.3.28).

Means, O Lord !

"From ignorance, lead me to truth, From darkness, lead me to light, From death, lead me to immortality, Om peace, peace, peace"

(http://aumamen.com/prayer/asatoma-sadgamaya-lyrics-and-meaning)

Explaining this *Yama,* Vyasa states: "Abstinence from-falsehood (satya) means speech and mind such as correspond to the object-intended; and speech and mind corresponding to what is seen or inferred or heard. If speech is spoken in order that one's own knowledge may pass to someone else, it should not be deceitful or mistaken or barren of information; [then it would be abstinence from falsehood]. It should be used for the service of all; not for the ruin of creatures. And even when used thus, should it be only for the ruin of creatures, it would not be an abstinence from falsehood; it would be nothing less than wrong. In so far as there would be a false kind of merit [and] a resemblance of merit, it would become the worst of evils. Therefore let [the yogin] consider [first] what is good for all creatures and [then] speak with abstinence-from-falsehood"—Tr. Woods (1914/2007, p. 178).

(C) ***Asteya*** means non-stealing and non-coveting others means and also not acquiring illegitimate wealth. In Hinduism it is advised to stick to *asteya* as a way of life.

When our means are insufficient to achieve something what we want, we may engage in acquiring that by stealing. Unceasing wish, thirst and desire give rise to theft. Thus Vyâsa explains this restraint: "Theft is the unauthorized (*apdstrapurvaka*) appropriation of things-of-value from another. While abstinence-from-theft, when free from coveting, is the refusal to do this"—Tr. Woods (1914/2007, p. 178).

Acquisition for material goods, particularly for money, is very compelling. Money is seen as a source of power, security, happiness, which can give social status. It is a resource that helps overcome calamities. However, when man's pursuits become targeted towards fulfilling his endless desires, unmindful about his *dharmic* obligations, one naturally remains busy acquiring wealth and his needs become greed.

One should earn money through righteous means after meeting own requirements, share the surplus back with society where from he has got it and focus on supporting those in need. This also results in social stability.

(D) ***Brahmacarya*** means abstinence-from-incontinence or the practice of continence. When controlled the part of human energy expressed in sexual urge becomes transmuted into a higher spiritual energy called *ojas* in *yoga*. This *yama* is described by Vyasa as "continence is the control of hidden organ of generation" –Tr. Woods (1914/2007, p. 178). Celibacy sublimates a person's urge into something more creative and frees him from sex. All spiritual men have practices continence and have also spoke at length about this *yama.* Suppression of sexual desire is not wanted, restraint is wanted. The sexual urge that is properly sublimated and practiced becomes a creative force that enables a spiritual practitioner to rise higher up on the path of spirituality.

(E) *Aparigraha* means the abstinence-from-acceptance-of-gifts. This *yama* is the opposite of *parigraha* acceptance of gifts from someone; which is a greedy or covetous nature of a spiritual practitioner. *Aparigraha* is a mental state in which all of the sensual cravings are dead. *Aparigraha* (abstinence-from-acceptance-of-gifts) bestows contentment and peace by removing at one stroke attachment, fear, anxiety, disappointment, anger, lust and jealousy. *Aparigraha* has been given the last position in the list of *yamas* (abstinences) because it is indeed an aid to *himsa* (injury) in that when the desire is not satisfied; then one can become angry and hates the person who is in the way of satisfaction of that desire. Then, the person who is in the need tries to harm such a person in different ways, starts speaking lies and begins to steal things to gratify his desires (Dwivedi, 2015, p. 39-40).

Atman-gyan (Knowledge of the self)

Atman-gyan is formed of two words *Atman* which means 'SELF' and *Gyan* which means 'KNOWLEDGE'. Together it means knowledge of the true self. Indeed the knowledge of the self is within us and since our childhood we have been conditioned to gain knowledge from the outside or the outer world. Throughout our lives we are gathering knowledge from outer side either by reading/listening or watching. We all have the knowledge of the outer world, but about the true self we do not have any knowledge at all. To know about the true self is the ultimate aim of the human life; because without realizing the true self we cannot experience our interconnection with the supreme-being and with all of the living creatures of this universe and also our existence in this universe is totally meaningless.

In the self-realization, a person experience that all of the living-beings are the part of the supreme power and that we all of the living-beings and the supreme-being are interconnected with one another. As mentioned in the Bhagavad Gita……

"sarva-bhuta-stham atmanam sarva-bhutani chatmani

ikchate yoga-yuktatma sarvatra sama-darshana"

(Bhagavad-Gita, Chapter 6, Verse 29)

A perfectly realized person (true yogi), uniting his consciousness with God (ultimate/supreme consciousness), and perceive the realized self in all living beings and in God and God in the self and in all of the living beings.

Meditation/Samadhi helps one to realize this connectedness between self-entity and supreme-entity. After knowing the true self one can realize the true meaning and purpose of the life. Then gradually proceed on the ladder of the spirituality and; ultimately attains the aim of this human life. That's why in Hinduism, it is recommended that one can attain *Atman-gyan* (knowledge of the true self) by practising meditation on the regular basis.

On the other hand, Mahatma Gandhi preferred the *Karma Yoga* as a way of self-realization (*atman-gyan*). In this concern he writes: *'this can be achieved by selfless actions, by renouncing fruits of action, and by dedicating all activities to*

God i.e., by surrendering oneself to Him – body and soul' (cited in Rao, 2012, p.158).

Tantra

Shri Shri Anandamurti (2017) explains the concept of *tantra.* He said, practical spiritual endeavour and practice is called *Tantra* that liberates the spiritual aspirant by helping him expand his mind and spirit. *Tantra* is "liberation through expansion".

This expansion, of mind, ideas, and human spirit, is the only *sadhana*. And when a *sadhaka*, spiritual aspirant, tries to enlarge his mind, naturally, debasing forces become very active. The *sadhaka* is to enlarge his mind and spirit by fighting at each and every step, and stage of life. In his mind, there will be two opposing forces; that is, the spiritual force and the debasing material force that will be in conflict with each other, in the mind.

In family, social and national life, in each and every stratum of life, there will be a fight. That is, those two fundamental, belligerent forces, will become active. One force will try to exalt you towards the Supreme Self, and the other force will want to degrade you, goad you towards crude materialism.

Now, a *Tantric sadhaka* is called, *sadhana samara*, a soldier in the battle of *sadhana. Samara* means war, battle, fight. The *sadhaka* is engaged in fight. It is for the brave and courageous people. And this cult is the cult of *Tantra*. Each and every *sadhak* should be ready for fight – fight in the mental stratum, fight in the family stratum, fight in each and every stratum of life. This is *Tantra*.

Now, in the realm of spirituality, there is little scope for theoreticians. It is 99% practical. *Sadhaka* means a practical man. *Sadhana* is yoga, not theory. This is subjective movement through objective adjustment ... that is, your movement is towards that Supreme Subject, not towards bookish knowledge. Not to aggrandise yourself, but to lead yourself unto the path of beatitude, towards the Supreme Subject. Yours is a subjective approach.

But while moving towards the Supreme Subject, and the culminating point of your life, you have to pass through the world of objectivities. The things of this physical world are all objectivities; but your march is towards the Supreme Subjectivity. So, within you, there must be equilibrium, balance, equipoise, between subjective approach and objective adjustment. You must pass through this world of objects keeping close contact and balance with this objective world; you must not ignore this world.

Don't neglect this world; don't cheat yourself by saying that everything is illusory, that it is nothing. No, it is not nothing; it is something. When you are speaking these words with the help of physical energy, and when you say, "It is nothing," then that "It is nothing" is also nothing. Because you are speaking with the help of energy. But if energy is nothing, vocal cord is nothing, sound is nothing, your utterance is also nothing. So, a *sadhaka* must have a clear-cut approach, a subjective approach through objective adjustment.

You must not neglect the world, but serve each and every object of this universe by ascribing consciousness to them. You are in the midst of so many minute expressions of Narayana, Consciousness.

Each and every expression is Narayana in a particular form, consciousness in a particular shape, Narayana in a particular style. You are to serve them, and serving Narayana in human form is your objective adjustment, and your movement towards the non-attributional Supreme Purusha is your subjective approach.

Moksha (Salvation)

Sanskrit term '*moksha*' literally means salvation, liberation and complete freedom from rebirth. It is the last one of the four aims of human life (*purusharthas-dharma, artha, kama, moksha*). *Moksha* means the complete freedom of the soul from the cycle of birth, death and rebirth; it may also mean the union of the human-soul with the universal supreme soul (*parmatman*) or God. In Hinduism, it is believed that every soul has to take birth on this earth again and again at least on eighty-four lack times in the different bodies of living beings before the soul obtains *moksha*. A soul can attain *moksha* in whatever body it has taken whether man, woman and even animal. There is no discrimination.

In Hinduism it is believed that the union with the supreme soul (God) can be attained by following the way of knowledge (*gyan marga*), way of work (*karma marga*) and the way of devotion (*bhakti marga*).

Gyan marga plays a role in achieving the ultimate goal of life called *moksha*. According to Ramanuja to attain the ultimate goal of life (*moksha*) is the purpose of every living begins in the world. To attain the *moksha*, one should be aware of his true nature as also the nature of the *Brahman* (God). When all of the hindrances to this awareness are removed, he attains the ultimate goal of life (*moksha*). *Saiva siddhanta* recognizes only the knowledge of the lord Siva (*patijnana*) leads to *moksha*.

In the Bhagavad Gita, Lord Krishna says that one who is full of faith, has mastered over his senses attains spiritual knowledge as follows:

Shraddhaval labhate jnanam tat parah samyatendriyah !

Jnanam labdhva param shantim achirenadhi-gacchati !!

(Bhagavad-Gita 4. 39)

"One with full faith, attentively focused, who has conquered the senses, attains (transcendental) knowledge, and also quickly attains super peace" (Rao, 2012, p. 160).

Further, Lord Krishna says that a sinner can crossover all these sins, through the boat of spiritual knowledge. Spiritual knowledge also leads to eradication of all of the sins, like fire burns all wood to ashes.

Api chedasi papebhyah sarvebhyah pap-krt-tamah !

Sarvam jnana-plavenaiva vrjinam santarisyasi !!

Yathidhamsi samidognir bhasma sat kurute'rjuna !

Jnanagnih sarva-karmani bhasma-sat kurute tatha !!

(Bhagavad-Gita 4. 36 and 37)

"Even if you are most sinful of all sinners, yet you will cross over all sins and miseries, by the boat of transcendental knowledge. O Arjuna, just as a blazing fire turns wood to ashes, similarly, the fire of knowledge turns all reactions from actions to ashes" (Rao, 2012, p. 161).

This transcendental knowledge helps one to discriminate between real or real and unreal, the material body and *Atman* and the ultimate distinction between *Atman* and *Parmatman*. Transcendental knowledge also enables one to attain realization.

The second way to attain liberation is ***Karma marga***. It is a path of detachment from the fruits of actions or rituals means selfless actions. Lord Krishna teaches that one should conduct all of his duties according to the *Dharma*. Without being attached to the results of those actions, as an offering to the God; could be a powerful source for the liberation. Because conducting actions without any expectation (Nishkama karam), purifies the mind and also leads towards the spiritual path. The lord Krishna advocates '*Nishkama Karma*' as following-

Karmany-evadhikaraste ma phaleshu kadachana !

ma-karma-phala-hethur bhur ma te sangoosty akarmani !!

(Bhagavad-Gita 2. 47)

"You certainly have the right for prescribed activities but never at any time in their results. You should never be motivated by the results of the actions, nor should there be any attachment in not doing your prescribed activities" (Rao, 2012, p. 157).

In the next *sloka*, Lord Krishna advises Arjuna that *Karma* Yoga is a state of equanimity. One should be balanced in both victory and defeat while doing such *Karma*, as follows:

Yoga-stah kuru karmani sangam tyktva dhananjaya !

Siddhi-asiddhyoh samo bhutva sampatvam yoga uchyate !!

(Bhagavad-Gita 2. 48)

"O Dhananjaya, established in the science of Yoga in action, perform your activities giving up attachment and maintain equanimity in both success and failure" (Rao, 2012, p. 158).

Lord Krishna explains over here that in the *Karma* Yoga, one should maintain equanimity in both victory and defeat and discard mental attachment to his actions. One should perform actions as a matter of duty (*karma*) because such actions are not disturbed either by benefit or loss in such actions. One who performs *karma yoga* sincerely successfully proceeds on the spiritual path.

When a person does Karma without expectations (*Nishkama-karma*) belief and surrenders the self to the supreme-being and constantly meditating upon that through mind, body and speech, is really following the '***Karma-marga***'.

The third way of attaining salvation as prescribed by Bhagavad Gita is ***Bhakti-marga***. It is a way of worship of the God with deep devotion. Bhakti is a feeling of the power of delight of the supreme-being and through bhakti the devotee becomes united with that supreme-being (God). Bhakti marga is certainly the most popular sâdhana. Complete surrender to the lord, firm and unshakeable love of the God (bhakti) is one of the means of liberation. So Bhakti marg is a path of devotion to the God and self-forgetting love to attain spiritual freedom (liberation).

In the Bhagavad Gita, Lord Krishna declares that as compare to the greatest yogi his devotee is superior for him:

Yoginam api sarvesham mad-gatenantaramana!

Shradhavaan bhajate yo mam sa me yuktatamo matah!!

(Bhagavad-Gita 6.47)

"Amongst all yogis (or those perfected in the science of the individual consciousness attaining communion with the ultimate consciousness), one who in full faith is always thinking of me within, deeply dedicated to me, rendering devotional service to me is the most superior of all" (Rao, 2012, p. 159).

Further, Lord Krishna explains that those devotees have achieved Him through Bhakti Yoga, have achieved perfection and they are not subject to reincarnation (continuous cycle of birth, death and rebirth) as follows:

Mam upetya punar janma dukhalayam asasvatam!

Napnuvanti mahtmanah samsiddhim paramam gatah!!

(Bhagavad-Gita 8.15)

"The great souls having achieved perfection take refuge in Me, never again assume this transitory birth (Punarjanma) full of misery" (Rao, 2012, p. 159).

Lord Krishna, concluding the *Bhakti* Yoga (Gita 12. 6 and 7) says that "But those who surrender all activities unto Me, meditate on Me with single minded devotion, I become their deliverer without delay from the ocean of death in the material existence" (Rao, 2012, p. 160).

He further assures in the next *sloka* that:

Mayya eva mana adhatsva mayi buddhim nivesaya!

Nivesisyasi may eva ata urdhvam nasamsayah!!

(Bhagavad-Gita 12.8)

"Concentrate the mind upon Me, establish spiritual intelligence in Me, verily you will reside with Me, after this existence without doubt" (Rao, 2012, p. 160).

Thus in the Bhagavad Gita, Lord Krishna assures that if His devotees focus their minds upon Him, He will quickly deliver them from this material existence (*Samsara*) exclusively in the *Bhakti* Yoga. So concluding the *Bhakti* Yoga it can be said that in the *Bhakti* Yoga the practitioner need a figure (a personalized form of divine) and that figure may be Brahma, Vishnu and Mahesh or anybody, but the practitioner need a focus of devotion. In the *Bhakti* Yoga the sadhaka fall in love with his Lord. So if the *Gyan* Yoga is the way of mind to attain Moksha, the *Bhakti* Yoga is a way of heart to attain the *Moksha*.

Indriyas (Sense Organs)

We have the five *indriyas* (sense organs) - eyes, ears, nose, tongue, and skin. We have been given these senses to help us to know what is good and what is evil. Evil destroys the individual; good, on the contrary, accepts the individual and wants him to grow to his supreme fulfilment. Good stands for a society of free individuals. Spiritual person has the power to grasp and discriminate through senses. Spirituality emphasizes the need of our sense organs because they impact on our behaviour. The *indriyas* must follow the path of truth. We have to strive for positive uses of senses to lead a spiritual life. The Bhagwad Gita says that a person whose senses are under control is in equipoise.

There are 10 *indriyas* or sense organs: five sensory (*Jnanendriyas*) and five motor (*Karmendriyas*). ***Jnanendriyas*** (knowing senses) are the five entrance doors. They are: organ for seeing (Eyes), organ for sound (Ear), organ for smell (Nose), organ for touch (Skin), and organ for taste (Tongue), and their functions respectively are: to see, to hear, to smell, to touch, and to taste. ***Karmendriyas*** (action senses) are the five exit doors. They are: vocal cord, hands, legs, anus, and genital organ, and their functions respectively are: to speak, to work, to move, to let out the waste, and to give birth.

According to inherent *Samakara*, the sensory organs (*Jnanendriyas*) are the receivers of vibrations and the motor organs (*karmendriyas*) are the creators of vibrations. The main cause of person's sensual desires is conflicting emotions in his mind and gradually he becomes a slave of his senses and finally his mind becomes instable. With the help of '*indriya-nigraha*', self discipline development of detachment to sensory objects and also with the practice of renunciation this instability of the mind has to be controlled.

Karma (Action)

The term '*karma*' is derived from the Sanskrit word '*karman*', which means 'action'. *Karma* as a doctrine encompasses a number of quasi-independent concepts: rebirth (*punarjanman*), consequence (*phala*) of actions as either 'good' (*punya or sukarma*) or 'bad' (*papman* or *duskarman*). The well known text, Bhagavata purâna representing the principal elements of the *karma* doctrine: "the same person enjoys the same fruit of the same sinful or a meritorious act in the next world in the same manner and to the same extent according to the manner and extent to which that (sinful or meritorious) act has been done by him in this world" (6.1.45; tagare1993: 779).

The belief in the law of *karma* is one of the common Hindu beliefs, also known as the law of moral causation. The law of *karma* is a moral law similar to the physical law of causation. The law of *karma* works in the moral world just as the law of cause and effect works in the physical world.

The law of *karma* implies the moral law as—every soul in this and subsequent births follow the results of good and bad deeds (*punya- paapa*). According to Rao (2012), in the Srimad Bhagavad Gita Lord Krishna explained that everyone should perform his duties according to his *dharma* and at that time he should not attach himself to the results, also the *karma* done regardless of any expectation, leads towards the spiritual path (p. 4). In the scriptures, *karma* is treated as an instrument for maintaining social order correctly. The result of *dharma* described by *Chandogya Upanishad*' as follows:

"Those, whose conduct here has been good, will quickly attain a good birth, the birth of a Brahman, the birth of a *kshatriya*, the birth of a *vaishya*. But those, whose conduct here has been evil, will quickly attain an evil birth, the birth of a dog, the birth of a hog or a birth of *chandala*." (5.10.7) (tr. Dr. S. Radhakrishnan).

It means that the conditions of the future or the next birth are determined by the actions (*karma*) whatever we do in the present life. Since a person can modify his fate (destiny) by performing actions, consciously, so this cannot be explained as fatalism.

So it is clear from the above description that in relation to the 'law of karma' Hindus believe in the concept of *paapa* and *punya*, unique for Hindu *dharma*. These are considered as the 'Bank accounts' in the life of an individual. It is believed that through *sansara* and *karma* these two (*paapa and punya*) follow the individual from one life to another, And also in the choice of one's subsequent births, they are responsible (collection) the accumulation of the effect of bad deeds can be described as '*paapa*' in the life of an individual. In the same way the accumulation of the effect of good deeds can be described as '*punya*' in the life of an individual. One can accumulate *punya* and work towards *moksha* simply by following the rule of actions (precepts) prescribed by *dharma* in life because *punya* is considered to be *Dharmic* in nature and vice versa *paapa* is considered to be against of *Dharmic* nature.

"tasmad asaktah satatam

karyam karma samacara

asakto hy acaran karma

param apnoti purusah"

(Bhagavad Gita, 3.19)

"Therefore, without being attached to the fruits of activities, one should act as a matter of duty, for by working without attachment one attains the Supreme".

http://vedabase.net/bg/3/19/en

Tapas (Austerity)

Tapas means austerity or the practice of penance. It also means meditation and restraints of the senses. *Tapas* leads to control of the mind. Austerities like observing silence and occasional fasting increase the power of tolerance/endurance. Vyâsa commented on this type of self-observance as “Austerity is the capacity to bear the opposites; and the opposites are hunger and thirst, cold and heat, standing and sitting, absence of all expressions and absence of speech. They also include vows such as the fasts of *krcchra, candrayana,* and *santapan*a”–Tr. T. S. Rukmani (1983, *Yogavarttika* of *Vijnabhiksu,* Volume II, p. 196).

According to Sri Sri Ravi Shankar (2018), “*Tapas* is endurance of discomfort or restraining the senses. The practice of knowledge, wisdom, meditation, yoga, *pranayama* and fasting all come under *Tapas*” (p.8). *Tapas* can help us how to get out of unhappiness or sorrow. It purifies our minds, consciousness and actions. Practices associated with *Tapas* are essential for spiritual growth. It connects us to God. Whenever we get time, we should practice it. Adopt *tapas* as a practice in day-to-day life.

As compare to the physical austerity; mental austerity is more powerful. He who tolerates heat and cold practice physical austerity and his power of endurance increases but he may not be able to tolerate insult (mental austerity). He will be easily upset by an unkind or harsh word for he has disciplined his body for tolerating the physical extremes only. Actually, mental austerity is keeping a balanced mind in all of the conditions of life to tolerate insult injury and persecutions, to remain serene, contented and peaceful and to remain calm and cheerful while facing extremely adverse conditions. Such a *Yogin* practices to have fortitude in meeting danger and develops forbearance and patience. In this manner this self-observance prepares a practitioner to maintain his composure and not to be upset on a trifle matter. It develops in a practitioner such type of mental preparedness that he concentrates on the practice of penance only and waits for its fruition. This definitely does not happen through osmosis; we must do our work and let the benefits unfold in time.

Ananda (Bliss)

Ananda literally means bliss or happiness. In the Hindu Upanishads, Vedas and Bhagavad- Gita, *ananda* signifies eternal bliss which accompanies the ending of the cyclical life process (*samsara*). Those who completely surrender themselves, and renounce the fruits of their actions to the divine will achieve the final termination of the birth-rebirth cycle to enjoy eternal bliss (*ânanda*) in perfect union with the Godhead. The tradition of seeking union with eternal bliss (God) through passionate commitment is referred to as *bhakti*, or devotion.

"bahya-sparshechvasaktatma vindatyatmani yat sukham

sa brahma-yoga-yuktatma sukham akchayam aœhnute"

(Bhagavad Gita 5.21)

Those who are not attached to external sense pleasures realize divine bliss in the self. Being united with God through yoga, they experience unending happiness.

"prashanta-manasam hyenam yoginam sukham uttamam

upaiti shanta-rajasam brahma-bhutam akalmacham"

(Bhagavad Gita 5.27)

Great transcendental happiness comes to the yogi whose mind is calm, whose passions are subdued, who is without sin, and who sees everything in connection with God.

"yunjann evam sadatmanam yogi vigata-kalmacha

sukhena brahma-sansparœham atyantaA sukham ashnute"

(Bhagavad Gita 6.28)

Consistently experiencing in this way the realization of the self, one perfected in the science of uniting the individual consciousness with the ultimate consciousness is freed from all material contamination easily attaining transcendental happiness being in realization of the ultimate truth.

So, it is clear from the above mentioned verses of the epic Bhagavad Gita that *ananda* (bliss or transcendental happiness) is a feeling of connection of the self or individual consciousness with the supreme or ultimate consciousness and to live within the connection. According to Swami Vivekananda, within the various schools of Hindu thought, there are different paths and ways of achieving transcendental happiness. The main four paths are *Bhakti* yoga, *Jnana* yoga, *Karma* Yoga and *Raja* Yoga (DeLuca, 2006).

Being soul, we comprise of *sat+chit+anand*. We have inbuilt desire to become happy. Although striving hard for many years to become happy, we see happiness slipping from our hands now and then. It is not eternal. Though the desire to be happy, to be in bliss is always there.

Conclusion:

We would have no prejudice if we practice spirituality with soulfulness. If we develop this vision we will feel connectedness at the level of the soul. In order to cultivate *adhyatmikta* into the spiritual realms, we see that the ***Atman, Dharma, Havan/Homa, Yama, Atma-Gyan, Tantra, Moksha, Indriyas, Karma, Tapas*** and ***Ananda*** would increase consciousness and give impetus towards understanding it. So let's become *Adhyatmic*, by following the above mentioned dimensions of *Adhyatmikta.*

An individual cannot evolve until he maintains a balance between responsibilities and rights. Attitude towards *adhyatmikta* should be applicable to all individuals, family, institutions, societies, and nations. The lack of balance in human behavior creates many disorders. We can live happily in this and other world if we adopt spiritual lifestyle. *Adhyatmikta* can makes our life more meaningful when we feel bored.

Notes

Satyam yatharthevanmanase. Yatha drstam yathanumitam yatha srutam tatha vanmanasceti. Paratra svabodhasankrantaye vagukta sa yadi na vancita bhrantava pratipattibandhya va bhavediti. Esa sarvabhutopakarartham pravrtta na bhutopaghataya. Yadi caiavamapyabhidhutyamand bhutopaghataparaiva syanna satyam bhavet... tasmatpariksa sarvabhutahitam satyam bruyat. Vyasabhasya on Yoga-Sutra, II.30.

Steyam as astrapurvakam dravyanam paratah svikaranam, tatpratisedhah punaraspriharupamasteyamiti.- Vyasabhasya on Yoga-Sutra, II.30.

Brahmacaryam guptendriyasyaopasthasya samyamah—— Vyasabhasya on Yoga-Sutra, II.30.

Tapo dvandvasahanam. Dvandvasca jighatsapipase sitosne sthanasane kasthamaunakaramaune ca. Vratani caisam yathayogam krcchracandrayanasamtapanadini.—— Vyasabhasya II. 32.

Chapter Two

WHAT IS SPIRITUALITY?

Everything in existence is surrounded by spirituality. Human beings with limited knowledge should try to know him in the domain of spirituality. Spirituality is guided and practiced by own philosophy. A human being can know and experience him through different facets of spirituality. Since the spirituality remains unknown to people, so the human mind moves towards it. And this movement towards unknown aspects of spirituality is the human quest.

In English meaning, "spiritual" was a phrase used to disparity house of worship life with "worldly wise" or acquisitive ways of being (Rizzuto, 2005). In the 19th century, spirituality was not only used as in commonly but as referred as spirit and other psychic phenomena. According to Dossey, Keegan, and Guzzetta (2000), "spirituality is the essence of who we are and how we are in the world and, like breathing, is essential to our human existence" (p. 92).

The role of spirituality in Psychology is recognized by the Psychology of Religion and Spirituality – Division 36 of the American Psychological Association, the Spirituality and Psychiatry Special Interest Group of the Royal College of Psychiatrists (Royal College of Psychiatrists, 2013), and the World Psychiatry Association Position Statement on Spirituality and Religion in Psychiatry (Moreira-Almeida, Sharma, Van Rensburg, Verhagen, & Cook, 2016).

Jung is considered the first contemporary psychologist to suggest that spirituality is innately seated within the psyche; for Jung, the psyche is "by nature religious" (Dunne, 2002).

Spirituality has been defined variously in the past thirty years. According to Shults and Sandaga (2006, p. 14), there are more than a hundred definitions for spirituality, but none of these is alone able to define the phenomenon sufficiently. We consider spirituality as a multidimensional phenomenon that any attempt to encompass it in one definition is seems to be an arduous task. Recently, spirituality has been defined variously, but quite a few definitions of spirituality are known within the field of spiritual psychology. However, many definitions fall short, in providing a wide foundation for understanding the spirituality. By combining a number of different points of view and approaches to spirituality, it is possible to arrive at an understanding the meaning of this term 'spirituality.' Some of the notable definitions are given below:

Definitions of Spirituality: An overview

In the present chapter, we want to explore the dimensions of spirituality by thorough understanding of its definitions. By and large there are three major dimensions which emerges from the definitions on spirituality are: transcendence, sacred and practice.

Spirituality as Transcendence

Logically, it is important to first overview some of the general definitions of spirituality that are more reflective and provide better understanding, and to identify potential commonalities on the basis of which conceptual and methodological approach to the topic may be evolve. There appears to be a fair amount of consistency in most of the definitions on spirituality. That is, they put emphasis on transcendence as a core feature. For instance, Elkins, Hedstrom, Hughes, Leaf, and Saunders (1988) define spirituality as "a way of being and experiencing that comes about through awareness of a transcendent dimension and that is characterized by certain identifiable values in regard to self, others, nature, life, and whatever one considers to be the Ultimate" (p. 10). Spirituality as discussed by Zinnbauer and colleagues (1997) is regarded as individual phenomenon and identify with such things as personal transcendence, supra-consciousness sensitivity and meaningfulness.

The Fetzer Institute/National Institute on Aging Working Group (1999) characterize spirituality as being "concerned with the transcendent, addressing ultimate questions about life's meaning, with the assumption that there is more to life than what we see or fully understand" (p. 2). According to Gladding (2000), spirituality refers to the transcendent dimension of a person's life.

According to Benson, Roehlkepartain, and Rude (2003), "Spirituality development is the process of growing the intrinsic human capacity for self-transcendence in which the self is embedded in something greater than the self, including the sacred. It is the developmental engine that propels the search for connectedness, meaning, purpose and contribution. It is shaped both within and outside of religious traditions, beliefs and practices. The cognitive, emotional and behavioural characteristics that operationalize spirituality and religiosity are not present in the new born. These characteristics develop across the life span."

Koenig (2010) sees spirituality as "distinguished from all other things—humanism, values, morals, and mental health—by its connection to the sacred, the transcendent... Spirituality is intimately connected to the supernatural and religion, although it extends beyond religion" (p.116–117). More recently, de Jager Meezenbrock and colleagues (2012) define spirituality as "one's striving for an experience of connection with oneself, connectedness with others and nature and connectedness with the transcendent" (p. 338).

From the above mentioned definitions it appears that there are different areas of across researchers. Moreover, the definitions utilize the concept of transcendence and, more specifically, transcendent reality as the basis for how to understand spirituality. Helminiak (1996, 1998, 2008) argued that such a term is presumptively linked to religious and theological systems that themselves are concerned with what is essentially metaphysical/ supernatural and do not fit well with the contemporary scientific worldview.

Such a definitional approach follows the work of several researchers and theoreticians; for instance, Grof (1985, 1988) has argued that spirituality is a natural human developmental potential which involves shifts and transformations in conventional personality functioning that result in higher modes of health, integration, and well-being. Hay and Socha (2005) have offered that spirituality is a natural human phenomenon which has both evolutionary and socio-cultural significance. Finally, through the concept of self-transcendence, Cloninger, Svrakic, and Pryzbeck (1993) has incorporated spirituality into his bio-psychosocial model of temperament and character.

Spirituality as Sacred

Another dimension which appears from the previous definitions of spirituality is 'sacred.' The sacred dimension appears to be closely related to the spirituality. Sacredness in everything inculcates spirituality in a person. Nowadays, the term 'spirituality' is frequently used to indicate *the experiential and personal side of our relationship to the transcendent or sacred* (Emmons & Crumpler, 1999; Hill, Pargament, Hood, McCullough Jr, Swyers, Larson, & Zinnbauer, 2000). The term "search for sacred" is commonly acknowledged explanation of spirituality. Pargament and Mahoney (2002) also defined spirituality "as a sacred….." and elaborated, "People can take a virtually limitless number of pathways involve systems of belief that include those of traditional organized religion, newer spirituality movements, and more individualized worldview" (p. 647). These pathways to the sacred also may be described as spiritual strivings, which include personal goal associated with the ultimate concerns of purpose, ethics, and reorganization of the transcendent (Emmons, Cheung, & Tehrani, 1998).

According to Jones (1995), the most central concept of spirituality is transcendent dimension to life, something or someone beyond our ego and experience. The experience of connection to this larger, sacred reality is what gives our lives ultimate meaning. Thus, spirituality also has to do with a sense of connectedness and interrelatedness, and with the search for meaning and purpose in life. Spirituality has been called the concept "which integrates everything else into meaning" (pp. 2-3).

According to Hill and Pargament (2003), "The sacred which includes the divine and the transcendent, is the common denominator of religious and spiritual life. Spirituality is the search for the sacred, a process through which people seek to discover, hold on to, and, when necessary, transform whatever they hold sacred in their lives" (p. 65). Peterson and Seligman (2004) said that "Although the precise content of spiritual belief differs, all culture have a thought of an ultimate, transcendent, scared, and divine force" (p.601). Zinnbauer and Pargament (2005) have defined spirituality as a "personal or group search for the sacred" (p.35). Pargament (2007) has defined spirituality as the "sacred domain" which concerns "ideas of God, higher powers, divinity, and transcendent reality" (p. 32).

Pargament, Mahoney, Exline, Jones, and Shafranske (2013) define spirituality as "the search for the sacred", with sacred referring not only to God/higher powers, but also to " other aspects of life that are perceived to be manifestations of the divine or imbued with divine-like qualities, such as transcendence, immanence, boundlessness and ultimacy" (p. 14).

Rao (2011) has suggested that "there is a general consensus between the Indian and Western perspectives that the common ground between religion and spirituality is the sacred. The sacred may refer to different things such as God, divinity, ultimately reality and so on. The common denominator of all of them, it would seem, is transcendence. Transcendence implies going beyond what is given in one's normal sensory experience. In the spiritual tradition of India, whether Hindu or Buddhist, there is overwhelming emphasis on transcendence as a state of being that goes well beyond sensory awareness. Spiritual pursuit is an exercise for transformation of the human condition to achieve transcendence" (p. 9).

Spirituality as Practice

Spiritual practices are the most endearing tradition of all time among the followers of different religious faith. These are nurtured and kept alive by generations of parents to their children through the socialization process. Spiritual practices protect the morality of children. And even when we grew up then we were grateful to our parents who provide us such an excellent path for the spiritual well-being.

In the words of Ram Dass, "Spiritual Practices help us move from identifying the ego to identifying with the soul. Old age does that for you too. It spiritualizes people naturally" (Husain, Beg, & Dwivedi, 2013, p. 120)

"Spiritual practices include any activity that one associates with cultivating spirituality. Spiritual practices help us to integrate and deepen our awareness of human experience. The purpose of spiritual practice is to realize happiness within – a fundamental purpose of life experienced in every waking moment" (Singh & Husain, 2015, p. 5). Husain, Singh, and Khan (2016) classified spiritual practices for Muslims into three categories, namely, individual, collective and sacred practices.

Waaijman (2000) classified spiritual practices into four categories:

1. **Somatic practices**, especially deprivation and diminishment. The deprivation purifies the body. Diminishment concerns the repulsement of ego-oriented impulses. Examples are fasting and poverty.
2. **Psychological practices**, for example, meditation.
3. **Social practices**, examples are the practice of obedience and communal ownership reform ego-orientedness into other-orientedness.
4. **Spiritual practices** aim at purifying the ego centeredness, and direct the abilities at the divine reality.

According to Waaijman, spiritual practices would mean shedding hostility, anger, jealousy, impulsivity etc. Love, piety, deity, kindness, altruism, empathy are not possible until an individual is able to rise high of small petty issues to develop a sense of appreciation for others.

The Spiritual Science Research Foundation (SSRF, 2013) defines spiritual practice as honest and sincere efforts done consistently on a daily basis to develop divine qualities and achieve everlasting happiness as Bliss. Another way of defining spiritual practice is our personal journey of going inward beyond our five senses, mind, and intellect to experience the soul (the God) within each of us. One of the qualities of God is perceptual Bliss and so by tapping into the soul, we too experience bliss.

Zhai, Ellison, Stokes, and Glenn (2008) demarcated spirituality as "widely perceived to be more individual and subjective, reflecting personal practices and experiences that may diverge from religious orthodoxy or convention" (p. 381).

Students and teachers of the Brahma Kumaris World Spiritual University studies and practices spirituality at four levels:

"Our understanding of and relationship with ourselves as the spiritual beings, giving life to our physical bodies";

"Our understanding of and relationship with the physical aspects of the world around us – food, wealth, environment and the maintenance of health";

"Our understanding of and relationship with other human souls";

"Our understanding of and relationship with the One, who is called by many names: God, Allah, Ishwar, Jehova, Shiva and so on. God is seen as the seed or "Supreme Parent" of all religions and not anyone exclusively" (O'Donnell, 2010, p. 4).

According to Henry (2013), "Spiritual practice often encourages people to go within, root out their feelings, and develop the capacity to attend others kindly. There is a greater focus in Eastern spiritual practice on acceptance and detachment from desires than the seeking and striving after goals found in many Western forms of psychological development. An increasingly numbers of new interventions, such as mindfulness, compassion therapy, and reconciliation, draws our attention on spiritual practices for inspiration" (p. 421).

Dwivedi (2015) discusses self-restraints (*yamas*) and self-observances (*niyamas*) practices as aids in inculcating spirituality in Hinduism. Self-restraints and self-observances are foundations to all yogic thoughts. *Hathayoga Pradipika* and different *Puranas* have described ten techniques of self-restraints (*yamas*): abstinence-from-injury, truthfulness, abstinence-from-theft, abstinence-from-incontinence, abstinence-from-acceptance-of-gifts, abstinence-from-impatience, abstinence-from-non-stead-forwardness, abstinence-from-cruelty, abstinence-from-non-steadiness, and abstinence-from-unwanted desires. Similarly, the *Skanda* and *Purana* lists ten techniques of self-observances (*niyamas*): cleanliness, bathing, penance, charity, observing silence, sacrificing in the holy fire, study of religious texts, observance of various *vratas,* fasting and controlling one's sensuous desires. Literature on spirituality and religious practices labels them as relating to spirituality.

Spirituality as related to Purpose/Meaning in Life, Values/Virtues, Beliefs and Experiences

Spirituality does not necessarily refer to religious doctrines. It could be some one's philosophy, values, or meaning of life (Kellehear, 2000). Albanese (1990) indicated that spirituality is human beings' awareness of details in existence and it revealed in-depth connections. Gawain (2000) suggested that, on the contrary, most of the people in modern times are lost and insecure because of an inner spiritual shortage. Therefore, spirituality could stabilize the will of the people and purify the soul.

Spirituality forms the basis of meaning and purpose for many people (Foglio & Brody, 1988). Kellehear (2000) defines spirituality as the pursuit of meanings and existence essence. Spirituality is the awareness of existence; it transcends material life and involves profound consciousness of the people, individual belief, and values.

Miller (1999, p. 499) defines spirituality as 'an innate actualizing tendency that directs an individual towards knowledge, love, meaning, hope, transcendence, connectedness, and compassion … creativity, growth, and the development of a value system'.

Spirituality makes us to think beyond our daily experiences, consequently, making a transforming impact on our lives, relationships and on our actions too. Up till now, we have talked about its theoretical aspect, but practically it includes a search for higher values, inner freedom and things that provide meaning into life (Shannon, 2000; Vergote, 2003). While for some, it refers to as search for God, and for some as quest for meaning (Mansager, 2002).

Spirituality has been described as "the way in which people understand and live their lives in view of their ultimate meaning and value" (Muldoon & King, 1995, p. 336), as "a subjective experience of the sacred" (Vaughan, 1991, p. 105).

Murray and Zenter (1989) define spirituality, as a quality that goes beyond religious affiliation that strives for inspiration, reverence, awe, meaning and purpose, even in those who do not believe in God. The spiritual dimension, tries to be in harmony with the universe, strives for answers about the infinite, and comes into focus when the person faces emotional stress, physical illness or death (p. 259).

Howden (1992) defines spirituality "as the dimension of one's being that is an integrating or unifying factor and that is manifested through unifying interconnectedness, purpose and meaning in life, innerness and inner resources, and transcendence."

Beck (1992) described the concept of spirituality on a set of human qualities rather than a search for the sacred or transcendent. Among these are insight and understanding; an awareness of the inter connections among and between personal and other life forms, an experience of mystery and awe; and a posture of generosity and gratitude. Spirituality "gives expression to the being that is in us; it has to do with feelings, the power that comes from within, with knowing our deepest selves."

Huddleston (1995) describes spirituality as "the manner, mode, or way in which a group lives its religion". She describes spirituality as – "putting into practice in the concrete conduct of life specific proclamations, doctrines, ideas, values, hopes, commandments, instructions, traditions, or habits of Christians (or other religious) faith by a particular way of living" (Huddleston, 1995, p. 20). She describes religion (Christianity) as "the graced, culturally conditioned, holistic response of the human individual or group to the gratuitous self-bestowal (love) of God..." (p. 21).

According to Miller (1995), "spirituality is the vital force, the life principle, or essence of being that permeates life and is expressed and experienced in multifaceted connections with the self, others, nature, and God or life force. Shaped by cultural experiences, spirituality is a universal human experience" (p. 258).

According to Vrinte (1996), "spirituality is impaired and sustained by transpersonal experiences that originate in the deepest recesses of the human being and they are but the natural manifestations of that domain of the human psyche that contain the greater depth of life" (p. 77).

Three common components included in most of the definitions of spirituality are (Bouchard, 1997):

- An understanding of self that is defined in the context of relationships to others,

- An understanding of a creation story and symbols of faith,
- An understanding of greater power that is outside of the self, you intimately connected with the sense of self.

Canda (1988) defines spirituality as the "human quest for personal meaning and mutually fulfilling relationships among people, the nonhuman environment, and, for some, God" (p. 243).

According to the Consensus Document of National Institute of Health Care of Research, Hill, Pargament, Swyer, Gorsuch, Mcullough, Hood, and Baumister (1998), spirituality can be defined as, "the feelings, thoughts, experiences, and behaviors that arise from a search for the sacred" (p. 21). In other words, we can say that, a set of beliefs and practices that directs and influences the behaviour of an individual is spirituality i.e., the spiritual attitude, behaviours and an awareness of spiritual side in oneself were the important component of this dimension. The spiritual beliefs constitute an orientation to a power greater than self, awareness of cosmic consciousness, a belief in God, and an interconnectedness of self to everything in this world and also beyond this world.

Spirituality generally refers to meaning and purpose in one's life, a search for wholeness, and a relationship with a transcendent being. One's spirituality may be expressed through religion or religious involvement, which generally refers to participation in an organized system of beliefs, rituals, and cumulative traditions (Fukuyama & Sevig, 1999).

Krishna Mohan (2001) advocates that "spirituality may be understood as an innate human capacity to transcend the egocentric perspective from which people experience and evaluate their lives in the process to attain full enlightenment. Spiritual people have thoughts and feelings of connectedness with the universe and a sense of moving towards personal wholeness by experiencing transcendence and immanence”.

Spirituality is rooted in an awareness that is part of the biological composition of the human order. Spirituality is present in all individuals and it may patent as inner peace and strength derive from a perceived relationship with a transcendent God or an ultimate reality or whatever an individual value as supreme (Narayanasamy, 1999, p. 124).

According to Puchalski and Romer (2000), “spirituality is that which allow to person to experience transcendent meaning in life…whatever belief and values give a person a sense of meaning and purpose in life” (p. 129).

Koenig, McCullough, and Larson (2001) described spirituality as ‘The personal quest for understanding answers to ultimate questions about life, about meaning and about relationship to the sacred or transcendent…’ (p. 18).

Swinton (2001/2003) writes: “The human spirit is the essential life-force that undergirds, motivates and vitalizes human existence. Spirituality is the specific way in which individuals and communities respond to experience of spirit.”

Griffith and Griffith (2002) provide a contextual and relational definition of spirituality. According to them spirituality is “a commitment to choose, as the primary context for understanding and acting one’s relatedness with all” (p. 15).

Frame (2003) has emphasized the various components of spirituality in her definition: “Spirituality includes one’s values, beliefs, mission, awareness, subjectivity, experience, sense of purpose and direction, and a kind of striving toward something greater than oneself. It may or may not include a deity” (p.3).

According to the American Academy of Family Physicians, "spirituality is the way you find meaning, hope, comfort and inner peace in your life. Many people find spirituality through religion. Some find it through music, art or a connection with nature. Others find it in their values and principles."

Peterson and Seligman (2004) define spirituality as "both the private, intimate relationship between humans and the divine, and the range of virtues that result from the relationship" (p. 602).

Heelas and Woodhead et al. (2005) consider spirituality as part of a person's life and experience; methods used in the behavioural sciences are naturally helpful for gaining information about spirituality as a universally human experience.

Mohr (2006) defines spirituality as "a person's experience of, or a belief in a power apart from his or her own existence" (p. 378). According to Husain (2007), "Spirituality implies thinking, mental knitting, meditating, praying, worshipping God, giving voice to God, growth, imagination and creativity."

Spirituality is an old vision, but a new and ultimate reality. It refers to an ultimate or an alleged immaterial reality; an inner path enabling a person to discover the essence of his/her being, or the "deepest values and meanings by which people live" (Sheldrake, 2007).

According to Roy (2011), "Spirituality is present in so many diverse ways in our thoughts and actions that it cannot be exactly specified or characterized and that makes us aware of the wide range and vast scope of the concept" (p. 309).

According to Astin, Astin, and Lindholm (2011), "spirituality is a dynamic construct that involves the internal process of seeking personal authenticity, genuineness, and wholeness" and "deriving meaning, purpose and direction in life". They argue that spirituality is a source of inner strength, moral orientation, and connection that brings faith, hope, peace and empowerment.

Husain, Jahan, Nishat, Siddiqui, and Akram (2011) have defined spirituality in terms of the sense of purpose and maintenance of discipline. Husain, Luqman, and Jahan (2012) have defined spirituality in terms of spiritual personality. They says that "as a process by which an individual who knows how to anchoring his lifestyle around his noble attitude toward others and follow the path of moral rectitude (p. 2). Husain and Anas (2018) revised spiritual personality inventory in which they says: "Spiritual personality takes a holistic view. Having a holistic perspective it requires spiritual virtues, positive outlook on life, spiritual discipline, goodness, spiritual service and moral rectitude. These are essential aspects and are deeply ingrained in a spiritual person" (p. 11).

According to Ramakrishna Rao (2013), "Spirituality is to religion what science is to technology. Seen in this light, science and spirituality are two truth-seeking activities that seem to run parallel to each other" (p. 5).

According to Taylor, Peterson, Oyedele, and Hasse (2015), spirituality serves as a foundation for and is antecedent to the development of one's spiritual perspective, a term that conveys each person's unique forms of spiritual awareness, beliefs, practices and experiences, beginning in childhood and extending over time. They have discussed and defined the following spirituality-related constructs.

> ***Spirituality:*** An inherent quality of all humans referring to their seeking and expressing meaning and the way they experience their connectedness to the moment, to self, to others, to nature and or the significant or sacred.

***Spiritual perspective*:** Each person's unique development of spiritual awareness, beliefs, practices, and experiences, beginning in childhood and extending over time.

Religion: A search for non-sacred goals (such as identity, belongingness, meaning, health or wellness) in a context that has its primary goal, the facilitation of the search that receives validation and support from within an identifiable group of people.

***Religiosity*:** Institutional and outward expressions of the sacred, including dimensions of devotion, holiness, and piousness expressed through religious organization's membership, attendance, beliefs and acceptance, and faith expressions.

***Spiritual/Religious Coping*:** Efforts to understand and deal with life stressors in ways related to the sacred.

"Based upon this small sampling of definitions which have appeared across four decades of research, one might conclude that the most efficient and straightforward way of construing spirituality is to define it as that aspect of human functioning, experience, and existence which concerns the transcendent" (MacDonald et al., 2015, p. 4).

Spirituality as Religious/Non-religious

Moberg (1971) provided a comprehensive definition of spirituality. He proposed that the spirituality pertains to an individual's inner resources, ultimate concerns, and the central philosophy of life, regardless of whether it is religious or nonreligious. He believed that all people are spiritual. According to Brown (1987), for nonreligious people, almost anything such as gardening, ecology, music, or humanism can be a form of spirituality. Ganje-Fling and McCarthy (1996) defined *spirituality* as "a complex, multifaceted construct that involves ultimate and personal truths that individuals hold as inviolable in their lives. This definition of spirituality is broad enough to incorporate religious, existential, and unstructured orientations, as well as concepts such as God, Higher Power, and spiritual source" (p. 253).

Spirituality is a harmonious connectedness to inner strengths and to any source which enhances one's sense of purpose or transcendence. In a study in Illinois of outpatient 65-year-olds, 80% believed that their religious faith was the most important influence in their lives (Koenig, Moberg, & Kvale, 1988).

Dimensions of Spirituality

Capps, Rambo, and Ransahoff (1976) offered six spiritual dimensions within religion: the mythological, ritual, experiential, dispositional, social, and directional.

Spirituality has been described and defined in humanistic-phenomenological terms (Elkins, Hedstrom, Hughes, Leaf, & Saunders, 1988). They define spirituality in the following terms: "Spirituality which comes from the Latin *spiritus,* meaning 'breath of life', is a way of being and experiencing that comes through awareness of a transcendent dimension and that is characterized by certain identifiable values in regard to self, others, nature, life, and whatever one considers to be the Ultimate" (p. 10). The Spiritual Orientation Inventory (Elkins, Hedstrom, Hughes, Leaf, & Saunders, 1988) consists of nine categories and is broadly referenced by therapists working in religious and spiritual areas (West, 2004): Transcendental dimension, Meaning and purpose to life, Mission in life, Sacredness of life, Material values, Altruism, Idealism, Awareness of the tragic, and Spiritual fruits.

LaPierre (1994) suggested the following six dimensions of spirituality:

1. Journey: Belief that life has meaning and purpose.

2. Transcendental encounters: As above, belief in a higher level of reality.

3. Community: Belief that personal growth should occur within a loving community.

4. Religion: Beliefs and Practices relating one to a supreme being.

5. Mystery of creation: Sense of connection to an environment, its creation and creator.

6. Transformation: Sense of personal change in relation to social involvement—of becoming.

Elkins, Hedstrom, Hughes, Leaf, and Saunders (1988), and LaPierre (1994) dimensions suggest directions for operarationalizing spirituality. They also suggest that it will be difficult, if not possible to assess spirituality in a holistic manner.

According to Sims (1994), there are five domains of spirituality. These are: meaning in life, interrelatedness, wholeness, morality, and awareness of God.

According to Mitroff and Denton (1999), there are eight key elements of spirituality:

- Not formal, structured, or organized,
- Non-denominational, above and beyond denominational,
- Inclusive, embracing everyone,

- The ultimate source and provider of meaning and purpose in life,
- The awe we feel in the presence of the transcendent,
- The deep feeling of interconnectedness with all,
- Inner peace and calmness, and
- An inexhaustible source of faith.

Wilber (2001) traces two paths of spirituality – the ascending path towards a higher transcendence and the descending path towards this world – in the evolutionary record. 'Evolution is best thought of as Spirit-in action, God-in-the-making, where Spirit unfolds itself at every stage of development' (Wilber, 2000, p. 9).

Salsman and Carlson (2005) have divided ways of being spiritual into intrinsic and extrinsic components. People for whom spirituality is an internal, guiding, and significant impact on their everyday lives were describes as manifesting an intrinsic orientation. In contrast, individuals for whom spirituality was more peripheral for how they lived and conducted their lives were said to have extrinsic spirituality. Their spirituality was often determined by external forces or need—such as the need to be a member of a community. Individuals who are still seeking their own spirituality have been described as having a quest orientation.

According to Bhajanananda (2011), there are two main streams of spirituality:

> *(1) Religious Spirituality* is spiritual life lived within the bounds of a religion. In the Indian tradition, religious spirituality exists. In religions of Indian origin spirituality has always formed the mainstream.

(2) Secular Spirituality is spiritual life lived without any affiliation to institutional religions. Secular spirituality exists mainly in the West. This is chiefly because the foundations of faith in religion have been undermined by the dominance of science, by the materialistic ideologies and rationalistic thought.

Hardt, Schultz, Xander, Becker, and Dragan (2012) reported that there are four dimensions of spirituality, namely, belief in God, search for meaning, mindfulness and feeling of security.

The three major forms of spirituality or 'hypergood' today are entailed in: exclusive (scientific) humanism, also received as scientism; Christian or theistic humanism; and neo-Nietzschean anti-humanism with its emphasis on exploring the Dionysian appetites whatever they might be, including a philosophy of cruelty and sadism. Early modern history scholar Brad Gregory (2012) adds a fourth (extreme view) with avant-garde trans-humanism. These people want to remake the human, or invent the human through various forms of manipulations (genetic, technological means among them). Taylor focuses attention on the first three feeling that this point of discussion is where the greatest increase in understanding of our twenty-first century modern identity is available. They are vital for discernment of the age we inhabit. They provide the hermeneutical key on contemporary plausibility structures with which people identify, structures which drive research and drive culture. Despite some naïve perceptions, we are not talking about a mono-culture.

Definitions and Dimensions of SPIRITUALITY based on acronym

Husain (2011) viewed spirituality in terms of knowledge and practice. He suggested twelve components of each dimension.

Knowledge includes the following: sacredness, positive energy, intellect, reasoning, inner experience, transcendence, universalism, awareness, life force, intuition, transformation and yearning, Practice includes the following: sacraments, perfection, initiation, renunciation, illumination, temperance, unity, awakening, love, imagination, tranquility, and yoga. He regards knowledge and spiritual practices as ways for understanding the spirituality. Although it is true that our spirituality can be founded on knowledge and practice, there are yet some limitations of which we need to be aware.

Husain (2015) defines spirituality in terms of "The state of consciousness and experience in which the feeling and act of spiritual service, spiritual perfection, spiritual intuition, spiritual revelation, spiritual intelligence, spiritual transcendence, spiritual unity, spiritual awareness, spiritual love, spiritual immunity, spiritual transformation, and spiritual yielding are established" (p. 353).

Husain (2016) also discusses a number of spiritual practices connected with Islam such as submission to Allah, prayer, infallibility, remembrance of Allah, intercession, truthfulness, unity, ascetic life, love, *istikharah*, thankfulness, and yielding. These practices have been acknowledged in the verses of the Holy Qur'an and Hadith. Believing in such practices is essential because these were practiced by Prophet Muhammad (PBUH). Islamic practices share the reward and make one an ideal Muslim and spiritual. In this context, 'SPIRITUALITY' has been defined as "the Islamic and Prophetic way of life."

Husain has made an attempt to understand and define the phenomenon of 'SPIRITUALITY' as an acronym. A major advantage of defining spirituality in this manner is that it permits for its inclusion of the use of religious and theological ideas but, at the same time, these definitions incorporate knowledge and practice aspects as a system of thought for the interpretation of spiritual phenomena. These definitions opens up the possibility of exploration and investigation of a number of religious practices embedded in Hinduism and Islam such as prayer and meditation as ways for the spiritual development and maintenance of spirituality. Definitions suggest that religion is not wholly synonymous with spirituality; religion can be regarded as a major means for understanding of spiritual beliefs, practices, and experiences and its significance for self, other, and reality without conducting scientific inquiry.

From the above definitions it can be inferred that religion is identified with the individual or the community. There is also distinction made between the manner or practice of spirituality and the holistic response of religion, making the meanings of the terms quite clear.

Furthermore, Husain and others explain a better understanding of spirituality on the basis of empirical studies conducted on various aspects of spiritual perspectives such as spiritual personality, spiritual practices, spiritual belief, spiritual values, spiritual support, spiritual distress, spritual fitness, spiritual health and spiritual coping. Their ideas serve as significant guideposts for understanding spirituality. Hindus and Muslims' spiritual perspectives have been studied among solace seekers, religious devotees, *Kalpvasis*, adolescents, stress-related diseases patients, HIV/AIDS clients, and students' population. They introduce these concepts and approaches which can be used in studying spirituality.

Conclusion

All the above-mentioned definitions of the concept of spirituality accumulate to form an understanding of spirituality.

There is no single definition which alone could serve as the basis for an effective exploration of spirituality. In this chapter we presented a broader view of spirituality. This means that all the definitions mentioned above are relevant and applicable, at least to some extent, for the identification of dimensions of spirituality based on acronym.

Spirituality is a multi-dimensional concept involving sacredness, transcendence, religious/non-religious practices, purpose/meaning in life, values/virtues, faith, beliefs and experiences aspects.

Chapter Three

SPIRITUALITY: A Right Path to Knowledge and Practice

In Ramz-e-Bekhudi Allama Iqbal says “Spirituality is not something mundane to attain, the way we put all our efforts into achieving an object in life. It occurs like a bolt from the blue when you least expected it.”

India is known as the land of *Saints, Sufis, Avtars*, and *Spiritual Gurus*. This land with spiritual people encourages and breeds spiritualism. This great land has produced many spiritual personalities like Gandhi, Swami Vivekananda, Sant Kabir, Guru Nanak, and others who have left indelible impact on world history. Sufism allowing every religion to thrive, flourish and prosper. No wonder *Sufis*’ thoughts and their practices are said to be cultural, religious and spiritual hub for the citizens of the world. Sufis with progressive minds have transformed themselves into the most powerful culture of India. With their purified hearts, they have created wonders. Inner spirits have been the continuous source of motivation for them.

People of India have travelled more on the road of spirituality. Even though they know it is very long journey but it can begin with a single step. The single step may be more effective if it is in the right direction. Spirituality is the realm of causality which is found in almost every person. Throughout their life people try to locale themselves on the path of spirituality. As a phenomenon it has heuristic value, it lights the jewels and shines like a diamond in our socio-cultural milieu. Spirituality is marked by both a process and its result. It enhances the inner wisdom and maintains intrinsic as well as extrinsic environment.

Specific teachings and beliefs vary amongst Indian People. There is an almost universal belief in the importance of spirituality and the influence of spiritual forces in the balance of one’s life. It is said that we are spirits on a human journey. In this journey, health and well-being are a result of the complex interplay between the physical world (i.e., our bodies), our mental processes (our thoughts and emotions), our environment (our family, culture, etc.), and the spiritual forces outside of us and the spiritual learned practices that become part of us. This perspective is sometimes referred to as the relational world view.

For the purpose of this chapter, we define spirituality broadly. It is more than religion. It is the power of the human spirit. It is the complex and often conflicting nature of spiritual teachings, a sense of purpose and being, a sense of future, a sense of a higher power guiding and shaping our existence. It is a sense of seeking understanding of the mystery of human existence. It includes religion and religious teachings from every conceivable point of view. This world view, in which well-being is balanced between mind, body, spirit, and context, teaches that these elements of life have equal weight; achieving balance among these various functions is in essence the objective of our human existence. To be well is to have these things in balance. Spirituality is a cornerstone of existence.

One of the most important reasons for the universal appeal of the highly evolved culture and civilization of India has been its unique heritage of spirituality. It can be found in nature, music, art or a secular community. Spirituality found an echo in the hearts of the Indian people from the very ancient times because it focuses on the 'unity of being and sacredness' which elevate and enrich human life. Gradually, the concept found its way and reached different parts of the world, partly through the teaching of the Seers in this land but largely due to the knowledge and wisdom which was transmitted from this country. Increasingly people of various cultures, languages, customs and traditions began to adopt spirituality as a way of life. With the passage of time and inputs from different schools of thought, it began to acquire richness, complexity and wisdom. India embraced spirituality and wove it with great finesse in its religious traditions and customs and thus it remains the hallmark of the Buddhism and Hinduism, since spirituality is a source of excelling in good deeds, it is totally in consonance with the essence of religion.

Spirituality provides us with the right philosophy of life. Spirituality is a helpful means in times of difficulty. It saves us from succumbing to adversity. It is the art of crises management, from which we derive intellectual inspiration when in need. Everyone is in need of spirituality, whether rich or poor, powerful or powerless. Spirituality provides a man with a starting point for life. Anyone who is deprived of spirituality will also be deprived of this starting point. It guides those whose behavior is virtuous. Spirituality will always guide them to the right way and always promote them to think positively for others.

Spirituality guides people in terms of good and spiritual life, laws to build harmonious societies, and unity among members of the society. Spirituality is more rational, if people are encouraged to apply their mind and faculties on various spiritual laws and principles propounded and understand its meanings as times and perspectives change. Sometimes spirituality can be irrational, if followers are required to follow its tenets and practices blindly without applying their mind or questioning its doctrine.

Spirituality can answer the questions, 'Who am I? What is the purpose of my life? What is the creation plan of the Creator? A seeker is able to find true spirituality by finding rational answers to such questions, whereby he receives spirituality at the mind or thinking level. True spirituality is based on contemplation and reflection, it is an intellectual activity. When an individual discovers the truth, his life enters a new phase – that is, building his personality according to spiritual principles. This intellectual journey is two fold, one is to solve the riddle of why human beings undergo negative experiences in this world and the other is to offer positive solutions. It addresses the paradox of human beings having been given the freedom to make their own moral choices, and their frequent misuse of this freedom – a course of action which causes them to repeatedly face situations in which people harm each other, losses are incurred because of others' injustice, severe provocation are suffered because of untoward experiences. At such times spirituality helps us to convert negativity into positivity.

The spiritual path enables us to see things that remain invisible to the physical eye. It enables us to learn lessons from the past and see the future in the present. It is the source of human progress. Repeatedly, we find occasions in life, when we feel helpless. It is when we feel that life has become rudderless without direction that a spiritual savior holds out hope, as a source of courage and conviction.

Spirituality produces God-oriented thinking in individuals. His life thus becomes a God-oriented life. That is what makes a spiritual person unassailable. A spiritual person enters into such profound communion with God that he becomes very powerful indeed. Human beings revolve around spirituality. The uniqueness of the spirituality is that it envelopes our entire body, soul, or spirit. It helps us in connecting to the inside and outside world. Spirituality is the path of people which unites tradition and modernity.

Spirituality encourages all efforts to overcome human barriers such as race, religion, politics, caste and ethnicity and works to build bridges of reconciliation, cooperation and peace. The universe is relational in nature. Spirituality teaches us the lesson of give and take action leading towards peace when the action is guided by the principle of living for the sake of others. Lasting human development has its foundation in unselfish give and take action.

With the arrival of scientific age, speculations about alien being passed from theologians to science fiction writers, story in the films, but the spiritual dimension remained just below the surface. For thousands of years, spirituality has a deeper significance and greater endurance in human beings. In India, there is a rich tradition of spirituality which provides us knowledge and also helps in the practical application of new methods and strategies for the benefit of humanity.

Spirituality is the divine path and it is the path of love. Spirituality lies within an individual heart's hidden core. Search it and move from brain to heart to spirit or soul. In the present era, we cannot stop talking about it. Transformation of limited love which is manifested to others into divine love is the goal of spirituality. Spirituality focuses attention on the spirit and therefore one need to look within.

There is an endless greed for spiritual happiness. People find the very blissful and peaceful co-existence within the realm of spirituality. Through spiritual attitude we feel connected to life and to entire humanity. Some people experience a larger connection with humanity, while others do it out of a sense of gratitude and love. Spirituality is the resource for the expression of 'we-self' rather than 'my-self.' As a result spirituality gives the feeling of happiness.

Spirituality helps in evolving psychologically; therefore it is a phenomenon of an evolved person. Spirituality helps in finding yourself, growing in love and gratitude. To understand the deeper meaning of spirituality, experience it. Once you understand it, you may experience personal transformation and develop the spiritual self.

Spirituality has a higher and natural power that ordered the seen and unseen aspects of life. People knew through experience that spirituality helps in exploring the manifestation of the Unseen, Supreme Power. Faith in God springs forth our hearts intuitively. People who submit completely to God's will, they received God's message wholeheartedly.

Spirituality is one which being on higher spiritual state, can promote tranquility, regardless of the circumstances. It exists within its own self. No external event can disturb its inner peace. Spirituality develops relationship with the Supreme that provides meaning of life and sense of purpose. It helps an individual in better understanding the meaning of life and death. It allows acceptance for others who see the world differently from me. Spirituality provides a sense of peace and serenity. It helps an individual to integrate his experiences and belief into action and make sense of the world. Spirituality encourages an individual to exercise his freedom and to assume the responsibility for the direction of own life.

The best and the only practical method to purify the mind and spirit is spirituality. Attitude towards spirituality keep the mind and its thought-process active. Spiritual awareness should be continued in our relationship with people, ideas, and things. It can be towards a living person or ideation. Spirituality gives us inner freedom to listen to problems without being influenced by its reactions. It has capacity to watch with full attention our own psychological problems.

Spirituality provides an opportunity for us to purify ourselves and thus maintain mental equilibrium, because everything in life takes place according to the Cosmic Will. If we wish to reach the supra-mental state of Divinity, we should not overlook the paramount importance of the spiritually disciplined life, due to too much preoccupation with worldly entanglement. We should maintain the practice and technique of meditation as a daily activity.

Spirituality has contribution in terms of the development of Divine human qualities. Therefore, a man is always in the spiritual state at any given point of time. Good behaviour, gentleness of speech, and positive thoughts are the basic principles for the purification of the mind, heart and spirit. In all our physical, mental, and spiritual activities there should be awareness and clarity of consciousness.

Spirituality shows us the path how to move from the real world into spiritual living. We can never know our real Self as long as we are falsely identified with the ego-senses. Spirituality directs the people to cherish the awareness of the existence of the Reality behind the changing world of name and form. God is beyond the comprehension of human speech and mind, and therefore, when we realize existence of God, we become silent and merge in the bliss of infinity. Meditation serves as a spiritual link to God.

At a certain stage of spiritual development, an individual grows more complete in his contemplation and finds fulfillment in perfect oneness in the Divine Unity. Spiritual people see everything as Divine because their vision is such that they have reached the transcendental state, in which exalted state the Supreme Consciousness prevails in them, and in that perfect liberation they lead the life of fullness and blessedness. The spiritual state remains forever outside the power of thought-waves; it is essentially pure, enlightened, and free. Spirituality is the essence of Reality, attribute-less Supreme Consciousness, and indivisibility. Psychologically speaking, this state is seeing in wisdom, the truth as the truth, falsehood as falsehood, free from delusion and ignorance. Spiritual awareness is not an ordinary perception of something, but actually an experiencing of the Truth at that moment in which the ego is completely lifeless. We, therefore, recommend that in preference to worldly pursuits we must work for the spiritual freedom of ourselves and for the good of the people, family, society, and the whole world. As we approach the supreme state of self-realization we are even better equipped to encourage others spiritually. Since spirituality promotes peace of mind therefore it is a universal longing of every human being.

Spirituality cultivates sense of enlightenment. Spirituality develops the feeling of contentment and inner peace. It is an approach to life which is practical one. From this perspective, it is possible to accept life in its totality. It brings happiness in one's life. It involves developing a quality of wisdom and cultivates contentment. Spirituality cultivates righteousness, purity, truthfulness, perfection, love, wisdom and truthfulness values.

Spirituality is not about religion. Spirituality has been portrayed as a way of knowledge and also as a way of love. Many people today would say they are spiritual but not very religious. Spirituality is about meaning, inspiration and wisdom. It is about a deeper sense of purpose. It is about connectedness and the highest aspirations of the human spirit. It is also a way of experiencing spiritual states beyond our limited waking states.

Conclusion

Spirituality is the way through which one can find meaning, hope, happiness and inner peace in his life. Many people develop spirituality through religious practices. Some people discover it through connection with nature, whereas others find it in their values or virtues.

Apart from providing opportunities to the students to learn fundamentals, effort should be made to develop their vision, problem formulation and solution which will expose them to solve their real life problems and will motivate them in pursuing their goals.

Spirituality played a central role in the development of personality as well as in the lives of the majority of the global population. Spirituality is a central feature of human nature. To understand the role of spirituality in positive psychology means addressing a series of questions those were raised by the psychologists. From this perspective, spirituality guides a person what is correct in terms of his life as a whole. Positive psychology, on the other hand, focuses on people developing signature strengths without attending to practices cultivating all the major virtues. In this chapter we have discussed a number of thoughts related to spirituality and positive behavior that have an important place in the current scenario.

Spirituality should be considered as the righteous path in 21st century which has been preached for thousands of years in followers of different religions. Spiritual lifestyle has become necessity for peoples living in a democratic world for their existence.

Chapter Four

HOLISTIC SPIRITUALITY

Spirituality is a mere bounty of God's grace. It encompasses everything. It is eternal. The 21st century can be considered as the 'spiritual century.' Because scientists have virtually conquered the planet, explored the moon and did the technological advancement, improve the travel and communication facilities, can control our environment, eradicate poverty, markedly reduced communicable disease, extend our lifespan, significantly modify our behaviour, and overall we are moving towards human flourishing.

Spirituality is part of our history, culture and tradition. It is in our poetry, literature, dance, music, art, painting and sculpture. Spirituality is one of the most important characteristic of man. It is common knowledge that human beings have always existed in terms of bodily, mental and emotional states. But the state of spirituality suggests the ways of leading life in this world i.e. 'self-oriented' and 'God-oriented.' There are many people who have spiritual personalities and they are able to explore their true potential before their worldly life ends. Spirituality helps people to recognize their strengths and become a capable of independent thinking. This is a gift to mankind by the Creator.

Spirituality is the powerful provider of moral and spiritual guidance. For me, spirituality is a concern of man who is inclined for the welfare and service of all. Spirituality establishes the Kingdom of Heaven. Spirituality is a way of life; it heavily relies on the principle of unity of all being, truthfulness, piety and righteousness. It is the original nature according to which God created mankind. Spirituality is real and natural. It can help us to become more creative, patient, persistent, honest, kind, compassionate, wise, calm, hopeful and joyful.

Spirituality as a Perfect Virtue

Spirituality implies a total commitment of the body, the soul, and the sprit. It is not only concurred for outer perceptions, or inner faith, but in addition to these a total disengagement from worldly concerns at all times and an openness to that which God wills. One who has come to the stage of *ihsan* is, in a way, no longer in possession of himself. In fact, according to the words of the Prophet to the archangel Gabriel, this stage of perfect virtue consists "of adoring Allah as though that didst see Him, and if thou dost not see him He nonetheless seeth thee." The man who is in a state of *ihsan*, the *muhsin*, is truly the *Khalifah*, the vicegerent of God on earth. He rediscovers "the most beautiful form" in which he was created (according to the Quran XCV, 4), because his heart is like a pure, well-polished mirror in which the Divine can be reflected.

The present chapter discusses the concept of spirituality as a perfect virtue, definitions and dimensions of spirituality. The dimensions of spirituality suggested in this chapter are: sacredness, purpose and meaning in life, inner harmony, rituals and righteousness, intuition, transcendence, unifying interconnectedness, awareness, light and love, immersing, transformation, and yearning.

Dimensions of Spirituality

We need a thorough definition of the term 'spirituality' to understand it completely. We consider devotional life and spiritual practices such as sacredness, purpose and meaning in life, innerness, rituals and righteous life, intuition, transcendence, unifying interconnectedness, awareness, light and love, immersing, transformation, and yearning as the dimensions of SPIRITUALITY.

Sacredness: Sacredness is one of the old dimensions of spirituality. It existed in India as the sacred arts, painting, sculpture, music, dance, and culture traditions. These traditions exist to reveal the One Transcendental Truth.

According to Storr (1988), this is a way of putting the individual in touch with his deepest feelings. Sacredness of nature may unearth one's spirituality. Wikström (2004) describes the element of the sacred in ordinary terms and in connection with the common life. In his view, a longing for the sacred is an inborn human quality.

Perrin's (2007, p. 84) succinct statement about the element of the sacred effectively summarises the essential point: "People have come to discover that it is not in hardy logic of religious rules that we find answers to our deepest questions of life; rather we find them in meaningful encounter with the sacred dimension of life, which surfaces in various ways."

Linardakis, Papadaki, Smpokos, Sarri, Vozikaki, and Philalithis (2015) have suggested that religiosity/spirituality have a 'sacred core', including feelings, thoughts, experiences, and behaviours. A spiritual person tends to be sacred and believes in maintaining peace as the fundamental to meaningful human existence.

Purpose and meaning in life: It is defined as the process of searching for or discovering events or relationships that provide a sense of worth hope and/or reason for living/existence. The description of this concept is generally based on the work of Frankl (1962). Frankl found that prisoners who could find a purpose or goal in life could survive. He theorized that when a person's striving for meaning is frustrated a neurosis pertaining to the spiritual core may develop. An outgrowth of his theory was the development of the psychiatric treatment modality, termed "logotherapy", which treated this spiritual neurosis.

Owe Wikström suggests that spirituality is about the quest for the meaning of life and about gaining a comprehensive understanding of one's life and existence. Thus the search for meaning, meaningfulness and purpose of life is ontological by nature. The significance of meaning is an essential feature of Swinton's (2001/2003) approach to spirituality. He explores the aspect of meaning in relation to religion and religious participation. He argues that the most important factor in religion is not being religiously active, but rather the meaning this has for the individual.

Iqbal (2012) advocates that in Islam, spirituality is defined as the linking of actions to the purpose of life and this purpose is to worship ALLAH (The Qur'an, 51:56). In Islam worship does not mean only observance of certain religious rituals but to lead complete life in all spheres according to the will of ALLAH. By this definition, all actions undertaken for the pleasure of ALLAH are spiritual because they link material action with the purpose of life. From this perspective nearness to ALLAH is synonymous with spiritual development and distance is indicative of spiritual fall. Allah is the source of your goodness, purpose and meaning in life.

We have limited perspective about who we are and the purpose of life. The purpose and meaning in life is an essential element in the spiritual quest. Spirituality is a major source of all things which is purposeful and meaningful in that pursuit. We are not able to appreciate the fact that the greatest crisis can become a means for our self-growth, progress and manifestation of truth if we can have purpose and meaning in life. God's remembrance and presence means the meaningfulness and purposefulness of life. God's remembrance ensures the consciousness of spiritual personality. The warning in *surah al-Hashr*—"Do not be like those who forgot Allah."

Innerness: Innerness, or inner resources, is explained as the process of striving for and/or discovering wholeness, identity, and a sense of empowerment. It manifests the feelings of strength in times of crisis, calmness or serenity in dealing with uncertainty in life, guidance in living, being at peace with one's self and the world, and feelings of ability. The description of this term derived from the work of Vaughan (1986) who viewed spirituality as "radiating from an inner source" (p. 87).

Sinnott (1969) described the spirit as "a reservoir on which man may draw" (p. 358); and Burkhardt (1989) who described inner strength as including "one's inner resources, awareness, consciousness and sense of sacred source" (p. 72). Spirituality activates our inner strength which helps us to differentiate between right and wrong.

Rituals and Righteous Life: The practice aspect of spirituality is linked with rituals. Rituals are in the form of purity, prayer, and fasting. These forms of rituals are well connected with divine assistance and consciousness. The model of ritual was given by the *sunnah* of Prophet Muhammad (SAW). Rituals establish the relationship between the self and God. Maulana Abul Kalam Azad has taken a liberal view which accords with the changing spirit of time. He maintains: "But ritual was not religion, said the Quran, nor the criterion of truth." It was merely an outward aspect of religion. The spirit was something superior to it, and that alone was *Din* or religion. Religion in reality was devotion to God through righteous living, and was no exclusively heritage of any single groups of people.

Some ritualistic behavior, for example, prayer and fasting; require therapeutic action that promotes well-being. Therapeutic action encouraging containment of the expression is important in all aspects of individuals' lives, including the religious/spiritual dimensions of their lives.

Rituals develop your responsible behaviour and personality in the right direction. An example, it is the following verse of the Qur'an:

Enjoin prayer on thy people, and be constant therein. We ask thee not to provide sustenance: We provide it for thee. But the Hereafter is for righteousness. (20:132).

Righteous life is not possible without practising rituals. The whole life of the Prophet Muhammad (SAW) was righteous. Spirituality develops righteousness and put an individual on the path of Self-enquiry. The definition of righteousness is highly spiritualized. This is a supreme virtue.

Intuition: It guides us in spiritual matters where we have insufficient information. Our minds have innate intuition. Our bodies can also tell us when something is out of balance in our lives, even if this knowledge is unclear in our conscious minds. If we are to fully heal, we must bring our attention to messages our bodies relay through intuition. But we also need logic and facts to fully understand which imbalances in our lifestyle are affecting our health. We need to balance emotions and intuition with logic and fact. Both – extreme logic without intuition, and intuition without logic – breed disaster.

Transcendence: In simple terms, "transcendence" means "going beyond." Jackson (1980) described transcendence as the self going beyond itself. It is explained as the ability to reach or exceed the limits of usual experience; the capacity, willingness or experience of rising above or overcoming bodily or psychic conditions; or the capacity for achieving wellness or self-healing. The definition of transcendence was taken from the work of Frankl (1962), who defined transcendence as the ability to rise above inflictions of the body or psyche.

Spirituality is pure and transcendental in nature. Reed (1987) viewed transcendence as "reflective of the human capacity to extend the self beyond common boundaries of the immediate context and achieve new perspectives and experiences" (p. 335).

Hardy (1984) suggests that spirituality is something yet more specific than a mere human quality or dimension. He defines spirituality in the following way: "It seems to me that the main characteristics of man's religious and spiritual experiences are shown in his feelings for a transcendental reality... a feeling that 'Something Other' than the self can actually be sensed; a desire to personalize this presence into deity and to have a private I-Thou relationship with it, communicating through prayer" (p. 131).

In the light of Islam people are to be transcendent while in Eastern religion people are Immanence. Each and every one has faced the transcendent part of life, something that obtains us away from our present way of thinking, feeling, or acting. Every single aspect of behavior is self-transcendence and is also logical; it can recognize the system of processes, talent, and decisions behind each of these new behaviors. It can refer to these condition as offering a kind of weak transcendence, a little that is beyond us but also within our reach—transcendence "of an internal and human sort" (Nussbaum, 1990, p. 379). However, people also experienced more radical forms of strong transcendence that have the courage to understanding, accepting, and control. This occurs when we find that life despite our best effort life is not on one way there is some ups and downs has been came. So we have overcome these hurdles and make the life in the form of strong transcendence.

A truly spiritual person would always prefer to transcendent from what is given to the future vision. He would be engaged in creating new world as what is given is never perfect. There are some characteristics associated with transcendent people. They are: unity, truth and goodness. According to Rao (2010), spiritual pursuit is an exercise for transformation of the human condition to achieve states of transcendence.

Unifying Interconnectedness: This dimension is characterized as the feeling of relatedness or attachment to others, a sense of relationship to all of life, a feeling of harmony with self and others, and a feeling of oneness with the universe and/or a universal element or Supreme Being. The term derived from the work of Hungelmann and others (1985) who defined the term "harmonious interconnectedness" in a phenomenological study to describe spiritual well-being in persons 65 years of age and older. The term was coined to define a concept which they believed exists throughout and beyond time and space.

Awareness: Spirituality develops high level of awareness which helps an individual to flourish. Knowing the 'Self' depends much on awareness. "Awareness of any spiritual aspect makes a man noble (Husain, 2011, p. 37). Man's creative abilities can be nurtured through awareness. Awareness is an essential element for human beings, both mentally and spiritually. Islamic spirituality triggers awareness of higher Self within the earnest seeker, drawing the aspirant into an inner state of reality beyond the mind. Those who are spiritually aware and awake have the responsibility to call for those who remain spiritually blind, knowing that there is no guarantee of a response.

Light and Love: Spirituality is a source of spiritual light. Spirituality gives light to those who are living in darkness on this earth. The object of light is an inner illumination. The dimension of love includes all modes of spiritual union. Love is a divine attribute. But surely loving God presupposes being conscious of Him. To be conscious of Him is to fix the heart in remembering of the Divine. Love is the attribute which unites the soul of man to God. Love alone is desire of possession or of union with opposite sex and God. Love is the positive disposition. Human love is fickle, selfish, fragile and imbued with egoism. Remember Divinity. His love is pure and everlasting.

The dimension of love is the very source of life. It is this that truly develops a sense of belongingness. In every human being, love is a source of life. This is why human beings seem to live in a constant struggle between the self and others. When you love others, you have the consciousness of being more than physical and social.

One of Mother Teresa's first followers Gertrude Gomes wrote: "A light has dawned in the darkness of the slums." Labouring joyfully and selflessly to dispel the darkness of disease, suffering, death, poverty, rejection and female infanticide, Teresa took upon her frail shoulders the immense responsibility of being mother, mentor, nurse, sister, friend and 'light' to thousands of those whom she considered sisters and brothers of her 'spouse' Jesus. Teresa remained uncompromisingly committed to love and serve God's children.

Swami Kriyananda gave the explanation of light in one of his songs, "What we need is Light! You cannot drive out the darkness with a stick." When Light fills us, where can darkness dwell? Swamiji's focus upon Light was more than "positive thinking." It explains that we can view of "reality" by our state of mind and spirit.

Sheldrake (2007) points out John Wesley's emphasis on love and service for one's neighbour as the key concepts of his spirituality. Our hearts need to be saturated with love, for love is the light that will illumine the world. For this, we need illumined hearts that can behold the vision of fellowship, unity and brotherhood. Love is what we need to build a new world of universal brotherhood and peace. Love is universal permeating all of nature. We seek Divine Assistance or blessing in the form of light. Spirituality nurture feeling of love and compassion. What we need is more of love and to show the light to build the foundation of one world family - *Vasudhaiva Kutumbakam*.

Immersing: One should try to immerse himself in doing creative work. We all need to learn to immerse, through focusing on what is important to beneficial our creativity and any task undertaken. It makes possible while visiting to a Holy Shrine. Visiting to a shrine is a spiritual activity which has a long tradition, but it still represents a valid aspect of spirituality in our time. There is something about the movement involved in going to a shrine. There are certain positive thoughts that induce and invite your mind to get immerse. Immersing might be difficult to some people, but it makes much more rewarding and deep spiritual experiences. A spiritual person who belongs to any religion, for him immersing in deity is a self-realization.

For many people practising spirituality means immersing. This implies “withdrawal” or going to a “solitary place” i.e. Holy Shrine. In India, we have many shrines, irrespective of the religious faith; people sought peace and solitude in order to find a more meaningful relationship with God through observing prayer, contemplation and meditation.

Transformation: Spirituality initiates and works the desired transformation at the mental level. Psychiatrist Curt Thompson (Anatomy of the Soul, 2010, p.7) gave surprising insights on the connections between neuroscience and a transformative relationship with God—a means to integrate the self and move us from insecurity to security: “The importance of spiritual development is now acknowledged by many researchers and respected clinicians as one of the most important lenses through which we should view our lives." What if God's fundamental orientation toward his entire creation (including humans) was one of deep, compassionate affection and intense interest in its well-being (Psalm 139)?

Leffel (2007) seeks to construct "an integrative psychology-theology framework for studying the *affective basis of spiritual transformation.*" He suggests that in attempting this "the relational spiritual paradigm provides an important theoretical advance in how we model the relationship between personality structure... and spiritual transformation..."

Aurobindo argues that 'Man' is born ignorant, and he does not know the nature of Reality. In addition, man experiences life through division and conflict. To overcome these limitations, man must embark on a process of self discovery in which he uncovers the divine nature. This discovery is done through a three step process (Rao, 2012, p. 205).

1. Psychic Transformation: A search within to discover his evolving soul. He understands the oneness and unity of Creation, and the harmony of all opposites experienced in life.

2. Spiritual Transformation: Then his mind expends and experiences knowledge through light, intuition and revelation, culminating in spiritual transformation.

3. Supra-mental Transformation: The first two steps lead to the complete transformation of the mind, heart, emotions as well as the physical body.

This evolution enables the soul to fulfill its human aspirations and realization of god. Aurobindo's philosophy extends beyond the perfection and transformation of the individual. It includes the evolution and transformation of human society in general.

Transformation implies believing in spiritual continuity and rebirth. Belief in God transforms man's thinking he begins to look at things not in relation to human beings but in relation to God. This is because, God infused spirit among us. Spirituality has transforming effects on our lives and relationships. The solution of most of the worldly problems is possible through spiritual transformation. Spiritual virtues from A to Z such as Assertiveness, Benevolence, Compassion, Devotion, Excellence, Faithfulness, Gratitude, Humility, Integrity, Justice, Kindness, Love, Modesty, Non-violence, Orderliness, Peacefulness, Quiet, Righteousness, Strength, Truthfulness, Uprightness, Vision, Wisdom, X, Yearning and Zeal are the greatest forces of transformation.

Yearning: Husain (2011) posits that yearning "is a comprehensive attitude to life in which of self-interest is martyred and replaced by positive yearnings to search for the self and fully realize through complete identification with the Will of God" (pp. 41-42). "Follow your heart's boundless desire. It takes you out of yourself and fosters an appreciation for the multidimensional pleasures of life" (Frederic & Brussat, 1996).

Yearning is associated with wellbeing and universal love. Many spiritual activities in our daily lives form an integral part of it. In order to find explanations to our lives, we developed yearning with God. Any activity in which you are in communication with God or Spiritual Guru, pursuing a goal implies that you are creating something new. What we understand in the past, today, and tomorrow as yearning with God in the form of worshiping. People should have sense of yearning to become truthful.

Conclusion

Practised properly, spirituality develops sacredness, purpose and meaning in life, inner harmony, rituals and righteousness, intuition, transcendence, unifying interconnectedness, awareness, light and love, immersing, transformation, and yearning. These are the infinite spiritual qualities within the human being. The dimensions suggested here is the innermost part of individuals' integrated well-being. These dimensions may have a great deal of concern at the conscious and practical levels about one who wants to become spiritual. A spiritual person will have self-perfection in his behaviour and will be centered, having experiential knowledge of the 'Self' which is reflected in the oneness of God. The central aim of spirituality is to get immersed with these dimensions at the individual level, and maintain spiritual health. Man can make psycho-spiritual progress through these ways. We are to follow these practices on earth; they will lead us to the way of God.

A number of definitions of spirituality are known within literature, serving their purpose well in the context for which they have been designed. By combining a number of different points of view and approaches to spirituality by the authors of this book and others, it is possible to arrive at an understanding which covers the meaning of this term more comprehensively so that it is applicable to give the operational definition of spirituality. The dimensions of spirituality suggested here pave the way to capture the essence of spirituality and to study it scientifically, using the accepted and sound methodology. Hence the concept of spirituality must be understood holistically.

The contribution of Husain and others may effectively describe the conceptual and dimensional aspects of spirituality as a phenomenon, but their contribution is substantial in defining what spirituality is. The phenomenon of spirituality requires tremendous understanding and exploration. Since spirituality is experiential in nature, mere investigation of the theoretical issues attached to it will not yield all its hidden secrets. Spirituality is like a river that is flowing, moving incessantly. Unless you follow with it is generously, with happiness, yearning with divine, you can see and experience the full beauty of that river.

Chapter Five

PRACTISING ASPECTS OF SPIRITUALITY IN HINDUISM

Hinduism can easily be divided into two phases: the *Vedic* phase and the *Puranic* phase. The *Vedic* phase focussed on ritual, while the *Puranic* phase is about narrative. The *Vedic* phase therefore continues to be mysterious, even out of reach, while the *Puranic* phase with its heroes and villains seems to make immediate sense. Historically, the *Vedic* phase begins 4,000 years ago and wanes after the arrival of Gautama Buddha, 500 BCE. The *Puranic* phase follows the rising appeal of the Buddha and his teachings, something that continues today.

The *Vedic* phase is associated with the hymn collections or *samhitas* - *Rig, Yajur, Sama, Atharva* - the ritual manuals or Brahmanas, and the philosophical texts known as *aranyakas* and more prominently, the *Upanishads*. The *Puranic* phase is associated with the great epics, the *Ramayana* and *Mahabharata*, and with the chronicles known as *Puranas*. There are many *Puranas*: 18 major ones, hundreds of minor ones, including those restricted to a particular place (*sthala-purana*) or to a particular community (*jati-purana*). It is through the *Puranas*, that *Vedic* wisdom reaches the common man.

Some see *Vedas* and *Puranas* as two distinct traditions that have nothing to do with each other, *vedas* being the creation of *Aryans* and *Puranas* being the creation of non-*Aryans*, who mingled with the Aryans. They see *Puranas* as a Hindu reaction to Buddhist monasticism, which is why the *Puranas* and temple traditions celebrate the householder's life over the hermit's.

Others see *Vedas* as superior and *Puranas* as inferior, a hierarchy that was common amongst Greek aristocrats, and later colonial orientalists, who preferred philosophy over poetry and saw 'logos' as superior to 'mythos'. This was adopted by many Hindu 'reformers' of the 19th century, who were ashamed of Hindu customs such as what they perceived as 'idol' worship.

At the heart of the *Vedas* is *brahmavidya* or *atman-gyan* - a deep understanding of human nature, which does not change with time (*Sanatan dharma*). The sages struggled to communicate this idea. First they used rituals, hence the *Vedas*. Later, with increased confidence, they used stories, hence the *Puranas*.

The Bhagavad Gita says: "Never was the spirit born; neither will it cease to be; it is beyond time; ends and beginnings are dreams; Birthless, deathless and changeless remains the spirit forever; Death hath not touched it at all, dead though the house of it seems."

In Hinduism, spirituality is practiced by doing yoga, meditation, *reiki*, prayer, reading scripture, fasting, service, *ragas* and music, *satsang,* meditation, and silence. Spiritual practices are universal but action depends on the faith of the person. Spiritual practices bring changes in behaviour. Spiritual practices are a set of behavioural, cognitive, and spiritual exercises and strategies aimed at to modify the behaviour of individuals for the purpose of enhancing spiritual growth. Hindu spirituality is regarded as a symbol of *dharma* and righteousness.

Spiritual practices are the most endearing tradition of all time among the followers of different religious faith. These are nurtured and kept alive by generations of parents to their children through the socialization process. Spiritual practices protect the morality of children. And even when we grew up then we were grateful to our parents who provide us such an excellent path for the spiritual well-being. Spirituality has hidden treasures of deep mystical knowledge.

According to Pradhan (2014), Indian spirituality seeks to explore the experience of true nature of soul or consciousness in one's being. It is not only a set of generalized principles but it is also a set of practice that can be used for the transformation of the human condition towards perfection. Indian spirituality stresses self-inspection and self-introspection to achieve self-mastery and perfection. It exhorts discipline of oneself, not of others .Wisdom is acquired by introspection, reflection and experimentation with one's own self in the light of spiritual knowledge or self-knowledge (*Atman–gyan*). It has redefined the goal of life from the pursuit of happiness to freedom (*Moksha*) revealing fantastic understanding of the order of the inner world (Pradhan & Shukla, 2010).

According to Yogi Indra (2017), "Our spiritual traditions focus on simple thing; to evoke the knower in us, for only then can one become one with Brahmn, and know that the world is nothing but a 'Belief'. And all beliefs are nothing but distorted perspectives, not the Truth" (p. 12).

In Hinduism, spirituality is purely practice-based; such kind of spirituality can provide a person solace. The present authors suggest spiritual practices based on the term SPIRITUALITY. The twelve practices which have been practised by Hindus are: ***Samskaras*** (sacraments), ***Prarthana*** (prayer), ***Indriya-nigraha*** (control over the senses), ***Ragas***, ***Invocation of OM*** (chanting of OM), ***Tarpan*** (libation), ***Upavaasa*** (fasting), ***Anubhava*** (experiences), ***Lokasamgraha*** (welfare of all), ***Ishwara-pranidhana*** (surrender to God), ***Tirth-yatra*** (pilgrimage) and ***Yoga***. These may involve the series of movements to create consciousness and establish connectedness with God.

Samskaras (sacraments)

The Sanskrit term '*samskaras*' means rituals and rites in one's life cycle. *Samskaras* place someone in the condition of salvation and perfection. Usually it is translated as 'sacrament', 'tradition rite', or 'rites of passage' but these terms do not completely convey its significance. *Samskaras* are more than traditional rites and ceremonies in fact they constitute a belief, an idea about human beings and their development in the world. *Samskaras* also taken to mean to perfect, polish, train, cultivate, refine, educate and prepare the human life cycle. They formally mark in the different stages of physical, psychological and moral development of a person and also preparing spiritually, socially and culturally the person to assume the *dharmic* duties and responsibilities of a good person especially in adulthood. To perfect and sanctify the whole human being, *samskaras* shape and educate a person's moral values. We find the evidence of these life cycle rituals (*samskaras*) in the ancient Vedas. In the performance of most of these rituals 'mantras' are recited, draw from the *Vedic* corpus of hymns, prayer and blessings. The Hindu tradition have more than forty *samskaras* (approximately forty eight) in the more comprehensive lists which included daily sacrifices, whereas some sources include only twelve *samskaras* finally by the medieval period, many authorities agreed on a common set of sixteen *samskaras* of the body. A good *samskaras* is believed to help the soul to get a higher level of birth. *Samskaras* signifies cultural beliefs.

Even before birth *samskaras* begin with the sanctification of the womb and seed in the prenatal knows as ***garbhadhana samskaras*** immediately performed after the marriage because to secure progeny is the prescribed purpose of wedding. In Hinduism it is believed that to born a male child is a sacred ritual. ***pumsavana samskaras*** conducted to ensure a male fetus. According to Manusmiriti it should be prescribed in the fourth month of pregnancy. An additional ***samskara*** of ***simantonnayana*** also conducted before birth to ensure the safe development and delivery of the child during the last trimester, which entails a ritual parting of the pregnant woman's hair. Remaining life-cycle rituals are conducted after the delivery and before the umbilical cord is cut. It includes several minor rites: as unequal proportions of ghee and honey on to the lips of newborn's to ensure strength and intelligence, uttering the name of those who have lived a long life to ensure the longevity of the newborn's, place the child on the lap of the father who whispers various sacred syllables, secret name and the "*vac*" word (speech) in the child's ear three times. ***Namakarana samskara*** is the naming ceremony of the new born child, conducted after eleventh or twelfth days of birth. ***Niskramana samskara*** is a newborn child's first outing. According to Manusmiriti this *samskaras* should be conducted during the fourth month after birth. ***Gannaprasana samskara*** is the first feeding of solid foods (mash, kheer) conducted in the sixth month after birth. ***Cudakarana samskara*** is the first hair-cut of the newborns, conducted in the first or third year of birth, meant to remove the impurities. ***Karnavedha samskara*** is ear-piercing *samskara*, conducted before the age of four of a child. In the human life the process if learning or study begin with the ***samskara*** of ***vidyarambha*** and in the period of studentship (*brahmacarya*) is further refined and solemnized and also inaugurated by the ***upanayana samskara.*** Traditionally this *samskara* was recommended for Brahmans in eighth year, *ksatriyas* in their eleventh year and *Vaisyas* in twelfth year of their age. During *upanayana* a student donned a sacred thread called *yajnopavita* for wearing daily, which reminds him his responsibilities to a life of purity and righteousness. Although traditionally, *Brahman*, *Ksatriyas* and Vaisyas were eligible to undergo *upanayana*. The ***samskara*** of ***veedarambha*** usually fall during a boy's studentship, a ritual initiation of a student into Vedic studies and ***kesanta samskara***, first ritual shaving of a boy's beard performance in his sixteenth year of age. ***Samskara*** of

samavartana performed when the stage of studentship completes and the student leaves the teacher and return to his home. As a part of this *samskara*, the student presents a gift or honorarium (*dakshina*) to his teachers (*guru*) signifying his respect and thanks also asks the permission of his teacher to take leave. The central of all the *samskaras* is ***vivaha samskara*** (marriage). It is considered as the initiation of men and women into the householder life and responsibilities. According to Manu it is as the highest dharma of both men and women. ***Antyesti samskara*** is a death rite (final ritual) in which the deceased body consigned to the fire (*agni*), from which the *samskara* gets its other name cremation. After the cremation within three days, the remaining ashes and bones are collected by the chief mourner and ritually throw into the following water river. ***Sraddha*** is an ancestor rituals. *Sraddha* rites are in the memorial ceremonies respect and tranquillize the deceased ancestors. *Sapindikarana* is a special *Sraddha* performed on the twelfth day after death. *Sraddha* must be performed at regular intervals, the memorial rite for the forefathers.

Prarthana (prayer)

In Hinduism, prayer/worship is the expression of devotion, for worship the Sanskrit word '*Prarthana*' is used, derived from two words '*pra*' and '*artha*' meaning pleading fervently. So '*prarthana*' means to ask the God for something with intense yearning (Vedanta- A Way of Life, 2011). It includes faith, pleading, love and respect. It is an act or invocation to activate a rapport with the universal power through deliberate communication. The aim of prayer is to enable a person to gain the direct experience of the recipient. If one offers prayer with spiritual emotions, the God protects him from distress. Prayer (*prarthana*) is the essence of worship (*puja*). *Puja* is overt and *prarthana* is covert. It cannot be observed but done by the worshiper with faith and devotion (*Bhakti Bhav*) or spiritual emotion.

According to Spiritual Science Research Foundation (2013) there are of two types of prayer

(i) *Sakam prarthana* (prayer with expectations) for worldly benefit.

(ii) *Nishkam prarthana* (prayer without expectations) for spiritual growth.

Sakam prarthana is done for the fulfillment of worldly desires such as wealth, health, worldly pleasures and progeny etc. *Nishkam prarthana* is done for surrendering oneself unto the God or the spiritual teacher (*guru*) without any expectation or objective. This type of prayer is done always in the context of spiritual progress. *Sakam prarthana* is inferior while that done *Nishkam prarthana* is superior for spiritual upliftment. Prayer may be performed anywhere and anytime either in personal or in the group but faith is necessary in the God.

Prayer connects with the Supreme. It is the direct path to approach the Higher Power. Prayer is well-directed, adequate effort, your commitment to the pursuit. You must persevere and continue to practice it with the pursuit until it is accomplished. Prayer cultivates perseverance. Prayer could be facilitating to overcome obstacles in the way of accomplishing the goal. Our knowledge is very limited to cope with the problems. Prayer has enough power through which obstacles can be avoided. It recognizes that there are unknown factors that make the difference between success and failure.

Benefits of worship: According to the Hindu Prayer Book (2014, p. 73) worship of the God purifies the heart, mind and soul. It helps the devotee to communion and sit near the God. It fills the mind with pure love and emotions (*suddha bhava*). By it may gradually transmutes into the divine being. It destroys egoism, anger, hatred etc. It turns the mind of the worshiper inward and eventually brings the worshiper face to face with the lord.

Indriya-nigraha (sense of control)

Indriya-*nigraha* means control or mastery over the senses. There are 10 *indriyas* or organs: five sensory (*Jnanendriyas*) and five motor (*Karmendriyas*).

Jnanendriyas: The five cognitive senses are the five entrance doors, which are called *jnanendriyas*. *Jnana* means knowing. *Indriyas* are the senses. They are: organ for seeing (Eyes- ***Chakshu***- *Indriya*), organ for sound (Ear- ***Karna***- *Indriya*), organ for smell (Nose- ***Nasika***- *Indriya*), organ for touch (Skin- ***Sparch***- *Indriya*), and organ for taste (Tongue- ***Swad***- *Indriya*), and their functions respectively are: *Darsana* (to see), *Sravana* (to hear), *Agharana* (to smell), *Sparsana* (to touch), and *Asvadana* (to taste).

Karmendriyas: The five exit doors are five means of expression, which are called *karmendriyas*. *Karma* means action. *Indriyas* are the means or senses. They are: vocal cord (***Vak***), hands (***Pani* or *Hasta***), legs (***Pad***), anus (***Payu***), and genital organ (***Upastha***), and their functions respectively are: to speak (*Kathana*), to work (*Silpana*), to move (*Carana*), to let out the waste (*Varjana*), and to give birth (*Janana*).

The instability of the mind has to be controlled with the help of '*indriya-nigraha*', self discipline, development of detachment to sensory objects and also with the practice of renunciation.

Renunciation means '*sanyas*' in the present day context renunciation does not mean to renounce home and family ties, but renunciation of one's desires, affection and attachment. It leads to stability of the mind, greater devotion to the supreme divine (God) and a smoother sailing in the path of self-realization. As it has been described in the Hindu scriptures that if one wants to realize the God then it is not necessary to become a '*sanyasi*' and renounce the world. A person who is having his family can also realize the God through spiritual beliefs utter devotion (*bhakti*) and practices like prayer, chanting the mantra (*japa*), meditation, worship, singing of hymns and *bhajans*, psalms that glorify the God selfishlessly. In *dharmic* life the control of *indryas* is considered imperative. So in the spiritual sphere Hindus will have to exercise to control over the sensory and motor organs.

According to Rao (2012), "one has to adopt the well established practice of 'Renunciation' of the following acts (through mind, speech and body):

(a) All forms of evil acts (*Nishiddha karma*) which are prohibited by scriptures- theft, adultery, deception, fraud, utterance of false-hood, oppression, violence, taking of prohibited drinks and food, wrong doing, cursing in the name of God, etc.

(b) All acts (including auspicious acts like worship, sacrifice, etc.) done with a selfish motive and for getting objects of enjoyment-like women, progeny, wealth, etc. The desire for honour, fame and social prestige, are considered products of '*Prarabdha karma*.

(c) Expecting money or service from others, acceptance of gifts or service from others with a selfish interest is to be totally renounced.

(d) All acts enjoined in the scriptures (worship of Gods, service of parents and elders, performance of sacrifices and charities, sustenance of the body, etc.) should be performed by duly renouncing every form of desire.

(e) One should have a sense of detachment for all work done through mind, speech and body as well as over all worldly objects and family ties. Regarding them as impermanent" (p. 44).

Indriya Nigraha is the most important prerequisite for spiritual development in Hinduism. How to perform *Indriya Nigraha*, and why it is mandatory is mentioned in Hindu scriptures like Bhagavad Gita, *Upanishads* and *Yogasutra* of Patanjali. The Bhagavad Gita says a person whose senses are under control is in equipoise. It is one of the basic requirements for a peaceful and prosperous life on earth. To ensure avoidance of unwanted inputs to our mind from our five sense organs, we need to develop a system that filters and controls the input. This control system which Patanjali Maharshi explains in the *Yoga Sutras* is *Indriya Nigraha*, an ability to shut out or restrain from the information and related instinctive reactions from the five sense organs at our choice.

Indriya Nigraha involves the control of both internal and external senses. The internal senses arise in the mind and are due to false identification of the soul, ignorance and lack of proper guidance. The internal senses are desire, lust, anger, egotism, strength and pride. The external senses are hearing, sight, touch, taste and smell.

As per the Bhagavad Gita, the tendency of the mind to waver makes the controlling of the senses difficult, but constant practice and detachment are the ways to control the senses. The person who has achieved the control of senses is firmly resolved, restrained, and peaceful and is a yogi.

Ragas

Ragas are highly spiritual in nature. The singer/artist tries to reach God through his *ragas*. Indian classical music in the form of *ragas* is a journey of the *Jeevatma* or the soul towards the *Paramatma* or the Divine.

'*Sangeeta sadhana*' or the practice of classical music is the key to attaining the Divine.

The *"Ranjayati Iti Raaga"* is the Sanskrit definition given to the word, 'raga'.

That which pleases the ear is referred to as a raga. The raga can be defined as a melodic type or melodic mould. It is a collection of notes in a particular order, giving rise to a melody type. The raga is the very soul of Indian music.

There are two main classical Indian music traditions, North Indian (*Hindustani*) and South Indian (*Carnatic*), and the concept of *raga* is shared by both. *Ragas* are also found in Sikh traditions such as in *Guru Granth Sahib*, Buddhism and Jainism. Raga is also a part of the *qawwali* tradition found in Sufism. Some popular Indian film songs and *ghazals* use *ragas* in their compositions.

As Powers (1959) states, "A *raga* is not a tune, nor is it a 'modal' scale, but rather a continuum with scale and tune as its extremes." The Indian raga is far more complex than the simple modal scale and encompasses in itself a variety of ways in which you can treat its notes or swaras. The raga is also much more complicated than just a tune. The raga can also present itself as a method of on-the-spot creative improvisation (like the *Alapana* or the *raga vistara*) by the musician/artist.

Ragas are ever-changing, dynamic entities. They veritably pulsate with life and help produce an almost unlimited flow of ideas in the artist. Raga is the pivotal concept of Indian music. It is uniquely melody-based and is a fine example of 'absolute music'. Nowhere else in world music can you see the existence of a phenomenon like the *raga*. Hence the Indian *raga* system generates much interest among musicians and musicologists of world music.

Indian music, on the other hand, stresses on scales of unequal temperament, or what is termed as 'just intonation' or 'correct intonation'. Here, the notes of each raga or melody are rendered in different raga. The notes of a scale are embellished with shakes and oscillations, which enhance the beauty of the *raga*. These shakes are referred to as '*gamakas*'.

Spirituality is the main feature of all ragas. There are several types of *ragas*: raga – *Bhairav*, raga – *Malkauns*, raga – *Hindol*, raga – *Deepak*, raga – *Shri*, and raga – *Megh*. This system of *raga-ragini* classification was also accepted and upheld by the Tansen school of thought. Kumar (Cited in Binathi, 2014, p. 5) feels that *Swar-sangatis* of particular ragas evoke feelings of spirituality, especially in raga '*Bhatiyar*' the *swar-sangatis*. *Ragas* have a mystical quality that leads one to introspect and paves the way for divine experiences. Every raga, other than its physical form, has its own essence in the internal form also that enables the artist and the audience to develop oneness with the Supreme Being.

Spiritual essence can be attained through performance of ragas with *bhava* that helps an artist or a devotee to reach the heights of spirituality to some extent. *Ragas* have the quality of expressing the feelings to God without the necessity of language. "*Raga* is *rasa* and *rasa* is *anand*", therefore, Abhinavgupt, (a successor to Shankaracharya from Kashmir period 950 A.D. to 1025 A.D.) has compared rasa with God i.e. "Bramhanand Sahodar" (Bahore, 2005; Mathire, 1997; Singh, 2005).

Ragas in Indian music are known to have healing properties. While ragas like *Sahana* heal the body of mild ill-health, *Todi* relieves severe sinus headaches. Singing the Carnatic ragas *Bharavi* and *Athana* restore sagging spirits and bestow a feeling of well-being both on the singer and his audience. During performance when the true artist sings in deep devotion and goes into a trance state, this becomes a spiritual experience.

Invocation of *'OM'*

In Hinduism one of the most chanted sound, symbol is 'OM'. It has a profound effect on mind and body of the person who chants it and also on the surroundings. Most of the *Vedic* prayers and mantras start with "OM". "OM" is also known *pranava* mantra means, "that (sound or symbol) by which the God is praised". In the word "Om" the entire essence of the Vedas is enshrined. It is believed that after chanting "OM" and "*Atha*" the God started to create the world. For any work that we want to undertake, its sound is considered to create an auspicious beginning. This Mantra is also chanted in the prayer that helps to generate spiritual emotions (*Bhav*) and to reach the chanting to the God. No matter, chanting is done with or without faith but one derives benefits from it, though that is limited to worldly benefits only. But if chanting is done with faith, added benefits are increased because when one chants with faith he feels more the presence of God, means his spiritual emotions (*bhav*) are increased. Due to chanting, the mind remains peaceful, so one is free from psychosomatic illness, disturbed by stress and enjoys good health. So chanting is able to cure malfunction of an organ (**Physical benefits**).

Psychological benefits of chanting: Through chanting the mantra the subconscious mind gets purified, because when we chant, spiritual emotions (*Bhav*) are increased and due to this *bhav* emotions like-devotion to God, love, respect and fear of wrong actions, etc. increase progressively. Through chanting we can gain the control over our six internal foes (anger, greed, attachment, pride, envy and passion). Chanting is also very beneficial in the treatment of a majority of psychiatric disorders like – obsessive compulsive disorder, anxiety disorders. Through chanting one can increase and develop his ability to concentrate on the study. It also develops introspection and introversion. Today our daily life becomes stressful and chanting leads us to a stress-free life.

Spiritual benefits of chanting: Due to chanting the mantra one's spiritual emotions and spiritual growth increases. An individual experiences the connection with the God, presence of God, a calm state of mind or internal satisfaction (Ananda) Bliss. Chanting of 'OM' eliminates distress and sorrow and we experience more Bliss (Ananda). In Hinduism, it is believed that through chanting one can acquire supernatural powers (*siddhis*) and dissolves the "ego". It also gradually reduces the attachment towards the external objects.

Tarpan (libation)

Tarpan is a Sanskrit term in the Vedic practices which refers to the offerings made to divine entities prescribed to perform by male descendant who does not have a living father. It is one of the rituals of offerings made to the manes (*bhuta yagna*), which is one of the five daily obligations (*pancha-mahayagnas*) prescribed to perform on the daily basis in the religion of Hinduism. It consists of standing in water after bathing in a river or tank and offering holy water thrice taking it in the joined palms of hand to the forefathers at regular intervals with appropriate *mantras* to all beings of creation from Brahma down to the blade of grass.

It can be done by just offering holy water only on the daily basis and food at the first annual *shraddha* (death anniversary) and during subsequent annual *shraddhas*, *amavasyas* (new moon days), *sankramanas* (solar ingresses), eclipses, and during visits to selected holy places of pilgrimage. Hindu Janajagruti Samiti. (2014) explain *Brahmayadryanga* (performed during sacrificial fires), *snananga* (performed every day after bathing), *shraddhanga* (performed during *Shraddha*) as the various *Tarpans* that are a part of various rites and should be performed during the respective occasions.

It is believed that one's *pitrus* will be eagerly waiting for *tarpana* on all the above-mentioned occasions. If no offering is made, they will return to their places disappointed, and the descendant misses their blessings which he would have received, if he had performed his filial duties. By doing *Tarpan* one learns that he is connected with the departed souls of his forefathers as well as he performs some rites relating to appease the souls of the forefathers and help them on their path to spiritual liberation (*Moksha*) and to seek their blessings as well.

Upavaasa (fasting)

In Hinduism fasting is called upavaasa derived from two words "*upa*" and "*vaasa*". "*upa*" means "near" and "*vaasa*" means "to stay", therefore *upavaasa* means staying near the God, the attainment of close mental and spiritual proximity with the God. In Hinduism, fasting is not encouraged for a long period of time but for a day on the eleventh day of the month and required in certain months, is encouraged. It is very good for the entire body especially for the digestive system, so sometimes it involves the regulation of the food eaten for longer periods of time. By fasting the mind becomes alert and pure because during the fasting one may either totally abstain from taking the food or eat simple, little food (fruits or special diet). Since it is a self-imposed form of discipline that is why it also observed at times in the preparation of special religious ceremonies.

Upavaasa revitalizes body, mind and spirit. It alters dietary pattern and behavior of people during fasting days. People who observe fast will not only observes abstinence from eating and drinking but develop positive feelings and emotions. Fasting involves the process of self-purification. This practice has a number of psychological and physical benefits. For example, it leads to tranquility and calmness in the face of adversity. It helps one to cultivate patience. Fasting helps to cultivate control over senses, guide the mind to be poised and at peace and also sublimate (purify) the desires. Fasting orients the observer to maintain the balance in spiritual and physical needs. It awakens the mind and develops positive thinking, and God consciousness. Spiritual faculties get awakened and the observer received blessing from God during the fasting days.

Anubhava (subjective experiences)

The way to Cosmic Consciousness is to practise *Ashtanga Yoga* (the eight limbed yoga). Firstly, free your mind from the influence of the *pranendriya* and motor organs and lead it towards consciousness. Then, the *karmashaya* becomes flooded with more and more consciousness. And through the practice of *asanas* and *pranayama*, one could increase the degree of control of the mind over *prana*. During the first stage of *sadhana* mind and body become increasingly pure. This is *anubhava*.

In all spiritual traditions, we have the desire to experience; it comes from clarity. When our mind is clear, we feel *anubhav* with the source. That is how i got back my peace of mind. For spiritual progress, *anubhav* is required. Attachment is what causes problem.

Awareness is dawns in the mind. Neuro-theology attempts to explain religious experience, transcendental states, and faith. *Anubhav* phenomena explain subjective experiences of spirituality.

Experience and emotions vary widely in different people subjected to similar sensory inputs. Experience tagged with a subjective affective component. Experience in many ways is central to a proper understanding of the nature of consciousness.

Lokasamgraha (welfare of all)

Lokasamgraha is a well-known concept of Bhagvad Gita which means welfare of all (society). *Lokasamgraha* provides the goal, direction and therefore it is the technique of performing one's action and duty. The compound word *lokasamgraha* means social-harmony and welfare as well as world presentation because its two component words *loka* and *samgraha* have more than one meaning each. For example, '*Loka*' denotes mankind or the world, and '*Samgraha*' stands for protecting, keeping, regulating etc.

Lord Krishna explains the concept of '*Lokasamgra*' in Bhagvad Gita. The underlying teaching of the Gita is that mere theoretical knowledge about what is good and real is not enough unless this knowledge is reflected in one's conduct (Bhagvad Gita, 3.21). As explained in Gita, *Lokasamgraha* has the social and universal dimension of Krishna's teaching.

Since *lokasamgraha* means bringing about a unity of purpose and co-operative effort in the society for a just cause, Lord Krishna asks the wise men not to be content by their own actions, but also to encourage others to act as well.

"na bhudhi bhedanam janayed ajnanam

jo sayet sarvakarmani vidvan yuktah samacaran"

(Bhagavad-Gita, 3.26)

The underlying message here is not to push people around, against their will but it is to perpetuate their ignorance. The place is in favour of a slow and steady effort to educate common people and to encourage them to follow voluntarily the example of the wise. By adopting the approach of the Gita, Gandhi achieved considerable success in obtaining mass support for his *satyagraha* movements based on the technique of *ahimsa*, which for him was a matter of deep conviction and practice.

To perform our duty towards society, i.e. the duty of *lokasamgraha* or our duty towards social welfare the attempt has been made to explore the concepts of '*yajna*', 'freedom' with reference to the wellbeing of the society. Bhagavad-Gita provides us effective guidelines to have effective social leadership. Our actions have to be conducive toward maintenance of the social and worldly order. The fundamental criterion of moral goodness is the promotion of dharma or order, and the result of it is peace, happiness and harmony.

Lokasamgraha follows naturally from the unattached action (*niskama karma*) which is the central theme of Krishna's teaching. If the action is to be selfless and is to be without reference to the fruit thereof (in relation to the actor) then the question naturally arises-why should anyone persist in a course of action? According to the theories of *yajna*-the action is to be performed to please the Gods and to derive worldly benefits through them. Bhagavad Gita emphasizes *lokasamgraha* as the welfare of the world which is the purpose of all actions.

The social theory linked with the *lokasamgraha* doctrine is derived from the Bhagvad Gita. The conception of the world order which is the duty of the individual to uphold by dedicating his activity towards that end runs through all the teachings of the Gita. The doctrine of sacrifice is thus given a wholly different meaning in the Gita, where action dedicated to God is called "*Brahmayajna*".

Londhe (2014) explained the concept of *Lokasamgraha* in detail. This concept was well explained by Swami Vivekananda in terms of 'social service'. Vivekanand translated *lokasamgraha* as 'working for the good of others', and added that this is "a very powerful idea-which has become the ideal in India" (Swami Vivekananda, 1972).

Sri Aurobindo elaborated it in terms of integral yoga. Sri Aurobindo translates *lokasamgraha* as the "holding together of the people". However as he moves from the status of a *karma* yoga to that of a *purnayoga* his concept of *lokasamgraha* undergoes a modification.

Tilak explained it in terms of *karma*-yoga. Tilak is the first commentator on the Gita who attach the importance of *lokasamgraha*. Lokmanya Tilak also elaborated the concept of *lokasamgraha* which was intended to show to the social reform oriented, educated Indians that their attempts at copying the West arose only because they had not understood their own scriptures properly. Tilak chooses to awaken the people to their right to freedom and their duty to fight for it. He realizes that through Gita we can connect to the people of the country irrespective of caste, creed or even religion.

According to Tilak (1936), 'It is an important duty of a man who has become *a jnyanin*, to remain himself in worldly life for the purpose of *lokasamgraha*, in order to give a living example of performing righteous, desireless action'. He says, the *jnyanis* perform all actions according to their dharma for the purpose of universal welfare (*Lokasamgraha*), looking upon it as an objective of the utmost importance and necessity, and though they may not need to perform such actions for their own benefit.

However, Tilak's interpretation of *lokasamgraha* was modified by Gandhi in the sense that '*ahimsa*' was made an inseparable element. Gandhi made non-violence as an essential prerequisite for *lokasamgraha*. Every person should involve himself in *lokasamgraha* in daily life for doing good.

Lokasamgraha i.e. the integration of life forces around the concept of the good is a feature of *karma* yoga and cuts at the roof of the exclusive claims of *sanyasa*. *Karma* yoga does not take a negative attitude either to *sanyasa* or *bhakti*. In fact knowledge is the basis and *bhakti* is universality of feeling, constitutes the spirit of *karma* yoga. The broad based *karma* yoga mingled with the essentials of *jnyana* and *bhakti* is advocated by Gita as the unexceptional rule of morality for all men under varied circumstances. And the Lokmanya Tilak exerts himself to bring out this truth to serve the interests of the people. This is the *lokasamgraha* according to Gita (Agrawal, 1997).

Interdependence is also a main characteristic of *lokasangrha*. It is there not only in the organizations but in the society as well. One is never independent. Others are affected by what he does and vice-versa. If he does not do what is expected from him, his duty, someone else is going to suffer. His freedom is limited by the impact of his actions will have on others. Even in a position of authority, he cannot do whatever he wants to do. He cannot be arbitrary.

"yadi yahyam na varteyam jatu karmanyat itindritataha

Mama vartanat anuvartante manushyah partha sarvashaha"

(Bhagavad-Gita, 3.23)

It means, if I ever failed to engage in carefully performing prescribed duties, certainly all men would follow my path (Swami Prabhupada, 2002). 'If I do not take part in action, all men will follow in all respects the path followed by me' (Tilak, 1971).

All our thinkers and leaders were having their own ideologies which are based on various ethical ideals. The ultimate goal of everyone was to render a peaceful living for all i.e. '*Lokasamgraha.*'

Radhakrishnan (1973) says, "*Lokasamgraha* stands for the unity of the world, the interconnectedness of the society, the Gita requires us to lay stress on human brotherhood." Vinoba Bhave interprets *Lokasamgraha* as "keeping people together and on the right path: He says that *Karma* Yoga technique of getting rid of selfishness by the method of diffusion. A personal, individual desire may be given a general, social application in order to cross over from attachment to non-attachment." (Vinoba, 1966)

Ishvara Pranidhana (surrender to God)

The term '*Ishvara Pranidhana*' is made up of two Sanskrit words; *Ishvara* and *Pranidhana*. *Ishvara* means 'Supreme Being', 'God', 'Brahman', 'Ultimate Reality' or 'True Self' and

Pranidhana means "surrender", "dedicate", "devote" or 'fixing'. So here we are advised to 'surrender' self completely to the Supreme Being, which in essence means cultivating a deep and trusting relationship with the universe, and making each action as an offering to something higher than us.

Ishvara Pranidhana is listed as the fifth *niyama* by Patañjali. In other forms of yoga, it is the tenth *niyama*. In Hinduism, the *Niyamas* are the "do list" and the *Yamas* are the "don't do" list, both part of an ethical theory for life.

Ishvara pranidhana is the spiritual practice of surrendering the self fully to God to guide the life and actions of the self in order to work in the world. In surrendering the ego to the Supreme Being in humility, it is thought that the character of the divine can be attained. In Patanjali's Yoga Sutras, this can be exercised through practicing the *asanas* along with a mantra and *mudra*, through meditation and prayer, and/or through one's actions of daily living. In yoga philosophy, one does not have to choose a personal deity of focus in order to practice surrender in this way, but an idea or spiritual wisdom that gives one inspiration.

Swami Satchidananda's translation of *The Yoga Sutras* mentions the practice of *Ishvara Pranidhana*. He says that if you can master this one, then there is no need to practice any more of the *Sutras* because you will already have attained *samadhi*, which is the state of oneness which is the final limb of yoga. He defines *ishvara pranidhana* like this: "By total surrender to God, Samadhi is attained." Particularly, he makes a point of stating that '*Ishvara Pranidhana*' means offering of our actions up to 'the divine' and humanity; because as we have all heard many times before that we are in fact all one. In the Upanishads, the word *Ishvara* means 'a state of collective consciousness', which tells us in this sense - that there is not a God like figure we are supposed to devote or worship our actions to that at all, rather 'God' represents this collective consciousness, and therefore represents all of us too.

Therefore, the practice of *Ishvara Pranidhana* means that if we are able to completely surrender our individual ego identities to God (our own higher self) then we will attain the identity of God. If we can dedicate our lives to serving the God that dwells within all other beings, human and non-human alike, we will move beyond all feelings of separateness, because in our modern culture the feelings of separateness and disconnection prevail. Then we will be freed from the stress, anxiety, self-doubt and negative karma that arise from our reliance upon our egos to determine which actions we take in our lives. *Ishvara pranidhana* will help to cure the afflictions of the mind that cause pain and suffering, as it is designed to redirect our energy away from our selfish desires and work towards the ultimate pursuit of Oneness.

Tirtha-yatra (pilgrimage)

In Hinduism, pilgrimage is considered as an essential part of their religion. *Tirtha-yatra* is integral to Hinduism. *Tirtha yatra* is a journey to a holy shrine or shrines where a divine world meets or touches the human world. In other words, *tirtha* is a holy place where the transcendent comes to the earth; the sacred meets the everyday to everyone and where the higher realms meet the lower realms. Therefore a *tirtha* is a mediate point between two realms (higher and lower). On pilgrimage one gets away from his daily routine of life and become free from his every responsibility and economic hindrances obstruct and dismiss the spiritual/religious practices. The pilgrims worship on a holy place (*tirtha*) and submit before the Lord to see that all people are equal before the Lord, in whatever place or form the Lord is worshiped. Pilgrims come to know and cherish the fundamental unity of bhârata, as they mix together from all over India and worship at the great holy shrines. Pilgrimages to the holy shrines are undertaken for appeasing of the deities in times of misfortunes, for completion of vows, of gaining good fortune and prosperity and as one of the simple religious practices of the God.

Toward the end of life people are more inclined to go on pilgrimages to holy shrines because at this stage of life the pettiness of the worldly life seems to be faded and they are expected to be more Godly-oriented. The son, after the death of a parent go to perform the ceremonial rites for his dead parent to Banaras, Gaya and Allahabad, and there is also strong urge for the Hindu devotees to join the pilgrimages at the time of the great festivals because at that time thousands of pilgrims gather to witness the ceremonies.

Special holy pilgrimage shrines: Each part of our country has its favorite shrines of pilgrimage to which hundreds and thousands of pilgrims come daily and on special occasions. Special sacredness is associated with the *câr dham* (four sites of the lord). These *câr dham* of the lord marking the boundaries of the sacred land of India, Puri in the East, Dwaraka in the West, Badarinath in the North and Rameswaram in the South. There is another *câr dham* in the Himalayas, consists of Gangotri and Yamunotri (the sources of two holy rivers), Badarinath (Lord Vishnu) and Kedarnath (Lord Shiva).

Pilgrimages to the seven holy shrines are highly prized among Hindus to Mathura, Dwaraka, Ayodhya, Varanasi, Hardwar, Ujjain and Kanchipuram. Mathurâ is cherished as the place of the youthful achievements of the lord Krishna. Dwaraka is the site of the kingdom ruled by the Lord Krishna and also the sacred place from which he left the world. Ayodhyâ is a sacred place dedicated to the memory of the Lord Rama. It is his birthplace and capital.

Varanasi, from the earliest times, it is believed among Hindus that Varanasi is a sacred place of salvation (*Moksha*) if someone dies over here. Varanasi is the great cremation ground (*mahasmasana*), it is also believed that all pilgrimages places united in the one and all of the Gods are gathered here. It is the most popular among all of the pilgrimage places. Haridwar is considered as gateway to the Lord Shiva the lord of mountains (Hari-ka-dwar). It is the holy place where the holy river Ganges from the Himalaya comes down to the ground. Ujjain is also a popular pilgrimage holy place and also one of the twelve *jyotirlingas*, perennial phallic forms of Shiva, these are especially sacred pilgrimage places. Kanchipuram, it is the stronghold of the worship of the mother Goddess.

There are also fifty-one sacred pilgrimage shrines, known as *pithas* (footrests). These shrines are dedicated to the divine mother (wife of the Lord Shiva). These shrines marking the places where her different parts of the body fell to earth, when the lord Vishnu, by his wheel cut the different parts of her dead body at the time when the Lord Shiva roamed India carrying her body, grief-stricken. The seven sacred rivers of India are themselves holy pilgrimage places, with the greatest sacredness attached to the places where to or more rivers join and where a river enters the sea. These seven holy rivers are Gangâ, Yamuna, Godavari, Sarasvati, Narmada, Kaveri, and Sindhu (Indus), even among all of these the Ganga occupies a special place and is often considered as a symbol of the sacred river itself. It is believed that bathing in these sacred rivers gives pilgrims a sense of union with his fellow beings and the creature

At Allahabad, Haridwar, Nasik and Ujjain, Kumbha-melas are held at every twelve years. The most bizarre is held at Allahabad where the three sacred rivers Gangaes, Yamuna and invisible Sarasvati are joined. It is believed that to bath here at an auspicious time according to the movement of the Jupiter planet is sacred to pilgrims. Mahakumbh melas attract the huge crowds especially at Allahabad to bathe in the rivers.

Though there are some less universally well-known specialized *tirthas* such as there are many goddess sacred places specialize in rites pertaining to male children, as their first hair offering, many places specialize to request the birth of male children.

Yoga

According to Rao (2012), there are three forms of yoga for attaining self-realization- *Karma* Yoga, *Bhakti* Yoga and *Gyan* Yoga.

(i) *Karma* Yoga: (path of action): According to Rao (2012), *karma* yoga is a path of selfless actions, means the detachment from the fruits of actions or rituals. Lord Krishna in the great epic Srimad Bhagavad Gita teaches that one should conduct his all of the actions (duties) as per his Dharma, without being attached to the results of those actions, as an offering to the God, that could be a powerful growth for the spiritual freedom (liberation). Because conducting the selfless actions (*Nishkama–karam* or actions without any expectation), purifies the mind of one and also leads towards the spiritual path.

When one does *Karma* without expectations (*Nishkama-karma*) beliefs and surrender himself to the God and constantly meditating upon God through mind, body and speech, is really performing the '*Karma*-Yoga'. Mahatma Gandhi preferred the *Karma* Yoga as a way of self-realization (*atman-gyan*). In this concern Gandhi writes: "this can be achieved by selfless actions, by renouncing fruits of action, and by dedicating all activities to

God i.e., by surrendering oneself to Him – body and soul" (cited in Rao, 2012, p.158).

(ii) *Bhakti* Yoga: (path of devotion): *Bhakti* is a way of the worship of the God with deep devotions, where one show reverence, remembrance and love to the God. So *Bhakti* yoga is a path of self-forgetting love and devotion to the God to attain spiritual freedom (salvation). Many devotional schools teach that to achieve spiritual freedom, *Bhakti* yoga is the easiest only practical way for a devotee. Ramanuja, Chaitanya and Madhva and many other saints proposed that *Bhakti* yoga is as a superior way to spiritual freedom (*moksha*/ salvation). Ramanuja advocates pure surrender and devotion to the God as the only way to spiritual freedom.

(iii) *Gyan* Yoga: (path of spiritual knowledge): *Gyan* Yoga means spiritual knowledge. *Gyan* Yoga is a path of spiritual knowledge (transcendent divine knowledge) to attain spiritual realization and also to attain '*Moksha*' or salvation. *Gyan* Yoga teaches the practitioner to identify and realize the Ultimate Truth through the power of discrimination between real and unreal. Here the practitioner does not need a personalized form of divine but he can meditate on a flame on emptiness and whatever.

The three paths of yoga described by the Hindu's great scripture Srimad Bhagavad Gita, for the realization of the self with the universal-self (God) are complementary in nature, like a *Karma Yogi* needed the concentration of the mind to discharge his duties effectively. In the same way, *Bhakti* is required to offer the fruits of his all of the actions to the God. *Gyan* is to understand the true nature of the God that is an important aspect of *Bhakti*. Although it is believed that a true is one, who exhibits his pure devotion to the God and also discharges his duties through *karma* without expectations (*Nishkama-karma*) that are necessary to acquire the spiritual knowledge. Only this is the path to liberation and realization of the God.

Apart from these paths of yoga described by the Lord Krishna in the Bhagavad Gita, according to Flood (2004), in the Upanishads the word of 'yoga' was used as a way of controlling the senses, the yoga Upanishads, *yoga-tattava* describe about four types of yoga by following any one of them one can attain liberation. These are: *Raja* Yoga, *Mantra* Yoga, *Laya* Yoga, *Hatha* Yoga etc.

(iv) *Raja* Yoga: Yoga is a state of *dhyan* (concentration) in which the mind is controlled and made to be single-pointed. Through developing eight limbs of the patanjali's yoga-sutra one can control his/her mind. These eight limbs are: *yama* (ethics or restraint), *niyama* (discipline), *asana* (body postures), *pranayama* (breath control), *pratyahara* (sense-withdrawl), *dharana* (concentration), *dhyana* (meditation), *Samadhi* (absorbed concentration). Raja yoga deals with the control of the senses and concentration of the mind through eight fold path of yoga. In the *Dharana* and *Dhyan* steps of the *Raja* Yoga *kundalinies* are awakened.

Raja Yoga is concerned with developing mental concentration in order to experience *samadhi*. According to Kaarthikeyan (2007, p.161), the state of pure experience of the divine and transcendence is the state of 'Samadhi'. According to Singh (2007, p. 31), in the *Raja* yoga breathing, *asanas* (specific body postures) and *kundalini,* spiritual experiences come into the practitioner.

(v) *Mantra* Yoga: According to Bhattacharyya (1953), *mantra* yoga is also known as *japa* yoga. In the *mantra* yoga, disciplines are adjusted to the intellectual abilities and to the emotional temperament of the devotee and he directs his devotion to the chosen deity and recites the appropriate *mantra*. According to Rao (2012), *mantra* yoga is a path of salvation through *japa* or the repetition of the appropriate *mantra*.

(vi) *Hatha* Yoga: According to Flood (2004), *Hatha* yoga is also known as the yoga of force. This type of yoga consists of some difficult body postures accompanied by breathing techniques. *Hatha* yoga must be performed under the close supervision of a guru, mastered in the *Hatha* yoga. The aim of the *Hatha* yoga is to realize liberation during life and realization can be possible through cultivating the body made divine or perfect in the 'fire' of yoga, because in the realization of liberation the self-awakens to its inmates identity with the absolute (*sahaja*). According to Rao (2012), *Hatha* yoga gives primary importance to better physical health and the longevity of life.

(vii) *Laya* Yoga: According to Bhattacharyya (1953), "*Laya* yoga rests on the effectiveness of practices which brings about the merging of the spirit through the annihilation of the personality of the worshiper" (p. 198).

Conclusion

In fact, spirituality should be the very purpose of whole lifetime. The spiritual practices suggested above will lead to the quality of an enlightened person. Hence these should be taken and adopted in one's life. We should do commitment in order to get clarity and understanding and then commitment towards practicing spirituality. All great Sages and Spiritual Gurus had commitment towards practicing spirituality and consequently purify their mind, heart, and soul. Once our mind, heart and soul are purified, we feel elevated and adopt the way leading to righteous life. Spiritual practices are very important towards self growth and enlightenment. Spiritual practices bring certain changes in behaviour, develop synergy level and maintain homeostasis in your whole being. We need to integrate both knowledge and practice oriented devotion. These are important in all walks of life for a spiritually oriented person.

Spiritual practices represents that one should be attached to anything. Spiritual practices bring changes in our behavior, so have the attitude of doing these. We suffer because we do not practise and driven by expectations in our life. Spiritual practices require special effort and allowing oneself to guide. Hindu practices are simple and have intuitive power which guides your life without desires.

Chapter 6

SPIRITUALITY WITHIN YOGA

Yoga is considered as a spiritual exercise to enhance our physical, mental, social, emotional and spiritual health. The various *asanas* and *niyamas* develop the fitness, strength and energy levels. They work on the body, mind, and soul, thereby strengthening the triune aspects of our existence. Yoga enhances awareness at the bodily and mental levels. It promotes healthy sexual activity arising out of biological and organic soundness; and healthy relationships with others and your spouse. Yoga increases the blood flow into the genitalia. Those who practice yoga, they are spiritual.

Yoga as an exercise is supposed to be beyond any other healthy practice. If the mind keeps thinking about the term unthinkable to focus on, that is also limited in sphere. Yoga is a challenge which one has to do it to attain by not pursuing anything with an intention to pursue, by becoming absolutely holistic.

According to Flood (2004), in the yoga tradition, Patanjali's yoga sutra is most significant. Patanjali defines yoga as: "yoga is a cessation of mental fluctuations". Yoga increases our existential well-being. It reminds us that we are not separate from the world we live in. What yogic exercises we do, we do for our well-being.

According to Husain (2016), there are four elements of yoga, namely, yearning, observances, God-consciousness, and abstentions and awareness. Yearning revolves around the individual's personality. The basic yearning is to live better. Observance is one of the Patanjali's eight limbs of Yoga. Observance helps to strengthen the effectiveness of Yoga practice. Through yoga, we develop God-consciousness which connects with our deeper sub-conscious and higher self that make us feel stronger and peaceful. The relationship between yoga and consciousness is fascinating. Every one of us has the ability to move beyond it and directly use consciousness, and yoga is the tool used by the soul. The yogi's experience is filled with universal God consciousness. Abstentions include non-violence, truthfulness, non-stealing, chastity, and non-greed. These qualities purify our body and mind. This is the principle of right action. Awareness is a state of being. Awareness is what you are. Any *asana* or *niyama* is performed to develop spiritual awareness will lead to attachment and single-minded devotion for the Supreme. A yogic person radiates the breath of spirituality and spiritual awareness into us.

In this chapter we will explain different types of yoga and integrate them with the phenomenon of spirituality. The twelve forms of yoga integrated into twelve letters of the concept of SPIRITUALITY are: **S** *Sahaja* yoga, **P** *Paranv* yoga, **I** *Iyengar* yoga **,** **R** Restrorative yoga**,** **I** Integral yoga**,** **T** *Tantra* yoga**,** **U** *Udgeeth* Pranayama**,** **A** *Ashtanga* yoga**,** **L** *Laya* yoga**,** **I** *Isha Kriya*, **T** *Trataka* yoga**,** and **Y** Yogeshvara's yoga (*karma* yoga, janan yoga and *bhakti* yoga). These are the practicing aspects of yoga to improve our well-being.

Sahaja Yoga

This is one of the yogic techniques for managing our mental, physical, psychological and spiritual well-being. H. H. Shri Mataji Nirmala Devi has popularized this technique in over 120 countries and had helped people to cope with stress and suffering.

What does *Sahaja* Yoga means? *Saha* means with us, *ja* means born and Yoga is union. *Sahaja* Yoga is therefore spontaneous *Sahaja* yoga is the *kundalini*, the divine energy, which lies below the sacrum of the bottom of the vertebral column, which when stimulated ascends through the *sushumna nadi*, the spine and corresponds to the parasympathetic nervous system. There are three *nadis* in our body, namely, *ida*, the sympathetic nervous system on the left which controls our temperament; *pingala*, the sympathetic nervous system on the right, which controls our physical and mental well-being and *Sushumna nadi*, the parasympathetic nervous system at the centre which has chakras to give us our qualitative attributes. If a person activates the chakras in this *nadi*, he would attain spiritual ascent and enjoy life to the fullest.

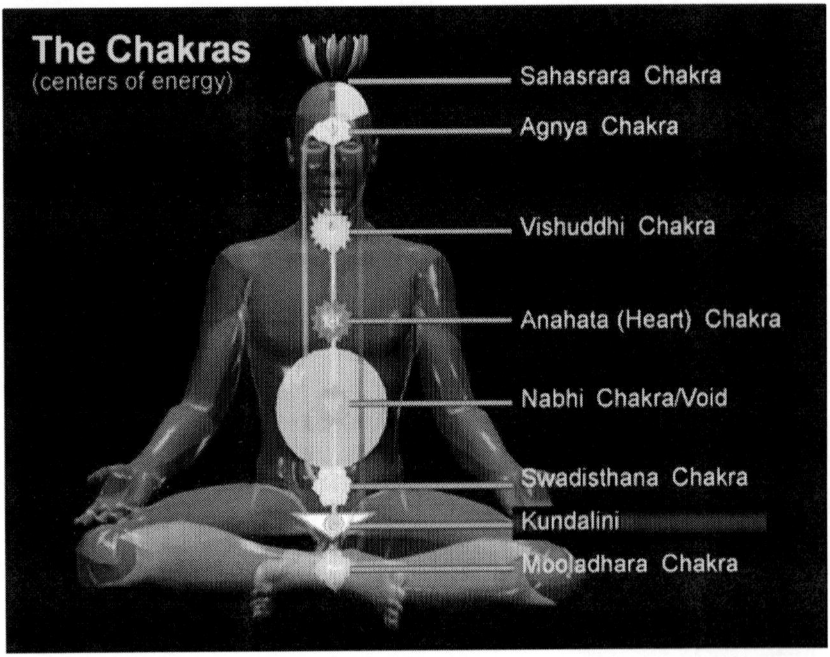

Image Source: Google

Stress is the effect of today's competitive which adversely affects our body system. But *Sahaja* Yoga is an easy way to cope with distress. It makes us experience love and compassion. *Sahaja* Yoga helps us to achieve a complete balance in our lives on the physical, emotional, mental, and spiritual levels. It aims at achieving holistic health of people.

There is a spontaneous awakening and the union of our primordial energy with the all pervading power of the divine. The awakening of the *kundalni* allows divine energy to pass through the seven chakras of energy centers which take care of the physical, mental, psychosomatic and spiritual aspects of the body.

Sahaja Yoga considers seven chakras; the first *chakra-mooladhara chakra* depicts the element earth and attributes qualities of innocence and wisdom. The *swadisthana chakra* represents the element fire and is responsible for creativity and divine knowledge. *Nabhi chakra*, representing water, gives us sustenance and dharma. *Anahata chakra* represents air and attributes the qualities of love, *maryada* and fearlessness. It awakens the *atman* or soul. The *Vishuddhi chakra* representing the element either is associated with divine diplomacy. *Agnya chakra* also called *guru chakra* or third-eye chakra is the subtle center of energy, believed to be located between the eyebrows, located behind it along the subtle (non-physical) spinal column. *Sahasrara chakra* maintains integration between mind and speech. Speech is important and a proper coordination between thought and speech assures better communication. This chakra attributes the qualities of collective consciousness and integration. All these correspond to a particular place on the hand and to a particular element of the universe. Each is attributed with special qualities.

Sahaja Yoga is a master key to solving the problems of the mind and the body. People who live in a normal life can tap to their inner spiritual power through daily *Sahaja* Yoga meditation. One has to learn to awaken one's *kundalini* to experience happiness and enjoy the fruits of *Sahaja* Yoga. (Chandra, 2011, p. 16).

Pranav Yoga

According to Swami Ramdev the last seventh pranayama is *pranav*. After practicing all of the six *pranayamas* (*Bhastrika,*

Kapalbhati, Bahya, Anulom Vilom, Bhramari and Udgeeth pranayama) concentrate the mind on inhaling and exhaling for some time is called ***Pranav pranayama***. This is very simple form of meditation. *Pranav pranayama* is the most important *pranayama* to experience spiritual and mental energy.

Image Source: Google

Maharishi Patanjali in his Yoga Sutras advocated that *pranayama*, 'control of the life force' is a prerequisite for the deepest states of meditation. Such control also gives one more control over feelings and emotions including spiritual intelligence to awaken higher human qualities such as benevolence and to live happily in all circumstances. Going deep into a true meditation path is therefore the most practical thing that one can do. The changes caused by deep meditation are responsible for the deep compassion that the yogis express in their service to others.

Procedure:

1. Sit in any meditative posture (*Padmasana*, *Sukhasana* or *Vajrasana*) quietly. Both the hands should be in *gyan*

mudra (Touch the tip of the thumb to the tip of the index finger and both the hand placed on the knees, close the eyes).

2. Breathe normally and concentrate mind on rhythm of the breathe in and breathe out, and meditate upon *udgitha* (OM) with your *prana* (breath).

3. While practicing this *pranayama* don't think about anything. Think about God and feel the presence of God everywhere and in each particle.

4. Imagine that God is in every particle and everywhere.

Try to look at the breath inside. In the beginning, the breath will be felt in the nose only. Gradually one shall be able to feel the touch of breathe deeply inside you. Thus, by chanting 'Om' with every breath, one automatically starts going into meditation. Mind will become highly one-pointed, identified with and absorbed in 'OM'. Along with '*Pranav*' the great Gayatri mantra should be recited and chanted.

Duration: Practice for 4-5 minutes to 1 hour depending on your ability and available time. Gradually increase the practice and try to breathe in and breathe out once in one minute.

Benefits:

1. Spiritual development and to widen the perspective so that you begin to realise the one in all and the all in one.

2. It gives physical and spiritual energy.

3. Gives good health.

4. Strengthen and calms the mind.

5. Good for meditation (*Samadhi*).

6. Improves concentration.
7. Releases stress and depression. ("*Pranav* pranayama – meditation and spiritual development," n.d.).

Precautions for all Yogas and Pranayama

1. *Pranayama* should be practiced early in the morning on an empty stomach.
2. *Pranayama* should be practiced in fresh air.
3. *Pranayama* should be practice under expert guidance.

Related Studies

Harinath et al. (2004) conducted a study to examine the impact of practicing '*Omkar* meditation' and '*Hatha* yoga' daily for 3 months on psychologic profile, melatonin secretion and cardiorespiratory performance. The sample of the study consisted of 30 healthy males with age ranging from 25 to 35 years. Subjects were divided into 2 groups: intervention group (n= 15) practiced some selected yogas for 45 minutes, and *pranayama* for 15 minutes during morning only and during evening practiced preparatory yogic postures and *pranayama* each for 15-15 minutes and also performed meditation for 30 minutes every day for 3 months. Control group performed slow running for 20 minutes, body flexibility exercises for 40 minutes during morning and, during evening played games for 60 minutes daily for 3 months. Results indicated an improvement in psychologic profile, cardiorespiratory performance and in plasma melatonin after 3 months of yogic practices. It was also found that in the yoga group the maximum night time melatonin levels significantly correlated with well-being scores.

Gurjar, Ladhake, and Thakare (2009) conducted an experiment to study the effect of 'OM' on nervous system.

Recordings of 'OM' chanting served as a database of this experiment. The recordings were made in a quiet room at 44.1 kHz sampling rate using a close-talk microphone. All files were segmented manually. Male and female speakers of age group 30 to 40 years did the entire recording in evening time after a day work before dinner by sitting in a *padmasana* position, which is best position for mediation. Recording is done for about 10 minutes. With proposed algorithm analysis has been carried out for the divine sound OM. By this analysis we could conclude OM is therefore serves as a brain stabilizer, which is also an energy medicine for human being under stress.

Kumar, Nagendra, Manjunath, Naveen, and Telles (2010) explore the significance of the syllable 'OM' from ancient texts and effects of 'OM' meditation in contemporary science. The descriptions of 'OM' have been taken from four Upanisads (*Mundaka, Mandukya*, *Svetasvatara*, and *Katha*), the Bhagvad Gita, and Patanjali's Yoga Sutras. Autonomic and respiratory studies suggest that there is a combination of mental alertness with physiological rest during the practice of 'OM' meditation. Evoked potentials studies suggest a decrease in sensory transmission time at the level of the auditory association cortices, along with recruitment of more neurons at mesencephalic-diencephalic levels. It was concluded that a person who realizes 'OM', merges with the Absolute. Scientific studies on 'OM' suggest that the mental repetition of 'OM' results in physiological alertness, and increased sensitivity to sensory transmission.

Kalyani et al. (2011) conducted a study to explore the "neurohemodynamic correlates of 'OM' chanting by using a sample of 12 healthy participants aged 22-39 years (mean ± SD=28±6 years) using fMRI (functional Magnetic Resonance Imaging). Four persons participated in the yogic meditation and compared with a rest state as well as pronunciation of "ssss" limbic deactivation was indicated by the neurohemodynamic correlates of chanting 'OM'. As in the VNS (vagus nerve stimulation) treatment used for epilepsy and depression recorded the same observations.

Joshi (2012) conducted a study to study the remedial effect of *Nadishodhana pranayama* and 'OM' chanting on memory enhancement of college students with age group 20-35 year more specifically. The sample of 50 students was included. The subjects have been selected by using Quota sampling technique. The time duration for yogic practice was 30 days for 30 minutes. *Nadishodhana Pranayama* 20 min and 'OM' chanting 10 min. Results of the study suggest that *Nadishodhana Pranayama* and 'OM' chanting cause a significant positive effect on memory of the students.

Joshi (2013) conducted an experimental study to examine the effect of 'OM' chanting and Bhramari *pranayama* on anxiety level among adolescents. 30 subjects (15 male & 15 female), were selected with age range from 20 to 30 years. The subjects underwent 20 days 'OM' chanting and Bhramari *pranayama* around 25 minutes daily. The results indicate that the practice of 'OM' chanting and Bhramari *Pranayama* is quite effective in reducing anxiety in adolescent life.

Dinesh, Sharma, Jeyakumar, Sunder, Gopinath, and Bhavanani (2013) conducted a study to find out the positive beneficial effects of *pranav pranayama* training on pulmonary function parameters in young healthy, volunteers of both the genders. Totally 12 healthy volunteers of both genders were included as the study sample. Among them 6 were males and 6 were females. The mean age was 18.58+0.66 years. Pre and post pulmonary function parameters such as FEV1, FVC, FEV1/ FVC,

FEF25-75, MVV were taken using the spirometer at the end of 8 weeks *pranayama* training. Results showed a significant difference in pulmonary function parameters. 8 weeks of *pranav pranayama* training in the young, healthy volunteers showed increase in the commonly measured pulmonary function parameters, but the increase was not statistically significant probably because of short duration of training. By increasing the duration of time the reliable goal can be achieved.

Pandya (2014) conducted a study on the basis of 'an Indian spiritual practice called the *Sudarshankriya* and *Pranayama* (SK & P) developed by a new popular religious movement- 'Art of Living Foundation' started by Sri Sri Ravi Shankar in India. The study was conducted to explore the effect of this spiritual and meditative practice in promoting well-being, using the experiences of 828 its practitioners. The findings of the study indicated that this practice is effective in order to reduce the level of stress as well as in promoting sense of overall well-being, enhancing coping and optimism.

Mooventhan and Khode (2014) conducted a study to evaluate the effect of only Bhramari *pranayama* and 'OM' chanting on pulmonary function in healthy individuals. A total of 82 subjects were randomized into the study group (SG) (n = 41) and control group (CG) (n = 41). Baseline assessment was performed before intervention for both groups. SG practiced Bhramari *pranayama* and 'OM' chanting for the duration of 10 min (5 min for each practice)/day for the period of 6 days/week for 2 weeks and CG did not practice so. After intervention post-assessment was performed for SG (n = 40) and CG (n = 39). Findings indicated that Bhramari *pranayama* and 'OM' chanting were effective in improving pulmonary function in healthy individuals.

Rajak, Rampalliwar, Verma, Singh, and Shiralkar (2016) conducted a study to investigate whether regular practice of Yoga for three months can reduce cardiovascular and respiratory reactivity induced by cold pressor test by using 60 male medical students of 18 to 22 years of age. After recording the basal blood pressure and pulse rate, and rate of respiration the cardiovascular and respiratory reactivity of all the 60 students was measured by application of cold pressure test devised by Hines and Brown (1936). Thirty five students were found to be hyper reactor to this test. These hyper reactors underwent *Yogasana*, *Nadishodhana*, *Bhramari Pranayama*, *Omkar* Chanting and meditation for the duration of 12 weeks. After the yogic training period the mean blood pressure and mean pulse rate/ min and rate of respiration / min was again measured which was found to be significantly reduced.

Jain (2016) conducted a study to find out the effect of 6 weeks *Pranav* yoga training on cardiovascular parameters of prehypertensive young adults. Sixty subjects were divided into two groups of 30 each. Group A (control group) comprised normotensive subjects and Group B comprised prehypertensive subjects. Cardiovascular parameters were recorded using impedance cardiovasograph and mercury sphygmomanometer before the training. After training of pranav yoga, subjects of Group B practiced it for 15 min daily for 6 weeks. All parameters were recorded in both groups after 6 weeks *pranav* yoga practice also. Results showed that in comparison to Group A, all cardiovascular parameters were significantly higher ($p < 0.05$) in Group B before the training and but did not show a significant difference ($p > 0.05$) after 6 weeks training of *pranav* yoga.

Amin, Kumar, Rajagopalan, Rajan, Mishra, Reddy, and Mukkadan (2016) conducted a study to assess the effectiveness of 'OM' chanting on depression, anxiety, stress and cognition in elderly women with hypertension. A total of 40 elder women (age 50–60 years) with diagnosed hypertension were included. After selection of the participants, baseline values were recorded and they were randomly assigned into two groups: Group A: (n=20) Control group (Only medications and 'OM' chanting was not performed) Group B: (n=20) Intervention group (OM chanting performed for six months along with medications). Intervention group participants performed 'OM' chanting once in a day at 7:30 daily at *Sattva* cultural space for six months under the supervision of yoga teacher. Results indicate that pre intervention depression, anxiety, stress and Mini Mental State Examination (MMSE) scores, blood pressure and pulse rate were not significantly different between the groups. However, following by six months of 'OM' chanting, systolic and diastolic blood pressure, pulse rate, depression, anxiety and stress decreased significantly among the participants of intervention group. MMSE scores also improved significantly followed by 'OM' chanting.

Vasanthan, Madanmohan, Bhavanani, Hanifah, and Jaiganesh (2017) compared the effect of 6 months of training in relaxing *asanas* and *pranayamas* on blood pressure (BP), pulse pressure (PP), heart rate (HR), and rate-pressure product (RPP) in young healthy volunteers. A total of 109 healthy volunteers aged 20-25 years were divided into 3 groups consisting of *asan* (n = 38), *pranayam* (n = 38), and control group (n = 33). The Yoga training was given 25 min/day for 6 days/week for 6 months. *Pranayam* group received relaxing *pranayam* (*pranav*, *savitri*, *nadi shuddhi* and *chandra nadi*), *asan* group received relaxing asan (*pawanmuktasana*, *balasan*, *dharnicasan*, and *shavasan*) and waiting list were kept as a control group. Results showed that after training significant decreases in systolic BP and diastolic BP as well as PP, mean arterial pressure and RPP were found in both *asan* and *pranayam* group as compared with control. There was, however, no significant difference between *asan* and *pranayam* group.

Rani and Deo (2017) conducted a study to examine the effect of *asana* and 'OM' chanting on memory in school going children. Sixty children were selected from Govt. Primary School, Sahu Hisar (Haryana) between the age group of 10 to 11 years. The data clearly indicated that after one month of *asanas* and 'OM' chanting result showed improvement in memory, learning ability and short term memory in school going children.

Iyengar Yoga

Image Source: Google

B. K. S. Iyengar founded the Iyengar Yoga. Iyengar yoga is a form of *hatha* yoga based on the traditional eight limbs of *astanga* yoga founded by Patanjali in his Yoga Sutra. It has an emphasis on precision, details and alignment in the performance of body postures (*asanas*) and breathing techniques (*pranayamas*). This type of yoga consist of more than 200 classical yoga postures (*asanas*) and 14 different types of breath control techniques (*pranayamas*) ranging from basic to advanced. In the Iyengar yoga props like; belts, wooden gadgets, blankets are often used. These props help practitioners to perform the *asanas* correctly and also minimizing the risk of strain or injury, and making the *asanas* accessible to all from young to old. *Asanas* are held for a long period of time and often modified with the help of props. The Iyengar yoga is designed to systematically cultivate stability, strength, flexibility, and awareness, and also can be therapeutic for specific conditions.

Iyengar was a key part of the movement that brought Yoga from India to the West in the early 1950's. He has written many texts and trained vast numbers of teachers in the Iyengar method, making it one of the most widely known and well established forms of modern Yoga practice. Iyengar yoga is a way of life and is meant for all. Types of *asanas* include standing, sitting, forward bending, back bending, twisting, and inversions, supine.

Students of Iyengar Yoga begin with basic/elementary postures, with an emphasis on the standing postures (*asanas*). In the time, other *asanas* are added, including forward bends and back bends, twists, inversions and restorative poses. *Salamba Sarvangasana* (Shoulder Balance) is introduced as soon as practitioners are ready because it has many therapeutic benefits. Each class ends with corpse pose (*Savasana*) or deep relaxation in which the practitioners learn to rest in a profound way, completely releasing the body while drawing the mind towards the peace within. As the student progresses, *Pranayama* (breath control technique) is introduced.

Teachers devise sequences of poses, which build skill and understanding, from posture to posture, and from class to class. Practitioners are encouraged to do their own home practice; without that, the study of yoga is incomplete. The main aim of the Iyengar Yoga is to unite the mind, body and spirit by practicing asana with great precision. Regular practice of Iyengar Yoga definitely integrates the body, mind and emotions.

Benefits: Iyengar yoga increase flexibility, tone muscles, calm mind, and help to relieve neck and back pain. It helps you strengthen the muscles of the body which are responsible for posture like back, legs and core. It also helps to improve the overall functioning of the body—from the lymph systems and circulatory, to the digestion and nervous system. It also helps to improve breathing ("8 Reasons to Practice Iyengar Yoga – DO YOU YOGA," n.d.).

Related Studies

Crow, Jeannot, and Trewhela (2015) conducted a systematic review of the existing research within Iyengar yoga method and its effectiveness on relieving back and neck pain (defined as spinal pain). Overall six studies with 570 patients showed, that Iyengar yoga is an effective means for both back and neck pain in comparison to control groups. This systematic review found strong evidence for short-term effectiveness, but little evidence for long-term effectiveness of yoga for chronic spine pain in the patient-centered outcomes.

In a study of healthy people (Woolery, Myers, Sternlieb, & Zeltzer, 2004) with mild levels of depression, the classes emphasized yoga postures thought to alleviate depression, back bends, standing poses, and inversions. The participants showed significant decreases in self-reported symptoms of depression and trait anxiety. These effects emerged by the middle of the yoga course and were maintained by the end. Changes were also observed in acute mood, with subjects reporting decreased levels of negative mood and fatigue following yoga classes. These findings provide evidence of the utility of Iyenger Yoga *asanas* in improving mood.

Evans, Moieni, Taub, Subramanian, Tsao, Sternlieb, and Zeltzer (2010) conducted a study to investigate the feasibility of a single-arm, group administered, six-week, biweekly Iyengar yoga (IY) program for eight young adults with Rheumatoid Arthritis (RA). Findings indicate that Iyengar Yoga is a feasible complementary approach for young people with RA, although larger clinical trials are needed to demonstrate safety and efficacy.

Shapiro, Cook, Davydov, Ottaviani, Leuchter, and Abrams (2007) presented further data on the intervention, focusing on individual differences in psychological, emotional and biological processes affecting treatment outcome. Significant reductions were shown for depression, anger, anxiety, neurotic symptoms and low frequency heart rate variability in the 17 completers. Eleven out of these completers achieved remission levels post-intervention. Participants who remitted differed from the non-remitters at intake on several traits and on physiological measures indicative of a greater capacity for emotional regulation. Moods improved from before to after the yoga classes. Yoga appears to be a promising intervention for depression; it is cost-effective and easy to implement. It produces many beneficial emotional, psychological and biological effects, as supported by observations in this study.

Streeter et al. (2017) conducted a study to assess the effects of an intervention of Iyengar yoga and coherent breathing at five breaths per minute on depressive symptoms and to determine optimal intervention yoga dosing for future studies in individuals with major depressive disorder (MDD). They found that during 12-week intervention of yoga plus coherent breathing, depressive symptoms declined significantly in patients with MDD in both the high-dose group (HDG) and low-dose group (LDG). Both groups showed comparable compliance and clinical improvements, with more subjects in the HDG exhibiting BDI-II scores d”10 at week 12.

Tiedmann, O'Rourke, Sesto, and Sherrington (2013) evaluated the feasibility and effect of a 12-week Iyengar yoga program on balance and mobility in older people. The intervention group (n = 27) participated in a 12-week, twice-weekly yoga program focused on standing postures and received a fall prevention education booklet. The control group (n = 27) received the education booklet only. The findings of the trial indicate that the intervention group significantly improved compared with control group on standing balance, sit-to-stand test, 4-m walk, and one-legged stand with eyes closed.

Restorative Yoga

Restorative yoga is derived from Iyengar Yoga which was invented by B.K.S. Iyengar. Restorative yoga is a series of body poses which enable one to create deep relaxation which release muscle tension in the body. Its poses provide relaxation, healing and restoration. Traditional restorative poses uses some props like; blankets, pillows, etc., however these poses can be done with or without props. Its poses are held for a long period of time and often modified with props.

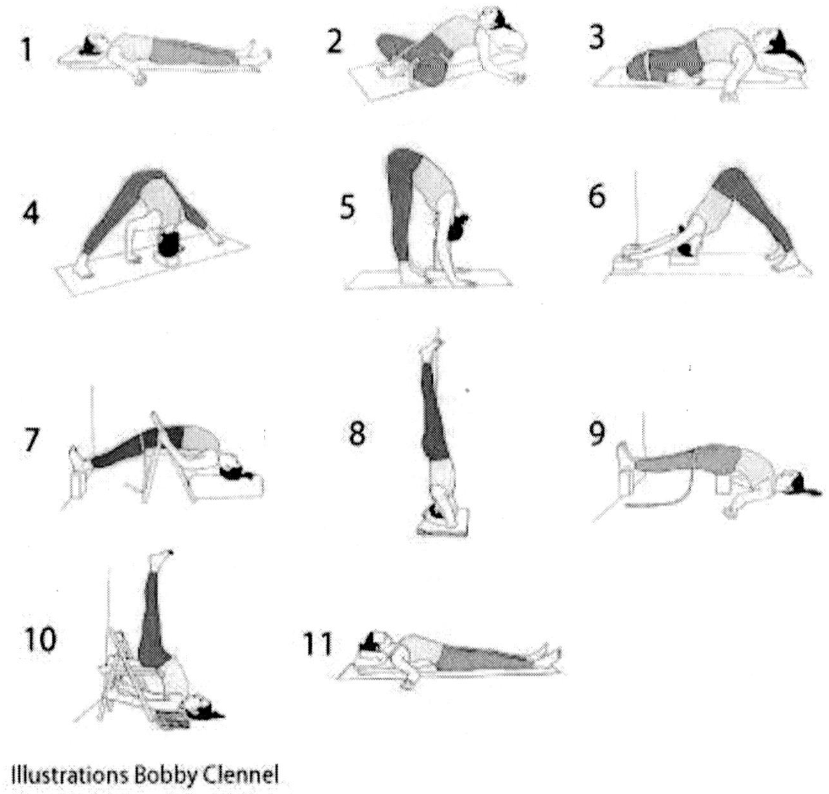

Image Source: Google

Procedure: Before one starts to perform the poses, first of all he/she should be warm-up, which can be done by performing the sun salutation (*Surya Namskara*). Poses has to be held for few minutes, and it can be as long as 10 to 15 minutes. Most commonly practiced yoga poses include:

- Legs against Wall pose- Performed with pillow under legs, back.
- Child's Pose - Tuck heels under hips and cradle a pillow with your upper body.

- Reclining Bound Angle pose- Performed with pillow under head, arms and legs.
- *Savasana* (Relaxation) - Rest the head on a pillow, legs on a bolster and feet on blanket.

While you practice restorative yoga poses, your yoga master may suggest you to use a blanket to cover your body, so that you will feel more comfortable.

Benefits: Enhances flexibility, deeply relaxes the body, stills the mind and enhance better sleep, improves capacity for healing and balancing, balances the nervous system, boosts the immune system, develops qualities of compassion and understanding toward others and self, enhances mood states by decreasing stress hormone cortisol ("Why Restorative Yoga? – Ekhart Yoga," n.d.).

Related Studies

Danhauer, Tooze, Farmer, Campbell, McQuellon, Barrett, and Miller (2008) conducted a study using fifty-one women with ovarian (n = 37) or breast cancer (n = 14) with a mean age of 58.9 years. All study participants participated in 10 weekly 75-minute Restrorative Yoga classes. Study participants completed questionnaires at baseline, immediately post-intervention, and 2 months post-intervention. Significant improvements were found for depression, negative-affect, state anxiety, mental health, and overall quality of life. Fatigue decreased between baseline and post-intervention follow-up. Health-related quality of life improved between baseline and the 2-month follow-up. Qualitative feedback from participants was predominantly positive.

Kanaya et al. (2011) tested a restorative yoga intervention vs. active stretching for metabolic outcomes. They conducted a

48-week randomized trial comparing restorative yoga vs. stretching among underactive adults with the metabolic syndrome. Their findings of the study suggest that restorative yoga was marginally better than stretching for improving fasting glucose but not other metabolic factors.

Integral Yoga

The founder of the integral yoga was Sri Aurobindo. It focuses on self-realization through personalized yoga practices. It does not focus solely on physical fitness but also takes a more spiritual approach. According to the teachings of Sri Aurobindo, integral yoga is directed towards the union of one's self with the divine consciousness and harmony. It is concerned with attaining oneness or union with the highest possible level of divinity and universe. In integral yoga, psychology is not separate from spirituality. According to Sri Aurobindo there should be complete synthesis in body, mind, and psychology spiritually to bring about a more charismatic world.

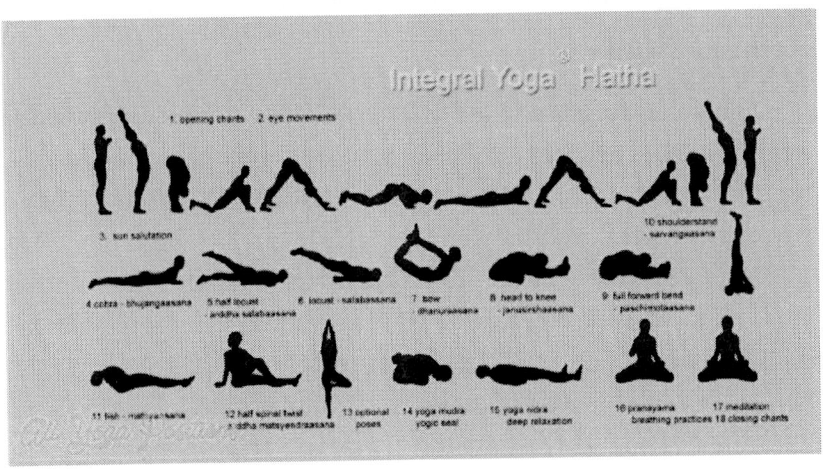

Image Source: Google

Most of the yoga focuses greatly on the development of a single aspect of the self like achieving a state of transcendence and liberation, or the achievement of optimum physical fitness, while integral yoga seeks a complete transformation of the entire being. The main aim of integral yoga is to integrate the body, mind and spirit, to achieve harmony and union with the karma. So, the basic intention of Integral yoga is to provide the practitioner with the tools necessary to live a peaceful, healthy, and joyful life.

Benefits: Purification of the mind is not possible without good thoughts which channelized to heighten the mental aspects. Regular practice of the poses of integral yoga helps to receive the solar energy to upgrade the life. Practicing integral yoga also helps to increase the stamina and endurance of the practitioner. It also helps to maintain proper focus in life. Most people are trapped of anxiety, frustration and ignorance. They desire need a force that give them the energy to succeed. In order to allow more effective contemplation, integral yoga brings spirituality under better scrutiny. (Introduction to Integral Yoga, n.d.)

Related Study

Khemka, Ramarao, and Hankey (2011) conducted a study to evaluate the effects of integral yoga practices on certain psychological and health variables and also the consistency of correlations observed between them. 108 subjects age range from 17 to 63 years were used. The study was a pre-post intervention study. The variables measured were sustained attention, emotional intelligence, general health, *guna* personality – *sattva, rajas* and *tamas*. Results indicate significant changes in all variables ($P< 0.001$) except in *sattva*. It also confirms that emotional intelligence and general health variables correlate significantly with each other and negatively with *tamas*. Emotional intelligence and *tamas* form positive and negative predictors of health respectively. *Sattva* correlates positively with emotional intelligence suggesting that a sattvic personality indicates better self-control. This suggests that, by improving *guna* personality, long-term yoga practice may stabilize emotional intelligence.

Tantra yoga

Image Source: Google

The word "tantra" literally means a technology or a technique. It is also known as Maha (the great) yoga. This refers to an inner technology. Actually, whenever we think about Tantra yoga, usually it comes in our mind that it is something sexual. Here we are right but to some extent, not exactly, actually this is something more than that. Although it is true that it may improve sex life, but only because of that it helps one to get in touch with one's own body and energy. So, the best way to overcome this negative perception about tantra yoga is to become aware and well educated on the subject itself.

Tantra Yoga is a holistic approach to the study of the universe from the point of view of an individual: the study of the macrocosm through the study of the microcosm. Tantra Yoga draws on all the sciences- astrology, astronomy, chemistry, geometry, mathematics, numerology, physiognomy, physics, alchemy, Ayurveda (the traditional medicine of India), psychology and so on - to provide a practical means of realizing the highest ideals of philosophy in daily life. Tantra Yoga draws the different areas of human knowledge together instead of categorizing and separating them. Instead of limiting the tree of life to any single branch of itself, tantra yoga studies itself. This tree is a microcosm, a great organization of diverse elements linked together by a unifying law (dharma) that is inherent in their very nature. Tantra Yoga seeks to understand this law (Mini & Awasthi, 2015).

Tantra yoga works on the subtle energies within the body in order to enhance one's physical wellbeing and spiritual growth as well. The purpose of life and the connection with others can be understood in a new dimension through the exploration of these energies and their connection to the universe. This ancient practice is a powerful combination of mantras, asana, mudra, and bandha (energy lock) and chakra (energy center) that can be used to build clarity, strength and bliss in everyday life. The female deity represents change and creativity by embodying and harnessing the five forces of Shakti. Tantric Yoga suggests that we can move through the world with more contentment and confidence. Tantra yoga is the oscillating balance between Shiva and Shakti, male and female to find the balance within ourselves. It is believed that we learn and find our truth to live from tantra yoga. Tantra yoga guides us to a path which will lead us to the absolute personal freedom with a strong physical and mental practice. The basic objective of tantra yoga is to merge with the ultimate reality by the channelling and arousing of sexual energy. Tantra yoga is a practice that can be used to expand awareness in all of the four levels of consciousness (Jagrat or wakeful state, Swapna or dream state, Shushupti deep sleep & Turiya), the connection between a couple and creating a deeper spiritual bond with each other. Tantra yoga is a combination of the four main yogas (Mantra yoga, Hatha yoga, Laya yoga and Raja yoga).

Aims of *Tantra* Yoga:

According to Mini and Awasthi (2015), tantra yoga teaches us to identify the various factors that influence our feelings and thoughts and to transcend the obstacles to our evolution arising from intolerance, ignorance, selfishness and attachment to our animal nature. One learns to create peace, harmony, and order within the self by refining feelings and thoughts by means of the tantra yoga practices. Tantra yoga thus promotes a one-pointedness and centeredness that help one to free the consciousness from limitations. Tantra yoga offers practical tools for reprogramming the mind and desires. Tantra yoga helps to unfold our divine nature by means of breathing exercises (pranayama), visualization (of yantras and deities), contemplation repetition of a mantra (mantra japa), physical and ritual cleaning. When Tantra Yoga practiced consistently, it can help one to get in tune with who he/she is, achieve the goals of life, and, deepen the relationship and connectedness when done with a partner. So, the basic purpose of the tantra yoga is to bring the spiritual world and the material world into one.

Udgeeth Pranayama

Image Source: Google

It is one of the most important 7 pranayamas (*Bhastrika pranayama*, *Kapalbhati pranayama*, *Bahaya pranayama*, *Anulom Vilom pranayama*, *Bharamari pranayama*, *Udgeeth pranayama* & *Pranav pranayama*) and this breathing technique is performed after all of the breathing exercises. It is also known as *Omkara Japa* Breathing technique or Chanting breathing technique. According to Hindu philosophy, OM is the all encompassing chant that takes man closest to God. In Hinduism, it is also believed that the entire creation and universe was set in motion by this chant of sacred OM.

Procedure: Inhalation and exhalation both should be slow, soft, long and subtle. Sit on the *padmasana* and close your eyes, spine erect. Inhale for 3-5 seconds rhythmically and slowly, and while chanting the sacred word 'OM' methodically (steadily & slowly) for about 15-20 seconds breathe it out. After one chanting is complete repeat this practice again. While chanting OM, the O should be 3 times longer that of the M; like OOOOOOMM. As the practice increases, lengthen each breath (inhalation and exhalation) to 1-minute. Visualize that the inhaled breath entering and moving inside the whole body and purify every time while chanting OM. In all of the *pranayamas* breath plays a vital role. So, the practitioner should concentrate on the breath and feel that the positive energies come into the body while inhaling and negative energies go out while exhaling. Repeat this for 5 to 10 minutes.

Benefits: Good for insomnia and for deepening the quality of sleep and relieving bad dreams. Helps the mind to become one-pointed and facilitate the practice of conscious sleep (*Yoga Nidra*). It is a practice of meditation.

Udgeeth pranayama increases attention level, positivity and self-confidence. It unites consciousness with the universal power, helps in clearing out the respiratory system, cure sexual dysfunction (both males and females), helps the mind to concentrate in one particular thing and facilitate the practice of conscious sleep (yoga nidra). If practiced every day in the morning the practitioner attains many physical and spiritual benefits, gradually reduce premature graying hair, hair fall, diminution of eye sight and appearance of wrinkles ("Welcome to my intellect," n.d.).

If practiced during bedtime this can help to keep away nightmares thus you have a sound and peaceful sleep, very beneficial in migraine and headaches etc, improves the digestive system, useful in acidity, it calms the mind and brings stability, it also relieves tension, anger and anxiety, it is the excellent breathing exercises for mediation, effective against hypertension, it cures problems related to sleep (insomnia) and bad dreams, control the high blood pressure and cure it, cures the problems related to the nervous system, it improves memory power ("Udgeet pranayama – steps – benefits – health school," n.d.)

Related Studies

Dabre, Pingale, Dahake, and Humbad (2011) conducted a study to find out the effect of *suryanamskar*, *pranayama* and *yogasanas* training on the intelligence of school going children. 154 subjects were selected, learning in the standard 5th of the session 2006-07 and the same subjects learning in 6th standard of the session 2007-08. These subjects were divided into the controlled group and experimental group i.e. 84 in control and 70 in experimental group. The experimental group underwent training of the *Uttejak Vyayam* (warm-up exercises), before starting the *Suryanamskar* (*smantrak*), Asana (*Padmasana*, *Paschimottanasana*, *Tadasana*, *Bhujangasana*, *Sarvangasana*, *Shavasana* etc.), and *Pranayam* (*Udgeeth* [*Omkar*], *Anulom Vilom*, *Bhramri* etc.) each day in morning six-days a week for 10 months. The subjects of control group did not participate in any of the above program. Pre and post –test carried out with the help of the School Annual Examination results. It was found that the experimental group was good in the school results as compared to the control group.

Manaspure, Fadia, and Gowda (2011a) conducted a study to investigate the beneficial effects of *pranayama* with reference to FEV1, FVC and FEV1 / FVC ratio. The participants were divided into control and study groups with 45 members each at the age group of 20±2 years. The study group was asked to perform *Kapalbhati*, *Anulom Vilom*, *Bhramari* and *Udgeeth pranayama* during eight weeks. In study group, the FEV1, FVC and FEV1 / FVC ratios were significantly elevated (p=0.000) as compared to that of control group. Since the mechanical factors of the Lung –Thoracic System like FVC, FEV1, FEV1/ FVC did show statistically significant changes, the therapeutic exercise programs for sedentary young adults can be best designed to improve the mechanical efficiency of Lung- Thoracic System.

Manaspure, Fadia, and Gowda (2011b) conducted a study to study the beneficial effect of pranayama with reference to respiratory rate and breath holding time. Totally 90 participants were divided into control and study groups with 45 members each of both the sexes at the age group of 20±2 years. The study group was asked to perform *Kapalbhati*, *Anulom Vilom*, *Bhramari* and *Udgeeth pranayama*. The duration of the study was eight weeks. The respiratory rate and breath holding time in both the groups were recorded. Result indicates that in study group, the respiratory rate was decreased significantly (p=0.000) whereas the breath holding time was increased significantly (p=0.000) when compared to that of control group.

Mehrotra, Phadke, Kharche, Pranita, and Joshi (2012) conducted a study to assess effect of yoga practices on anxiety score (using Taylor's manifest anxiety scale) and resting heart rate. Study group included subjects who participated in yoga practices (*Suryanamaskar*, *Tadasana*, *Utkatasana*, *Ushtrasana*, *Ardhamatsyendrasana*, *Pavanmuktasana*, *Paschimottanasana*, *Halasana*, *Sarvangasana*, *Matsyasana*, *Bhujangasana*, *Dhanurasana* and *Pranayama* i.e. *Anuloma viloma*, *Kapalbhati*, *Bhastrika*, *Bhramari*, *Udgeeth*, *Omkar*, *Pranav*) for a period of 3 months. Control group included subjects who did not perform yoga or any exercise. Anxiety score and resting heart rate were recorded in both the groups before start of study and at end of the study. Results indicate that at the end of three months statistically significant decrease in anxiety score and resting heart rate was observed in the study group. Whereas, there was no statistically significant difference in anxiety score and resting heart rate of control group.

Holkar and Makhija (2015) conducted a study to observe beneficial effects of 3 month and 6 months of Yogic exercise on various anthropometric parameters in patients of hypertension with obesity. 60 subjects with an age group of 40-60 years, amongst these, 40 were male subjects and 20 were female who attended the Yoga Life Modification Programme (YLMP) conducted between. The practice session, 1 hour each day of a 7 days outpatient course, interrupted by a one day weekend break. Results indicate that, at the end of the study, there was a significant decrease in mean blood pressure as well as weight and BMI of patients.

Gandhi and Anbalagan (2016) conducted a study to analyze the effect of yogic practices combined with *varmam* on muscular strength endurance and flexibility among the middle aged men. Thirty subjects were included age ranged from 35 to 45 years. The subjects were divided into two equal groups. The study used a pre-test and post-test design. The subjects (n=30) were randomly assigned to two equal groups of fifteen subjects each. Experimental group assigned *Asana*, *Pranayama* (including Udgeeth pranayama) with varmam Training group and group II Control Group they were not given any specific training. All the subjects were tested immediately prior and after the experimental programme. Based on the result, it was concluded that Asana, Pranayama, Meditation combined with Varma (APMVTG) produced as significant development on the selected physical variables among the middle aged men.

Jain and Sharma (2017) conducted a study to study the effect of Yoga: *Pranayama* on anxiety and depression. A sample of 120 persons (60 males & 60 females) was selected and they were divided in two groups: Experimental Group and Control Group. A pre and post control group design was used. The experimental group was trained for Yogic Intervention the package of *Pranayama* of seven breathing exercises as suggested by Swami Ramdevji: *Bhastrika*, *Kapalbhati* , *Bahya Pranayama* (with *tribandh*), *Anulom-Vilom*, *Bhramri*, *Udgeet* '*Omkar*

Japa', *Pranav Pranayama* (Meditation of Om with Breathing). The research scholar has been trained in Patanjali Yogpeeth, Haridwar under the supervision of Swami Ramdev. Every subject had to do *Pranayama* in the early morning or at least with a gap of 4 to 5 hours after taking his meals. The duration was 20-25 minutes daily for three months. An analysis of results shows that the *pranayama* had positive effect in the management of anxiety and depression as well as in creating positive image about oneself in the experimental group while control group did not show any significant difference from the baseline records.

Ashtanga Yoga

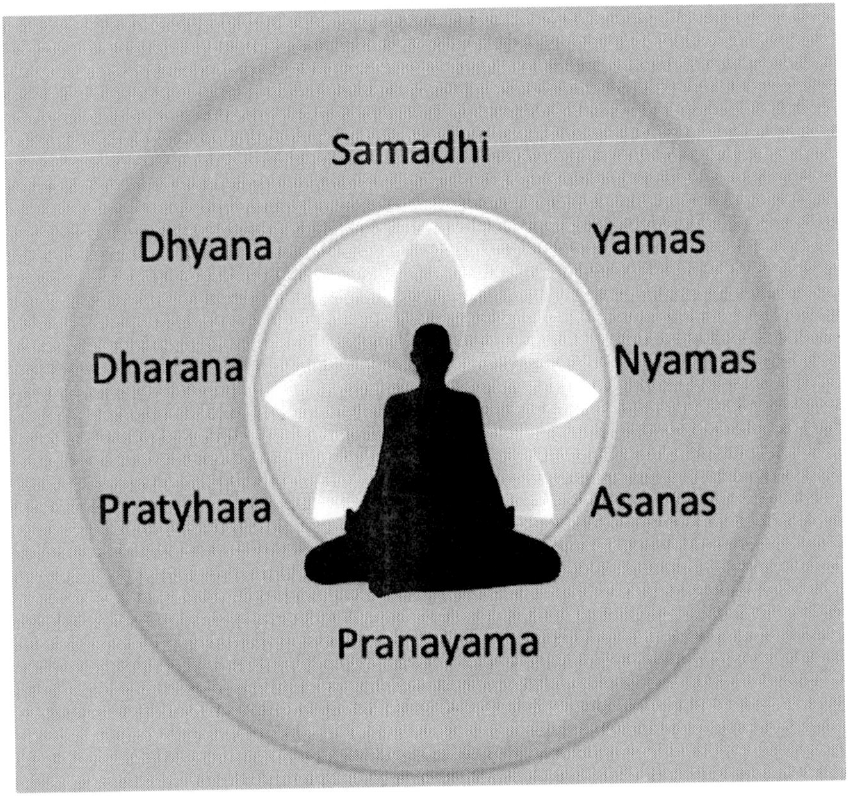

Image Source: Google

Ashtanga yoga is also known as *Raja* yoga which deals with the control of the'all senses and concentration of the mind through eight fold paths of yoga. In the *Dharana* and *Dhyan* steps of the *Raja* Yoga *kundalinies* are awakened. By following the eight steps of *raja* yoga the practitioner can attain inner clarity, peace, realization and self-control. These eight steps are:

1. *Yama* - Self-control
2. *Niyama*- Discipline
3. *Asana* - Physical exercises
4. *Pranayama* - Breath exercises
5. *Pratyahara* - Withdrawal of the senses from external objects
6. *Dharana* - Concentration
7. *Dhyana* - Meditation
8. *Samadhi* - Complete Realization

1. Yama - (Self-Control)

Yama consists of five principles: *Satya* (truth), *Asetya* (non-stealing), *Ahimsa* (non-injury), *Brahmacharya* (chastity) and *Aparigraha* (non-greed).

***A. Satya* - Truthfulness:** It is good and correct to always speak the truth, but more important is how the truth is conveyed. One has the capacity to convey the truth to someone like hurling a knife, but he/she also capable of telling the same truth using loving words.

***B. Asteya* - Non-Stealing**: One should never take anything else that rightfully belongs to others.

C. Ahimsa - **Non-Violence:** Ahimsa means not to cause pain or harm to any living being by thought, word or deed.

D. Brahmacharya - **Pure Way of Life:** It is often translated as sexual abstinence. But it actually consists of much more. It means that our consciousness should always be turned towards the God. We should fulfil our duties/responsibilities carefully, but always with the awareness that we are not the doer; in fact God only is the doer of all.

E. Aparigraha – **Non-greed:** It means that we should not collect goods, but only acquires and use what we need to live. One, who has many possessions, also has many worries. We are born without belongings and when we dead, we leave all behind in this world.

2. *Niyamas* (Discipline)

This consists of five principles: *Shaucha* (purity), *Santosha* (contentment), *Tapas* (self-control), *Svadhyaya* (study of the scriptures), *Ishvara Pranidhana* (surrender to God).

A. Shaucha – **Purity:** Everyone should maintain not only external purity, but also more importantly, internal purity. Our clothes, body, thoughts and feelings should be pure. For spiritual development good company of people should be kept which impart a good effect upon us.

B. Santosha – **Contentment:** One can attain contentment only when he/she recognises that inner wealth provides more happiness as compare to the material possessions and all the worldly goods bring disappointment.

C. Tapas - **Self-Control, Self-Discipline:** In life, when one encounters obstacles and adversities, he should never give up; should be continue on the chosen path honestly.

***D. Svadhyaya* - Study of the Holy Scriptures:** The Holy Scriptures (the Upanishads, the Bhagavad Gita, Patanjali's Yoga Sutras etc.) provide great assistance on our yoga path as well as impart valuable knowledge.

***E. Ishvara Pranidhana* - Devotion to God:** God protects all of them who surrender themselves to the God with faithfully and trustfully. It means to hand over all whatever you do to the divine self with pure devotion.

3. *Asana* - Physical Exercises

Asanas consists of physical exercises.

4. *Pranayama* - Breath Exercises

Raja Yogis in the process of controlling the body and breath, they also achieve control of the mind. This leads to the awakening of those inner powers which will guide one continuously on the spiritual path.

According to Baba Ramdev there are seven breath control techniques namely *(Bhastrika pranayama, Kapalbhati pranayama, Bahaya pranayama, Anulom Vilom pranayama, Bharamari pranayama, Udgeeth pranayama & Pranav pranayama)*.

5. *Pratyahara* - Withdrawal of the Senses

In the first stages of meditation we practice *Pratyahara*, keeping the body motionless, the eyes closed, the mind quiet and the attention directed inward. There are special techniques through which we can practice *Pratyahara*. Meditation exercise initially directs attention to external sounds, their nature, distance, etc. - simply observing the sound. Gradually awareness is withdrawn to one's "inner space" to the sounds within the body (heartbeat, blood circulation, etc.). It is only when one has mastered the step of *Pratyahara* that we can progress to concentration.

6. *Dharana* – Concentration of the mind

Dharana means to focus our thoughts and feelings upon a single object. Usually we succeed with this for only a short period of time, and then other thoughts come into the mind and distract our focus. So, after just a few minutes we become aware of lack of concentration. Until we are capable of concentration on a thought or object for a long period of time, in any situation, we still have not mastered *Dharana*.

Trataka (Candle meditation), *Pranayamas* (breathing exercises), specific *Asanas* (physical exercises), as well as chanting of *Mantras* greatly help in improving the ability of concentration.

7. *Dhyana* - Meditation

For true meditation, all meditation techniques are only the preliminary exercises. Meditation happens whenever the mind is in the state of peace. In meditation, we experience pure being. The moment the individual ego ceases to exist and the intellect is still, within the heart Divine light shines and we are one with it.

8. *Samadhi* - Complete Realization, Enlightenment, Union with the Divine

The state of *Samadhi* is where the knowledge, object of knowledge and knower unite. The knowledge (i.e. what is God), the object of knowledge (i.e. God) and knower (i.e. the person practicing) become one. This means that the human consciousness unites with the Divine consciousness. Those who attain *Samadhi* hear a heavenly sound, see a heavenly radiant light, and feel an infinite expanse within them. When *Samadhi* is achieved, one is like a river that finally flows into the sea after a difficult and long journey. All difficulties are overcome and the river unites with the ocean. In the same way, at the end a Yogi reaches becomes one with the Supreme Consciousness. The Yogi's consciousness finds eternal bliss, peace and quiet- means the Yogi is liberated (Raja Yoga, n.d.). "*Samadhi*" is the state of pure experience of the divine and transcendence (Kaarthikeyan, 2007, p. 161).

Raja yoga deals with the control of the senses and concentration of the mind through eight fold path of yoga described in the 'yoga darshana' by the father of raja yoga namely, Patanjali. Although Raja yoga consists of all of the *yogasnas*. It means yoga is a state of *dhyan* (concentration) in which the mind is controlled and made to be single-pointed (*ekagrata*). Through developing eight limbs of the Patanjali's yoga-sutra one can control his/her mind. In the *Raja yoga* breathing, *asanas* (specific body postures), *kundalini* and spiritual experiences come into the practitioner (Singh, 2007, p. 31). So, Raja Yoga is concerned with developing mental concentration in order to experience *samâdhi*. In *Dharana* and *Dhyan* steps of the raja yoga *kundalinies* are awakened.

Benefits of Raja Yoga: According to Brahma Kumaris there are many benefits of performing *raja* yoga ("Brahma Kumaris Official Website - Benefits of *Raja* Yoga," n.d.)

1. Enhance memory and concentration.
2. Create a sense of well-being.
3. Mind becomes more clear and focused.
4. Gain freedom from stress and anxiety.
5. Improve personal relationships.
6. Overcome negative habits.
7. Improve quality of sleep.

Physiological Benefits: According to Brahma Kumaris there are many benefits of performing *raja* yoga. The most important of those are as follows ("100 BENEFITS OF RAJYOGA MEDITATION... - Brahma Kumaris India | Facebook," n.d.)

1. Relaxes our nervous system
2. Cure headaches and migraines
3. Greater orderliness of brain functioning
4. Helps in post-operative healing.
5. Enhances the immune system
6. It lowers oxygen consumption.
7. It decreases respiratory rate.
8. It increases blood flow and slows the heart rate.

Spiritual benefits: According to Brahma Kumaris ("100 BENEFITS OF RAJYOGA MEDITATION... - Brahma Kumaris India | Facebook," n.d.)

1. Helps you discover your purpose in life.
2. Provides peace of mind, happiness.
3. Increased compassion.
4. Increased self-actualization.
5. Deeper understanding of yourself and others.
6. Growing wisdom.
7. Deeper Level of spiritual relaxation.
8. Brings body, mind, and spirit in harmony.
9. Helps learn forgiveness.

10. Increased acceptance of one self.
11. Creates a deeper relationship with your God.
12. Greater inner-directedness.
13. Changes attitude toward life.
14. Helps living in the present moment.
15. Increases the synchronicity in your life.
16. Discovery of the power and consciousness beyond the ego.
17. Experience a sense of Oneness.
18. Creates a widening, deepening capacity for love.
19. Experience an inner sense of Assurance or Knowingness.
20. Leads to enlightenment.

The basic difference between *raja* yoga and yoga involves exercise is that *raja* yoga directly connects the mind to the source of spiritual power. This creates a strong mind, peaceful personality and a healthy body. Yoga involving exercises focuses only on the body. The body relaxes, but other exercises are required for making the mind strong. So, these types of yogas connect human beings with human beings. *Raja* Yoga is not physical exercise; rather it is an easy mental exercise. *Raja* yoga connects human beings with the Higher Being (God). *Raja* Yoga transcends the mind beyond the body and creates long lasting peaceful experiences. ("Brahma Kumaris Official Website - What is Rajayoga?," n.d.)

Related Studies

Sukhsohale, Phatak, Sukhsohale, and Agrawal (2012) conducted a study to examine the effect of *Raja* Yoga meditation on physiological and psychological well-being. 100 practitioners of Brahmakumaris *Raja* Yoga meditation (33 men and 67 women) aged 30 years and above (mean age 52.06 ± 12.76 years). The subjects were divided into short term meditators (meditating for 6 months to 5 years with mean duration 3.37 ± 1.67 years) and long term meditators (meditating for more than 5 years with mean duration 11.19 ± 5.13 years). Physiological variables like heart rate (HR), respiratory rate (RR) per minute, systolic blood pressure (SBP) and diastolic blood pressure (DBP) were recorded before meditation practice and twice during the practice of meditation after every fifteen minutes. Also, detailed history regarding addictions, negative attributes and spiritual practices before and after practicing meditation was inquired as per the predesigned questionnaire. Fasting blood sugar was also estimated by glucometer. Results indicate that both short term as well as long term meditators showed a significant declining trend in HR, RR, SBP and DBP 15 minutes as well as 30 minutes after meditation ($P<0.05$). Subjects of long term meditation got rid of addictions (tobacco chewing, smoking, alcohol, non-vegetarian diet) and negative attributes (anger, mental stress, negative/waste thoughts and irritability) after learning and practicing meditation. Subjects also experienced various benefits in the form of mental peace and happiness.

Dhar, Chaudhuri, Rahaman, Majumdar, Biswas, and Goswami (2016) conducted a study to evaluate the effect of Raja yoga on stress management among healthy young adults. Hundred healthy young adults in the age range 18-35 years performing Raja yoga regularly were selected as study subjects, and hundred age- and sex-matched subjects from the local population were chosen as control group. Stress level in the subjects was assessed according to the presumptive life event stress scale (PSLES). Both the groups were age-, sex- matched, and their food habits were same. The presumptive life event stress scale (PSLES) showed no significant difference, but perceived stress score was significantly higher among control group. Body mass index and waist/hip ratio were significantly more in control group. Resting pulse rate, systolic blood pressure, and diastolic blood pressure were significantly lower in Raja Yoga group. Results of Orthostatic Tolerance Test (OTT) and isometric hand grip test showed significantly lower values in Raja Yoga group. Results of 40 mm endurance test were significantly raised in Raja Yoga group. Cardio-respiratory fitness parameters in young adults are correlated with perceived stress. Perceived stress shifts autonomic balance toward sympathetic dominance, hampering cardiovascular and respiratory functions. Practice of Raja yoga meditation can help in overcoming these bouts of stress and thereby stress-related hazards.

Laya Yoga

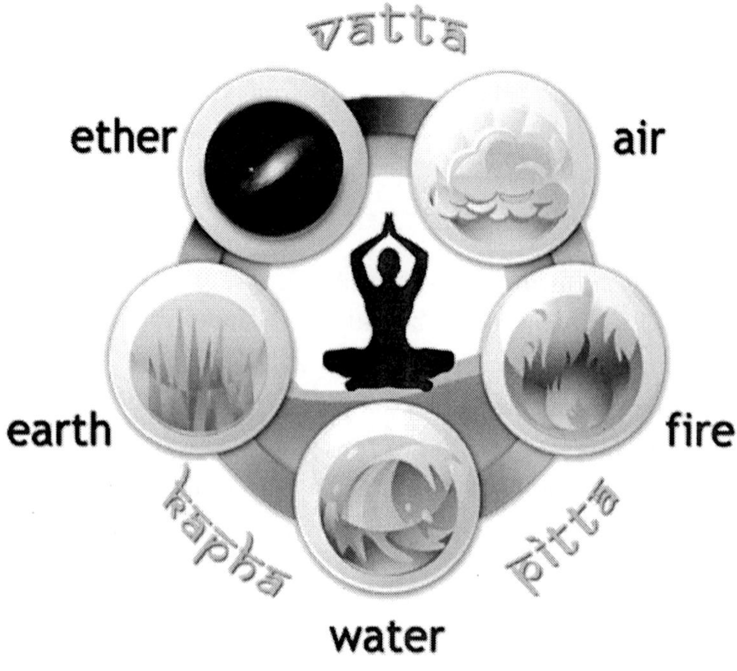

Image Source: Google

According to Sivananda (1994) in the *laya* yoga, *laya* is the state of mind when the practitioner gets absorbed into the object of meditation and forgets all of the objects of senses. *Laya* yoga is also known as *kundalini* yoga. *Laya* Yoga is a form of meditation. In Ayurveda and Indian philosophy, it is considered that the human body is made of five elements (tattvas) and these elements are: *Aakash* (ether), *Vayu* (air), *Agni* (fire), *Jal* (water), *Prithvi* (earth). So, Laya enables the practitioner of having a perfect control over these five *Tattvas*, mind and *Indriyas* (*Jnanendriyas*: ears, skin, eyes, tongue and nose; *Karmendriyas*: speech, hands, legs, genitals, anus). Laya also stops fluctuations of the mind and the mind, body and *prana* will be entirely subdued. The basic purpose of the *laya* yoga is to merge into the transcendental reality; means making an effort to obliterate the ego and deep concentration, thereby rising to *Turiya* (a higher state of consciousness).

Procedure: Sit in *padmasana* (lotus position); put the palms together in Prayer Pose at the center of the chest, or in *gyan mudra* with the wrists on the knees. Focus on the eyebrow point. Actually, s*ambhavi mudra* (the eyebrow center gazing gesture) is an effective method for *laya* yoga, in which the practitioner intently concentrates on any one of the seven Chakras (energy centers). There are seven chakras: *Sahasrara* (Crown Chakra), *Ajna* (third-eye chakra), *Vishuddha* (throat chakra), *Anahata* (heart chakra), *Manipura* (navel chakra), *Svadhishthana* (sacral chakra), *Muladhara* (root chakra); five in the spine and two in the head. In due course of practice, the Yogi gets established in *Samadhi*. He becomes a *Jivanmukta. Laya* yoga attempts to locate these chakras and awaken them through meditation.

Benefits: The ultimate aim of laya yoga is to attain supreme consciousness (*Turiya*, or the fourth level of consciousness), to cultivate spirituality and to achieve the state of *ananda* (a state of peaceful bliss) or ultimate happiness. By practicing *Laya* Yoga, yogi can be unified with the universal power and connect with the divine consciousness. *Laya* yoga heals and cleanses mind and body, uplifts the consciousness. In it the seeker locates different centers (*chakras*) and meditates on them, thereby transforming consciousness ("LAYA YOGA: Kundalini Tantra - Mantra - Siddhi Meditations," n.d.).

Isha Kriya

Image Source: Google

Isha literally means that it is the source of creation, ***Kriya*** refers to internal action towards that. *Isha kriya* created by yogi and mystic Sadhguru, who is the founder of *Isha* Foundation and a well known and respected spiritual master from India. The purpose of *Isha Kriya* is to help an individual to get in touch with the source of his/her existence, to create life according to his own vision and wishes. Daily practice of *Isha Kriya* brings health, peace, dynamism and wellbeing.

It is the vision of Sadhguru through *Isha Kriya* to offer "one drop of spirituality" to every individual seeking for. Through *Isha*

Kriya meditation, the possibilities of a spiritual process, which were once available only to ascetics and yogis, are now being offered to everyone even in the comfort of their own home.

Its simplicity and effectiveness makes *Isha Kriya* very special. It can be taught to anyone, anywhere, in a short period of time. 12 to 18 minutes of daily practice is all it takes to bring a profound transformation in the life.

Preparation: Sit facing East in a cross-legged posture, with your spine comfortably erect. Keep your hands upon your thighs, with your palms facing up. With your face slightly upturned, eyes closed, focus between your eyebrows. This meditation will happen in three stages:

Stage 1:

Inhale and exhale gently and slowly.

With each inhalation, mentally say to yourself: "I am not the body." The inhalation should last the whole duration of that thought.

With each exhalation, mentally say to yourself: "I am not even the mind." The exhalation should last for the whole duration of that thought.

Repeat this for 7 to 11 minutes

Stage 2:

Utter a long "A" sound (as the "a" in father). The sound should come from just below the navel. You need not utter it very loud, but loud enough to feel the vibration.

Utter the long "A" sound 7 times, exhaling fully into each sound.

Stage 3:

After the second stage, sit for 5 to 6 minutes with a slightly upturned face, and keep a mild focus between your eyebrows.

The total time of this practice should be between 12 to 18 min. The practitioner can sit longer if want.

Benefits: Daily practice of *Isha Kriya* will help one to reorganize his energy, improve health, heighten focus, enhance clarity and create peacefulness and joy.

Note: *While sitting for the Isha Kriya, do not pay attention to the activity of the body or mind. Whatever is happening in your body or your mind, just ignore it and simply sit. Do not take a break in between, as it will disturb the reorganization of energies that happens during the practice.*

It is recommended to do it once a day for 90 days, or twice a day for 48 days (a full *mandala*). It takes about 40 days for anything new to become part of your system. This is because the human physiology goes through a certain cycle every 40 to 48 days; this cycle is known as a '*mandala*'.

Trataka **Yoga**

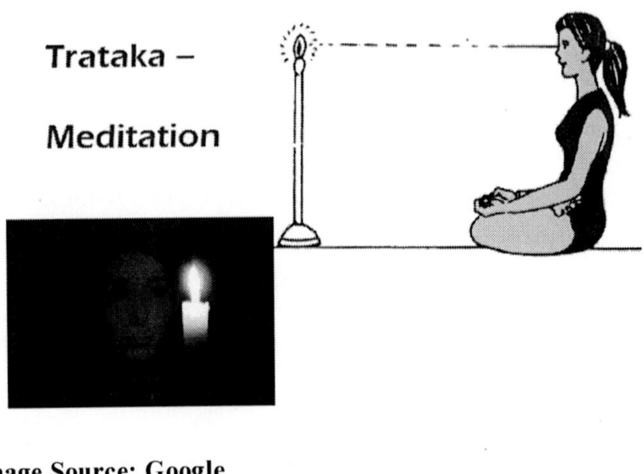

Image Source: Google

Trataka means visualisation, this technique involves steady gazing. *Trataka* yoga is one of the six components of *Hatha* Yoga including (*dhauti*, *vasti*, *neti*, *neuli*, *tratak* and *kapalbhati*). During waking hours, mind usually becomes filled with thoughts good and bad. The mind becomes in a state of disturbance and we have a propensity for being distracted easily. There are three types of *tratak* meditation.

The inner *tratak* is done by closing eyes. In this the focus concentration is within self, concentrate on the third eye. By focusing on the third eye one may feel pain and heat in eyes. However, with the passage of time you will feel normal.

In the **middle *tratak*** one need to keep the eyes open and concentrate on a flame of a candle or lamp, a crystal *Shivling*, or may be just a point. Whenever this is done one might feel a burning sensation in the eye. This is because of not to blink. Eyes can be closed if the irritation becomes too much and then repeat the same *sadhna* again. There is nothing wrong in doing so. The distance between the object from eyes must be at least twenty inches which is ideal for your eyes.

The last type of *tratak* is called the **outer *tratak***. It is the most complex of all *tratak sadhnas*. In this one needs to concentrate on any object like the stars, moon or sun. This can be done during day or night.

Procedure: Sit in the *sukhasana* (lotus posture) in front of a candle. Place the candle about 3 feet away from you with the wick of the candle at the same height as your chest and then light the candle. Close your eyes. Mentally chant the Mantra. Open the eyes and look at the flame without blinking for half a minute or for as long as you are able to keep your eyes open. The flame has three layers of colour. At the base it is reddish, in the middle bright white and at the tip smoky. So, you should concentrate on the upper brightest part of the flame with eyes open till tears come. When your eyes get tired, close them and visualise the after-image of the flame in front of you with closed eyes. Then open your eyes and again gaze at the flame without blinking the eyes.

Time: Do this for five minutes before going to sleep and before you begin your studies. This will do wonders to your power of concentration.

Benefits: This can help one to calm the mind, develop better intelligence and confidence. The ones who can perform inner *tratak* well can also hypnotize people from a distance. This also helps to remove all negative thoughts. It is therefore recommended for school children by strengthen the ability to concentrate. Improve spiritual power, memory, mental power, concentration (Secrets of tratak sadhana n.d.). It also helps to improve vision by purifies the eyes, strengthens the eye muscles. Helps people with sleeping difficulties and bedwetting. Develop the ability to visualize, intuition and willpower (*Trataka* n.d.).

Related Studies

Gopinathan, Dhiman, and Manjusha (2012) conducted a study to evaluate the efficacy of *trataka* yoga *kriya* in the management of timira (Ammetropia and Presbyopia). The study showed that none of the patient's aesthenopic symptoms were cured and markedly improved in eye exercises group. In *trataka* group, moderate improvement was observed in one patient, mild improvement was observed in 20 patients and no improvement was observed in 10 patients of timira. In Snellen's chart reading one line improvement was noted. There was moderate improvement in clarity of vision, contrast sensitivity, and fineness of objects. Though the degree of this improvement was almost similar in both the groups, a better relief was appreciated by patients of *Trataka* Yoga Kriya group.

Lolage and Jadhav (2013) conducted a study to measure the effect of yogic exercise on Myopia of high school girls. This experiment therefore included thirty (N=30) high school girls whose age ranged from 11 to 15 years. The subjects were divided into two groups i.e. control group (n=15) and experimental group (n=15). Initial test of Myopia was conducted to all subjects. In training of Yogic Exercise, *OM stawan*, *Anulom-vilom*, *Kapalbhati*, *Bhramari*, *Ujjayi Pranayama*, OM recitation, eye exercise *tratak*, palming and *Yoganidra*. In evening sixty minutes for each session of the day. The subject of control group did not practice in the above programmed. After one month training of yogic exercise final test was conducted for the entire subjects. It was found that due to the practice of yogic exercise eyesight of high school girls was improved.

Raghavendra and Singh (2014) conducted a study to assess the immediate effect of *trataka* on cognitive performance using the Stroop color–word test. They found better Performance on the Stroop color–word test assessed among 30 healthy male volunteers with ages ranging from 18 years to 31 years old (22.57 ± 3.65 years). The participants were tested before and after yogic visual concentration (*trataka*) and during a control session on two separate days.

Talwadkar, Jagannathan, and Raghuram (2014) conducted a study to test the effect of *trataka* on cognitive functions of the elderly (n=60). They found significant improvement in digit span scores ($z = 3.35$, $P < 0.01$) in the *trataka* group. SLCT scores ($t = 5.08$, $P < 0.01$) and TMT-B scores ($t = 4.26$, $P < 0.01$) improved immediately after the practice of *trataka* (when baseline compared to first follow-up). At 1 month follow-up, *trataka* group showed significantly better performance in the SLCT test compared to baseline ($t = 3.93$, $P < 0.01$) and TMT-B scores ($t = 7.09$, $P < 0.01$). So, the results of this study suggest that *trataka* can be used as a technique to enhance cognition in the elderly.

Rajpoot and Vaishnav (2014) investigated the effect of *trataka* on the level of anxiety among adolescents using a sample of 30 adolescents (age range 20-30 years) selected from Devsanskriti Vishwa Vidyalaya Haridwar using random sampling. Sinha's anxiety test was used for measuring the level of anxiety. Findings of the study revealed that *trataka* significantly decreases the level of anxiety among adolescents.

Soumya, Chhugani, and Tamang (2017) conducted a study to assess the effectiveness of *trataka* exercise on vision and on aesthenopia among student nurses. The sample comprised of student nurses belonging to the age group of 15 – 25 years studying at Rufaida College of Nursing, New Delhi. Pre – test Post – test Control Group Design was used. *Trataka* exercise was administered for 10 minutes in the experimental group for 2 weeks. No intervention was administered in the control group. On 15th day post- test vision and aesthenopia was assessed in both the groups. The results indicate that there was no significant difference in vision among experimental and control group after the intervention. On the other hand, there was significant difference in aesthenopia in the experimental group after the intervention of *trataka* exercise.

Karmakar and Pant (2017) more recently conducted a study to find out the effect of *Trataka Kriya* session on Visual Perception of elderly people. Sample of the study consist of 30 subjects. The age of the subjects was above 60 years. The design used for the study was pre-post design. OMKAR Chanting,

Trataka Kriya and Relaxation done by closing eyes until the inflammation feeling in eyes ends were used as the components of the session for a period of 6 weeks. Though there was not significant level of change in level of visual perception, yet there was a little improvement observed in case of visual perception after the end of session for 6 week. So, it was concluded that the session for a longer duration may have highly significant level of change in the level of visual perception of elderly people.

Yogeshvara's Yogas *(jnana* yoga, *karma* yoga *and bhakti* yoga*)*

Image Source: Google

According to Rao (2012) in the great epic Bhagavad Gita there are three forms of yoga for attaining self-realization- *Jnana* Yoga, *Karma* Yoga and *Bhakti* Yoga.

***Jnana* Yoga** (path of spiritual knowledge): In the Gita Lord Krishna says that one who is full of faith, has mastered over his senses attains spiritual knowledge as follows:

"Shraddhaval labhate jnanam tat parah samyatendriyah !

Jnanam labdhva param shantim achirenadhi-gacchati !!

(Bhagvad Gita 4. 39)

One with full faith, attentively focused, who has conquered the senses, attains (transcendental) knowledge, and also quickly attains super peace" (as Cited in Rao, 2012, p. 160).

Further, Lord Krishna says that a sinner can crossover all these sins, through the boat of spiritual knowledge. Spiritual knowledge also leads to eradication of all of the sins, like fire burns all wood to ashes.

"Api chedasi papebhyah sarvebhyah pap-krt-tamah !

Sarvam jnana-plavenaiva vrjinam santarisyasi !!

Yathidhamsi samidognir bhasma sat kurute'rjuna !

Jnanagnih sarva-karmani bhasma-sat kurute tatha !!

(Bhagvad Gita 4. 36 and 37)

Even if you are most sinful of all sinners, yet you will cross over all sins and miseries, by the boat of transcendental knowledge. O Arjuna, just as a blazing fire turns wood to ashes, similarly, the fire of knowledge turns all reactions from actions to ashes" (as Cited in Rao, 2012, p. 161).

This transcendental knowledge helps one to discriminate between real and unreal, the material body and *Atman* and the ultimate distinction between *Atman* and *Parmatman*. Transcendental knowledge also enables one to attain realization.

***Karma* Yoga** (Path of action): The lord Krishna advocates 'Nishkama Karma' as following-

"Karmany-evadhikaraste ma phaleshu kadachana !

ma-karma-phala-hethur bhur ma te sangoosty akarmani !!

(Bhagvad Gita 2. 47)

You certainly have the right for prescribed activities but never at any time in their results. You should never be motivated by the results of the actions, nor should there be any attachment in not doing your prescribed activities" (as cited in Rao, 2012, p. 157).

In the next *sloka*, Lord Krishna advises Arjuna that *Karma* Yoga is a state of equanimity. One should be balanced in both victory and defeat while doing such *Karma*, as follows:

"Yoga-stah kuru karmani sangam tyktva dhananjaya !

Siddhi-asiddhyoh samo bhutva sampatvam yoga uchyate !!

(Bhagvad Gita 2. 48)

O Dhananjaya, established in the science of Yoga in action, perform your activities giving up attachment and maintain equanimity in both success and failure". (as cited in Rao, 2012, p. 158).

Lord Krishna explains over here that in the *Karma* Yoga, one should maintain equanimity in both victory and defeat and discard mental attachment to his actions. One should perform actions as a matter of duty (*karma*) because such actions are not disturbed either by benefit or loss in such actions. One who performs *karma* yoga sincerely successfully proceeds on the spiritual path.

***Bhakti* Yoga** (Path of devotion): In the great Bhagavad Gita, Lord Krishna declares that as compare to the greatest yogi his devotee is superior for him:

"Yoginam api sarvesham mad-gatenantaramana!

Shradhavaan bhajate yo mam sa me yuktatamo matah!!

(Bhagvad Gita 6.47)

Amongst all yogis (or those perfected in the science of the individual consciousness attaining communion with the ultimate consciousness), one who in full faith is always thinking of me within, deeply dedicated to me, rendering devotional service to me is the most superior of all" (Cited in Rao, 2012, p. 159).

Further, Lord Krishna explains that those devotees have achieved Him through *Bhakti* Yoga, have achieved perfection and they are not subject to reincarnation (continuous cycle of births and deaths) as follows:

"Mam upetya punar janma dukhalayam asasvatam!

Napnuvanti mahtmanah samsiddhim paramam gatah!!

(Bhagvad Gita 8.15)

The great souls having achieved perfection take refuge in Me, never again assume this transitory birth (*Punarjanma*) full of misery" (as Cited in Rao, 2012, p. 159).

Lord Krishna, concluding the *Bhakti* Yoga (Gita 12. 6 and 7) says that "But those who surrender all activities unto Me, meditate on Me with single minded devotion, I become their deliverer without delay from the ocean of death in the material existence" (as cited in Rao, 2012, p. 160).

He further assures in the next *sloka* that:

Mayya eva mana adhatsva mayi buddhim nivesaya!

Nivesisyasi may eva ata urdhvam nasamsayah!!

(Bhagvad Gita 12.8)

"Concentrate the mind upon Me, establish spiritual intelligence in Me, verily you will reside with Me, after this existence without doubt" (Rao, 2012, p. 160).

Thus in the Bhagavad Gita, Lord Krishna assures that if His devotees focus their minds upon Him, He will quickly deliver them from this material existence (*Samsara*) exclusively in the *Bhakti* Yoga. So concluding the *Bhakti* Yoga it can be said that in the *Bhakti* Yoga the practitioner need a figure (a personalized form of divine) and that figure may be Brahma, Vishnu and Mahesh or anybody, but the practitioner need a focus of devotion. In the *Bhakti* Yoga, the *sadhaka* fall in love with his Lord. So if the *Gyan* Yoga is the way of mind to attain *Moksha*, the *Bhakti* Yoga is a way of heart to attain the *Moksha*.

Conclusion

The twelve forms of yoga explained above are: *Sahaja* yoga, *Pranav* yoga, *Iyengar* yoga, Restrorative yoga, Integral yoga, *Tantra* yoga, *Udgeeth* Pranayama, *Ashtanga* yoga, *Laya* yoga, *Isha Kriya*, *Trataka* yoga, and *Yogeshvara's* yogas (*karma* yoga, *jnana* yoga and *bhakti* yoga). These are fundamental for the unity of existence. Yoga is a very rich tradition with different religious /non-religious lineages, so there are many techniques. Some of the above mentioned forms of yoga are the most well-known; the others are more specific or complex.

Yoga is ancient traditional wisdom to maintain the bodily, mental and spiritual health. We can take initiative to participate in any kind of yogic exercise that can improve our well-being. Yoga is about making your light weight and grows spiritually through slowly process and ultimately improves your well-being.

When you take full responsibility for your own spiritual life, you can attain the peak of spiritual progress and become fully established the solid ground of spirituality through *abhyasa* of yoga. When you accept something as absolute after due logical deliberation, you should develop *shraddha* or respect for yoga. One who does not perform yoga can never attain psychic balance and spiritual health.

Indian mental health professionals need to apply the psychotherapeutic system evolved out of yoga. Emphasizing the strength of yoga and showing paralles with psychotherapy. Lerner (1971) affirms that yoga is basically spiritual in its thrust and suggests that Western psychotherapists might benefit from yoga knowledge as it has therapeutic and growth qualities. If adopted in psychotherapy and community health development programmes, yogic practices might promote well-being.

Chapter Seven

RUHANIAT

***Ruhaniat* (Spirituality)** is the origin of all sciences. True love and true happiness is possible though spirituality. Spirituality is an integral part of our lives. This is an existential philosophy of our existence. *Ruhaniat* is the sum total of everything. It exists before birth and will exist after death. *Ruhaniat* manifests in the invisible form. It remains changing and requires a great deal of thought in understanding. *Ruhaniat* is the path to serenity. It is like the ocean of this and other world.

Ruhaniat promotes the principle of the oneness of human being. Human beings can understand the personal world and the world around them through *Ruhaniat* as the system of knowledge and practice. *Ruhaniat* directs our energies during the critical period of life towards the spiritual growth. This is one of the most precious gifts of God which everyone needs to practice it. Those engaged in practicing *Ruhaniat* should try to find it as the divine law that brought everything into being. *Ruhaniat* focus on higher levels of consciousness. It makes a greater partnership with human beings.

Spirituality is a gift of God for the benefit of the mankind and for the unification of humanity. It is the service to humanity and mankind. Its inception lies with the Adam and his community. Spirituality connects with human experiences. It is the highest expression of human behavior and experiences. Ruhaniat develop non-attachment. The more you develop non-attachment, the less vulnerable you will be. Every day you pray and make God responsible for your well-being.

Essential aspects of Ruhaniat

Ruh (Spirit)

The first and foremost concept regarding the inner nature of man is the one expressed by the term *ruh*. The term *ruh* (literally spirit, soul or breath of life) is used in the Qur'an to refer to numerous metaphysical varieties like angels, revelation or divine inspiration. But quite often it connotes the inner divine human nature or 'Soul' of metaphysical parlance. The spirit given by God to each person that contains a template of potential for that person.

According to Burckhardt (1983), spirit is a mediator between the Divine Being and the conditioned universe. The uncreated aspect relates to Divine Being whereas the created aspect is reflected in the universal soul, created intellect etc. Just as there is a universal Spirit (*al-ruh*) i.e., a realm of the Spirit.

You have the spirit within your body. Your body is extremely fragile, but you have a strong spirit. You have the body, mind, heart, and spirit; one has to respect take care of these. See the beauty of the body. The spirit is only the permanent. Learn to love the spirit which is permanent. Experience its elegance in perfection. There is so much beauty in it. Spirit is eternal and immortal.

Urafa (Gnostics)

'*Urafa* avail an inner and esoteric method, which consists of two aspects (i) positive and (ii) negative. The negative aspect of *urafa* refers to abstaining from certain things, '*Urafa* emphasizes physical exercises and abstaining from carnal desires. The positive aspect consists of strengthening the power of soul, self-training and remembering name of God and reminding the heart about the spiritual knowledge.

'*Urafa* consider rational arguments as weak. They pursue the goal of inner insight of the reality and rely on. One reaches to this stage through different spiritual exercises and the strengthening 'self'. In this way the heart of an Arif may prepare for inner insight of the ultimate reality. '*Urafa* do not presume intellectual and rational interpretation of being. Their main goal is attaining truth and reaching God; gaining intuitive insight into the reality of being and extension in it. However, apart from this ultimate goal, the '*Urafa* also presume the medium, sometimes, it is referred as the goal of 'Irfan.

Gnostics consider it very essential to follow a master who have gone through *Tariqah* and have reached unto *Haqiqah*. It is impossible to tread mystic path without a guide and a master. Such persons are remembered with the titles of master, (*Pir*) the guide (*Murshid*), saint (*Wali*), *Khizr*, heavenly birds (*tair-i Qudsi*) and perfect man (*Insan-i Kamil*).

Hikmah (Wisdom)

The Arabic term "*Hikmah*" literally means wisdom. It is a concept in Islamic philosophy and law. Mulla Sadra defined *hikmah* as "coming to know the essence of beings as they really are" or as "a man's becoming an intellectual world corresponding to the objective world" (Cooper. 1998). In the Qur'an, it means the knowledge and the understanding of the Qur'an and the *Sunnah* and one's ability to speak and act in the right way.

Hikmah (denoting 'wisdom') is a positive term used repeatedly in the Qur'an as a characteristic of the righteous [Qur'an 2:251; Qur'an 4:54; Qur'an 5:110]. Islamic Research Foundation International has defined wisdom as...

- The ability to make correct judgments and decisions.
- As foreseeing consequences and acting to maximize beneficial results.
- Making the best use of available knowledge.

- Thinking what is best and doing what is best in any given situation.

Hikmah is a gift that comes from Allah. Allah inspires the human's heart by giving *Hikmah*. It is Allah's light (*noor*) by which one can differentiate between the truth and falsehood. One knows the reality of the things (*Haqiqat*) and the secrets of the actions and deeds upon it. For an ordinary person, all that is in heaven and earth and thinks only that he can just cultivate land, raise flowers and cattle, do business [and just thinks that] *Allah* has done this for him. But, for a *Hakeem*, all of that which is between heaven and earth in the physical world are signs and similitude to guide him. They are all physical manifestations; physical or materialized forms of each and every word of Holy Qur'an.

'*Amal salih* (Good deeds)

The Qur'an gives us the concept of *'amal salih* which is translated into English as 'good deeds.' The key word here is '*salih*'. The root of the word is *slh* from which it is derived. There are so many words associated with this are to be good, to repair, to mend, to improve, to be righteous, to be efficient, to be suitable, peace and friendliness, reconciliation etc. thus it will be seen that *'amal salih* leads to a society which is reformed, good efficient, suitable (to humanity), improved and above all which is peaceful and friendly to all human beings. According to the Qur'an, *'amal salih* is very necessary for moral conduct. In chapter 103 of the Qur'an says, "By the time! Surely man is in loss, except those who believe and do good work (*'amal salih*), and exhort one another to Truth and exhort one another to patience."

The key concepts associated with *'amal salih* are truthful and patience. Man is surely in loss but those who perform good deeds are truthful and patient would not be. Thus, for *'amal salih'* truth and patience are highly necessary.

Niyyat (Intention)

This refers to intention behind action. Majority of us use this term with negative connotation. In the Qur'an it acquires a meaning which leads to a spiritual bond with the Almighty. In Islam it is derived from the word 'niyyah' which is the criterion of value in every act, including worship and it is the first obligatory act in prayer. *Niyyat* is the soul of *ibadat* (devotion and prayer) (Hassan, 2017). *Niyyat* is considered the pillar of *ibadat*. *Niyyat* with devotional practices such as reading Holy Scripture and prayer can take you closure to God. The most difficult tasks can be solved if we have pure and sincere *niyyat* to gain something.

Ruhaniat needs to be cultivated in such a way that we have to know everybody's *niyyat* before receiving any help. As mentioned in the Qur'an, "Your actions will be judged by your intentions." Our mission of life depends much upon the *niyyat*. We are constantly engaged in actions, but what motivates us to do anything is *niyyat*.

'Irfan (Knowledge)

The concept of *'Irfan* is discussed in detail by Naqvi (2016). According to him, both the terms, *'Irfan and Tasawwuf* are applied on all the three aspects of mysticism: social, theoretical and practical. Sometimes, these two terms are used in particular and more specific meanings. The word *'Irfan* is sometimes used for knowledge of God and sometimes for special kind of knowledge, gained through intuitive method of mysticism. In some cases, the word *Tasawwuf* is used to denote social aspect only and sometimes to denote practical and ethical aspects of mysticism. In socio-spiritual behaviour, *'Irfan* is used for theoretical knowledge and system of spiritual methods of living and behaviour. *'Irfan* is just like the knowledge of soul, purification of character, reaching to the 'state' of inner peace and abstraction of soul etc. *'Irfan',* as a cultural-intellectual system consists of two parts, namely, (i) theoretical and (ii) practical.

(1)Theoretical *'Irfan'* deals with knowledge. This suggests how to purify the heart from moral vices, to help produce moral virtues and thus to attain spiritual perfection. It also deals with regulating relationship of man with his 'self' and with the Almighty God. Mystics consider discussion of theoretical *'Irfan* confined to God, His attributes and his Sway Qaisari considers the divine person and his internal attributes, as the main subject of *'Irfan.* Some mystics emphasized that God is not the subject of *'Irfan*, rather it is the relation of God with the universe, that is the main subject.

Qaisari defines theoretical *'Irfan* as: "It consists of understanding God from the view point of His Names, Signs, Attributes and Manifestations. Likewise, it is to gain understanding of the beginning and end of the existence, knowing realities of the universe, and to realize how this multiplicity returns to celestial unity".

The word *'Irfan* is generally used in the meaning of knowledge and understanding. Fars bin Zakariya believes that *'Irfan* means understanding, its root being "'Urf", which means peace and calm. Therefore, the Arabs called this particular kind of knowledge as *'Irfan*, which gave them calmness and spiritual peace.

(2) Practical '*Irfan*' stipulates practical ways: how a person should start his journey unto God, from which stages gradually he passes in his spiritual journey, and what states his experiences. The '*urafa* (mystics) believe that one should pass these spiritual stages under the guidance of a perfect saint, who knows and has experience of these stages; and has reached to perfection. Such a spiritual master is called celestial bird (*tair al quds*), or *Khizr*. Generally, this part of '*Irfan* is referred as a science of spiritual exercises (*Sair wa suluk*). This part of '*Irfan* in a way resembles ethics, as it is also concerned with how to produce moral and spiritual virtues. However, there are some fundamental differences between '*Irfan* and pure ethics. Firstly, the main concern of practical '*Irfan* is relation of man unto God and how to bring man nearer to God. Secular ethics is not concerned with God, but is concerned only with producing virtuous behaviour. Secondly, while practical '*Irfan* is based on theoretical gnosis and special theosophical view of God and Man, Ethics does not have such philosophic foundation. Its foundations are different from that of practical 'Irfan. Thirdly, '*Irfan* and ethics pursue different goals: while the goal of practical '*Irfan* is to expand and enrich human consciousness by removing barriers and to take man's consciousness to the stage of *fana if Allah* (annihilation unto God), the goal of present day ethics is purification of character and inner reform of human conduct and behaviour as per the principles of morality with no reference of the Creator.

Issues in '*Irfan*: In theoretical terms, '*Irfan* is the nature of emanation of multiplicity, the One Being, and the manifestations of God name or attributes i.e., of God. Other issues of practical '*Irfan* include the nature of spiritual exercises and meditations, the 'states' and 'stations' on the path of spiritual journey unto God, and also the results of these spiritual exercises.

Thus, the issues of '*Irfan*, like Philosophy carry their descriptive nature; and, the issues of practical '*Irfan* like ethics, have their normative nature. Practical '*Irfan* also deals with descriptive aspects like the description of 'states' of soul and the realities that are seen by *Arif*.

Fundamentals of '*Irfan*: Fundamental of '*Irfan* include its definition, its benefits and concepts and also those principles on which science of mysticism is based. In fact, the issues of mysticism are based on fundamentals and intuitive knowledge that is by a mystic through the way of inspiration and intuition; though, it is described in rational terms. The basic difference between '*Irfan* and Philosophy is that a philosopher does not know the results of his researches before hand. It is through the rational method that he reaches to philosophical conclusions. However an *Arif* (theosophist) is after rational affirmation and interpretation of the knowledge that he has already gained through meditation and inspiration. As he goes ahead reaches and of the states, and 'stations' he is in a never ending spiritual journey.

Principle and Issues of Practical Mysticism *(Irfan e 'Amali): Shari'at, Tariqat, Haqiqat*

In the view of Gnostics (*Urafa*), this discussion constitutes the base of practical mysticism. Other discussions of practical mysticism are organized on this foundation. In the view of 'Allama Mutahhari, one of the major causes of difference between the Gnostic and others, especially the clerics and scholastics, *fuqaha* and *mutakallim*, is the special view of 'Urafa about *Shari'ah, Tariqah,* and *Haqiqah*.

Shari'ah, means the collection of Islamic rules and precepts that are described in the Holy Qur'an and the *Hadith*. The jurisprudence derives these principles from these two sources.

The jurisprudent and theologians believe that the principles of *Shari'ah* are based on realities and real interests, and by acting upon these principles, man reaches to success and salvation. Therefore, worship and action following *Shari'ah* is a way to attain perfection and salvation.

Thus, on the one hand Gnostics believe that in between *Shari'ah* and *Haqiqah* there is another mediator, namely, *Tariqah.* It is essence of religion and higher stage than Shari'ah, while the goal is reaching to *Haqq.*

However, another group of 'Urafa' do not subscribe to this view. In Islam there is so much importance of *Shari'ah* that a Muslim can be hardly a Muslim without following the *Shari'ah* precepets. Sheikh Abu Sa'id Abul Khair says: "Shari'ah is practice".

Akhlaq (Character)

We maintain ***Akhlaq*** to initiate and nurture relationships with our spouse, partners, close friends, and spiritual guides. *Akhlaq* elevates intense interaction and mutual understanding. It has relations with emotions and enriches one's life. *Akhlaq* develops warmth and good behaviour. Through *akhlaq* we create our destiny. It plays a unique and great role in our lives. It motivates us to keep doing good to ensure a happy future for oneself. *Akhlaq* is a great and powerful virtue to win or gain respect from others. It is a value system through which one can recognize others. *Akhlaq* is the means through which we judge others and form opinion about others.

Akhlaq denotes the inner strength of man which leads to behavior (Zaqzuq, 2000). There is no doubt that the most important contribution of religion Islam to the progress of mankind has been morality. According to Zaydan (2000), *akhlaq* is a set of qualities which are embedded in the soul of a person which leads to good or bad behavior. According to al-Ghazali (2000), *akhlaq* is a state of the soul which easily leads to behavior without having to first deliberate. If the resulting behavior is good, then the state of *akhlaq* is good, likewise a bad *akhlaq* results in bad behavior. Thus *akhlaq* is divided into two, good *akhlaq* (*al-akhlaq al-mahmudah*) and bad *akhlaq* (*al-akhlaq al-mazmumah*). According to al-Ghazali (2000), good *akhalq* consists of *mahmudah* (praiseworthy) qualities such as repentance, patience, gratitude, fear, hope and so on, whereas bad *akhlaq* includes gossiping, prejudice, love of the world, arrogance and so on.

Tawajjuh (Meditation and Focus on God)

Spiritual masters do recommend meditation to enable one to overcome with depression. *Tawajjuh gives* inspiration to uncover scientific truths. It is the main door to enlightenment. *Tawajjuh* creates space to breath in breath out. It is the state of Godhood - and the state of action in every sense. It cultivates patience, continue to imagine and think to do good things.

Why do we need *Tawajjuh*? We need to develop mental and spiritual strengths to pursue the most fruitful action. It keeps us happy and healthy. If we can become completely silent even for a moment, that is the real state of God-realization. In deep sleep, we may attain this stage. It is very difficult to become completely thoughtless. After remaining blank for a while one may feel sleepy but even then it is worth practising. The effort to do *Tawajjuh* is a mental and spiritual exercise and action. So that action should not be discarded. To imagine a point and then to focus on it is also an action. But as a beginner, we may take some form or light and remain blank which may ultimately lead to the state of nothingness and thoughtlessness.

God is unspeakable. One who realizes the existence of God cannot utter a word about it. It is for individuals to experience it. We should follow the path of *Tawajjuh* and human welfare and to perform this selflessly. Connectedness with God is becomes possible only for a meditator at heart. We can thank to God through good works. During the process of *Tawajjuh* you need to be left alone. *Tawajjuh* makes us stronger and develops positive thoughts. *Tawajjuh* changes behaviour and keeps us focussed at the inner and outer levels. This is a great bonding exercise during travelling. This is an exercise which keeps us happy and energized. Through *Tawajjuh* one can express gratitude to God.

Conclusion

Practise *'RUHANIAT'* as a right livelihood. *Ruh, Urafa*, *Hikmah*, '*Amal salih, Niyat*, *Irfan*, *Akhlaq* and *Tawajjuh* determine the quality of ways to reach a blissful state i.e. *Ruhaniat. Ruhaniat* is a pre-requisite to lasting happiness. Those interested in applying *Ruhaniat* in their daily lives should test the above mentioned essential concepts; they will find the solutions of their problems. There is no valuable therapeutic agent than *Ruhaniat*.

Chapter Eight

SPIRITUALITY AT THE WORKPLACE

Interest in spirituality has grown considerably in various disciplines such as psychology, medicine, nursing, social work, counseling, sociology, and organizational management. Indian organizations have major challenges especially in terms of work culture and productivity. If we look at the dynamism of spirituality, it would definitely be fast track to organizational change and development. India has a rich heritage of spirituality. Work is a precious resource for meaningful in life. Every person does work according to his ability, interest and aptitude. There are some persons who enjoy doing work at their respective workplace, whereas others do work to earn money, gain power and occupy certain position in the organization.

Spirituality has the potential to be beneficial for people's mental health, happiness and well-being. For instance, being part of a team at workplace, learning new skills and solving problems are all aspects of work which can add to workers' happiness and general life satisfaction. It is not the workplace that is a problem, but also the nature of job what you get.

God gave us energy, talent, and intelligence; even then most of us do not bring these into the workplace. We can take you to the world of work through certain spiritual paths such as 'work is worship', organized, renunciation, knowledge, power of devotion and determination, love to work, active contemplation, competitiveness, and excellence. These are the means to discover the end of your existence at workplace.

Husain and Khan (2014) advocated that the topic of spirituality in the workplace is gaining importance among academicians as well as business professionals currently. Spirituality is extensively incorporated either tacitly or explicitly in public or private, and profit or non-profit organizations across the world.

Spirituality has a direct bearing on job performance of employees, balance in our quality of personal, family, and work life. Spirituality helps us to develop our vision, effectiveness and leadership skills. It improves our performance and enables us to get involved in personal growth and learning interpersonal relationship skills.

Organizational psychologists often appreciate the integration between spirituality and workplace, but frequently say that they are not sure how to bring spirituality into their professional work, training and skill. They can bring spirituality at workplace by protecting the health and well-being of employees. The workplace spirituality sets out the key principles for supporting employees to make healthier and more informed choices about their own well-being.

Specifically, on the subject of spirituality at workplace, very few empirical studies have been conducted. We normally work to gain employment, earn money and fulfill the need of the family, and for existential pleasures. A spiritual person takes pleasure in work itself, irrespective of its outcome. He enjoys living most of his time in the world of activity leading to his dream, rather than dwelling on the dream itself. He feels contented and happy at each moment of his work, with whatever fruit comes by the Will of God. He tries to excel in his work every moment, giving each moment his best to attain the fruit. A spiritual person experiences happiness at every moment of work. He enjoys selfless devoted service as rendered by spirituality.

There are multiple definitions in literature for workplace spirituality. Depending on their interests and disciplines, theorists include words like energy, meaning, and knowing in their explanations; others explain that workplace spirituality comes into play when we decide to do what's right (whatever that may be);

yet others explain that spirituality at work is about employees who understand themselves as spiritual beings whose souls need nourishment at work. An overall theme seems to be "connectedness" and a search of the working souls for depth of meaning and significance under the surface appearances of things in our world.

Workplace spirituality recognizes that people have an inner life that nourishes and is nourished by meaningful work that takes place in the context of community (Ashmos & Duchon, 2000). Organizations that promote a spiritual culture recognize that people have both a mind and a spirit, seek to find meaning and purpose in their work, and desire to connect with other human beings and be part of a community.

Spirituality is the 'basic desire to find ultimate meaning and purpose in one's life and to live an integrated life' (Mitroff & Denton, 1999). Jurkiewicz and Giacalone (2004) define workplace spirituality as "A framework of organizational values evidenced in a culture that promotes employees experience of transcendence through the work process, facilitating their sense of being connected to others in a way that provides feelings of connectedness and joy." Spirituality is a concern 'with our deepest sense of meaning, purpose and interconnectedness with one another and the earth we live on' (Costello, 2006).

Spirituality considers work as worship, attaches importance to organizational values, brings spiritual knowledge, power of devotion and determination, love to work, involve active contemplation, and cultivate excellence at the workplace. The spiritual service is in harmony with humankind's *dharma* or eternal existential purpose. When we are engage with spirituality at the workplace, our own needs are taken care of mystically, by the God.

Prophet Muhammad (SAW) said: ***"God loves a believing, skillful servant."***

There are eight principles of spirituality in the workplace. They are: spirituality in creativity, spirituality in communication, spirituality in respect, spirituality in vision, spirituality in partnership, spirituality in energy, spirituality in flexibility, and spirituality in finding you (Husain, 2005). In the present chapter, we are discussing the nine essential elements of 'WORKPLACE' associated with spirituality.

Work is Worship

Believing in 'work is worship' is not suffice only; our mind and heart must be inspired by this. If the case is such then all will be effective and productive. We have faith on it but not with firm conviction. 'Work is worship' provides strength and determination in ourselves. People who have dynamic sincerity with it drive them to spectacular actions. 'Work is worship' is not built in-resource in any individual. A spiritual person focused on 'doing of work' itself without the job anxiety of a distant outcome at the end of the work.

Prophet Muhammad (SAW) said on this topic: "One hour of meditation on the work created by God is better than seventy years of prayer." According to Husain and Khan (2014) "Those who believe that "work is worship" should do hard work and shape their skills. Whatever our job description, we should face the challenge and try to bring satisfaction, equality and joy to work world" (p.204). We have to cultivate spirituality in ourselves since beginning i.e. during the time of study or education and to transcend it to our workplace.

Bhawuk (2011) states "the *Bhagavad Gita* recommends the practice of *Karma* yoga, or the path of work (or doing one's prescribed duties), as the intervention to avoid the unhappiness resulting from the pursuit of desires. This is done through *manan* and *chintan* or self-reflection and contemplation" (p. 117).

Students need to transform at the thought and action levels when they discover for themselves the purpose and goal of their life. Similarly, the workers must have faith on 'work is worship' then they should discover with definite convictions to provide selfless service to the organization. Having this idea in our own mind and thought in our heart; then we can discover new horizons to our work life. Workers need to apply themselves in action in their workplace and to adopt 'work is worship' as a way of work life. If this is practiced regularly with deep sincerity and firm determination, the positivity in our work life will respond in harmony with our motivation to work.

Organizational Values

The organizations should give priority to organizational values. That is, setting of excessively high standards for performance of workers. Workers should be trained in such a way that they should not set unrealistic standards for themselves and tends to overly focus on their flaws, and tries to avoid failure. Organized organizations should encourage their workers to set possible goals for self and others, no need of approval by workmates, fear of taking risk, extreme competitiveness and difficulty in accepting criticism.

Organizations are capable of leading to self-development, provided the workers seek to discover and makes the most of the potentialities for their growth. If organizations have value systems then they can do the proper assessment of the employees' job performance and the working environment, and practices which lead to organizational health and development. Policies and practices which benefit employees' health can improve productivity in the organized sector. Organisations that are perceived to be healthy tend to have clear policies and active methods of dealing with employees problems.

It is necessary to emphasize the organizational values that promote personal and collective well-being of employees. Healthy organizations need to emphasize the organizational values and personal values in the lifestyles modifications program oriented toward workers' well-being. The scope of spirituality in the workplace or organization could be enhanced if we incorporate the following organizational values: integrity, teamwork, innovation, performance priority, quality, accountability/ responsibility, trustworthiness, self-motivation, safety awareness, continuous improvement, open communication, service to others, diversity, respect for the individual, and community involvement.

According to Kumar and Kumar (2013), the Gita teaches us to do work without thinking of its results (work with intrinsic value) because attachment with the results leads to stress, competition and aggression. Understanding *Karma* yoga and its practice lead an individual towards work and leading to a satisfied life.

It is therefore asserted that the organizational values must be fine-tuned to the employees behavior and their capabilities. That is, focusing on performing *karma* without getting entangled in the bondage of earthily desires must be obvious to employees so that they can reorient their behaviour towards attaining spirituality at the workplace. True spirituality can only be demonstrated through work.

Reward

When we do any work with devotion and determination, and gratitude, we receive reward in the form of blessings and grace from God. Reward reinforces our talent, skill and capacity towards excellence. Reward is everywhere and in everything provided that if we recognize its value.

Knowledge

Acquisition of knowledge is the ultimate reality. Spirituality is the fountainhead from where all knowledge flows. Acquisition of knowledge is linked with spiritual knowledge about the soul. It helps one to maintain equanimity in loss or gain, success or failure.

Acquisition of knowledge is necessary to transform spirituality at workplace. Knowledge is not mere information; it requires the person to act upon his beliefs and commitment to the goals which he aims at attaining. In brief, we would like to say that the theory of knowledge is needed to develop insight and social action as its ingredients. Vedas are an excellent means of knowledge about the Supreme Truth. To gain excellence, we need to acquire knowledge in all aspects of life.

It may be said that Islam is the path of "knowledge." No other religion or ideology has so much emphasized the importance of 'ilm. In the Qur'an the word '*alim* has occurred in 140 places, while *al-'ilm* in 27. In all, the total number of verses in which '*ilm* or its derivatives and associated words are used is 704. The aids of knowledge such as book, pen, ink etc. amount to almost the same number. *Qalam* occurs in two places, *al-kitab* in 230 verses, among which *al-kitab* for *al-Qur*'an occurs in 81 verses.

The sacred path to spirituality at the workplace emerges from a deep knowledge of scriptures and instructions of an employer.

A life worthy of the Lord is necessarily along with increasing the knowledge of Him "To lead a life worthy of the Lord, fully pleasing to him, bearing fruit in every good work and increasing in the knowledge of God" (Col. 1: 10). Such a life, according to this verse, is pleasing and fruitful in every good work.

Power of Devotion and Determination

Prophet Muhammad (SAW) declares: "When you do something, God likes you to do it perfectly". What one is expected to do is to work with devotion and determination, and submission to the God, without expecting the fruits. All fruits of action are designed by God. When you work with devotion and submission to the Divine will, spirituality will be attained. Devotion and determination paves the path to spirituality. Workers should do work with devotion and determination no matter whether they will exceed on excellence.

Working with devotion and determination throughout his or her period with the organization includes training for the job, training in general aspects of health and safety and support offered through the provision of adequate management of the social and technical aspects of an employee's working life. Good management practices have a role of spirituality both in terms of devotion and determination of employees at workplace.

Devotion and determination are the eternal natural energy of the soul. It simply means that we should repose the affection that we have within our hearts towards God in a favourable way that pleases Him. That is all that we have to transform spirituality in workplace with devotion and determination. The spirit of devotion involves into work. When the devotion and determination of workers is serious, their efficiency gets enhanced, and the organizations flourish.

Love to Work

This is the only energy that can make you feel satisfied with the job. You can bring love in the workplace. Work fulfills a large part of your life, and the only way to be truly satisfied is to do great work. To do great work is to love what you do. Love to work is one of the ways of soulfulness. Love eliminates the difference between employer and employees. If love to work creates energy at your work then you would not need a holiday from work. Love develops motivation to work and enhance your productivity. Love develops positive relationship and builds interpersonal trust among workmates. When you truly love the other workmates, team spirit develops. Love to work enhances the power of commitment at the individual and organizational levels. Love gives the power of experience to perceive others in the cooperation and competition situation. Understanding develops when you get an opportunity to work in either of the situation.

Acknowledging love to work is necessary and appropriate to bring spirituality in the workplace. Organizations can be developed and flourish if you learn to explore and bring love as the basis of your work. If this is your real goal, then your work life is truly fulfilling. If workers could understand and realize the importance of this positive emotion which is a huge source of energy and the process through which they may be able to use this energy they could reorient their aggressive impulses through sublimated channels. Love to work would act as a key to a better psychological health and in the long run prove beneficial to healthy organization.

Be it the dissatisfaction with job, it is better for us to love to work. Love yourself and your work. When we love to work, our action becomes perfect. A worker's attitude generates excellence.

Active Contemplation

In the workplace active contemplation is the high ideals of practicing spirituality. Active contemplation encouraged love to work. There are at least two forms of it, i.e. constant remembrance of God and longing of a higher order while doing work. Work actually pertains to the spirit of action. Every action needs contemplation. Attaining quality of work life is impossible without active contemplation. Workers should properly practice it at the workplace. Active contemplation is very important to inculcate in a worker at the thought and reflection level that he should work conscientiously and abstain from unlawful things. It is the path through which one should lead a life of thankfulness to God. When a worker continues to do active contemplation in the workplace, he will receive all kinds of blessings in this world.

Active contemplation matters at the workplace. This requires training and practice. It can enrich the job; organizations should promote it and try to give employees as a challenge. Active contemplation is needed wholeheartedly at the workplace because it is superior among all spiritual practices. If we are not contemplating at the workplace, it simply means that we need to enhance our effort. The crucial components of this effort may be in terms of quietening of mind and feel contentment. The active contemplation helps one to improve the quality of work and job performance.

Competitiveness

Along with the improvements during the scientific era and the rapid development of information, competitiveness among working people has become increasingly intense. A consequence of this competitiveness is stress. Moving away from studying to work decides the lifestyle of a person which he or she would adopt in the future. A good academic result may place the student in a better college but it does not guarantee whether he or she will be able to combat the stresses and strains one faces in their daily lives. To equip oneself with armor in the workplace, one needs to have an understanding of his potential, as it is this self-awareness which would help to identify one's area of competence and face competition in the corporate world.

We expect from all organizations to introduce competitiveness among workers. Supervisors and managers should be competent in introducing such behaviour which is needed for good management, healthy development and team unity in the workplace. Supervisors and managers have an important role in developing the organizational culture and promoting healthy competition and dignity of each employee within the team, department and overall organizational development.

Excellence

Workplace spirituality promotes human excellence. Excellence is needed if we practice spirituality as the domain of workplace. Excellence reflects the uniqueness of human being. Workers need to attain their goals and fulfill their aspirations through excellence instead of mediocrity. Excellence enriches your work life. It is most precious gift if you live for others. If you invest your time and energy in achieving excellence through spiritual paths such as doing hard work and performing duties conscientiously; you will get reward in terms of what God envisioned you to become a spiritual person. As a worker invest your life in achieving excellence at the workplace. Your excellence reflects your priorities in the way you want to bring changes in the organization and the way you want to improve your quality of work life.

The employer should also be concern about the excellence of the employees. The employer needs to know is it possible to raise the level of excellence of the employees in the organization. If raising excellence concerns are seen as a work strength, the employee can rightly claim to the employer to prevent the organizational culture and environment. Therefore, excellence needs to be prioritized and constantly reinforced among employees. Workers should try to excel in their respective fields by working hard.

A worker's attempt should be to do the best at the workplace to attain excellence. To achieve excellence, a worker must have the talent and skill in the specific field and he should work sincerely and have the right attitude. If excellence is not developed in all aspects of life then you will face failure. At the workplace when we combine all internal resources and when the body, mind, intellect, and spirit are integrated, a certain amount of work efficiency increases.

Conclusion

Let us introduce spirituality in workplace through 'Work is Worship', Organizational values, Reward, Knowledge, Power of devotion and determination, Love to work, Active contemplation, Competitiveness, and Excellence to attain and improve quality of work life. We are convinced that spirituality is selfless service that is why it has potential for action and solution. By understanding and imbibing these concepts, we are sure that the organizations will be stronger and healthier. While addressing workplace spirituality can be challenging, it can also be a path for positive change, for better and more productive relationships at work and for increased creativity and productivity of employees.

Future researches need to verify the present model and continues to show the practicing aspects of spirituality especially at workplace, is very much related to how work makes us feel happy and satisfied. In turn, how we feel when at workplace and how we feel about our spirituality influences when we engage with work, how productive we are and how convivial we are in our working relationships within a department, a team or a larger work group.

Overall, we have few evidences to show that spirituality exist at workplace. This is a concept which necessitates that there is still a lot of work to be done in this field for deeper and clearer understanding and application of the concept. It is time for government and private organizations in India to draw attention upon their great ancient spiritual traditions (e.g., Bhagvad Gita, Upanishad) to bring spirituality in the workplace.

Chapter Nine

SPIRITUAL RESOURCES AS THE MEANS FOR HEALTHY LIVING

Every person has the desire for health and well-being. Spirituality is the ultimate desire of life and self-existence. Those who seek spiritual health should strive for the achievement of spiritual perfection, then the urge for self-existence. There are some psychospiritual factors which form the basis of spirituality and the source for health and well-being. In recent years, spirituality has become luminous in the mind, heart, soul/spirit of people.

The very concept of spirituality evokes positive behaviour and experiences. This is perhaps the only philosophical and conceptual contention of positivism. Spirituality has put so much emphasis on man's behavior and his experiences. Spirituality makes a man directly responsible for his good behavior and actions. Hard work is needed to enhance spirituality. Spirituality is needed when you have something of value, truth, love, enlightenment. Spirituality is in finding the truth.

Spirituality is full of connections through which we come to grips with the negative or positive aspects of life. So we have to be very careful about availing opportunities afforded by natural relationships formed in the course of our existence. Spirituality makes us believe that we are living a good life. Spirituality is scientific, it is repeatable and so this is blissful experience. It does not happen by chance but by destiny.

Spirituality is the Supreme Energy taking care of the well-being of all people living in this world and hereafter. The stability of spiritual system depends on how the overall energy of the system is balanced. Spirituality can increase the energy level. Through spirituality one can liberate the negativity of personal world. Spirituality shows the right direction for a meaningful life.

The physical creation is for a materialistic purpose and the spiritual is to uphold dharma. All through our lives once the purpose is fulfilled, we returned to other world. Spirituality is the force which bound in the experiences and manifestations pertaining to physical creation through right practice of yoga with the guidance of an able *Guru*.

We should do yoga till the body feels energetic, active and feel at that time it makes difference. Do not wait when the vigour and vitality of the body begin to diminish, problems start; and once strength goes away, living with one's own body becomes a burden. Yoga develops the strength and capability in the body, mind and spirit. We need to do meditation and yoga, if the intellect does not really function.

The 21st century is very significant in the sense that it witnessed spiritual belief systems and practices grow simultaneously. Spirituality is the very existence and purpose of human beings and their life on earth. Spirituality is the assessment of meaning in life and its purpose. The essence of spirituality realizes the presence felt in this world and other world. Spirituality is delving into life and human experiences. The very moment you breathe implies you live or exists.

We will discuss spiritual awareness and spiritual experiences, righteousness, peace, reading scriptures, *sadhana,* compassion and graceful life, positive thoughts, relationship of spiritual values with spiritual life and prayer and ultimate goal of life in this chapter. These are helpful resources for healthy living and in the process of spiritual growth.

Spiritual awareness

This is an important component of spiritual resources. Spirituality is relating to a higher Power that is benevolent and good. Spiritual people tend to align with God. We are born with a natural sense of the spiritual. Spiritual awareness flows in human beings.

In ancient India, everyone was exposed to spiritual knowledge at age seven. Spiritual values empower people and give them a sense of direction. Their talent and energies will be used positively. Yet, there is little attempt at cultivating this most important aspect of life in children. Sages prescribed different paths to the Spirit to suit varied natures of people.

Spiritual Experiences

Spirituality is a continuous flow of various kinds of thoughts, will, intuition, imagination, ideas and so on. The mind is the instrument of our experiences. It is the mind alone that performs all actions. It is much better to understand its functioning in search of happiness; the mind follows the senses into the world of objects and enjoys various experiences. Spirituality makes us feel and experience that it is the ultimate destination. It is creativity and expression of love to God and others.

One does not need to yearn for it or crave for it; the daily practice establishes the experience. Meditation is so designed by masters of the Vedic tradition that if it is learned systematically and practised twice a day, the experience will come. You know only the body, mind and intellect. Rise above their limitations to experience the power, serenity and bliss of *Atman*, your real Self.

Peace through Spirituality

Everyone wants to live in a peaceful state. People want peace in their personal world - in their home, city and in their country. How can we achieve this universal dream? We believe that we can have global peace through spirituality which is the study of our own inner self. It is the path of discovering who we are, why we are here, life after death. It is the science of uncovering the greatest mysteries of the universe - God and our soul. Building a peaceful world begins with the first foundation stone - our own selves. We must first find peace ourselves through spirituality to attain global peace.

What can a single individual do for attaining world peace? By attaining world peace inner peace at the personal level is needed. Human beings can make a difference for all humanity and for posterity by the actions they choose to take. Let us begin with our own transformation in the pursuit of peace. If you want to attain inner peace you have to develop a world whose principles rest on peace.

We propose that everyone in the community, society and nation be peaceful. We need to make all cities and countries peaceful. All the efforts in the world will not make others peaceful. All we can do is work on ourselves. If we find peace within ourselves, our life will be transformed and others will be curious as to why we are experiencing such joy and happiness in our life. They themselves will want to learn how we achieved it.

Righteousness comes from Spirituality

Most scriptures agree that love is an important manifestation of a man's spirituality or religiosity. Righteousness is a virtue expected in a spiritual person. Holiness is nothing but righteousness. When righteousness prevails in a society, its effect is justice and peace. The concept of righteousness varies from person to person. This is coloured by an individual's world view, environment and other factors. In fact, everyone need to look for righteousness. Human nature of man is to be more inclined to be self-righteous. For righteousness to prevail, we need to overcome the hate, selfishness and greed that distress our hearts.

Reading Scriptures

"Many good sayings are to be found in holy books, but merely reading them will not make one religious. One must practice the virtues taught in such books in order to acquire love of God."

Ramakrishna Paramahansa

Scriptures clearly discusses concepts, values and practices. The religious teacher or Guru is considered indispensable in explaining scripture and providing religious guidance based on it. Reading scripture is crucial to the whole process of development. Human beings have unique perspective. Reading scripture implies to the execution of human duties, both spiritual and social. Reading scripture is an act of evolved beings.

We have an input of spirituality-related concepts in the sacred scriptures like Holy Qur'an, Bible, Bhagwad Gita, Ramayana, Upanishad, Guru Granth Sahib, etc. Scripture is the foundation of every religion. Studying the scriptures help us to attain the ultimate goal of life and self-realization. Reading scripture is the spirituality, We are referring to, because it has a universal application. There is no conflict with any religion with regard to the sacred scriptures. Each one read faithfully one's own scriptures. Every scripture is an embodiment of Truth-Knowledge-Bliss. The process, path and goal of studying scriptures should be pious.

Muslim Scripture

Reading scripture i.e. Qur'an is obligatory after the age of four years and four months among Muslims. It is believed that a child is ready for formal education. Traditionally, the Qur'an is taught as part of education. After the completion of Qur'an, the Maulvi and parents bless the child.

Holy Qur'an clearly informs us that God Almighty sends his prophets with a mission to inculcate the very highest possible standards of spirituality in mankind by forming a close union with God. Through that union man comes to fulfil not only the rights of God, but also by displaying the very highest moral standards they are led to fulfilling the due rights of God's Creation.

Studying the scriptures give us strength to live harmoniously and peacefully in our daily life. Reading scriptures protect us in life obstacles. It is the path of peace invocation. While studying scriptures we directly experience blessings by God. The underlying meaning of reading scripture is more enlightening. Holy Qur'an is the religious and scientific treatise. The various principles are scattered in the Scriptures, at various verses, some in abstract form and most are explanatory in nature. Islam promise heavenly existence and spiritual way of life. The knowledge and practice of the Spirit is Spirituality. The Qur'an deals with a number of psychological and sociological problems which can be made use of, in living an ideal and practical life.

Hindu Scriptures

Hindu sacred texts can be classified as the six scriptures: (i) *Srutis*, (ii) *Smritis*, (iii) *Itihas*, (iv) *Puranas*, (v) *Agamas* and (vi) *Darsanas* and the four secular writing: (a) *Subhashitas*, (b) *Kavyas*, (c) *Natakasand*, (d) *Alankaras*.

The Bhagavad Gita is one of many scriptures sacred to the Hindus. Hinduism has close to 900 million adherents worldwide and can be traced back to ancient Indian cultures along the Indus valley. Hindu believes in supreme God that is worshipped through various deities.

Today, although in the Hindu religion there are many scriptures, many sayings and many books. Hindus have chosen

Bhagavad Gita as their guideline and guiding light, because it is the scripture which Lord Krishna himself told Arjuna, when Arjuna was in a state of deep depression. He was not sure what to do, what decision to make, and at that particular time Lord Krishna guided him. There is one verse from Bhagavad Gita in which Krishna says: 'Always think of one. Become my devotee. Worship me. And offer your homage unto me, thus you will come to me without fail. I promise you this because you are my dear friend' (18.65). Because Gita's message is for the whole universe, not only for Hindu community and not for India. Lord Krishna has spoken about mankind because Gita tell us what is the aim of life, what is happiness, what is death; all these problems are caused by ignorance.

If we follow the path of Lord Krishna's teachings, all the problems which we are facing can be addressed, because Gita is the message of oneness, Gita is message for love and service to those who need it.

Every religion cultivates goodness, harmony, tolerance, love, wisdom, and brotherhood and does not differentiate between the believer and his fellow brother and calls for a mutual respect, regardless of differences in belief or opinion.

All the heavenly messages are based on sacredness, nobility, and purification; all those who believe in God believe in brotherhood of nations, justice and pure faith in God. The pure objective of all religions is reformation, creation of peace, love and understanding and all the ways and methods in implementing it.

Reading scripture is of paramount importance for enhancing spiritual well-being. Fortunately, the followers of Islam practice it as simply rituals. Recent researches have shown the medical benefits of reading scripture in terms of recovery of clients but how many of us have understood the consequences associated with this spiritual exercise.

Sadhana

This is a spiritual practice. A Guru guides the disciple in his *sadhna* to achieve a particular goal of religion, his great knowledge, wisdom and authority. Wisdom dawns on those who do intense *sadhana* and *dhyana*. In Hinduism, find out a true spiritual *Guru* is required for self-realization.

Spirituality helps you progress in the *sadhana*. Among the various layers of creation unfold in front of you and you realize that the physical, which a majority of people spend their life, is just a small aspect of creation, a layer which is directly controlled by the world is spiritual, this is the subject of yoga and meditation.

A unique combination of knowledge and devotion is what we get to see in the tradition of one of the religious reformist of the fifteenth century, Sant Kabir Das. The essence of his message is *sadhana* of *nirakar*- practice of the formless - which he expresses in mystic form. Usually, *nirakarbadis* believe only in the *sadhana* part, not in feelings. But Kabir knew that the dry path of *sadhana* cannot be sustained for long by many.

Moreover, in order to collect the mind in the first stage there is the need of feelings. So in his compositions Kabir suggests that your lover is within you; reflect and contemplate on yourself, and proceed towards the secret door of your existence. Then break open the door and let your union take place.

This unique combination of spiritualism and romanticism -romanticising spiritual *sadhana*- is a remarkable feature of Kabir's contribution in the field of literature and spiritualism. Besides, his articulation and style of presentation are highly engaging; even incomparable. The path of mystic love remains prominent in subsequent literary contributions as well as in spiritual approaches other than Kabir's tradition.

The mention of mystic sound is another important part of the *sadhana*. The sound, as Ramakrishna explained, can be heard after performing *tapasya* for many years, and following that sound one can reach the ocean of *samadhi*. The mystic sound as Kabir describes it is echoing in the darkness of the night against the starry sky - as if someone is moving from star to star and the mystic sound keeps flowing. Listen to that sound and follow it to attain the state of liberation; *jivanmukti*! Raja Ram 'Saheb' all day and all night engaged in deep *sadhana*, listening to the eternal mystic sound and remaining engrossed in it. He is so deep in thought that he at times is not aware if a visitor has arrived. aware if a visitor has arrived.

You may watch him from a distance, reading from some of the texts of Kabir and discussing with himself. Sometimes he is engaged in deep conversation with no physical being around. As you make him feel your presence he might return to this world and greet you with great affection. The next moment, after exchange of a few pleasantries, he might try his best to take you to the spiritual world.

Step-by-step he would start his guidance. It may begin with some of the texts of Kabir which he may like you to read out and then he himself would explain and simplify the mysticism. How to transform your entire physical and mental existence to one single vibration produced without any friction (the *anahatsabda*) and then how to hold on to that vibration and move towards *samadhi*- that is the essence of his guidance. He advises us to develop the practice of *sadhana* so that in the midst of all your activities you are able to remain aware of the mystic sound. Realization of the state of nothingness gives you the energy to work for human welfare selflessly and effectively.

In Hinduism, the practice of cultivating spirituality is known as *sadhana*. This is the main theme of spiritual life. Spirituality is an attribute of a good citizen and it is the starting point on the path of *sadhana. Sadhana* first requires mental equilibrium. This is an exercise through which we can lead spiritual life. Whatever you do, you do it with a view to promote your *sadhana* and help the *sadhana* of others. Human beings come to earth to practice *sadhana*, to move closer to *Ishvara*, the Supreme Goal - to come closer to *Parama Purusha*, the Supreme Consciousness. Whatever human beings will do; they will do in such a manner that progress in their *sadhana* will go on accelerating.

The *sadhana* starts spiritual practices with the principles of morality. *Sadhana* devoid of morality will divert people again towards material enjoyments and at any moment they may use their mental power, acquired with much hardship, to quench their thirst for physical objects. Even before beginning *sadhana* one must follow moral principles strictly. Those who do not follow these principles should not follow the path of *sadhana*; otherwise they will bring about their own harm and that of others. *Sadhana* is to be pursued with patience. It can then slowly take us from the physical world to spiritual world.

When human beings attain proficiency in controlling *vaekhari* power by dint of spiritual *sadhana*, it is called *vaekhari siddhi*. Even without following systematic spiritual practice, through continuous normal practice also one can gain control over this *vaekhari shakti*, though only to some extent.

Leading Compassion and Graceful Life

We should understand and obtain benefit for the soul which is attainable through compassion and grace. It is better to live the spiritual life at all times and in all ways throughout the life. Try to obtain the absolute natural bliss of God, who by His Grace has made all the universes, worlds, things, living beings, ways of living.

That spiritual life can be obtained only by Grace which can be obtained only by leading a life of compassion towards all living beings - not even a little of it can be obtained by any other means. This is because Grace is God's mercy, natural manifestation; compassion means living beings' sympathy or their souls' natural manifestation. Therefore, it is certain that by sympathy we can get mercy and by manifestation, get manifestation. Grace can be obtained only by being compassionate to other living beings.

When compassion to living beings manifest, knowledge and love will blossom along with it; therefore 'helping power' manifests; because of that all good benefits will appear. When compassion to living beings disappears, knowledge and love will disappear immediately, therefore 'helping power' will disappear, and when it disappears, all evils will appear. Virtue is nothing but showing compassion to living beings, and vice means to be without compassion to living beings.

Enlightenment coming from leading a life of compassion towards living beings is Enlightenment of God, and bliss coming out of leading a life of compassion towards living beings is Divine Bliss. But, what is meant by leading a life of compassion towards all living beings? It is to live, worshipping God, by the melting of the soul of living beings, towards other living beings. What is the spiritual need to have compassion towards other living beings? All living beings are created by God as part and parcel of the natural truth and are of the same quality; so they are all brothers with the same right.

Some people, even on seeing other living beings suffer, do not have compassion towards them and are hard-hearted; there is no fraternal right to these people. Their spiritual awareness has become very dim because compassion to living beings did not arise. From this it is learnt that those who have compassion towards other living beings have enlightened spiritual vision or perception.

Positive Thoughts

Most of the time, thoughts prevent you from experiencing the moment. Whenever there are thoughts, you are closed to this moment. Thought is an expression of memory. Memory pulls you backward and not towards the present moment. Life is in the present moment, and not with the past. When the thoughts are overused or used wrongly, causing inner chaos.

In spiritual life, you move on the sacred path. What appears as positive thinking is nothing but an association with the present and projections into the future with some hopefulness. Life's existence or the root is in the present, and most of us are flying with the thoughts of the past or imagining an illusory future. Present oriented consciousness is needed to cultivate positive thoughts. Being unconscious of this fact is misery. So, one has to learn to look into present consciousness. Such looking is not through thought but silence, which is a state of no mind or a state of thought-free awareness. So, transform the energy from thinking to present consciousness.

Consciousness can only guide you. When we get identified with negative thoughts, we get identified with our past. We live our past. We are not living in the world, but we live our minds. When we get identified with thoughts, we are flowing with our beliefs. Thought is rooted in some belief, an idea, or dogma.

Thought tells us that the future will be your saviour if you will be happy. Mind or thought convinces you that the future or attaining happiness will make you fulfilled. Once this happens, your thoughts will gain strength. During this process, something else silently happens. You will be telling yourself that though you are unhappy now, you will be happy in the future. Thought, with its likes and dislikes resides in an inner space and this space is beyond thought. The thought centre is pure and has empty space. Learn to discover the thought process.

As you think positively, so you become spiritual. You have been thinking of body, mind and intellect continuously, so you have become weak. Think of spirit with the same dedication and consistency.

Relationship of Spiritual Values with Spiritual Life and Prayer

As the relationship between spiritual values and prayer is proved by the laws of nature, it is also proved by the testimony of the Holy Qur'an and other sacred books. It is often observed that spiritual living incline by natural principles like prayer and almsgiving develops piety. This is an argument that the spiritual values of man have, from the beginning, directed all peoples that they should not separate prayer from spiritual well-being but should evolve meaning in life with prayer. Cultivation of values is necessary to realize the consequences of prayer. The good fortune of man depends much on how he seeks help through prayer from God.

Ultimate Goal of Life

Bliss or Ananda has been the goal of seekers and saints since ages. A few experience it, many claim to attain it, still many imagine that they are in bliss, and yet many more think that this is some kind of spirituality. The reality of bliss is that it is inherent to life. *Vedanta* says *Sat, Chit,* and *Ananda*, or the inherent nature of life, is eternal bliss consciousness. It is just a matter of experience.

Bliss consciousness is nothing but the simplest form of our own awareness. Also called Transcendental Consciousness, it is the most expanded state of our 'Self ', which is Pure, Absolute and most importantly, attainable by all and that too without any effort, control or concentration.

Our mind which is active all the time, entangled in thoughts, problems or simply nothing except unnecessary clutter. This active mind which has not known silence, transcends. It does so in a very systematic, easy and effortless manner and becomes its own expanded Self, silent, pure, unbounded, aware and full of bliss.

Why spirituality gives meaning to our lives? The humanities might be called the 'why' of spiritual life. Spirituality can help us better understand why we do, or ought to do, certain things. Spirituality teaches us how to do things. We might know how to get people to live through personal experience. Why spirituality is for existence -to protect a loved one and to manage to find how to survive?

Conclusion

Spirituality as a principle of life is what makes our spiritual life run smoothly. If you enter spiritual life, first having learnt to make adjustments within the Self. For a better quality of life, you need something more - that is spirituality. So, you have to accept that spiritual experiences are an inescapable part of life. And you have to be capable of adopting a spiritual attitude within self. You must realize that spirituality is a blessing for you. Connect with the same world that is now. And the same world that is now you will become enjoyable.

The psychic and spiritual potentialities of human beings are immense, but people do not utilize them because they think that their valuable time is wasted in spiritual activities such as meditation and yoga. How much time do people really get to devote to spiritual practices? We should devote some time to do meditation in order to control over our breathing and respiratory system, because the waves of respiration control wave of thinking. Whenever you are doing something creative, your respiration becomes very active; and when you are thinking of something subtle, it becomes extremely low. Hence some degree of control over respiration is essential.

Chapter Ten

SPIRITUAL PRACTICES FOR THE INNER TRANSFORMATION

Practitioners indulging in various spiritual exercises eventually undergo similar experiences. One may wonder how the widely differing spiritual practices lead to congruent experiences. Does the different spiritual practice lead to similar changes deep inside? The answer to questions like this lies in the fact that the spiritual journey essentially requires transcending the lower nature of self and detaching it from all the materialistic belongings. This transcendence leads to few early stage rewards such as flow of creativity, hearing of soothing sounds, experiencing of colorful light flashes and filling of the heart with joy etc., and are the indicators of a deeper reality experienced by man. In fact different sounds and colours appear in a definite order indicating the spiritual progress undergone by the man on the path and mostly seekers are aware of these.

There are many ways to begin this rewarding journey. J. Krishnamurthi in his ten-page masterpiece 'At the Feet of the Master' says we can start by doing three things:

(1) **Tame your body and mind**: We are more than the sum of our physical, astral and mental bodies to perform our tasks smoothly. For example, when there is an opportunity to help someone, the physical body might feel tired and want us to rest. The astral body has its desires; it wants us to say sharp words, feel jealous, be greedy, and envy other people's possessions. While the mental body is absorbed in the thoughts of self and pay little attention on others. Each one of them pretend to be our real self wanting us to pursue selfish motives. But as we want none of these things, it must always be us who should control our physical, astral and mental bodies and not the other way round. The body must be treated well, fed on pure food and drink, and kept clean, for without a

perfectly clean and healthy body we cannot do the work of preparation or wish to shine or appear clever.

Speak little; better still say nothing, unless we are quite sure that what we want to say is true, kind and helpful. We must always control anger or impatience, so that our thoughts remain calm and unruffled.

(2) **Consider sufferings as healing**: For people taking the journey, God's grace allows past karmas to bear fruit in an accelerated way in only one or two lives whereas usually it might take hundred lives or more. The resultant suffering thus is like the healing of the patient and should be embraced with cheer.

(3) **Always watch for an opportunity**: To help others through selfless and unattached actions. Any set of spiritual practices with the above mindset will transform us into channels through which divine energy and love can flow. The more divine love flows through us to help others, the higher we rise on the evolutionary ladder. We rise as we help others rise. This resolve must fill our whole nature, and no temptations should ever turn us away from this. This is the common thread running across all deeper practices.(Quoted by Srivastava, 2017).

Spiritual Walking

This is like physical walking. Everyone is spiritual in nature. In spiritual walking we move towards productive goals like creating happiness, nurturing loving relationships, inner growth, spreading peace, serenity and tranquility.

Spiritual walking creates energies and helps in coping with stress, dysfunction and regression. But there is an inner momentum, and if we make the right choices, that will keep pushing us forward till we realize our destiny.

People have very different conceptions of reaching to their final destiny. Some think in terms of annihilation and cessation of all our functions. Others believe that beyond death there is eternal life which keep walking. If we walk in the presence of God on this earth, we do it partially. In the after-life, we believe that we will do spiritual walking to approach God.

Spiritual walking is important so long as we remain detached from the diseases. Through spiritual walking we can attain our goals in this life. During spiritual walking we create motion and energy with creative forces in the universe; spiritual walking with the positive attitude influences our choices, goals, intellectual and emotional life.

Through spiritual walking we can integrate our body and mind. It boosts us to move forward as the spiritual forces help us to overcome stress. In spiritual walking we are accompanied in spiritual journey with the God. By spiritual walking, we move to higher levels of consciousness. In spiritual walking, we carry people along with us. We influence the 'other' and establish connectedness with significant others and with those who boost our energies. Also we learn to establish connectedness with God through walking with others. The deepest sense of connection comes from learning to see God through walking.As a spiritual being, let us keep walking, to cope with distress, despair and fear and hopefully we will attain eternity.

Consciousness and Flow

Attitudes would not change until there is an expansion of consciousness. A new consciousness of unity is needed for flow. The role of flow is to become agents of change towards greater cooperation and competition, especially at work, where competition is still highly rewarded.

Everyone has an urge of expansion of consciousness. If an individual wants to expand his level of consciousness, it implies that knowingly or unknowingly, he wants to move towards the Supreme. If we see God in the faces of others, we will naturally feel a deep sense of connectedness with everyone. Even to hold a fraction of that consciousness radically changes the nature of our relationships.

If the content of consciousness is low, life is low, and if the content is high, life is high. To check and be alert to the content of consciousness is an indispensable part of spiritual health. If the content of consciousness is hurt, jealousy, anger, ego, it pulls us down. If it is love, gratitude, compassion, then life will be elevated.

Energy flow: Create a magnetic upward flow of energy. An important principle is to create a positive flow of energy up through the spine to the spiritual eye. This upward flow of energy through the chakras creates a magnetic field that connects us with others. A downward flow, on the other hand, increases our separation and disunity.

If we find ourselves slipping into a negative or complaining attitude, we should work first on controlling the flow of energy rather than on trying to convince the mind to be more positive.First feel the energy in the heart and make it positive. A little moment of appreciation works wonders! Then direct the heart's feeling upward to the spiritual eye. We will find that our thoughts turn positive as soon as the life-force begins to flow upward.This upward direction of energy will also make us magnetic, and positive magnetism will attract positive people.

Once you can produce a positive flow, consciously let it stream out to those around you. Become a wellspring of kindness and support.When we make the welfare of people our main priority, we generate the positive magnetism that causes the right things to happen, and in the best possible way.

Harmonious flow: The deep sense of connectedness to God and other people that we gain in meditation is a large part of what produces an attitude of unity. Yogananda said that meditation should be active service and that service should be active meditation.

If we can approach our work with a deep inward consciousness, our outer and inner life will begin to mould together into a beautiful, harmonious flow. The particular area of our work is not nearly so important as the quality of consciousness with which we work. Therefore we must make it fun, joyful, cooperative, and holy.

Meditation

Modern science now attests to the wide range of healing properties of the ancient art of meditation. Meditation helps in controlling our thought and breath. If one's mind is agitated, one's breathing will not be calm. During the process of meditation there is a deep communication between the meditator and God. In order to understand ourselves- and the cause of our own suffering, meditation is the way and it leads to inner transformation.

Meditation has been clinically proven to relieve chronic pain, reduce stress, slow ageing, lower blood pressure, improve heart and lung function, reduce depression, and improves sleep and memory. Many see meditation as a solitary activity better suited to loners, but it has been found to increase one's sense of connection to others and improve one's emotional intelligence. Meditation may also change brain and immune function in positive ways, and it has been seen to improve one's ability to regulate emotions. It also energizes body and mind. Vaswani (2018) says that "Meditation also helps the mind to relate to our inner instinct-intuition. This connection aids our creativity and innovative thinking. Thus meditation is a systematic method of tapping human brilliance" (p. 12).

Some are under the impression that meditation is just sitting, doing nothing, and therefore a waste of time. But it has been found to increase one's focus and attention, improve the ability to multitask, and enhance memory, all of which boosts productivity.Meditation develops good health, peaceful mind, confidence, harmonious relationships and meaningful life. Meditation can help you in exploring the unknown and untapped power of thought. Meditation is the best possible way to contemplate from zero point to that transcendent point where there is no division between oneself and Divinity. If we can live in such a reality eternally, there will be pure bliss. Spending time in silent meditation helps us commune with our true self and the divine power that created us. Those moments are thus filled with bliss, peace and love.

Vaswani (2018) explained five types of meditation advocated by Buddha. The **first is meditation of love** in which we so adjust our heart that we wish for the happiness of all living things, including the happiness of our enemies. The **second is meditation of compassion** in which we think of all beings in distress, vividly representing in our imagination their sorrows and anxieties so as to arouse a deep compassion for them within us. The **third is meditation of joy** in which we think of the prosperity of others and rejoice with their rejoicing. The **fourth is meditation on impurity** in which we think of the evil consequences of immorality and corruption. In this meditation, we realize how trivial is the pleasure of the moment and how fatal are its consequences! The **fifth is meditation on serenity** in which we rise above love and hate, tyranny and oppression, wealth and want, and regard our own fate with impartial calm and perfect tranquility.

Mindfulness

The practice of mindful breathing and walking are not too difficult; they enable us to go back to the here and now in order to live deeply for every moment given to us to live. When you breathe in or breathe out mindfully, or when you walk mindfully, with every step, you generate the energy of mindfulness.

Mindfulness is the kind of energy that allows us to know what is happening in the present moment; it is always mindfulness of something. When you breathe in mindfully, that is the mindfulness of breathing. When you drink your tea mindfully, that is mindfulness of drinking. When you walk mindfully, that is the mindfulness of walking. When you are doing anything mindfully, you are always in the here and now and are living deeply every moment.

Mindfulness considers reactance to thoughts and feelings as the most crucial factor in managing any behavioural disorder. Thus one may have a problematic thought or feeling; but what maintains this is once reactance to this particular thought or feeling. Mindfulness-based intervention encourages the individuals to view one's 'thoughts as thoughts' and 'not as facts' and this reduces the person's reactivity to thoughts.

Compassion with Love

Deep listening and loving speech can help remove obstacles between teachers and students. If you listen with compassion and love you can help the other person to suffer less. You know that suffering is in you, but in him there is also suffering. When you see the suffering in the other person you do not blame or accuse them anymore. Instead you want to help them. Coupled with mindful listening, is the practice of loving speech. We try to tell the other person the truth about the suffering in us and in him, using gentle speech to help the other person open his heart. The way we speak, helps the other person recognize the suffering in him, and in you. We therefore, need to become compassionate with love.

Compassion with love gives us inner strength, self-confidence and keeps our mind calm. According to The XIV Dalai Lama (2018), "A calm mind is very important. It doesn't matter, our physical situation; mental calmness is most important" (p. 14).

Speaking Truth

This is a practice and an art. The 'Truth' is our natural state. Sometimes it is very difficult to maintain it because of what we do and what others expect from us. Initially, it is difficult to look inside and differentiate what is true and what is false. Negative influences can easily translate into false habits and erode health. Speaking truth provides the key to happiness and total well-being.

Speaking truth is beneficial to health. Although telling a lie can often become a shortcut, but it depends on how we use it. The truth is constantly pointing to a greater harmony and higher perfection and so is the cornerstone of all integral health.Truly, there is a unique spark within all things, waiting for the right conditions to appear. Speaking truly is the need of the times. Its blossoming depends upon worldly existence. The truth is dynamic and governs every process unwinding in the universe. Anything false will one day be obliterated.

When we speak the Truth we fulfill our religious duty and collaborate with the divine work. We find a way to live in freedom and harmony.Anyone called upon to give evidence in a court of law is required to take an oath "to speak the truth, the whole truth and nothing but the truth." The oath is necessary because half-truths can be more misleading than the whole truth. Speaking truth is simply because it came from a person who had taken an oath to always speak the truth.Similarly, speaking anything more than the whole truth can also lead to dire consequences.

From a moral and ethical point of view, the truth helps one to enter into paradise.'Truth Alone Triumphs.' Therefore, all of us, in whatever capacity we are working, need to abide by the truth in all circumstances.Truth cannot be hidden forever and ultimately one will have to pay the price for withholding truth from the people. As Emile Zola has said, "If you shut up truth and bury it under the ground, it will grow and gather to itself such explosive power that the day it bursts through, it will blow up everything in its way," (Mathur, 2017).

Realization of the Inner Light

Illuminate life at both spiritual and personal levels. Inner light awakens knowledge and truth in our hearts and minds. It develops our innate brilliance and goodness.Realization of the inner light shows the seeker, the path of righteousness even at the darkest of times and places. The awakening to one's true Self, introduces one to immense peace, universal compassion, love and awareness with the oneness of all things -that is cosmic knowledge.

Sant Rajinder Singh (2018) says that: "As we enter the inner core of our hearts, we find that there is a light within us. That Light is the Light of the Creator: The realization drawn on us that the same Light that is within us in all other human beings"(p. 12).

People need to reflect on and evaluate their thoughts, words and actions through realization of the inner light. Realization of the inner light helps the process of transformation within and to discover how we are more loving, kind, respectful towards us and others. As a spiritual practice, realization of the inner light is a symbol of the divine. Illumination promotes awareness of the inner light that is the core of every human being. Spending sometime and energy in cleaning and purifying our mind and heart from the inside, is the true meaning of celebration and realization of inner light.

Let every one of us illumine our hearts and be the source of light and happiness, for everyone who comes in contact with us. Love unconditionally, forgive unconditionally, and be in alignment to receive the cosmic abundance of love, light and happiness. 'Lokasamastha sukhinobhavantu.' Let all beings experience happiness.

Mental Cleansing: Just as our body need to do cleansing every day, similarly it is also necessary that we keep getting rid of all negativities from our minds from time to time. For it is only when valuable space is cleared of clutter that we can furnish it with things that are more useful and functional and could engender our aims and goals. Cleansing the outdated thoughts from the mind will help in clearing mental space and will be resulting in a feeling of lightness and infuse vitality in our lives. Through this the human mind moves towards the inner transformation.

Clutter in the mind blocks the flow of vital energy, adversely effecting relationships, growth, health and productivity. This clutter could include things that have become outdated and have no utility, in the present or future. We need to throw the dirt out of our mind. In place of that we can be jewel things that are useful for us depending upon our needs. *Rishis* of ancient India taught us "You are what you think."

Thoughts are important aspect of our lives. If we allow negative thoughts and feelings to take root in our minds they will destroy not only our chances of success in what we do but also negatively impact our peace of mind. Like pessimism which detracts from us our enthusiasm and makes us fear the future; greed which tempts us into unethical and sometimes dangerous situations; ambition which makes us rotate like spinning top relentlessly at the cost of bodily and mental harm; anxiety, depression, and stress which destroy our peace of mind. In fact,these negative psychological states affect our abilities and prevent us from enjoying what life offers us.

By helping the practitioner cleanse the mind and clear the intellect, Raja Yoga enables correct perception and right decision-making. Ego, anger and other weaknesses may no longer cloud the mind, and one is able to see the larger picture. In this way Raja Yoga helps one think beyond the bounds created by one's fears and desires.

Spiritual Journey: By and large, it is observed that we are compelled to embark on a spiritual journey due to two reasons. Firstly, when a smooth, comfortable life is suddenly affected by some unforeseen catastrophe, leaving us gasping for breath, we intuitively seek solace through visiting holy places. During spiritual journey we search for the light within and the seeds of goodness germinate.

Secondly, when all our material needs and sensory desires have been fully satiated but we still find ourselves floundering in a sea of unhappiness and discontentment, the moment of epiphany comes. Spiritual journey is guided by our own philosophy and belief. Spiritual journey is the gateway to quest for eternal happiness and achieving goodness.

Conclusion

Time should be spent while doing all these exercises because it would yield and benefit one at intellectual or spiritual level. Spiritual practices tend to improve coping skills and social support, foster feelings of optimism and hope, promote healthy behavior, reduce feelings of depression and anxiety, and encourage a sense of relaxation. By practicing meditation and mindfulness we can increase our awareness and transform our life.

References

100 BENEFITS OF RAJYOGA MEDITATION... - Brahma Kumaris India | Facebook. (n.d.). Retrieved May 9, 2017, from https://www.facebook.com/Brahma.Kumaris.India/posts/314406922008041

8 Reasons to Practice Iyengar Yoga – DO YOU YOGA. (n.d.). Retrieved May 31, 2017, from https://www.doyouyoga.com/8-reasons-to-practice-iyengar-yoga/

Agarwal S.P. (1997). *The social role of the Gita: How and why*. New Delhi: Motilal Banarsidass Publications.

Albanese, C. L. (1990). *Nature religion in America: From the Algonquian Indians to the new age*. Chicago and London: The University of Chicago Press.

Al-Ghazali, Abu Hamid Muhammad Ibn Muhammad (2000). Ihya' 'ulum al-din. Kaherah: Dar al-Taqwa li al-Turath.

Alister, H. (1984/1979). *The spiritual nature of man: A study of contemporary religious experiences*. Oxford: Clarendon Press.

Amin, A., Kumar, S. S., Rajagopalan, A., Rajan, S., Mishra, S., Reddy, U. K., Mukkadan, J. K. (2016). Beneficial effects of OM chanting on depression, anxiety, stress and cognition in elderly women with hypertension. *Indian Journal of Clinical Anatomy and Physiology, 3*(3), 253-255.

Anandamurti, S. S. (2012, July 09). Ten characteristics of Dharma. Retrieved December 28, 2018, from https://www.speakingtree.in/article/ten-characteristics-of-dharma

Ashmos, D.P. & Duchon, D. (2000). Spirituality at work: A conceptualization and measure. *Journal of Management Inquiry, 9*(2), 134-145.

Astin, A. W., Astin, H. A., & Lindholm, J. A. (2011). Assessing students' spiritual and religious qualities. *Journal of College Student Development, 52*(1), 39-61.

Aurbindo, Sri (1949). *Essays on the Gita*. Calcutta: Arya Publishing House.

Aurobindo, Sri. (1971). *The synthesis of yoga.* Pondicherry: Sri Aurobindo Ashram Birth Centenary Library Edition.

Azad, M. A. K. *The Tarjumn al-Quran.* Vol. I by Syed Abdul Latif, p. 160.

Bahore, R. (2005). *Bharateeya sangeet ke pramukh sthamb.* New Delhi: Classical Publishing Company, Pt. Madan Lal Vyas Krut.

Bansal, P., Kaur, R., Gupta, V., Kumar, S., & Kaur, R. (2015). Is there any scientific basis of *Hawan* to be used in epilepsy-prevention/cure? *Journal of Epilepsy Research, 5*(2), 33-45.

Bhajanananda, S. (2011). Swami Vivekananda's concept of spirituality: Transformation of consciousness from the human to the Divine through synthesis of yogas. In *Spirituality and science of consciousness.* Kolkata: Ramakrishna Mission Institute of Culture.

Bhattacharyya, H. (1953/2006). Yoga psychology. In H. Bhattacharyya (Ed.), *The cultural heritage of India* (Volume III, pp. 53-90). Calcutta: The Ramakrishna Institute of Culture.

Bhattacharyya, S. (1953). Religious practices of the Hindus. In K. W. Morgan (Ed.), *The religion of the Hindus.* New York: The Ronald Press Company.

Bhave, V. (1966). *Steadfast wisdom.* Varanasi : Sarva Seva Sangh Prakashan.

Bhawuk, D. P. S. (2011). *Spirituality and Indian psychology: Lessons from the Bhagavad-Gita.* New York: Springer.

Binathi, G. (2014). Essence of spirituality in the ragas of Hindustani and carnatic music systems. *Sangeet Galaxy, 3*(1), 2-11.

Bouchard, N. (1997). Seminar Presentation. Denver: Society of Certified Senior Advisors.

Brahma Kumaris Official Website - Benefits of Raja Yoga. (n.d.). Retrieved May 9, 2017, from http://www.brahmakumaris.org/us/massachusetts/typeb.2009-07 23.5593975822/typec.2009-07-23.9541270677

Brown, L. B. (1987). *The psychology of religious belief.* London: Harcourt Brace Jovanovich.

Burkhardt, M. A., & Nagai-Jacobson, M. G. (1985). Dealing with spiritual concerns of clients in the community. *Journal of Community Health Nursing, 2*(4), 191-198.

Canda, E. R. (1988). Spirituality, religious diversity, and social-work practice. *Social Casework-Journal of Contemporary Social Work, 69*(4), 238-247.

Capps, D., Rambo, L. & Ransohoff, P. (1976). *Psychology of religion.* Detroit, MI: Gale Research.

Chandra, K. K. (2011). *Times of India*, New Delhi Saturday February 26, 2011, p. 16.

Cloninger, C. R., Svrakic, D. M., & Pryzbeck, T. R. (1993). A psychobiological model of temperament and character. *Archives of General Psychiatry, 50*, 975–990.

Cooper, J. (1998). Mulla Sadra (Sadr al-Din Muhammad al-Shirazi) (1571/2-1640)". In C, Edward. *Routledge Encyclopedia of Philosophy*. 6. London; New York: Routledge. pp. 595–599.

Costello, T. (2006). Spirituality and love at work. In C. Barker and A. Payne (Eds.) *Love and work.* Qld: John Wiley & Sons/Australian Institute of Management.

Crow, E. M., Jeannot, E., & Trewhela, A. (2015). Effectiveness of Iyengar yoga in treating spinal (back and neck) pain: A systematic review. *International Journal of Yoga, 8*(1), 3-14.

Dabre, P. C., Pingale, P. V., Dahake, T., & Humbad, P. N. (2011). Effect of suryanamskar, pranayama and yogasanas training on the intelligence of school going children. *International Journal of Sports Sciences and Fitness, 1*(1), 68-78.

Danhauer, S. C., Tooze, J. A., Farmer, D. F., Campbell, C. R., McQuellon, R. P., Barret, R., & Miller, B. E. (2008). Restorative Yoga for women with ovarian or breast cancer: Findings from a pilot study. *Journal of the Society for Integrative Oncology, 6*(2), 47-58.

Dasgupta, S. (1922/1991). *A history of Indian philosophy.* New Delhi: Motilal Banarasidass.

Dasgupta, S. (1953/2006). Introduction. In H. Bhattacharyya (Ed.), *The cultural heritage of India* (Volume III, pp. 3-26). Calcutta: The Ramakrishna Institute of Culture.

de Jager Meezenbroek E., Garssen B, van den Berg M, Tuytel G, van Dierendonck, D, visser, A., & Schaufeli, W.B. (2012) Measuring spirituality as a universal human experience: Development of the

Spiritual Attitude and Involvement List (SAIL). *Journal of Psychosocial Oncology, 30,* 141–167. doi: 10.1080/07347332.2011.651258 PMID:

DeLuca, D. (2006). *Pathways to joy the master Vivekananda on the four yoga paths to God.* Novato: New World Library.

Dinesh, T., Sharma, V. K., Jeyakumar, M., Sunder, A., Gopinath, M., & Bhavanani, A. B. (2013). Effect of 8 weeks of pranav pranayama training on pulmonary function test parameters in young healthy, volunteers of Jipmer population. *International Research Journal of Pharmaceutical and Applied Sciences, 3*(4), 116-118.

Dossey, B., Keegan, L., & Guzzetta, C. (Eds.). (2000). *Holistic nursing: A handbook for practice.* Gaithersburg, MD: Aspen Publishers.

Dwivedi, C. B. (2015). Inculcating subjecting well-being in Hinduism by adhering to a spiritual life style. In A. Shukla and A. Dubey (Eds.), *Mental health: Psycho-social perspectives* (Volume One: Issues and Interventions pp. 27-53). New Delhi: Concept Publishing Company Pvt. Ltd.

Elkins, D. N., Hughes, L. L., Saunders, C., Leaf, J. A. & Headstrom, L. J. (1988). Towards a humanistic phenomenological spirituality: Definition, description and measurement. *Journal of Humanistic Psychology, 28*(4), 5-18.

Emmons, R. A., & Crumpler, C. A. (1999). Religion and spirituality? The role of sanctification and the concept of God. *International Journal for the Psychology of Religion, 9,* 17–24.

Emmons, R. A., Cheung, C. & Tehrani, K. (1998). Assessing spirituality through personal goals: Implications for research on religion and subjective well-Being. *Social Indicators Research, 45*(1), 391-422.

Evans, S., Moieni, M., Taub, R., Subramanian, S. K., Tsao, J. C. I., Sternlieb, B., & Zeltzer, L. K. (2010). Iyengar Yoga for young adults with rheumatoid arthritis: Results From a mixed methods pilot study. *Journal of Pain and Symptom Management, 39*(5), 904- 913.

Fetzer Institute, National Institute on Aging Working Group (1999). *Multidimensional measurement of religiousness/spirituality for use in health research.* Kalamazoo, MI: Fetzer Institute.

Flood, G. (2004). *An introduction to Hinduism.* New Delhi: Foundation Books.

Foglio, J. P., & Brody, H. (1988). Religion, faith, and family medicine. *Journal of Family Practice, 27,* 473-4.

Frame, (2003). *Integrating religion and spirituality in counseling: A comprehensive approach.* Pacific Grove, CA: Brooks/Cole.

Frankl, V. (1962). *Man's search for meaning.* New York: Washington Square Press.

Frederic & Brussat, M. A. (1996). Reprinted by permission of the authors from *Spiritual Literacy: Reading the Sacred in Everyday Life* (Scribner, 1996; Touchstone, 1998), pp. 19-25.

Fukuyama, M. A., & Sevig, T. D. (1999). *Integrating spirituality into multicultural counseling.* Thousand Oaks, CA: Sage.

Gandhi, S., & Anbalagan, P. (2016). Effect of yogic practices combined with varmam on the selected physical variables among the middle aged men. *International Journal of Physical Education, Sports and Health, 3*(4), 333-336.

Ganje-Fling, M. A., & McCarthy, P. (1996). Impact of childhood sexual abuse on client spiritual development: Counselling implications. *Journal of Counselling & Development, 74*, 253-258.

Gawain, S. (2000). *The path of transformation: How healing ourselves can change the world.* California: New World Library.

Ghar, M., Chaudhuri, A., Rahaman, W. B., Majumdar, S., Biswas, A., & Goswami, A. (2016). A study of the effect of Raj yoga on cardiorespiratory parameters in young adult Indians. *Saudi Journal of Sports Medicine, 16*(2), 111-117.

Gladding, S. T. (2000). *Counselling: A comprehensive profession* (4th ed.). Upper Saddle River, New Jersey: Prentice-Hall.

Gopinathan, G., Dhiman, K. S., & Manjusha, R. (2012). A clinical study to evaluate the efficacy of Trataka Yoga Kriya and eye exercises (non-pharmocological methods) in the management of Timira (Ammetropia and Presbyopia). *Ayurveda, 33*(4), 543–546.

Gregory, B. (2012). *The unintended reformation: How a religious revolution secularized society.* Cambridge, Mass: Harvard University Press.

Griffith, J. L., & Griffith, M. E. (2002). *Encountering the sacred in psychotherapy: How to talk with people about their spiritual lives.* New York: Guilford Press.

Grof, S. (1985). *Beyond the brain: Birth, death, and transcendence in psychotherapy*. Albany, NY: SUNY.

Grof, S. (1988). *The adventure of self-discovery: Dimensions of consciousness and new perspectives in psychotherapy and inner exploration*. Albany, NY: SUNY.

Gurjar, A. A., Ladhake, S. A., & Thakare, A. P. (2009). Analysis of acoustic of "OM" chant to study its effect on nervous system. *International Journal of Computer Science and Network Security, 9*(1), 363-366.

Hardt, J., Schultz, S., Xander, C., Becker, G., & Dragan, M. (2012). The spirituality questionnaire: Core dimensions of spirituality. *Psychology, 3*(1), 116-122.

Harinath, K., Malhotra, A. S., Pal, K., Prasad, R., Kumar, R., Kain, T. C., ...Sawhney, R. C. (2004). Effects of hatha yoga and Omkar meditation on cardiorespiratory performance, psychologic profile, and melatonin secretion. *The Journal of Alternative and Complementary Medicine, 10*(2), 261-268.

Hassan, M. (2017). Niyyat in Islam is about purity of intentions. *The Times of India*, New Delhi, June 12, 2017, p. 10.

Hay, D., & Socha, P. M. (2005). Spirituality as a natural phenomenon: Bringing biological and psychological perspectives together. *Zygon, 40*, 589–612.

Heelas, P. & Woodhead, L., (2005). *The spiritual revolution: Why religion is giving way to spirituality.* Oxford: Blackwell Publishers.

Helminiak, D. A. (1996). *The human core of spirituality: Mind as psyche and spirit* (p. 307). Albany, NY: SUNY.

Helminiak, D. A. (1998). *Religion and the human sciences: An approach via spirituality* (p. 332). Albany, NY: SUNY.

Helminiak, D. A. (2008). Confounding the divine and the spiritual: Challenges to a psychology of spirituality. *Pastor Psychology, 57*, 161–182.

Henry, J. (2013). Quieting the mind and low arousal routes to happiness. In

S. David., I. Boniwell., and A. C. Ayers (Eds.), *The Oxford handbook of happiness* (pp. 411-26). London: Oxford University Press.

Hill, P. C., & Pargament, K. I. (2003). Advances in the conceptualization and measurement of religion and spirituality: Implications for physical and mental health research. *American Psychologist, 58*, 64- 74.

Hill, P. C., Pargament, K. I., Hood, R. W., McCullough Jr, M. E., Swyers, J. P., Larson, D. B., & Zinnbauer, B. J. (2000). Conceptualizing religion and spirituality: Points of commonality, points of departure. *Journal for the Theory of Social Behavior, 30*(1), 51 77.

Hill. P. C, Pargament, K. T., Swyers, Gorsuch, R. L., McCullough, M. E., Hood, R. W. & Baumiester, R. F. (1998). Definition of religion and spirituality. In D. B. Larson, J. P. Swyers and M. E. McCullough (Eds.) *Scientific research on spirituality and health: A consensus report* (pp. 14-30). Baltimore: National Institute for Health Care Research.

Hindu Janajagruti Samiti. (2014). Tarpan and Piru Tarpan. Retrieved July 12, 2018, from https:/www.hindujagruti.org/hinduism/tarpan

Hines, E. A., & Brown, G. E. (1936). Cold pressor test for measuring the reactibility of blood pressure. *American Heart Journal, 11*(1), 1-9.

Holkar, S., & Makhija, S. (2015). Alteration in anthropometric measurements before and after yogic exercises in patients of hypertension with obesity. *International Journal of Health Sciences & Research, 5*(4), 159-164.

Howden, W. (1992). Development and psychometric characteristics of the spirituality assessment scale. Dissertation, Texas Women University.

Huddleston, M. A. (1995). *Springs of spirituality*. Liguori, Missouri: Trumph Books.

Hume, R. E. (1921), *The thirteen principal Upanishads: Translated from the Sanskrit* (pp. 391–393). London: Oxford University Press.

Hungelmann, J., Kenkel-Rossi, E., Klassen, L., & Stollenwerk, R. (1985). Spiritual well-being in older adults: Harmonious interconnectedness. *Journal of Religion and Health, 24*(3), 407-418.

Husain, A. (2005). *Spiritual psychology*. New Delhi: Global Vision Publishing House.

Husain, A. (2007). Subjective well-being in relation to spiritual orientation among solace seekers. *Journal of Psychological Researches, 51*, 39-45.

Husain, A. (2011). *Spirituality and holistic health: A psychological perspective.* New Delhi: Prasad Psycho Corporation.

Husain, A. (2015). A new approach to defining applied spirituality. In N. Sanyal (Ed.), *Spirituality and positive psychology* (pp. 351-370). Kolkata: Ramakrishna Mission Institute of Culture.

Husain, A. (2016). Islamic spirituality in practice. In N. A. Ab. Majeed (Ed.) *Proceedings of the Two-day International Conference on Social and Spiritual Teachings of the Quran in Contemporary Perspective* (pp. 222-230). New Delhi: Excel India Publishers.

Husain, A. (2016). YOGA: a path for attaining spiritual energy and power. *International Journal of Yoga & Allied Sciences, 5*(1), 30-37.

Husain, A., & Anas, M. (2018). Manual Spiritual Personality Inventory – Revised. Agra: Agra Psychological Research Cell.

Husain, A., Beg, M, A., & Dwivedi, C, B., (2013). *Psychology of humanity & spirituality*. New Delhi: Research India Press.

Husain, A., Jahan, M., Nishat, A., Siddiqui, R. N., & Akram, M. (2011). Spirituality Attitude Scale. New Delhi: Prasad Psycho Corporation.

Husain, A., Kaneez, S., & Jahan, M. (2014) (Eds.). *Studies in spiritual psychology*. New Delhi: Research India Press.

Husain, A., & Khan, S. (2014). *Applied spirituality: Theory, research and practice*. New Delhi: Global Vision Publishing House.

Husain, A., Luqman, N., & Jahan, M. (2012). Spiritual Personality Inventory. New Delhi: Prasad Psycho Corporation.

Husain, A., Singh, R., & Khan, S. M. (2016). Spiritual Practices Scale (Muslims). New Delhi: Prasad Psycho Corporation.

Indra, Y. (2017). To know and not to believe (the speaking tree). *The Times of India*, New Delhi/ Agra Saturday, March 18, 2017.

Introduction to Integral Yoga. (n.d.). Retrieved May 13, 2017, from http://www.yogawiz.com/types-of-yoga/integral-yoga.html

Iqbal, N. (2012). Spirituality: An Islamic perspective. In A. Husain and N. Khatoon (Eds.) *Understanding spirituality* (52-68). New Delhi: Research India Press.

Jackson, G. (1980). Spirituality: A process theology perspective. *Studies in Formative Spirituality, 1*(3), 407-418.

Jain, S. (2016). Effect of 6 weeks pranava yoga training on cardiovascular parameters in prehypertensive young adults. *National Journal of Physiology, Pharmacy and Pharmacology, 6*(5), 416-419.

Jain, V., & Sharma, J. (2017). Effect of yogic intervention: pranayama on anxiety & depression. *The International Journal of Indian Psychology, 4*(3), 124-136.

Jaisingh, H. (2007). Understanding Hinduism. In S. C. Kashyap and A. Kashyap (Eds.), *Understanding India relevance of Hinduism.* New Delhi: Vitasta Publishing Pvt. Ltd.

Jitatmananda, S. (2007). Hinduism and modern times. In S. C. Kashyap and A. Kashyap (Eds.), *Understanding India relevance of Hinduism.* New Delhi: Vitasta Publishing Pvt. Ltd.

Jones, J. (1995). *In the middle of this road we call our life: The courage to search for something more.* New York: Harper Collins.

Joshi, K. (2012). Effect of Nadishodhana pranayama and Om chanting on memory enhancement of college students. *International Journal of Yoga and Allied Sciences, 1*(1), 52-57.

Joshi, K. (2013). Effect of Om chanting and Bhramari pranayama on Anxiety level among Adolescent. *International Journal of Yoga and Allied Sciences, 2*(1), 33-35.

Jurkiewicz, C., & Giacalone, R. (2004). A values framework for measuring the impact of workplace spirituality on organizational performance. *Journal of Business Ethics, 49*(2), 129-142.

Kaarthikeyan, D. R. (2007). Hinduism: A quest for the divine. In S. C. Kashyap & A. Kashyap (Eds.), *Understanding India: Relevance of Hinduism.* New Delhi: Vitasta Publishing Pvt. Ltd.

Kalyani, B. G., Venkatasubramanian, G., Arasappa, R., Rao, N. P., Kalmady, S. V., Behere, R. V.,... Gangadhar, B. N. (2011). Neurohemodynamic correlates of 'OM' chanting: A pilot functional magnetic resonance imaging study. *International Journal of Yoga, 4*(1), 3-6.

Kanaya, A. M., Araneta, M. R. G., Pawlowsky, S. B., Barrett-Connor, E., Grady, D., Vittinghoff, E., Schembri, M., ... Cole, R. J. (2011). Restorative Yoga and metabolic risk factors: The Practicing Restorative Yoga vs. Stretching for the Metabolic Syndrome (PRYSMS) randomized trial. *Journal of Diabetes Complications, 28*(3), 406-412.

Karmakar, K., & Pant, G. (2017). Effect of trataka kriya session on the visual perception of elderly people. *International Journal of Yoga, Physiotherapy and Physical Education, 2*(2), 45-48.

Kellehear, A. (2000). Spirituality and palliative care: A model of needs. *Palliative Medicine, 14*, 149-155. http://dx.doi.org/10.1191/026921600674786394

Khemka, S. S., Ramarao, N. H., & Hankey, A. (2011). Effect of integral yoga on psychological and health variables and their correlations. *International Journal of Yoga, 4*(2), 93-99.

Koenig, H. G. (2010). Spirituality and mental health. *International Journal of Applied Psychoanalytic Studies, 7*, 116–122.

Koenig, H. G., McCullough, M. E., & Larson, D. B. (2001). *Handbook of religion and health*. New York: Oxford University Press.

Koenig, H. G., Moberg, D. O., & Kvale, J. N. (1988). Religious activities and attitudes of older adults in a geriatric assessment clinic. *Journal of American Geriatrics Society, 36*(4), 362-374.

Krishna Mohan, K. (2001). Spirituality and well-being: An overview. C. In Matthijs (Ed.), *Consciousness and Transformation* (pp.227-253). Pondicherry: Sri Aurobindo Ashram Press.

Kumar, S., Nagendra, H., Manjunath, N., Naveen, K., & Telles, S. (2010). Meditation on OM: Relevance from ancient texts and contemporary science. *International Journal of Yoga, 3*(1), 2-5.

Kumar, A. & Kumar, S. (2013). Karma yoga: A path towards work in positive psychology. *Indian Journal of Psychiatry, 55*(6), 150-152.

LaPierre, L. L. (1994). A model for describing spirituality. *Journal of Religion and Health, 33*, 153– 161.

LAYA YOGA: Kundalini Tantra - Mantra - Siddhi Meditations. (n.d.). Retrieved June 1, 2017.

Leffel, G. M. (2007). Emotion and Transformation in the Relational

Spirituality Paradigm. Part 1. Prospects and Prescriptions for Reconstructive Dialogue. *Journal of Psychology and Theology, 35*(4), 253–280.

Lerner, M. (1971). Yoga concentration and psychotherapy. *Acta Psiquiatricay Psicologica de America Latina, 17*(6), 410-417.

Linardakis, M., Papadaki, A., Smpokos, E., Sarri, K., Vozikaki, M., & Philalithis, A. (2015). Are religiosity and prayer use related with multiple behavioural risk factors for chronic diseases in European adults aged 50+years? *Public Health, 129*(5), 436-443.

Lolage R., & Jadhav, N. (2013). Effect of yogic exercise on Myopia of high school girls. *International Proceedings of Economics Development and Research, 4*(2), 144–150.

Londhe, M. (2014). Concept of lokasamgraha – Lokamanya Tilak's perspective. *Online International Interdisciplinary Research Journal, (Bi-monthly), IV*(IV), 270- 277.

MacDonald, D. A., Friedman, H. L., Brewczynski, J., Holland, D., Salagame, K. K. K., Mohan, K. K., ..Cheong, H.W. (2015) Spirituality as a scientific construct: Testing its universality across cultures and languages. *PLoS ONE 10*(3). e0117701. https://doi.org/10.1371/journal.pone.0117701

Mahajan, B. (2017). Concept of Yajna, Sacrifice in the Gita. *The Speaking Tree, The Times of India,* Delhi, July 19, 2017.

Manaspure, S. P., Fadia, A., & Gowda, D. (2011b). Effect of selected breathing techniques on respiratory rate and breath holding time in healthy adults. *International Journal of Applied Biology and Pharmaceutical Technology, 2*(3), 225-229.

Manaspure. S. P., Fadia, A., & Gowda, D. (2011a). Effect of specific pranayama techniques on ventilatory functions of lungs. *Research Journal of Pharmaceutical, Biological and Chemical Sciences, 2*(4), 351- 357.

Mansager, E. (2002). Religious and spiritual problem v-code: An Adlerian assessment. *The Journal of Individual Psychology, 58*, 374–387.

Mathire, R. (1997). *Bharateeya Sangeet aur sangeetagn*. Jaipur: Bohra prakashan.

Mathur, M. M. (2017). Speak The Truth, Nothing But The Truth. Retrieved July 11, 2018, from https://www.speakingtree.in/article/speak-the-truth-nothing-but-the-truth

Mc Gee, M. (2004). Samskara. In S, Mittal & G, Thursby (Eds). *The Hindu world.* New York & London: Routledge Taylor & Francis group.

Mehrotra, R., Phadke, A. V., Kharche, J. S., Pranita, A., & Joshi, A. R. (2012). Effect of yoga on anxiety score and resting heart rate in young healthy individuals. *National Journal of Integrated Research in Medicine, 3*(2), 142-146.

Miller, G. (1999). The development of the spiritual focus in counseling and counselor education. *Journal of Counseling and Development, 77,* 498-501.

Miller, M. A. (1995). Culture, spirituality, and women's health. *Journal of Obstetric, Gynecologic, & Neonatal Nursing, 24*(3), 257-263.

Mini, K. V., & Awasthi, H. H. (2015). Tantra yoga and Kundalini yoga. *International Ayurvedic Medical Journal, 3*(9), 2814-2817.

Mitroff, I. I., & Denton, E. A. (1999). *A spiritual audit of corporate America: A hard look at spirituality, religion and values in the workplace.* San Francisco: Jossey- Bass.

Mitroff, I., & Denton, E. (1999). A study of spirituality in the workplace. *Solan Management Review, 40*, 83-92.

Moberg, D. O. (1971). Spiritual well-being: Background and issues of the technical committee on spiritual well-being. White House Conference on Aging. Washington, DC: U.S. Government Printing Office.

Mohr, W. (2006). Spiritual issues in psychiatric care. *Perspectives in Psychiatric Care, 42*(3), 174-183.

Mooventhan, A., & Khode, V. (2014). Effect of only Bhramari pranayama and OM chanting on pulmonary function in healthy individuals. *International Journal of Yoga, 7*(2), 104-110.

Moreira-Almeida, A., Sharma, A., Van Rensburg, B. J., Verhagen, P. J., & Cook, C. C. (2016). WPA position statement on spiritu-ality and religion in psychiatry. *World Psychiatry, 15*, 87–88. doi: 10.1002/wps.20304.

Muldoon, M., & King, N. (1995). Spirituality, health care, and bioethics. *Journal of Religion and Health, 34,* 329–349.

Murray, R. B., & Zenter, J. B. (1989). *Nursing concepts for health promotion.* London: Prentice-Hall.

Naqvi, A. M. (2016). *Introduction to Muslim spirituality, theology and philosophy.* New Delhi: Samath Publication.

Narayanasamy, A. (1999). A review of spirituality as applied to nursing. *International Journal of Nursing Studies, 36*, 117-125.

Nath, Y. R. (1983). *The Hindu believes* (ch-6, pp-185-186, 187). New Delhi: D. K Publishers distributors.

Nussbaum, M. (1990). *Love's knowledge* (pp. 281-282). Oxford: Oxford university press.

O'Donnell, K. (2010). Spirituality in uncertain times: A challenge for all. In A. Husain (Ed.), *Explorations in Human Spirituality* (pp. 3-30). New Delhi: Global Vision Publishing House.

Pandya. S. P. (2014). Sudarshankriya and pranayama: Insights into an Indic spiritual practice for promoting well-being. *Journal of Spirituality in Mental Health, 16*(1), 51-71.

Pargament, K. I. (2007). *Spiritually integrated psychotherapy: Understanding and addressing the sacred* (384 p.). New York: Guilford.

Pargament, K. I., & Mahoney, A. (2002). Spirituality: Discovering and conserving the sacred. In C. R. Synder, & S. J. Lopez (Eds.), *Handbook of positive psychology* (pp. 646-659). Oxford: Oxford University Press.

Pargament, K. I., Mahoney, A., Exline, J. J., Jones, J., & Shafranske, E. (2013). Envisioning an integrative paradigm for the psychology of religion and spirituality. In K. I. Pargament (Ed.), *APA handbook of psychology, religion, and spirituality* (Vol. 1, pp. 3-19). Washington DC: American Psychological Association. Doi: 10.1037/14046-001.

Perrin, D. B. (2007). *Studying Christian spirituality.* New York, London: Routledge

Peterson, C., & Seligman, M. (2004). *Character strengths and virtues: A handbook and classification.* Washington, DC: American Psychological Association.

Pilch, J. (1981). *Wellness: Your invitation to a full life.* Minneapolis: Winston Press.

Powers, H. S. (1959). The Background of the South Indian Raaga-System. Ph.D. dissertation, Princeton University.

Prabhupada, S. (2002). *Bhagavad-Gita as it is.* North America UK: The Bhaktivedanta Book Trust.

Pradhan, M. (2014). Spirituality and well-being: An Indian perspective. In S. Saini (Ed.). *Positive psychology in the light of Indian traditions* (pp. 132-146). Haryana: Indian Association of Health, Research and Welfare.

Pranav pranayama – meditation and spiritual development. (n.d.). Retrieved May 31, 2017, from http://eyogaguru.com/pranav-pranayama-meditation-and-spiritual-development/

Puchalski, C., & Romer, A. L. (2000). Taking a spiritual history allows clinicians to understand patients more fully. *Journal of Palliative Medicine, 3*(1), 129–137.

Radhakrishnan, S. (1973). *The Bhagavad-Gita.* New York: Harper and Raw.

Raghavendra, B. R., & Singh, P. (2014). Immediate effect of yogic visual concentration on cognitive performance. *Journal of Traditional and Complementary Medicine*, *6*(1), 34-36.

Raja Yoga. (n.d.). Retrieved May 9, 2017, from http://www.yogaindailylife.org/system/en/the-four-paths-of-yoga/raja-yoga

Rajak, C., Rampalliwar, S., Verma, R., Singh, P., & Shiralkar, M. (2016). Study of yogasana, nadishodhana, bhramari pranayama, Omkar chanting and meditation (yoga) on cardiorespiratory parameters in hyper reactors to cold pressor test in young healthy preclinical medical students. *World Journal of Pharmacy and Pharmaceutical Sciences, 5*(9), 1737-1750.

Rajpoot, P. L., & Vaishnav, P. (2014). Effect of Trataka on anxiety among adolescents. *International Journal of Social, Behavioral, Educational, Economic, Business and Industrial Engineering, 8*(12), 3989-3992.

Raju, P. T. (1985). *Structural depths of Indian thought.* New York: State University New York Press.

Rani, M., & Deo, G. (2017). Effect of asana and OM chanting on memory in school going children. *International Research Journal of India, 2*(9), 1-11.

Rao, D. J. (2012). *Essence of Hindu religion and philosophy*. New Delhi: Viva books Pvt. Ltd.

Rao, K. R. (2010). Psychology in search of the sacred. Keynote address delivered in the national seminar on spiritual psychology held on October 28-30, 2010, Aligarh Muslim University, Aligarh.

Rao, K. R. (2011). Indian psychology: Implications and applications. In R. M. M. Cornelissen, G. Misra, and S. Verma (Eds.), *Foundations of Indian Psychology (Volume1) Theories and Concepts* (pp. 7-26). Delhi: Pearson.

Rao, K. R. (2013). Indian psychology, parapsychology and spiritual psychology. *International Journal of Yoga - Philosophy, Psychology and Parapsychology, 1*(1), 4-14.

Reed, P. G. (1987). Spirituality and well-being in terminally ill and healthy adults. *Research in Nursing & Health, 10,* 335-344.

Rizzuto, A. M. (2005). Psychoanalytic considerations about spiritually oriented psychotherapy. In L. Sperry, & E. P. Shafranske (Eds.), *Spiritually oriented psychotherapy* (pp 31-50). Washington, DC: American Psychological Association.

Royal College of Psychiatrists. (2013). Recommendations for psychiatrists on spirituality and religion (3). Retrieved from http://www.rcpsych.ac.uk/pdf/Recommendations%20for%20Psychiatrists%20on%20Spirituality%20 and%20Religion%20Revised.w.pdf

Rukmani, T. S. (1983). *Yoga Vârttika of Vijñân Bhik°u* (Volume I). New Delhi: Munshiram Manoharlal Publishers.

Salsman, J. M., & Carlson, C. R. (2005). Religious orientation, mature faith, and psychological distress: Elements of positive and negative associations. *Journal for the Scientific Study of Religion, 44,* 201-209.

Saxena, M., Gupta, B. S., & Pandya, P. (2007). A study of the impact of Yagya on indoor microbial environments. *Indian Journal of Air Pollution Control, 7*(1), 6-15.

Secrets of tratak sadhana. (n.d.). Retrieved June 1, 2017, from https://www.lifepositive.com/secrets-of-tratak-sadhana/

Shankar, S. S. R. (2018). Joy of giving is greater than joy of receiving. The speaking tree. *The Times of India*, New Delhi/ Agra, Saturday, June 10, 2018.

Shannon, W. (2000). *Thomas Merton's paradise journey: Writings on contemplation.* Wellwood, UK: Burns & Oates.

Shapiro, D., Cook, I. A., Davydov, D. M., Ottaviani, C., Leuchter, A. F., & Abrams, M. (2007). Yoga as a complementary treatment of depression: Effects of traits and moods on treatment outcome. *Evidence-Based Complementary and Alternative Medicine, 4(*4), 493–502.

Sheldrake, P. (2007). *A brief history of spirituality*. USA: Wiley-Blackwell

Shults, F. Le., & Sandage, S. J. (2006). *Transforming spirituality: Integrating theology and psychology.* Grand Rapids, MI: Baker Books.

Sims, A. (1994). Psyche-spirit as well as mind? *British Journal of Psychiatry, 165*, 441 446.

Singh, L. K. (2005). *Kavya, Sangeet Sangeevani*. New Delhi: Kanishk Publishers.

Singh, L. P. (2010). *Tantra, its mystic and scientific basis* (p. 153). New Delhi: Concept Publishing Company Pvt. Ltd.

Singh, R., & Husain, A. (2015). Spiritual Practices Scale (Hindus). New Delhi: Prasad Psycho Corporation.

Singh, S. R. (2018). Direct your decisions & actions for unity. *The Speaking Tree.* The Times of India, Delhi. May 18, 2018.

Sinnott, E. W. (1969). Spirit. In W. Burnett (Ed.). *The spirit of man*. New York: Books For Libraries Press.

Sivananda, S. (1994). *Kundalini Yoga* (10th ed). Himalayas: Divine Life Society Publication.

Soumya, C. M., & Tamang, E. L. (2017). Assessment of effectiveness of Trataka exercise on vision and aesthenopia among student nurses with refractive error. *International Journal of Health Sciences and Research, 7*(4), 325-331.

Spiritual Science Research Foundation. (2013). What is the difference between prayer with expectations and without expectations? Retrieved January 14, 2016, from http://www.spiritualresearchfoundation.org/aboutspiritual research/SpiritualPractice/prayr/prayer_expectation.

Spirituality, (2016). Retrieved July 12, 2017, from http://psychiclibrary.com/beyondBooks/spirituality/

Srivastava, A. (2017). Service, A crucial part of deeper journey. *The Speaking Tree*. The Times of India, Delhi. October 26, 2017.

Storr, A. (1988). *Solitude: A return to self.* New York: Ballantine Books.

Streeter, C. C., Gerbarg, P. L., Whitfield, T. H., Owen, L., Johnston, J., Silveri, M. M.,... Jensen, J. E. (2017). Treatment of major depressive disorder with Iyengar Yoga and coherent breathing: A randomized controlled dosing study. *Journal of Alternative and Complementary Medicine, 23*(3), 201-207.

Sukhsohale, N., Phatak, M., Sukhsohale, S., & Agrawal, S. (2012). Does Raja Yoga meditation bring out physiological and psychological general well being among practitioners of it? *International Journal of Collaborative Research on Internal Medicine & Public Health, 4*(12), 2000-2012.

Swinton, J. (2001/2003). *Spirituality and mental health care: Rediscovering a 'Forgotten' dimension.* London and New York: Jessica Kingsley Publishers.

Tagare, G. V. (trans. 1993 [1976]. The Bhagavata purâna. Part 2 of 5: [skandhas 4-6]. Delhi: Motilal Banarsidass.

Talwadkar, S., Jagannathan, A., & Raghuram, N. (2014). Effect of *trataka* on cognitive functions in the elderly. *International Journal of Yoga, 7*(2), 96-103.

Taylor, C. (2007). *A secular age*. Cambridge, Mass: Harvard University Press

Taylor, E., Peterson, C., Oyedele, O., & Hasse, J. (2015). Spirituality and spiritual care of adolescents and young adults with cancer. *Seminars on Oncology Nursing, 31*(3), 227 241.

The Hindu Prayer Book (in Sanskrit and Roman with English translations). Retrieved on December 19, 2014, from http://www.lohana.info/data/culturecorner/HinduPrayerBook.pdf

The XIV Dalai Lama (2018). Compassion as the source of happiness. *The Speaking Tree*. The Times of India, Delhi. July 4, 2018.

Tiedmann, A., O'Rourke, S., Sesto, R., & Sherrington, C. (2013). A 12-Week Iyengar Yoga Program Improved Balance and Mobility in Older Community-Dwelling People: A Pilot Randomized Controlled Trial? *The Journals of Gerontology Series A Biological Sciences and Medical Sciences, 68*(9), 1068-1075.

Tilak, B. G. (1936). *Srimad Bhagvd Gita Rahasya*. Pune: Tilak Brothers.

Tilak, B. G. (1971). *Srimad Bhagvd Gita Rahasya* or Karma-Yoga Sastra, Translation by B. S. Sukhtankar. Pune: T. S. Tilak.

Trataka. (n.d.). Retrieved June 1, 2017, from http://www.yogaindailylife.org/system/en/hatha-yoga-kriyas/trataka

Udgeet pranayama – Steps – Benefits – Health School. (n.d.). Retrieved May 31, 2017, from http://www.healthschool.co.in/yoga/udgeet-pranayama-steps-benefits/

Vasanthan, S., Madanmohan, T., Bhavanani, A. B., Hanifah, M., & Jaiganesh, K. (2017). Comparative study on the effect of yogic relaxing asanas and pranayamas on cardiovascular response in healthy young volunteers. *National Journal of Physiology, Pharmacy and Pharmacology, 7*(1), 127-130.

Vaswani, Dada JP (2018). Practise meditation to energize body and mind. *The Speaking Tree*. The Times of India, New Delhi/ Agra, July 13, 2018.

Vaughan, F. (1986). *The inward arc*. Boston: New Science Library.

Vaughan, F. (1991). Spiritual issues in psychotherapy. *Journal of Transpersonal Psychology, 23*(2), 105–119.

Vedanta - A way of life. (2011, October 22). prayer-prarthana | Vedanta Philosophy | India. Retrieved on December 21, 2014, from http://www.vedantaindailylife.com/2011/10/practical-steps-to-spirituality-part 80.html

Vergote, A. (2003). Plying between psychology and mysticism. In J. Belzen, & A. Geels (Eds.), *Mysticism: A variety of psychological perspectives* (pp. 81–107). Amsterdam: Rodopi.

Vivekananda, S. (1972). *Complete works*. Calcutta: Advaita Ashrama, Fourteenth edition.

Vrinte, J. (1996). *The quest for the inner man: Transpersonal psychotherapy and integral Sadhana*. New Delhi: Motilal Banrasidas.

Waaijman, K. (2000). *Spirituality: Forms, foundations, methods*. Gent: Carmelitana.

Welcome to my intellect. (n.d.). Retrieved May 31, 2017, from http://www.myintellect.org/coursedetail.aspx?id=30

West, W. (2004). *Spiritual issues in therapy*. Hampshire: Palgrave MacMillan.

Why Restorative Yoga? – Ekhart Yoga. (n.d.). Retrieved May 31, 2017, from https://www.ekhartyoga.com/articles/why-restorative-yoga

Wikström, O. (2004). *Pyhän salaisuus: Kätketty todellisuus janykyaika*. Transl. by Oili Räsänen. Helsinki: Kirjapaja.

Wilber, K. (2000). *Integral psychology: Consciousness, spirit, psychology, therapy*. Boston: Shambhala Publications.

Wilber, K. (2001). *A brief history of everything*. Dublin: Gateway.

Woolery, A., Myers, H., Sternlieb, B., & Zeltzer, L. (2004). A yoga intervention for young adults with elevated symptoms of depression. *Alternative Therapies, 10*(2), 60-63.

Zaqzuq, Mahmud Hamdi (2000). *Mawsu'ah al-Mafahim al-Islamiyyah al-'Ammah*. Al-Qaherah: Majlis al-A'la lil shu'un al-Islamiyyah (baru jumpa balik rujukan ini…)

Zaydan, 'Abd al-Karim (2000). *Usul al-Da'wah*, Cet. ke-vii. Beirut: Muassasah al-Risalah.

Zhai, J. E., Ellison, C. G., Stokes, C. E., & Glenn, N. D. (2008). "Spiritual, but not religious:" The impact of parental divorce on the religious and spiritual identities of young adults in the United States. *Review of Religious Research, 49*(4), 379-394.

Zinnbauer, B. J., & Pargament, K. I. (2005). Religiousness and spirituality. In R. F. Poloutzian and C. L. Park (Eds.), *Handbook of the psychology of religion and spirituality* (pp. 21-42). New York: Guilford Press.

The Indian Diasporic Writing
(Theory and Discourse)

Edited by

Satyavir S Phulia

Principal, Govt. P.G. College,
Ambala Cantt (Haryana)

Hemant Verma

Asstt. Director Colleges
c/o Higher Education Commissioner
Panchkula (Haryana)

SHRI SAI PRINTOGRAPHERS
NEW DELHI

The Indian Disporic Writing: Theory and Disclosure

ISBN: 978-81-89996-07-9

Published in India by-
Shri Sai Printographers
101, 4787/23, Ansari Road,
Darya Ganj, New Delhi - 110 002
Phones - 23246222, 23246333, 41563422
Mobiles - 9312220441, 9811197091
e-mail - frienpub@yahoo.com,
sales@friendspublicationsindia.com

Laser Typesetting
Reliable Infomedia, Delhi

Printed in India
Navbharat Printing Press

CONTENTS

PREFACE

It was for the very first time that Government College, Ambala Cantt organized a seminar on literature in English on the thrust area "The Indian Diasporic Writing: Theory and Discourse." Though the college is very young (just 10 years old), it is striving hard to outshine in the orbs of academics and co-curricular activities. It has been a great privilege for this institute to be the host to the scholars from Indian universities and colleges for the scholarly contemplations in this seminar. These distinguished personalities, all of whom have earned a niche for themselves in their respective place of working, discussed in full details the issues, themes, theories, writers and artists of Indian diaspora. The coming together of so many luminaries resulted in far reaching deliberations and results thereof.

Seminars and conferences are always productive scholastic activities and they provide the teachers and researchers an apposite platform for the intellectual exchange. It also inculcates and imbibes the tendency of exploring new, unheard and finer nuances and ideas and the discussions of the same. I feel a real sense of pride that the college is developing a tradition of organizing seminars and conferences.

I am highly gratified and thankful to all the delegates from far and wide who spared so much of their valuable time to make this endeavor a grand success. Their contributions, which are there in your hands in the form of this book, would show the brilliance and high intellect. The Department of English and its faculty deserve all kudos for the thumping success of the seminar. The organizational skills and propensity with a lot of hard work and perseverance were the forte of my colleagues.

I acknowledge the contribution made by entire faculty and the supporting staff who remained a source of strength for me all the while during the seminar and but for whom the seminar would not have received the applause it did from all those who attended it.

I appreciate whole-heartedly the acumen, zealous and unrelenting efforts put in by Mr. Hemant Verma. The way he organized the proceedings with his adorable communication skills and his initiative to edit the papers in the present volume with a valuable introduction deserve all accolades. It is a well pain staking effort taken by him, which is there in the form of a compendium. The present book I must say is ***Love's Labour.***

This book will bring forward many new ideas and aspects of diaspora expressed by different scholars. Now these views will be disseminated widely among readers.

The memories of the seminar and the delegates still linger afresh in my mind. It was the start of an era in the history of Government College, Ambala Cantt. I hope that such efforts will be taken time and again by my colleagues and will add colour and grace to the profile of this college.

This volume will surely prove an asset to the students, researchers, and teachers of English Literature.

-Satyavir S Phulia

1

INTRODUCTION

-Hemant Verma

Diaspora - another beautiful offspring of globalization. Globalization is a fundoo term, which is very convenient to use, and it is all-inclusive. It is a phenomenon that tries to bring various people with various reasons together. It relates everything to everything. It is due to globalization, the term 'diaspora' or diasporic communities have seen the daylight. The term diaspora originally used for the Jewish externment from its homeland, is now applied as a 'metaphoric designation' for expatriates, refugees, exiles and immigrants. This term has its origin in Greek where it means "a scattering or sowing of seeds." It is used interchangeably to refer to the historical movements of the dispersed ethnic population of Israel, the cultural development of that population or the population itself. The probable origin of the word is the Septuagint version of Deuteronomy 28:25, "thou shalt be a dispersion in all Kingdoms of the earth." The term was incorporated from Greek into English in the late 20th Century with the establishment of the academic field of diaspora studies.

The 20th century was a spectator of the massive ethnic refugee crises, due to war and the rise of nationalism, fascism, communism and racism, as well as from natural disasters, economic collapse and Globalization. The West has always been an attraction to the people of Indian subcontinent. A very bright future and life style have always been a beautiful dream for the people of India Republic. Many Indians are settled in various countries of the world. The Indian Diaspora is a general term to describe the people who migrated from terrains that are currently with in the boarders of the Republic of India. It also refers to their descendants. The diaspora is currently estimated to number over twenty million. Indian citizens not residing in India (NRIs) and persons of Indian origin who have acquired the citizenship of some other country (PIOs) are used for Indian diaspora. The Indian diaspora covers practically every part of the world. Residing in distant lands, its members have succeeded amazingly in their chosen line of work by dint of their single-minded perseverance and hard work. What is more, they have retained their poignant, cultural and spiritual links with the country of their origin. This strikes a reciprocal arpeggio in the hearts of people of India. The symbolic relationship is fostering progressively. What is it that kindles the writers of diasporic writers to profess their feelings and ideas of their own country so painstakingly and candidly? There have been discussions and deliberations to probe into the recesses of the minds and psyche of diasporic writers of India and other countries. Diasporic literature is an amalgam of dual personality, cultural conflicts, questions of belongingness, placements and displacement, old values and new desires, identity crises, changing global conditions and psychological generation and de-generation. Diaspora, border, trans-national, transcultural, hybridity and diasporic are a few terms which are often used to denote the existence and emotions of dispersed people. "The term that once described Jewish, Greek and American dispersion now shares meanings with a larger semantic domain that includes words like immigrant, expatriate, refugee, guest worker, exile community, overseas community, ethnic community."(Tololian 1991: 4-5)

Diaspora, for the most part, necessitates longer distances and segregation more than expatriation. Diasporic forms of longings, nostalgic and (dis)location or identification are shared by a broad spectrum of minority and migrant populations. People disseminated from their native countries by vast oceans, political barriers and boundaries develop better relations with the aboriginal country due to the technological developments in the means of transport and communication. William Safran in his essay on Diaspora defines it as expatriate minority communities (1) that are dispersed from an original centre to at least two "peripheral" places, (2) that maintain a "memory, vision or myth about their original homeland,"(3) that "believe they are not-and perhaps cannot be-fully accepted by their host country," (4) that see the ancestral home as a place of eventual return, when the time is right;(5) that are committed to the maintenance or restoration of this homeland, and(6) of which the group's consciousness and solidarity are "importantly defined" by this continuing relationship with the homeland. (Safran)

It is an interesting paradox that a great deal of Indian writing in English is produced not in India but in widely distributed geographical areas of agreement ('Girmit') e. Indian Diaspora in the South Pacific, the Caribbean, South Africa, Mauritius and the contemporary Indian diasporas in the U.S.A., the U.K., Canada and Australia. Frankly speaking the very idea of "India" needs to the understood properly when contextualized in the backdrop of cultural study of the Indian Diaspora. Given the context does "India" mean a nation-state or a larger civilizational identity? And, if it connotes "South Asia", then how do South Asian diasporans articulate themselves today? These are certainly the issues which deserve serious attention.

With more and more writers of India origin settling abroad and engaging themselves in creating writing in the countries of their domicile, the theoretical problem is that of the critical parameters by which their works have to be defined and assessed. Although there are certain common resonances in the literary representations of the experience of the writers of the 'indenture' and the 'new' Indian diaspora, the responses and the narratives of the individual writers vary greatly. Writers like A. K. Ramanujan, Agha Shahid Ali, Bharati Mukherjee, David Dabydeen, M. G. Vassanji, Meena Alexander, Rohinton Mistry, Salman Rushdie, Satendra Nandan, V. S. Naipaul, to mention a few, differ from each other not only in their socio-cultural backgrounds and literary ancestries but also in their thematic preoccupations and literary styles. Further, the responses of the diasporic writers to India are also varied and not always adulatory; they range from sentimentality and nostalgia to a cynical celebration of their coming of age. However, their diasporic condition, their sense of exile and alienation and their efforts to seek replenishment by making symbolic returns to their origins bind all this writing into a unity. The theoretical and literary possibilities of the writings of Indian diaspora are immense.

There crops up many questions and concerns related to the theoretical and literary possibilities of the Indian Diaspora Writers. There are issues like nature of the diasporic aesthetics of the writers of Indian Diaspora in order to theorize the literature of Indian diaspora. How do the socio-political and cultural transformation, acculturation, adaptation, accommodation and integration in the diasporic communities happen? The questions of self/identity in the diasporic experience; cultural identity cross the class, gender and ethnicity, the issues of religion the challenges of linguistics, their economies and various diasporas like Punjabi and Gujrati need to be searched.

Why does diaspora writing evoke strong emotions? Colonial othering has been replaced or even displaced by neo-imperial forms of longing, lamentation, bewilderment, benevolence and malevolence towards the other. These feelings are fuelled and altered by increased globalization and panic at the visibility and ease with which the other appears to profit from its very otherness while participating in the practices of an everyday life in what should be for the other anything but ordinary.

Class and gender play crucial roles in the fashioning of not just the diaspora but also the diaspora's interaction with and investment in cultures that define an ethics of ethnicity. Newer diasporas are more concerned with trying to maintain umbilical ties with home/desh, even as the manner in which these ties manifest themselves vary generationally. A post '65 migrating generation imagines India very differently than say a post '80s generation and a post 2000 generation.

Sangeeta Ray exclaims in her online article 'Through the Looking Glass' that to generalize, one could say without much qualification that an earlier generation felt greatly unmoored and anchored themselves by holding on to an ethos characterized as, say India, evoking tradition as a key that helped them expand and share a common idea of home with other similar minded folks even as it helped keep at bay the immanent threat of an invading foreign public sphere. The separation of public and private so crucial to colonialism and nationalism resurfaces in the U.S., Canada, England, and Australia as a way of marking difference.

We are here but not quite. We want to be home but not yet and so we continue to recreate home as a desire to resituate the discourses of us versus them. The us has a cultural superiority rooted in ideas of tradition and community that confirms some of the fundamental tenets of an orientalist discourse. It is an anxious withholding of modernity in the face of a material modernity so desired by the us. The rituals of custom are furiously and often desperately maintained so that the us does not get swallowed up by the them who are merely dedicated to an ever developing materialist modernity.

In contrast, newer generations growing up in a much more hybrid world, a postmodern, globalized, digital, consumer capitalist world has less trouble negotiating the us and them divide. And again class is a crucial marker of Cosmo political ability-to be at home anywhere and everywhere. This is called cosmopolitics and not cosmopolitanism because the cosmopolitical while sharing non-nationalist ideals with the cosmopolitan enjoys the idea of home and this enjoyment while not entirely independent of gender is far more androgynous than ever imagined by an earlier migrating population.

Then there is the second generation of South Asian Americans-the unforgiving acronym of ABCD (American Born Confused Desis) only touches the tip of the cultural iceberg they are challenged to confront and negotiate. All this and more forms the content of many novels originating in the diaspora.

The effervescence of diaspora gives rise to a sense of disillusionment. The sense is infact, the consciousness of exile. Such a consciousness is a reflection of crises of the diasporic community, at being denied a central and nurturing tradition. The diasporic writing diverges from immigrant writing in its preoccupative with the attachment to the homeland. Exile and expatriate writings are more immersed in the situation at home and the circumstances that prolong the individual's exile or expatriation than with the émigré's or émigré community's relationship with the dominant society. Diasporic writing then is about or by people who are linked by common histories of uprooting and dispersal, common homelands, and common cultural heritages, but it develops different cultural particularities of the dominant society. Given its historical and cultural dualities, conflicts, contradictions, and ambivalences, diasporic writing has an inherent complexity, which is amplified when—as in literature at large—the writer's personal experiences are brought into the equation.

The literature of diaspora defines a space that can be distinguished from the literature of 'stay at home' writers. Texts that deal with the pain of having to live on the fringes of another society are in some ways easier to classify and group. The diasporic writings cause a sense of alienation and uprooted ness. The diasporic writers are often concerned with the outer reaches of the immigrant experience, the point at which it intersects with the larger community and causes discrimination and cultural conflict. These sorts of writings capture a feeling of space among the immigrant communities.

With a milieu of exile and expatriation, the diasporic writers portray their memories and experiences about the 'hyphenated' identity. Such an identity has developed a feeling of space—a space that the immigrant communities can declare as their own.

Through vividness, zeal and spirit, these diasporic writers have demonstrated the ambience and sensation of identity. They emphasize the ardent effervescence of warmth and vehemence of being segregated to a 'hyphenated' space, as well as identity, in the other multicultural country. So their writings usually focus on the discrimination, differentiation, and injustices, inequities that have been a part of almost every Indian immigrant. Such treatment of life has compelled them to become nostalgic. Perhaps that is the reason why, the diasporic writers tend to draw upon the reservoir of memories from their homelands.

Bhim S. Dahiya, a renowned scholar and academician explores the dynamics of diasporic discourse in his essay 'The Dynamics of Diasporic Discourse: An Overview'. Dahiya discusses at length the origin, the growth, formulation and explication of Diaspora 'the concept.' He argues that diaspora; the term does have not a stable meaning to be defined as a theory. This paper details the history of various diasporas in different ages such as the diasporic experience of those who were displaced within 'their own' homelands like the tribals and other poor communities and also dalits and adivasis. Then, there came the external diasporas in Europe and America the reasons for which was economic progress and development. Bhim S Dahiya says that the diasporic studies do not remain a matter of cultural domain alone and that we need to develop an equally complex discourse for comprehending and classifying the phenomenon of continual displacement. One can not subside the issues of inequalities on the basis of caste, class and gender in the writings of diaspora writers living outside country. Sometimes it is felt that diasporic discourse is insensitive to gender inequalities. Then Dahiya brings forth the views of Mathew Arnoldian on culture, civilization and barbarism. He further puts forth the ideas of Lionel Trilling on literature, socialization, mass culture and radical polities etc. He exhorts that the critical discourse of diasporic literature should be viewed in a larger context of post structuralist poetics. The established canon and its critical credo should be demystified. The demystified critics must act as models of what means to be intellectual freedom-fighters and should also show the resistance to the homogenizing discourse of globalization and the like.

Diasporic writings focus on an important aspect of the post modern condition in which responsibilities of citizens cross national boundaries. The earlier modernist notions of center and margin, home and exile, familiar and strong are falling apart. The power theory, community, space and time are replacing the geographical, cultural and ethnic borders. However, the present day theories are merely political and ideological unlike the earlier theories which were political, ideological, moral, aesthetic standards and all other new concerns.

Tejinder Kaur in her paper 'Portrayal of Diaspora Issues in Indian Diasporic Writings' presents various issues related to diasporic experience and writings, the literature and literary theory. Elaborating these concerns in the writings of many diasporic writers writing in English and other languages as well, she starts with defining the term 'Diaspora.' Tejinder Kaur deals with the nostalgia and yearnings of the diaspora in The Mystic

Masseur and The Mimic Men by V.S. Naipaul and Maluka by Sadhu Singh Dhami. According to Tejinder Kaur, the diasporas face cultural dilemmas, identity crisis and feel displaced. She also enables us to see through various terms like 'internal space,' 'diaspora consciousness', 'diaspora space', 'hybrid space', 'third scenario,' ' the third New World presence' given by different theorists like Homi K. Bhabha, Gayatri Chakroborty, Stuart Hall, Avtar Brah, Paul Gilroy, Robert Bromley etc. She prefaces that the main concerns about Diaspora issues are dislocation, marginalization, racial hatred, cultural and gender conflicts, subjectivities shown in the writings of Bharati Mukherjee, Meera Syal, Jhumpa Lahiri, Chitra Banerjee, Iqbal Ramoowalia, Susham Bedi,Jarnail Singh and Nakshdeep Panjkoha. The plight of the illegal immigrants, sexual abuse is detailed by Iqbal Ramoowalia, Bharti Mukherjee, Divakaruni and Susham Bedi. The pitiable conditions of immigrant children and the racial hatred find expression in Meera Syal, Chitra Benerjee and Susham Bedi's Havan etc. The Inter-generational gap between the first, and the second generations of diaspora is depicted ably by Jhumpa Lahiri in The Namesake and Meera Syal's Anita and Me. Tejinder kaur also discusses the works and themes of Punjabi writers like Dalip Kaur Tiwana, Nakshdeep Panjokha, Parvej Kaur Sandhu, Rani Nagender, Veena Verma and Gurpreet Dhaliwal. She pertinently observes, "out of these cross- cultural confrontations, interactions and dialogues, new hybrid subjectivities are getting formed which indeed are contributing to the growth of human consciousness and development both at the global and local levels.

The next article 'Indian Diasporic Writers- Living on the Margin of Two Societies' is mainly a survey piece wherein Ritu Sharma reviews various themes, the colonial processes, the experiences and nostalgia of the diaspora. Ritu Sharma finds that the diasporic community is very complex and full of variety and any attempt at homogenization leads only to over simplification. She discusses the bicultural pulls and the emergence of a new culture. Taking clues from Arnold Harrichand Itwaru and Vassanji, Ritu Sharma comments that the immigrant writer himself experiences all the diasporic experiences and becomes a custodian of the collective history of people. She very usefully helps us to pass the bridge between the first and the second generations of diasporas, their outlook and their thinking. According to her, "whenever we adopt from one-another's culture and our hopes and aspirations are redefined in this manner, this is a positive way forward. In anyway, culture is a moving phenomenon and not a static thing."

The main concern of Neer Kanwal Mani in her essay 'Word/ Image: Intersection of Literature and Art in the Diasporic Context' is the articulation of various issues of self and identity in diasporic experience that underwrite the literature and art being produced by women. Neer discusses at length the idea of the self and identity issues of women. Women have never got their real place in the works of male artists. So there is an emergence of feminist studies like cyber feminism and eco-feminism. This paper presents the representation of self in Meena Alexander's works and Chila Kumari Burman's art. Both these artists struggle hard to locate their identities and self due to their relocation in other countries. The autobiography of Meena Alexander Fault Lines represents her travails in establishing herself and her identity in another country, different surroundings. This self consciousness and quest for identity also finds expression in her poetry. Neer aptly examines the insights of Alexander in her poem 'Black River, Walled Garden' which regards childhood as the place when she started as a poet and her present day persona of being a poet. Similar are the experiences of Chila Kumari Burman for whom identity is the coming together of many unassimilable perspective. The conflicts of gender, culture, ethnicity are well woven in the collages of Burman. Neer says,

"Both Meena and Chila's works represent a desire to figure them afresh, and to make up their lives in a diasporic world." The question of identity in an alien country often leads to confusion; one identity is shed for another and another for another. Neer concludes her piece with Alexander's poem 'Night-Scene, the Garden' in which the poet feels that boundaries and borders are blurred into a "no man's land" and with Meena Alexander's comment "fluid selves, porous boundaries."

Anita Sharma assesses Gita Mehta's A River Sutra in terms of cultural space and diaspora in her paper 'Cultural Space and Diaspora.' Beginning her piece with the premise that Indian culture takes life as a pilgrimage and a sojourn on this planet where diaspora and diasporic journey becomes an appropriate metaphor for the human condition. Anita Sharma compares the journey of life till death and even after that as another dimension of diaspora. She defines diaspora as a shift from the unknown to the alien resulting in a social, psychological and cultural void and leading to a trishanku like situation. A River Sutra presents a diversity of cultures within India which are connected by the force of river Narmada and the narrator protagonist who is the 'Sutradhar'. It presents independent stories of Hindu and Jain ascetics, courtesans, minstrels, merchants, Muslim clerics and teachers etc. Gita Mehta's novel reflects the complexity of India's mythology and cultural heritage. Gita Mehta looks at her homeland from the distance in time and space and creates a miniature multicultural India within her novel. In this way, she tries to cope up with her isolation and ambivalent situation in a distant country. Anita Sharma concludes by saying that the movement away from the constricting traditional culture gives the writer a power to discover the 'self' and the cultural spaces within diaspora.

Kiran Kamboj in her essay 'The Indian Diaspora and Raja Rao as a Diasporic Writer' takes us to a beautiful journey in the history of Indian diaspora , its experiences, the past and the present conditions and the know-how of Indian diasporic writers of early 20th century. Her paper focuses on the works of Raja Rao and the influence of Gandhi, Sri Aurobindo, Rama Maharishi and Pandit Tara Nath etc.on the novels of Raja Rao beginning with Kanthapura, The Serpent and the Rope, and The Cat and Shakespeare.

We move to another aspect of diaspora with Alka Sharma in her piece 'Crisis of Unbelongingness in Raja Rao's The Serpent and the Rope'. Starting with the premise 'Home is where your feet are and may your heart be there', Alka Sharma introduces Raja Rao as a diasporic writer who lives the most part of his life in the West and had the nostalgic feelings of a diaspora. Alka tries to explore the cultural differences in the lives of an Indian Man and his French wife. Through Ramaswamy and Madeliene, Raja Rao brings home the fact that India can be known better living in the West. East and West are presented not only as geographical or historical entities but also as ideas, living traditions, cultural, racial, philosophical and metaphysical manifestation. The deep nostalgia for India can be felt in the lines in which Raja Rao says, '... I would go back to India, for that India was my breath, my only sweetness, gentle and wise; she was my mother...' Indian culture, history and literature are so much deep rooted in Ramaswamy that he feels alienated in France. The extent of his attachment to India is very much visible when he exclaims, 'Paris is a sort of Benaras turned outward.' Going through the saga of Ramaswamy, his relations with Madeliene and Savithri, his hypocrisy, his quest for self, existence, Alka Sharma concludes by saying that to belong to any place, a man should know himself.

In the next chapter, Bhan Singh tries to explore the community feelings of another famous diasporic writer Rohinton Mistry. The aspect which he has chosen is 'The Parsi Feelings in the novel Such a Long Journey'. Introducing Rohinton Mistry to the readers, his background, his works, his journey from India to Canada and the accolades which he received for his writings, Bhan Singh says that the backdrop of Such a Long Journey is Indo Pak war of 1971. The impact of the times on the lives of the hero, Gustad Noble and his family is very well depicted by Mistry. Noble's belief in the destiny that we should accept whatever is written for us. And his long journey in this feeling less and malevolent world is in a way the journey of an ethnic group, a community which is on the verge of extinction. Noble does not have very high dreams and ambitious. However, his modest expectations always receive jolts and denials. The role of fate and chance in the whole episode of Gusted Noble's life is very poignantly depicted in the novel. A sense of displacement which is always there in the diasporic writers is also presented in this novel in the exclamations of another character Dinshawji on the changes of street names. The novel ends on a note of reconciliation. This was a long journey in which there was good and evil as well. It presents Mistry's feelings for his community and country.

Elaborating Rohinton Mistry as a diasporic writer, Suman Bhatia delineates the theme of Oppression and Resistance in Rohinton Mistry's A Fine Balance in her paper. Suman grounds her essay in the statement that the Indian expatriates belong to a country which is not monolithic. Hence, all of them try to relate to their original homeland with its myths and culture. Suman very rightly and emphatically says that alienation is not a feature of the diasporic subject. And that inequality and disenfranchisement related to class, gender, sexuality and ethnicity inevitably produce alienated and marginalized individuals. This statement is being applied on the works of Rohinton Mistry where we have internal displacements and dislocations of class, gender, community with in the country. Mistry, a Zoroastrian Parsi, explores the feelings of Parsi community, their cultural identity and their different life styles. Bhatia says that Mistry loves to take the down trodden, oppressed and exploited people in Indian society. A Fine Balance is a story of Dina Dalal, a widow, Maneck Kohlah, Iswar Darzi, his nephew Om Prakash and Shanker, the beggar. These characters are brought together by the force of circumstance and necessity. All of them are repressed, poor and oppressed whose resistance is often subdued. And they also meet a tragic end. The survivors are those characters who have been able to maintain a fine balance in their lives.

The next paper gives us a comparative study of two diasporic writers attitudes towards West: Rohinton Mistry and Jhumpa Lahiri. Sarika Goyal's essay 'Different Attitudes Towards West: A Study of Mistry and Lahiri' presents how Rohinton Mistry and Jhumpa Lahiri take on the West. Sarika Goyal feels that writers of Indian diaspora feel an otherness, a rootless ness and apathy while living in other countries. The feelings are more or less the same but there is a difference of the milieu, gender, age, community and ideas. This is what Sarika endeavors to present through Mistry and Lahiri. Rohinton Mistry's writings are influenced by his being a Parsi, his maleness, his interest in politics, cricket etc. And Jhumpa Lahiri being a Bengali advocates Bengal, its cuisine, architecture, dresses and customs. Mistry's novels are full of ethnic consciousness and he tries to reshape his dissatisfaction into the blind acceptance of things or becomes critical at times. Whereas in Lahiri's The Namesake, the characters of the new generation are completely acclimatized and do not feel any diasporic pangs and traumas. Lahiri presents a multicultural society where the characters adjust themselves with the new environment for being successful. And Mistry shows varied trends in delineating human relationship with the Parsi threads always pulling back. Comparing and contrasting Mistry and Lahiri, Goyal shows that every writer should follow a global approach though being concerned about personal identity.

A. K. Singh assesses 'The Tiger's Daughter in terms of Bharti Mukherjee's Diasporic Experiences'. Mukherjee writes of identity issues, cultural clashes and belongingness. A. K. Singh says that some immigrants face dislocation and rootlessness and other relocate themselves. This relocation leads to the re routings of the self which forms the core of diasporic experience. The Tiger's Daughter is a study of the differences between the eastern and the western, the past and the present and the real and imagined selves. Tara, the heroine, her past, her settlement in New York, her stay in Bombay, her journey to Calcutta and her reaction to India as a diasporic and her cultural dilemmas between American and Indian way of life are well depicted in this saga of alienation and belongingness. The Tiger's Daughter presents the predicament of someone returning to her homeland and for whom home is not home again and who once again prefers the life of exile. For A. K. Singh, Mukherjee appears to be saying that passages to and out of India will cause pain and bewilderment. He concludes his essay by proclaiming that this novel brings to the fore the predicament of an Indian who wants to redefine her ties to her homeland.

Similar twinges and echoes can be heard in the next essay '(Re)membering Selves: Dislocation and Fulfilment in Chitra Banerjee Divakaruni's Arranged Marriage' by Sanjeev Kumar. Sanjeev starts this piece with Salman Rushdie's stance on Expatriates which says that physical alienation from our country means that we will not be capable of reclaiming the thing that was lost but can create that country in fiction, in imagination. And applying this statement to Arranged Marriage a collection of short stories by Chitra Banerjee Divakaruni, Sanjeev Kumar says that the expatiates try to forget their past and adopt new ways of living and thus give birth to a crisis of belonging to nowhere. They further face dislocation and try to get fulfilment and hence suffer. Elaborating this theme of dislocation and fulfilment, Sanjeev explores the stories and characters of

Divakaruni's Arranged Marriage. He analyses the 'dim-descried' future and unforgettable past which the protagonists like Sumita in 'Clothes', Jayanti in 'Silver Pavements, Golden Roofs,' Shona of 'The Word Love' share. Most of the stories present Indians caught in the conflicting values of east and west, fighting their sense of dislocation and preparing them to be a member of the new world while deciding not to remember the past. Kumar pertinently observes that the world of Arranged Marriage is a large room with many windows showing assorted experiences of Indian Americans on an isthmus of 'here' and 'there'. Chitra Banerjee touches upon the issues like interracial relationships, economic disparity, abortion, divorce, racial bigotry and the dilemma of Indian women caught between all these. There is an urge to locate their wounded selves back and a struggle to get fulfilment in the new world in all the protagonists.

In the next essay on Chitra Banerjee's Arranged Marriage, Amrit Kaur deals with another aspect of this very interesting writer which deals with old values and new desires. Amrit Kaur touches upon the experiences of émigré women in new country, in new culture and surroundings. In this paper, Amrit probes into the divergent experiences of women liberated and at the same time trapped in the conflicting worlds of home and host countries. Issues like extramarital relations, adultery, love, the issue of personal space, divorce have been shown light in the stories of the book. Amrit examines that most of the stories are told from the first person singular point of view, in the present tense with a female voice of intimacy and cinematic credibility. She delves into the world of the protagonists in 'Silver Pavements, Golden Roofs', 'Affair', 'Clothes', 'The Word Love' and concludes that every story presents a balance between old beliefs and values and new desires. Chitra Banerjee depicts her characters as victims of changed circumstances who struggle hard to survive in a distant country.

We see to another side of the Indianness through the eyes

of another diasporic writer Shashi Tharoor in the next article 'Voices of Sanity amid Communal Frenzy in Shashi Tharoor's Riot written jointly by Karan and Jyoti Yadav. Karan and Jyoti start the essay with the definitions of the term 'diaspora' and distinct diasporic literature and themes. The writers exclaim that the diasporic writings are marked by secular and not so secular bent of mind of the writers. Most of diasporic writers are not influenced by the dogmatic influences of their religions. They feel pain and anguish when they delineate the communal madness of their people and depict their hatred and harmony as well. Jyoti and Karan review communalism and sanity in Riot by Tharoor. Explaining communalism and then relating its implications in the society, the writers present a bird's eye view of the narrative of the novel Riot. Riot presents Priscilla Hart, her stabbing in Hindu Muslism riots of 1989, characters like Ali, Makhan Singh, Ram Charan Gupta, Geetha and there are other characters like Professor Sarwar, V. Laxman, Gurvinder and his father who voice sanity. The piece is concluded with the remark that secularism has been an incontrovertible part of Indian sensibility and Shashi Tharoor uses it aptly and emphatically.

In his essay, 'Diasporic Element of 'Liminality' in V.S. Naipaul's Early Novels and his Travelogues on India', Sanjiv Kumar quotes from Victor Turner to define diasporas as 'transitional beings' or ' liminal personae' because they oscillate between one culture and another. He further explains the term 'liminal' as belonging to the point of conscious awareness below which something can not be experienced or felt. V. S. Naipaul was two times displaced, first from the land of his ancestors and then from his birth place, Sanjiv contends that the conflict between the East Indian traditions and West Indian estrangement which is seen in the early novels of Naipaul is a result of this transition of culture. Naipaul's life had been a journey from one country to other, one culture to another and one house from another. A House for Mr.Biswas depicts Naipaul's father's life-long quest for a 'home'. Kumar also presents themes of his other three early novels Mystic Masseur, Miguel Street, Suffrage of Elvira and the autobiographical elements in A House for Mr. Biswas. Sanjiv also discusses Naipaul's vivid experienc es of his visits to India three times. He felt hurt on his first visit which he records in his book An Area of Darkness. He records the objective experiences of his second visit to India in 1975-76 in his travelogue India: A Wounded Civilization and his stance on communalism, minorities and dalits in his third travelogue India: A Million Mutinies Now. Sanjiv concludes his paper by asserting that Naipaul is different from other diasporic writers in the sense that he shows disinterestedness towards host culture and home culture as well. He is near to being liminal as he watches the world without being biased and does not feel any sense of suffering or alienation.

'Diaspora: Vision and Image' is a incredible version of diasporic experiences in sketches by Gagandeep Kaur.

The above papers discuss the Indian diasporic writings, the theory and the discourse as well. Most essays presented in this collection give us a sufficient insight into the many writers who do offer a deeper and more serious engagement with the Indian diaspora. Various theorists and novelists have been detailed. But it is felt that the undercurrent themes are more or less the same i.e. the alienation, the oppression, the nostalgia in the writings of many a writers. The paper writers deserve all accolades. I am too small and feel humbled to say anything on the writings but I am sure the endeavor will be appreciated.....

References

1. http//en.wikipedia.org/wiki/Diaspora
2. http//www.india-seminar.com
3. Tololian, Khachig. 1991, The Nation State and its Others: In Lieu of a Preface. Diaspora 1(1):3-7
4. Safran, William. 1991, Diasporas in Modern Societies: Myths of Homelands and Return. Diaspora 1 (1): 83-99

2
The Dynamics Of Diasporic Discourse: An Overview

Bhim S. Dahiya

Diaspora, like any other theoretical concept, has its own dynamics of origin and growth, formulation and explication. Originally used for the dispersed Jewish community living throughout the Gentile nations, the term has been extended to include other displaced populations due to slavery, colonialism, forced or wilful migrations. Thus, diaspora has now become "the domain", as James Clifford has remarked, "of shared and discrepant meanings, adjacent maps and histories, which we need to sort out and specify as we work our way into a comparative, intercultural studies."[1] In his editorial preface to the first issue of Diaspora, Khachig Tololian chose to describe diasporas as "the exemplary communities of the transnational moment," adding that "the term that once described Jewish, Greek, and Armenian dispersion now shares meanings with a larger semantic domain that includes words like immigrant, expatriate, refugee, guest-worker, exile community, overseas community, ethnic community."[2]

In the postmodern era of theorization, no term, including diaspora, is allowed to acquire a stable meaning, for the central premise of THEORY is to question whatever seems to have stabilized. Faced with too much theorization in our time, one begins to wonder with Lucian, a rhetorician of 2nd century A. D., if there could be a concept "not open to exception nor combated by one as soon as propounded by another."[3] It has become increasingly difficult in the reign of THEORY to define in distinct terms different paradigms; such as those of diaspora and borderland, for instance, which often overlap in the present-day world. For dispersed peoples, once separated from homelands by vast oceans and political barriers, now increasingly find themselves in broader relations with the homeland, thanks to the advancement of the technologies of transport and communication. A further mutation of the term emerges when one takes into account the diasporic experience of those displaced within "their own" homelands. These displacements include those of Tribals and other poor communities that are driven out of their settlements by big dams, multinational companies, and sheer necessity of subsistence. Arundhati Roy gives astounding accounts of such displacements in here recent book.[4] The displacements caused by these "temples of modern India," as Nehru described them, is estimated to be of 50 million people, mostly Dalits and Adivasis, which is almost 3 times the population of Australia, and 10 times the historical Indian displacement of 1947. Half the total number of them, by the way, is in India, which number over three thousand three hundred. These internal diasporas in our own land bring forth more touching narratives of displacement difficulties than those generated by the external diasporas in Europe or America. Communities, after all, are much smaller than nation-states and their displacement from their roots for reasons of development or devastation, economic disparity or ethnic dominance makes them experience the same diasporic feelings that the overseas Indians articulate in their narratives.

Then, there is a form of diaspora that over a period of time assumes the character of the colonizer, inviting as sharp resentment against itself from the native population as does the imperial power. The English diaspora in America underwent several changes of status, from diaspora to colony to ruling group, all in less than a span of two centuries. The Indian diasporas in Fiji, Mauricius, and several African countries have been viewed in that light by the native populations of those countries, inviting severe hostility against their alleged economic exploitation. Hence its status is not stable and permanent, it keeps undergoing change perpetually. We should not feel surprised if after 50 years, the Asian diaspora in England outnumbers the natives. Also, if at bottom what divides castes and classes, ethnic and tribal groups, is the disparity in economic position and developmental status among various populations, their diasporic studies don't remain a matter of cultural domain alone. In that case, it cuts across the boundaries of homeland nation-states. In other words, the diasporic discourse gathers metaphoric and symbolic meanings around an originally simple concept of demography. The internal caste and class-groupings within the diasporas, ranging from the exploiter to the exploited, cannot also be overlooked. Equally un-ignorable is the neo-colonial feeling of superiority which most overseas Indians display when they visit their homeland.

Another strand in the dynamics of the diasporic discourse is that of minority feeling, which is relative among different ethnic or caste communities. The antagonism among different ethnic and caste groups percolates to regions within a single state down to small localities within a single town. Viewed from this perspective no ethnic or cultural group can be said to have remained untouched by the perpetual phenomenon of dispersal and displacement. It also needs to be remembered that the phenomenon of dispersal and displacement was not gifted by 19th century European imperialism or colonialism; it has always been there all along the course of human history. Lucian, himself a diasporic writer in Athens in 2nd century A.D., discovers in his successful journey to Heaven, under the fictitious name Icaromenippus, that "there was a group of Gods whose alien origin left them in a rather doubtful position."[5] Thus, it can be seen that the subject of diaspora has grown into something quite complex, especially in the postcolonial and neocolonial globalized world of our time. Accordingly, there is a need to develop an equally complex discourse for comprehending and classifying the phenomenon of continual displacement.

Besides, we cannot afford to lose sight of the difference between the phenomenon of mobility triggered by economic globalization and the historical displacements of earlier times. The two phenomena are radically different from each other and create and promote two very different responses to the fact of distance from the homeland. As we go along in the various directions and at different depths of the problem we discover that the dynamics of the discourse of diaspora has gained stupendous magnitude in its vast range of meanings. As Gayatri Spivak has observed, international or post-colonial issues are often more comfortably dealt with than antagonisms closer to home, differences structured by race and class. For at the level of every day social practices cultural differences are persistently radicalized, classed, and gendered.[6] Diaspora theories also need to account for these concrete, cross-cutting structures. The point is that the inequalities fostered for long by caste and class, race and religion, in the name of customs and traditions are followed by the diasporas with as much zeal as by their communities back home. The charge from this viewpoint is that theories and discourses that diasporize or internationalize "minorities" can deflect attention from long-standing socially structured inequalities of caste and class, and politically fostered inequalities of dominant and disadvantaged groups.

An internal dissenting voice has also been rising from the female members of the diasporas, characterizing the diasporic discourse as insensitive to gender inequalities. The point made by this section of the diaspora is that the diasporic discourse talks of travel and displacement in unmarked ways, normalizing and universalizing male experiences. The pertinent question raised is: do diaspora experiences reinforce or loosen gender subordination? One cannot ignore to mention here the unflattering record of the overseas matrimonial practices in Punjab, responsible for all sorts of cruelties to women.

The ancient and medieval practices of rituals and ceremonies, feasts and festivals, tirades and traditions, which the diasporas perpetuate in the name of homeland causes and cultures, have only helped maintain the male dominance in the "community." Thus, diasporic discourse becomes a site for another form of gender conflict within the larger domain of the postcolonial reinterpretation of history and civilization.

Viewed historically, however, the present-day quarrel about culture springs from the Mathew Arnoldian formulation of a secular and humanistic view of culture, which seeks to do away with classes; to make the best that has been thought and known in the world current everywhere; to make all men live in an atmosphere of sweetness and light...[7]

Arnold had designed his weapon of culture as a shield against the dangers he foresaw from an arrogant aristocracy and an anarchic working-class. But Arnold's project got disrupted by the collapse of nineteenth-century Europe; the collapse was formalized by World War I. T. S. Eliot, essentially Arnoldian in his view of culture, attempted to reconstitute and redefine the highbrow (European) culture after the said collapse of the imperial Europe. For him, contemporary history had become, as Stephen Dadelus declares in James Joyce's Ulysses, "a nightmare from which he was trying to awake."[8] Significantly, Eliot, in his famous review of Ulysses, describes to novel's world, the contemporary Europe, as "an immense panorama of futility and anarchy."[9] Decidedly, very much like Arnold, Eliot was strongly smitten with the idea of civilization and the horror of barbarism.

The post-World War II exponent of highbrow culture, a direct descendent of Arnold and Eliot, Lionel Trilling, in his renowned essay, "on the Teaching of Modern Literature," expressed serious suspicion of the academization of knowledge. He puts his probing of the issue as under:

Can we not say that, when modern literature is brought into the classroom, the subject being taught is betrayed by the pedagogy of the subject? We have to ask ourselves whether in our day too much does not come within the purview of the academy. More and more, as the universities liberalize themselves, turn their beneficent imperialistic gaze upon what is called Life Itself, the feeling grows among our educated classes that little can be experienced unless it is validated by some established intellectual discipline.[10]

What Trilling actually seems to lament in the said essay is that university teaching often silences and domesticates radical and subversive literary works. In other words, it turns them into subject "of merely habitual regard." Interestingly, this process of what Trilling calls "the socialization of the anti-social, or the acculturation of the anti-cultural, or the legitimization of the subversive" leads him to "question whether in the Western culture the study of literature is any longer a suitable means for developing and refining the intelligence."[11] Obviously, Trilling is not asking here in a spirit of undermining the academy but rather of emphasizing the possible failure of the Arnoldian view of culture to contain what Trilling perceives as the philistine and anarchic alternatives becoming more and more available to students of the 1960's and the subsequent decades-namely, mass culture and radical politics.

With the decolonization of the third world (Asia, Africa and Latin America) in the later half of the twentieth century, the decolonized sensibilities crusaded civil rights, gender and ethnic movements. It is in this historical context that the diasporic literatures have secured their own spaces, within and alongside the mainstream literatures of the western world. The critical discourse of diasporic literature, too, has to be viewed in the same larger context of the post-structuralist poetics. Confirming Trilling's fears, the most illuminating mode of theoretical inquiry in the postmodern era has been the demystification of the established canon and its critical credo. All those who promote the new cultural politics of difference must perforce adopt the demystificatory mode of critical enquiry and interpretation. The stable springboards for the most desirable forms of critical practice which take history seriously include political and social analysis of empire, determinism, class, race, gender, nation and region. This mode attempts to trace the complex dynamics of institutional and other related power structures for disclosing options and alternatives in the service of transformational praxis. It also tries to grasp the manner in which representational strategies are creative responses to changing circumstances and conditions. No doubt, this method is partisan, partial, engaged, and crisis-centered. But it also keeps open a sceptical eye so that it can avoid dogmatic traps, formulaic formulations, or rigid conclusions. It is decidedly anti-canonist and anti-essentialist.

Such an approach is, however, not without attendant dangers or traps, the most formidable of which being reductionism, be it of sociological, psychological, or historical sort. One way to avoid this trap is to stay attuned to the best of what the mainstream has to offer in terms of its paradigms, viewpoints, and methods, and yet to maintain an orientation in affirming and enabling subcultures of criticism. The demystified critics must act as models of what it means to be intellectual freedom-fighters, striking their position within or alongside the mainstream critics, while clearly aligning with those who vow to offer resistance to the homogenizing discourse of globalization and like. As Cornel West has put it, "The new cultural polities of difference can thrive only if there are communities, groups, organizations, institutions, subcultures, and networks of people of colour who cultivate critical sensibilities and personal accountability-without inhibiting individual expressions, curiosities, and idiosyncrasies."[12]

The phenomenon of multi-culturalism, responsible for the production of diasporic writing, is itself an aspect of post-modernism, which proclaims multicultural and multi-ethnic societies, promoting the politics of difference. In this condition, identity is no longer unitary or essential; rather, it is fluid and shifting, shaped by multiple sources and assuming multiple forms. In other words, there is no such thing as woman or Asian. However curious it may sound, the post-modern condition typically connects the local and the global. As Krishan Kumar has remarked in his brilliant essay, "The Post-modern Condition," "Global development-the internationalization of the economy and of culture-reflect back on national societies, undermining national structures and promoting local ones. Ethnicity receives a renewed impetus. There is an upsurge of regionalism and 'peripheral nationalism' – the nationalism of small nations which have typically been incorporated in larger units such as the United Kingdom, France, Spain and other historic national groupings. 'Think globally, act locally,' the slogan of the 1960's, applies to a good number of new social movements, most noticeable the feminist,"[13] and, we may add, the diasporic. In other words, we notice today a new, or renewed, importance attached to place, leading to a sort or re-discovery of territorial identities, local traditions, and local histories. The tendencies stretch to the creation of imagined or even invented communities and nationalities. The concept of diaspora carries all these connotations, all of which need to be comprehended.

Diasporic writing draws our attention to an important aspect of the post-modern condition in which responsibilities of citizens go across national boundaries. The earlier modernist notions of centre and margin, home and exile, familiar and strange are falling apart. The borders defined in terms of geography, culture and ethnicity are being replaced by configurations of power, community, space, and time. Citizenship cannot any longer ground itself in forms of Eurocentricism and the language of colonialism. In our time, new spaces and identities and relationships have to be created which permit people to move across boundaries, to engage difference and otherness as part of a discourse of justice, social engagement, and democratic struggle. As Krishan Kumar puts it, "Academics can no longer retreat into their classrooms and symposiums as if they were the only public spheres available for engaging the power of ideas and the relations of power. Foucault's notion of the specific intellectual taking up struggles connected to particular issues and contexts must be combined with Gramsci's notion of the engaged intellectual who connects his or her work to broader social concerns that deeply affect how people live, work, and survive." [14]

Diasporic writing brings into focus, as matter of fact, not merely the role of the intellectual or the relationship of teaching to the evolution of democracy, but also the intellectual's need to move away from a mere language of critique for a redefinition as part of a language of transformation and hope. It is only on this premise that the struggle against racism, class structures, sexism and other forms of oppression would gather new momentum. This necessary and inevitable shift indicates that literary writers and critics combine with other cultural activities for inventing languages and providing critical spaces that offer new opportunities for a coming together of different social movements. By so doing, there can be a rethinking and reexperiencing of "democracy as a struggle over values, practices, social relations, and subject positions that enlarge the terms of human capacities and possibilities as a basis for a compassionate social order." [15]

However, after we have said all this, it seems equally necessary to remind ourselves that literatures like the diasporic are not perforce anti-universal or anti-value. Any art, if it is great and good, would transcend the transient and rise to whatever is universal and valuable in human experience. As Iris Murdoch has insistently asserted, "Art shows us the only sense in which the permanent and incorruptible is compatible with the transient; and whether representational or not it reveals to us aspects of our world which our ordinary dull dream-consciousness is unable to see. Art pierces the veil and gives sense to the notion of a reality which lies beyond appearance; it exhibits virtue in its true guise in the context of death and chance." [16]

What is being insisted upon here is the fact that despite our cultural concerns and political polemics in the study of literature, more so the diasporic, the aspect of literariness or artness of literary works would always remain a relevant and valuable consideration. Equally relevant and valuable will remain the concept of good and great art as against the inferior and frivolous art. No amount of deconstruction can demolish the difference, for example, between a Shakespeare and a Shobha De.

The problem with the present-day critical approaches under the blanket term theory, including the multicultural and the post-colonial, is that even though seemingly emancipatory, they tend to confine the business of literary criticism to the surfaces of whatever is represented or expressed in art. The questions being addressed today by Theory-of differing, of otherness and orientalism, of politics and ideology-are, in fact, not new; they have always been addressed, in greater or smaller measure, by writers as well as critics from the time of Homer and Plato to our own time. The only difference is that while the earlier critical approaches tended to include different kinds of questions arising out of the literary work, such as political, moral and aesthetic, the Theory prefers to remain restricted only to the political and ideological, disdainfully excluding the moral and aesthetic. We need, therefore, to restore to our reading or criticism of literature the wholeness of concerns. To do this, we have to admit that literature, including the diasporic, is ultimately an art, not journalism and politics, nor sociology and psychology, nor linguistics and anthropology, but rather a combination of all these, subjected finally to the laws of story-telling.

Our divisive critical concerns today are, in fact, symptomatic of a world divided against it. Forces of globalization are crossed by those of localization. More than at any other time, we need to emphasize, therefore, the essential humanism of all literatures, including the decadent and the diasporic. As Terry Eagleton has rightly observed, "if literature matters today, it is chiefly because it seems to many conventional critics (including myself) one of the few remaining places where, in a solidly material world, a rare glimpse of transcendence can still be attained...... For if even this precariously surviving enclave of art can be historicized, materialized, deconstructed, then where indeed one to find value in a degraded world is." [17] Let us, therefore, examine not merely the cultural and ideological meanings of diasporic writing but also its ethical and aesthetical meanings, and measure its worth by applying to it the normative standards with which we have always evaluated the greatness of literary works-of course, with the parameters of evaluation made large enough to encompass over new concerns, responsive to contemporary consciousness.

References

1. see "Diasporas," Cultural Anthropology 9˙(3):302-338
2. The journal was launched in 1991, which carried the cited observation on pages 4-5.
3. See "Icaromenipuus, An Aerial Expedition," Marchus Aurlius and His Times

(New Your:Walter J. Black)

4. see The Algebra of infinite justice (New Delhi: Penguin Books, 2002), 42-142

5. see "Icaromenippus," Marcus Aurellius And His Times, 235.

6. Gayatri Chakravotry Spivak,"Who Claims Alterity?" in Remaking History, eds. Barhara Kruger and Phil Mariani (Seattle:Bay Press, 1989), 269-292.

7. see Culture and Anarchy -An Essay in Political Criticism (1869; New York: Macmillan, 1925), p.67

8. see Ulysses (1922;New York:Random, 1934), p.35

9. see "Ulysses, Order, and Myth, "James Joyce: Two Decades of Criticism, ed.S. Crivens(New York:Vangurard,1948),pp.198-202

10. See Beyond Culture: Essays on Literature and Learning (New York: Viking, 1965), p.10

11. Ibid, p.26

12. see "the New Cultural Politics of Difference., "Education, and p.518

13. see "The Post-Modern Condition," Education, p.98

14. Ibid.,p.129

15. Ibid,p.129

16. see The Sovereignty of Good (London: Routhledge, 1970), p.86

17. see Literary Theory: An Introduction, Second Edition (1983; Delhi: Maya Blackwell Doaba publications, 2000), p.208

❑❑❑❑

3

Portrayal of Diaspora Issues in Indian Diasporic Writings

-Tejinder Kaur

Portrayal of the problems engendered by the experience of migrancy and diaspora such as displacement, rootlessness, fragmentation, racial discrimination, marginalization, crisis in identity, cross-cultural confrontation and many others in the changing global economic, political and cultural scenario has lately received a great attention in literary works, literary theory, cultural studies and films. The post-colonial theory and discourse along with other issues have also addressed themselves to analyzing various aspects, ramifications and experiences of diaspora.

The term 'diaspora' taken from the Greek to 'disperse' has been defined by Bill Ashcroft, Gareth Griffiths and Helen Tiffin as "the voluntary or forcible movement of peoples from their homelands into new regions...." (Ashcroft, 68). Robert Cohen describes diasporas as communities of peoples living in one country who "acknowledge that the old country, a nation often buried deep in language, religion, custom or folklore always has some claim on their loyalty and emotions." (Cohen, IX)

Though the term diaspora was initially used in connection with the scattering and exile of the Jews from their homeland and their nostalgia for their lost country and the isolation and cultural alienation experienced by them in the cultures of new location but in the seventeenth century with the advent of colonialism there was an upsurge in migratory moves. The nostalgia and yearnings of such people to return to their homelands that were displaced in the form of indentured labour have been captured very incisively by V. S. Naipaul in his early novels The Mystic Masseur and The Mimic Men. Many people were uprooted in the eighteenth and nineteenth centuries for serving the British Empire in various parts of the world. The yearnings of these displaced people for their homelands signified for them political freedom. In the early part of the twentieth century many Hindus, Muslims and mainly Punjabi Sikhs went to Canada for earning their livelihood and worked as lumber-jacks in saw mills. They had to work on lower wages and suffered racial hatred and discrimination too but the protest of this Indian diaspora in Canada against the atrocities caused on them united them in the form of 'Gadar Party' which became a leading force in the struggle for freedom going on in their homeland. Sadhu Singh Dhami in his novel Maluka (1997) has portrayed this phase of the Indian diaspora in Canada in the pre-partition period.

A new dimension to this life in exile got added in the Post-colonial situation in India when many people in the sixties and seventies started moving to the developed countries on their own accord to escape political or economic difficulties of their native lands or to study or as professionals which Gayatri Chakravorty calls as part of "the brain-drain". Since then this move to other countries has been continuing. What is important to note is that whatever the reasons for migration be, the immigrants do experience a sense of unbelonging and uprootedness in the new lands. They may try hard to assimilate or acculturate in the new cultures; they still remain on the periphery and are treated as the 'other'. While remaining on the margins of the 'host' cultures, they undergo complex experiences of anxieties, confusions, yearnings and aspirations. Of course, "the nature of the diaspora, and its cultural location, 'politics' and its behaviour also depend on the nature of the host countries and not just on that of the diaspora. These diasporas live in what Homi K. Bhabha calls "in-between condition" which is very painful for them and there is a yearning for "home" which remains a "mythic place of desire in diasporic imagination," according to Avtar Brah (Brah,192). They create "imaginary homelands" from the fragmentary and partial memories of their homelands. "Migrants" says Salman Rushdie, "straddle two cultures... fall between two stools" and "suffer triple disruption" comprising the loss of roots, the linguistic and also the social dislocation (Rushdie, 5 and 279). They undergo cultural dilemmas, feel culturally displaced and threatened of their cultural identity at the mockery of their cultural practices and icons whose baggage they carry with them and try to preserve it. They show resistance also to the discourse of power in the host culture in various forms.

Though the children born to migrants occupy different spaces in the representative culture because of their better assimilation and better settlements, and their confusions, feelings of rootlessness and displacements are also less intense and are not of similar nature but as John McLeod states "their sense of identity borne from living in diaspora community [is] influenced by the past migrant history of their parents or grandparents." (McLeod, 207)

Another fact of diaspora existence, reality and experience in the world polity is that the treatment meted out to them in the host country also depends on the colour of the skin of the diaspora. Blacks and Asians born even in the white countries, as Rushdie says in his essay "The New Empire Within Britain," are thought of as people whose real home is elsewhere.

But this is also a part of reality that living in the new locations diaspora identities do not remain isolated, static or pur, rather in interaction with the representative culture and other cultural communities they constantly produce and reproduce themselves "anew through transformation and difference" says Stuart Hall and they also intervene in the cultural discourse of the dominant culture (Hall). The transformation in the subjectivities and modes of thinking of diaspora becomes possible because they have the advantage of living on the border zone of two cultures and having relationship with two geographical spaces which "overlap" each other in their "internal space." This space formed in "diaspora consciousness" is called "diaspora space", "hybrid space" "third scenario", "the third New world presence" by different theorists. Robert Bromley considers this "third space" as "a vital space for revaluation" (Bromley, 20) as "within this liminal space traditions are engaged in dynamic process and weave into new cultures." Theorists like Homi K Bhabha, Stuart Hall, Avtar Brah, Paul Gilroy and Robert Bromley celebrate this in-between space and call it "the juncture point where cultural tributaries meet... where the creolization, assimilation and syncretism are negotiated" and which becomes a space of immense creativity and possibility." Hence, as Sura P. Rath observes, "The immigrants of diaspora who inhabit the third space live the third culture and shape the third history...." (Rath)

Since in the present day global scenario, with the interaction and commingling of the cultures, the new routes and modes of thinking about diaspora identities and belonging are emerging, these theorists feel that the discourses and narratives of nationalism, ethnicity or race which are the modes of belonging and place individuals in the certainty of roots are not suited anymore when the migrants are thinking in different ways about their relations to the new place, home and their past. Moreover, since a considerable change has been visible in the outlook, location and identities of diaspora, the diaspora individuals and communities can not be placed only in relation to some homeland to which they all want to return or at all costs must return. Avtar Brah and Uma Parmesvaram aver that diasporas after having crossed the political borders must cross the psychic borders and make a mark of identification and recognition for themselves in the realistic, historical and political space of the place of relocation because "Both exile and home are here, within the new homeland," believes Uma Parmesvaram.

The creative writers all over the globe have portrayed these multiple issues pertaining to diaspora lives and experiences from different angles and perspectives but the space occupied by the diasporas is so diverse that all the diasporas cannot be clubbed together. Moreover, their concerns and sensibilities vary to a great extent as per their generation, individual perceptions and community and race specific identities and issues but overall their dominant concerns pertaining to diaspora experiences have been of the similar nature as discussed so far.

Many Indian diaspora writers writing in English and other languages too have portrayed in their works certain community, region and culture specific conflicts in the new lands of location revealing the diversity of Indian culture. But their major common concerns about diaspora issues have been dislocation, fragmentation, nostalgia for home, marginalization, racial hatred, cultural and gender conflicts, identity crises, generational differences, transformation of subjectivities, emergence of new patterns of life with cross cultural inter-action and disintegration of family units of Indian diaspora leading to anguish, traumas and dilemmas suffered by the members of such families in varying degrees and mainly by the children of these unhappy and broken homes many of whom are shown going astray in the cultural lawlessness of the western countries and inclining towards drug addiction, homosexual and lesbian relationships.

Let us have a brief overview of the portrayal of different issues of Indian diaspora in a few Indian diasporic texts. The fictional narratives like Bharati Mukherjee's Jasmine (1990), Meera Syal's Anita and Me (1996), Jhumpa Lahiri's The Namesake (2003), Chitra Divakaruni's The Mistress of Spices (1996), Iqbal

Ramoowalia's The Death of a Passport (2004), Susham Bedi's HAVAN originally written in Hindi and translated into English under the title The Fire Sacrifice and the fictional texts written in Punjabi like Jarnail Singh Sekhon's DUNIYA KAISI HOI and Nakshdeep Panjkoha's PAAR BANAYE AALHNE show the Indians living in England, America and Canada where they have immigrated either to improve their economic condition to seek jobs because of unemployment at homelands or for better education of their children or for better professional opportunities. Their life of hard work, tensions and anxieties because of various existential problems have also been portrayed in these texts and many immigrants are shown not feeling a sense of belonging, and are yearning silently for home.

Iqbal Ramoowalia's The Death of a Passport and Bharati Mukherjee's Jasmine also bring out the plight of the illegal immigrants who have to do menial jobs at lower wages stealthily, living constantly under the fear of the police and the immigration authorities. Another aspect which emerges from these two novels and Divakaruni's The Mistress of Spices and Susham Bedi's HAVAN is the violence and sexual abuse suffered by Indian women both at home and at work place for various reasons such as incompatible marriages with NRI men, the feudal attitude of the Indian husbands towards their wives, and the sexual exploitation of Indian women by the comparatively better placed men of their own communities and even by the priests of temples and gurudwaras. But some of the female characters in these novels are also shown adopting different resistance strategies to assert their identities and live a life of dignity and self-respect by revolting against the oppressive relations and seeking the help of the police and the NGOs.

People of elderly generation are shown feeling isolated since every one in the home is busy from morn till eve. They are also presented feeling perplexed because of their inability to accept the new cultural ways adopted by their children and grandchildren. Torn between the non-fulfillment of their expectations from their children as per the Indian cultural codes and the loss of their hold on the family units, they pass their time either in front of the idiot box or in the company of the people of their own generation from their own communities if available in the neighborhood.

We also get glimpses of the life of neglect at home led by the children of the over busy immigrants and the racial discrimination suffered by them in the environment and at schools. Meera Syal through the mental torture suffered by the nine year old Meena and Chitra Divakaruni through the psychic repression and beatings hurled daily on Jagjit, a 12 year old Sikh boy by the white Amercian schoolmates because of his wearing a turban and being considered a Paki, project how the children of the Indian immigrants feel oppressed, struggle hard and look for different escape routes to make space for themselves in the culture of the natives. Like Jagjit some of them also get entrapped in the network of the Amercian mafia gangs for drug smuggling and other illegal activities, who give these neglected and bullyed children support, money, motor-cycles, and promise them guns, the symbols of power which they consider to be their "passport to real America". The narrator of the novel in Chitra Divakaruni's The Mistress of Spices is shown worried about the adolescent children like Jagjit who have entered the golden jaws of America and she wonders "in dismay, what went wrong. To ask myself over and was it him, was it his parents, was it America...." Raju's mother, Guddo in HAVAN when on finding so much money in his drawer asks him from where he had got it and where he was heading to, he replies that with this money he wants to do something big and special and establish a company which will be headed by him. These secret ambitions of the diaspora children speak of their frustrations and suppression in the foreign working systems. She warns him to stop this mad race but finds him lost in the destructive trap from which she knows there is not return. The presentation of these serious issues pertaining to the children of Indian immigrants who are joining mafia gangs, either out of frustration or to earn money or to resist and overpower the racial hatred and discrimination faced by them constantly in the discourse of power at every step in the country of the whites reveals the deep concern of the Indian diaspora writers for them.

How this problem of racial hatred took a terrible form in America for the South Asians and especially for the Sikh diaspora after 9/11 has been presented by Chitra Divakaruni in her latest novel The Queen of Dreams (2004) where a second generation Sikh young man Jaspal is given a horrible bashing by a few American youth, though he keeps on crying that he is an American like them, he feels sad for this incident and his sympathies are with America but "two of the men grab him and say " 'Looked in a mirror lately.' One of them spits. 'You ain't American! It's fuckers like you who planned thjs attack on the innocent people of this country. Time someone taught you faggots a lesson." During night the snack bar belonging to his Indian friends is burnt and the word "terrorist" is painted on its door. Rakhi, one of the owners of this snack bar and the representative of the America born and bred generation of Indian immigrants who have not seen even the face of India later asks herself this question "But if I wasn't American, Then what was I." This precarious situation of the diaspora poses a question before the theorists of diaspora identities as to which nation do the diasporas actually belong, the nation which their parents and grandparents had once left to settle in the other one or the one which they had adopted which never accepts them from the heart. Moreover, such reaction of the American youth towards Sikh diaspora and the South Asians also raises a few other issues: whether it was done because of their patriotic feelings and the sikhs suffered because of the mistaken identity or it is an expression of the feeling of anger and revenge against the diaspora communities who are entering their country in large numbers because of their country's liberal immigration policy and are snatching their job opportunities in their own country, the issue which has been pertinently raised by Susham Bedi in HAVAN.

Jhumpa Lahiri in The Namesake, Meera Syal in Anita and Me and Bhaji on the Beach, Ravinder Randhawa in A Wicked Old woman (1993).,Chitra Divakaruni in The Queen of Dreams have also portrayed the problem of inter-generational gap of the Indian diaspora where the first generation parents expect from their children to live by the value system of Indian culture which they impose on them at home through food, dress, customs, rituals, language, beliefs etc. but the children encountering different cultural environment outside, find the latter more fascinating. Sandwiched between the two cultures and confused like Gogol in The Namesake and Meena in Anita and Me , who daily hear and bear the racial comments because of their brown skin, they are not able to decide which is their real 'home', India or the country where they have been born and brought up. Jaiwanti Dimri has analysed these dilemmas of the IInd generation diaspora very appropriately: "Expatriate experience is problematic for the second generation immigrants of the third world for specific reasons. Born and brought up on foreign soil expatriation for this neo-class of immigrants hangs in the background as an imaginary reality. Free from the stigma of nostalgia and the popular symptoms of angst, loneliness, existential rootlessness or homelessness, their predicament is in many ways worse than that of their predecessors. Despite their assimilation and acculturation they cannot escape from being victimized and ostracized." (Dimri)

In many fictional narratives in Punjabi like Dalip Kaur Tiwana's BHAUJAL, Nakshdeep Panjkoha's PAAR BANAAYE ALLHANE and in a few short stories by Parvej Kaur Sandhu, Rani Nagender, Veena Varma, Gurpreet Dhaliwal and Lahiri's The Namesake and a few short stories, Ramoowalia's The Death of a Passport, Divakaruni's The Mistress of Spices and The Queen of Dreams, Susham Bedi's HAVAN, we find the portrayal of the crumbling family units of Indian diaspora because of the commercially negotiated marriages, fast growing divorce culture among the Indians, expectation of Indian values by the male Indian immigrants from their green card holder America/Canada born wives, changing power relations in the house and also because of cultural and racial clashes. However, Jhumpa Lahiri and Divakaruni and a few Punjabi writers have also shown, certain characters making conscious efforts to keep their family units intact and adapting themselves to the requirements of the culture and lifestyle of their children.

Harikunzru in his novel Transmission (2004) has dealt with another current realistic aspect of the professional Indian diasporas especially the InfoTech skilled ones whose dreams of making dollars and a name for themselves in the Silicon Valley of America get shattered because of the saturation of job avenues there. Out of frustration they find destructive means of taking revenge and expressing anger which prove disastrous for them there and for their families back home.

A few Indian diaspora writers like Sadhu Singh Dhami in his Maluka Jhumpa Lahiri in The Namesake and in her short story "The Last and Final Continent" and Kavita Daswani in her For Matrimonial Purposes (2003) have also presented the positive aspects of diaspora experiences which widen the horizons of the consciousness and bring transformation in the subjectivities of their characters. They have shown through their protagonists that the cultural interaction not only opens new routes for them relating to the culture of new location and of their homeland but also makes them mobile carriers of cultures and ways of thinking to both the lands and more lands and make a good synthesis of these, thus creating new third cultures and shaping third history. According to Vijay Mishra, the latest advancements in information and communication technology and the fastest means of transportation have enabled "the late modern hyper mobile diaspora" (Mishra) to make the cultural assimilation faster, bring global and local cultures together and transplant and reinvent their home cultures in new lands.

To sum up, I would say that the portrayal of the diversity and complexity of Indian diaspora issues, identities and experiences in the fast growing theory and discourse on diaspora indicates that Indian diaspora like all other diasporas in spite of suffering economic, political, racial, existential, emotional and psychological hazards in the lands of adoption does not want to return to real and imaginary homelands. Rather it has been struggling hard to create home away from home in the new lands and cultures of relocation. Out of these cross-cultural confrontations, interactions and dialogues, new hybrid subjectivities are getting formed which indeed are contributing to the growth of human consciousness and development both at the global and local levels.

Works/Articles Cited

- Ashcroft, Bill, Gareth Griffiths and Helen Tiffin. (eds) Key Concepts in Post-Colonial Studies (Routledge, 1998).
- Bhabha, Homi K. The Location of Culture (Routledge, 1994).
- Brah, Avtar. Cartographies of Diaspora : Contesting Identities (Routledge, 1997).
- Bromley, Roger. Narratives for a New Belonging : Diasporic Cultural Fictions (Edinburgh : Edinburgh University Press, 2000).
- Cohen, Robert. Global Diasporas : An Introduction (UCI Press, 1997).
- Dimri, Jaywanti. "Second-generation Feminist Discourse on Expatriation : A study of Ravinder Randhawa's A Wicked Old Woman and Atima Srivastava's

Transmission," Literary Voice Book Series-5, February 2000, pp 28-33.

- Hall, Stuart. "Cultural Identity and Diaspora" from Colonial Discourse and Post-colonial Theory : A Reader ed. Patrick Williams and Laura Chrisman (New York : Harvesta Wheatsheaf, 1994), 392-403.
- McLeod, John. Beginning Post Colonialism (New York : Manchester University Press, 2000).
- Mishra, Vijay. "New Lamps for Old : Diasporas Migrancy Border" in Interrogating Post-Colonialism: Theory, Text and Context, eds. Harish Trivedi and Meenakshi Mukherjee (1996: rpt. Shimla: IIAS, 2000) pp. 67-85.
- Rath, Sura P. Home(s)/Abroad Diasporic Identities en Third Spaces http:// social-chass/ncsu. edu/jouvert/v4i3/rath./.htm.
- Rushdie, Salman. Imaginary Homelands (London: Granta Books, 1991)
- Edition (1983; Delhi:Maya Blackwell
- Doaba Publications,2000), p.208

❑❑❑❑

4

Indian Diasporic Writers-living On The Margin Of Two Societies

-Ritu Sharma

It is evident in the history of mankind that man has always shifted from his social group to other communities. There have always been social, economic or literary exchanges between the people of diverse groups. It is the basic nature of human beings to know and explore the world beyond their boundaries and there is always a curiosity to know about the different ethnic entities. Human civilization and culture have always got enriched by this intermingling of ideas of different cultures. India has always been depicted in the literatures written in the West. It is rather noteworthy that generally these are the writers of Indian diaspora who have always tried to portray the country of their own or their forefathers' origin. In recent years, the diasporic writers have created a unique form of literature that indulges in nostalgia and at the same time attempts to forge identity with new place and people. The individual writers of this group make a rich and varied response to their experience of migration. One of the most important themes in this literature is the sense of homelessness and nostalgia for the lost heaven. Most post-colonial writers delve into their national past that has been distorted by the colonial process. In his essay "On National Culture" Franz Fanon says that "this passionate search for a national culture which existed before the colonial era finds its legitimate reason in the anxiety shared by native intellectuals to shrink away from that western culture in which they all risk being swamped."[1]

Broadly speaking, diaspora is any community of individuals who have shifted outside their homeland but still identify themselves with the people of their homeland. The members of such community act individually to express their identities. The word 'diaspora', in real sense, means a group of persons which may be treated as 'refugee' or 'ambassador'. Expatriate writing assumes an important place between countries and their cultures (native and the adopted ones). This very concept gives birth to new theories regarding new identity making a balance between different temporal and spatial metaphors. The shifting of the culture, getting adapted to it and again a change causes emotional amnesia in the individuals. Nostalgia for one's homeland often creates problems regarding the identity of an immigrant. The pull of the past and the attraction towards one's homeland disorients the immigrant to relocate himself in the new scenario of his adopted culture.

The literature of diaspora explores the cultural, intellectual and emotional dimensions and due to the increasing variety, comprehensive coverage and richness, this diasporic literature is growing into an independent branch in literature having international parameters in true sense. The writers of diaspora portray the social, professional and marital inter-mixture along with other verities. The writers who live abroad live on the margin of two societies. Many immigrants take a literary journey to their homelands due to this physical distancing. "The endeavour to write about one's native country on the basis of memory has been an irresistible challenge and a compelling necessity for a number of exiled or immigrant writers who have been cut off from their ethnic roots.[2] "Remembering the past is a strategy often employed by immigrant writers to reconstruct, re-define and re-shape their pasts."[3]

The diasporic community is very complex and full of variety and any attempt at homogenization leads only to over simplification. There is a wide gap for these immigrants between 'home' (represents the culture of origin) and 'world' (represents the culture of adoption). The contemporary literature deals with the emotional problems of modern man and clearly reflects his pathetic condition. The theme of 'identity atrophy' is highlighted in every detail- the uprooting from the native land and cultural traditions, his position as an unaccommodated alien or as a mere outcast. Various emotional and psychic lacerations are deeply dealt in these descriptions. The pathos and hardships to live between two worlds, neither of which promises hope of stability and happiness, finds the central place in these details. There is a significant cultural encounter that takes place in diasporic writing. There is the description of the bicultural pulls and the creation of a new culture which finally emerges.

Since the immigrant writer describes from margins, his focus is apt to be off-centered. Similarly, even the protagonist fails to take the centre stage because the story being narrated is never about him. The description lends voice to local or national politics, to community life or his pain of being marginalized or alienated. There is a double vision of the expatriates-both a looking forward and a yearning backward. Infact, it is the part of the human condition, part of every person's life. Even if, a person lives in the very same place all through his life-he looks at the past, at the lost moments, opportunities and the lost loves.

Expatriate writing is the outcome of the existential, political and metaphysical unsettlement. This unsettlement, in modern times, is due to the uneven capital development and the forced movement by the colonial powers. Though the tradition and culture of a particular society should be the base of a writer's individual talent but the modern literary imagination finds its real strength in its evocation of the individual's predicament in terms of alienation, immigration, expatriation, exile and linguistically estranged, his idea of social, emotional, ethnic or cultural identity gets mythic proportions and this becomes an unattainable ideal for him. The security of members seems to provide him an illusion of 'homes' and shelters him from an alien, unwelcoming and at times even hostile society. "Caught within a system of binary oppositions that labels them as the outsider and the others, they tend to highlight differences and assume a particularization that negates the universalizing principles within Western discourse."[4] In 'The Invention of Canada: Literary Text and the Immigrant Imaginary, Arnold Harrichand Itwaru writes:

"The immigrant writer is not merely the author who speaks about the immigrant experience, but one who has lived it, one whose response is an irruption of words, images, metaphors, one who is familiar with some of the inner as well as the outer workings of these particular contexts."[5]

A more serious consideration, apart from nostalgic reminiscences, can be found in these writers's attempt to recreate the past. In this manner, they become "folk historians, myth markers and custodians of the collective history of their peoples."[6] As Vassanji states, "this reclamation of the past is the first serious act of writing. Having reclaimed it, having given himself a history, he liberates himself, to write about the present."[7]

The inter-generational frictions, that exist every where, are being exacerbated through the concepts of 'home' within the diasporic community. This inter-generationality leads to several groupings rather than the most accepted one depending on age. This results into disparate "cultures" within diaspora. The second generation, that is born say in Canada or America, is definitely different from those who shift to these countries in their childhood. Their thinking of course is guided by their parent's economic, educational and cultural background and also on the time when they left India.

"Home" for those born in Canada, is very definitely Canada,

but because of force feeding of their parents "homeland" could still be India. Further, it does not help that they are often asked, "Where are you from? As though the colour of their skin automatically pushes them to another place. They are sandwiched between two rocks."[8]

The immigrant writers have the marked characteristic of multiplicity in authenticity and ambivalence. Their racial, cultural, geographical and political contexts validated their attempt at self-definition. These writers give their outpourings in the shifting, fleeting time space sequence and social specification in terms of class and gender. Reality is perceived as utterly fluid.

The problem faced by the immigrant writers is not that of dual reality of schizophrenia but one of that affirmation and re-affirmation and that too in a new perspective. They wrestle with the racism to figure out meaningful postures and to prove that their metaphysics of solidity is not negative but just a halt in their struggle of affirmation and concurrence. Despite the fact that these writers hail from different regions, their predicament is just the same. They all go through a sense of marginalization and at the same time they search for their roots and the visualization of their experience. The new world described in their writings is not an imagination; rather it is an attempt to erase the reality of the past and at the same time an effort of fulfilment, participation and readjustment. "The sense of release, freedom experienced in a new environment may present juxtaposed polarities between the indigenous culture and the culture of their adoption but the racial-historical –political equivocations are to be supplanted by the cravings of a new self, new equation that denote adjustment, order, harmony and solidarity."[9]

The immigrant writers register several tracks in their movement towards self-fulfilment and self-enrichment. Whenever power structures give way to new constructions, the emancipated psychic encounters various distortions within itself.

There is an ethos of unpredictability where an overwhelming sense of void, that the pain of dislocation leads to can only result into a temporary sense of helplessness. But with the passage of time, these private grievances lead to the ebullient spirit of self acceptance.

The expatriate writers face a number of problems. Their mode of operation is "subject to the memory of past, confrontation with the present and receptivity towards the future is continuously drawn towards the need for an integrative world which does not denote hegemony, racial, class solidarity but an organic connection between the subjective self and the objectivied narrations that complement one another in the newly traversed paths."[10] There seem to be no solution for the problems faced by the expatriates. There is no doubt regarding the fact that all expatriation involves anxiety and belonging to two communities that leads to a kind of struggle that others do not have to struggle with. Expatriate writers have also been engaged in a permanent act of uprootedness and dislocation through travel and travelogues. This growth may be painful but it is an inseparable part of the emigrant experience. In other words, it is an inseparable part of the emigrant experience. In other words, it is recognition of alternative realities, an acknowledgement of double ness. Whenever we adopt from one-another's culture and our hopes and aspirations are redefined in this manner, this is a positive way forward. In anyway, culture is a constantly moving phenomenon and not a static thing.

References

1. Fanon, Franz "One national Culture", The Wretched of the Earth, tans. Constance Farrington. Harmondsworth; penguin Books, 1967. 168-78. RPT in literature in the Modern World:Critical Essays and Documents. Ed. Dennis Walden, New York:OUP, 1990.265

2. Goel, Savita, "A literary Voyage to India:Rohinton Mistry's A Fine Balance." Writers of the Indian Diaspora. Ed. Jasbir Jain, New Delhi:Rawat Publications, 2003.189.

3. Baxi Sonal. "The World of Neil Prissoondath Ideology in /and practice". Writers

of the Indian Diaspora. Ed. Jasbir Jain, New Delhi Rawat Publications, 2003. 130.

4. Jameela Begum A. "Locating the Exile's Culture Shyam Selvadurais funny boy". Writers of the Indians Diaspora. Ed. Jasbir Jain . New Delhi: Rawat Publications, 2003. 139.

5. Itwaru, Arnold Harrichand . The Invention of Canada Literary Text and the Immigrant Imaginary. Toronto :TSAR 1990. 25.

6. Asnani, Shyam M. "Identity Crisis of Indians Immigrants: A study of three Novel". Writers of the Indians Diaspora. Ed. Jasbir Jain, New Delhi: Rawat Publications, 2003. 75.

7. Vassanji, M. G. "The Post Colonial writers: Myth Maker and the Folk Historian." Ed. M. G. Vassanji. A Meeting of Streams: South Asian Canadian literature. Toronto; TSAR. 1989. 63-67

8. Parameswaran, Uma. "Home is where your feet are, and may your heart be there too!" Writers of the Indian Diaspora. Ed. Jasbit Jain. New Delhi:Rawat Publications, 2003. 28

9. Nagpal, B. R. "south Asian Immigrant Women Poets: Postmodernist contexts". Writers of the Indian Diaspora. Ed. Jasbir Jian, New Delhi: Rawat Publications, 2003. 84.

10. Ibid.83

❑❑❑❑

5

WORD/IMAGE: INTERSECTION OF LITERATURE AND ART IN THE DIASPORIC CONTEXT

-Neer Kanwal Mani

I have chosen to study a poet and writer like like Meena Alexander; and then further, I study an interaction between her and a painter like Chila Kumari Burman, where both have focused their Gaze on the creative process, and found their own particular voice to portray the complex realities they live in and the Self they answer to.

This defines the title of my paper, 'Word/Image' as I am concerned with articulation of the various issues of self and identity in diasporic experience that underwrite the literature and art being produced by women. I argue that the complex reality of being a woman and so many 'others'; of the multi-layered, shifting selves which is expressed through various creative acts is, at heart, the search for a place where one is most truly oneself; and where one most truly is one's own person.

I

Nothing in our world seems more obvious, real, and commonsense than the idea of the self. Self lies at the heart of much of what we do and what we think about, including politics, religion, psychology, economics, psychotherapy, relationships, nationality, gender, and race. But in the fast-changing contemporary world, the traditional concept of the bounded, internal, stable self is under siege and may well be headed for extinction sooner than any of us suspects. Women have always acted as agents in sustaining the links between tradition and modernity. But today, we come across the ossified forms of women, where they are ascribed pre-decided needs, desires and ambitions.

These elements have been the instruments in construction of identity of women and remain at the heart of the experience of being one and/or many. With regard to the materiality of identities, the issues of restricting conditions in developing (and sustaining) identity, borders, states, isolation, imprisonment, war, media exposure, mental problems, sexual questions: all have contributed to production and construction of women's identity. So becoming one's own person in a world of multiple taxonomies still remains a concern of theory and theorizing domain.

Women's studies/feminist theory has had very little to say about women artists as producers of culture compared to the work on woman in terms of representations within culture. As one can not conceive of an ahistorical, objective, essential self free from all cultural determinants, it is imperative to contextualize specific views of self and to analyze such views in terms of the dynamic, dialectical relations between self and culture.

The different forms of analysis of women as producers of culture also has to be studied in relation to a wide variety of feminist theories of gender, politics, experience, social and cultural mores, historical understanding - and this has to be taken as an open-ended enquiry, and not as a fixed position or as one type of approach or method.

Although gender unites women artists as producers into a marginalized group in culture and in popular perceptions of cultural value - in terms of representation, gender alone rarely structures their interests or concerns as individual artists. There are nevertheless subjects which women artists have tackled which have never been tackled in the work of male artists because of their experiences as women in the world. Women artists' approaches to their chosen subjects have been consistently different from the work of their immediate (male) peer group as much work in feminist art history and art criticism has continually shown.

Here I would assert that the contemporary woman in creative fields has emerged as a speaking subject, a gazing subject who is beginning to own spatiality in areas which once depended on her invisibility, her silence and the suppression of her subjectivity. These themes provide a space for emerging debates. Thus focus on 'Women and New Media' and 'cyber-feminism' in the visual arts is the new and emerging focus of study. Other concerns as in Performance Arts, on Sculpture/Public Art and Installation and Ecological (which has two very different ideas within it - the first, ecology and eco-feminism, the second, systems of logic in women's work) can serve to open up avenues for future enquiry.

II

The Luminous Palimpsest of Self: Meena Alexander

As a result of her family's relocations as a youth, Alexander struggles to forge a sense of identity, despite (or because of) a past full of moves and changes. Her autobiography, an unraveling of her past, is titled Fault Lines, and which revolves around the theme of establishing one's self, an identity independent of one's surroundings. In her autobiography she writes: "I am, a woman cracked by multiple migrations. Uprooted so many times she can connect nothing with nothing."[1] Alexander's writing is lyrical, poignant, and sensual, dealing with large themes including fanaticism, ethnic intolerance, terrorism, interracial affairs and marriages, and it is about what it means to be an Indian- American.

As she herself comments: "Sometimes I think that at the heart of what I write is a struggle to define the self. And for people like us, Indian-Americans, that self is complex, multiple, fissured."[2] Alexander has often been remarked upon for her acute consciousness of self that flows through her poetry and fiction. She defines her quest as poet: "... but deeper, under all that I know there is some deep dark turn I need to make. Some underground water I must draw into the river of words, so that the richness, the complexity will grow, so the 'self' and what an odd word that is can keep flowing. And when I say 'self' in that way, I hardly mean the 'I.'"[3] Her concept of charting out maps of that inner life, is the process that has to be gone into again and again, till this 'self'is a 'luminous palimpsest' to her.

Talking of the social responsibilities of the artist, Alexander stresses the need for thinking in a larger perspective. To her, space and language have to be thought in terms of elements that construct our everyday reality:

"At the rim of a new century, with its massive migrations of peoples, ceaseless circulation of goods and knowledge, cities that multiply their inhabitants, glittering Web sites and cyber knowledges working terror, working hope, we need to think space. To think space, through our blood and bones. We need to think out how space permits language, encodes the poem. By which I mean it grants the poem a cadre interieur. I borrow that phrase from the Cubists to mean an internal index of sense."[4]

Alexander regards childhood as the place she began as a poet and it has taken her all these years to find this place of a poet: A girl child hidden in a tree. In lines of poem called Black River, Walled Garden, alluding to that time of childhood she has written:

"I swayed in a cradle hung in a tree
and all of the visible world --
walled garden,
black river -- flowed in me."[5]

And in a unique free- flow between childhood memories

and the present day persona of being a poet, she offers this insight:

"It is where I began as a poet and it has taken me all these years to find this place. A girlchild hidden in a tree. She refuses to come down. She will not enter a world marked by the cross-hatch of aerial routes, rough sea voyages, the morass of intercontinental crossings. Will the child render back what the grown woman in her search for meaning making has lost? The glimmer of leaves, fragrance of fruit, whispering of many mouths in the tree of life."[6]

III

Fluid Selves, Porous Boundaries: Chila Kumari Burman

Chila Kumari Burman was raised by East Indians who emigrated to the impoverished Bootle district of Liverpool in the '50s. She was taught early and young to look for identity between the cracks of culture. Burman uses memorabilia from her past -- shards of humor, pain, and the unexplained -- to create a persona. Her collages are the perfect medium for addressing the conflicts she's experienced in creating herself -- conflicts of gender and ethnicity. Burman works by analogy: identity is not a seamless entity but, like a collage, an amalgamation of unassimilable perspectives.

This is a way in which the subcontinent underwrites both Chila Burman and Meena Alexaander. As Meena remarks on the links that join both of them: "A subcontinent, colonized, torn apart by Partition, yet remaking itself and us in this late twentieth century so that memories and fantasies that pour through our skins, some memories that we cannot even name, become, in their very exigency the route we take to our own bodies."[7]

Burman too, through her works, makes us aware of how ridiculous but common this notion of Third World women is. She suggests that the way the West has demeaned the East and the way men have demeaned women are wedded in a dangerous and seductive tangle of power and pain.

Meena asserts that it is an act that the postcolonial daughters have to undertake, in their art, and in their writing. Being cast outside every border, what other genealogy can they have, except to commit to the truth of their art. Chila Burman also attests to a similar truth when she paints a collage that shows a body scrawled over by the borders women have crossed, scrubbed out in the high glare of the streets.[8]

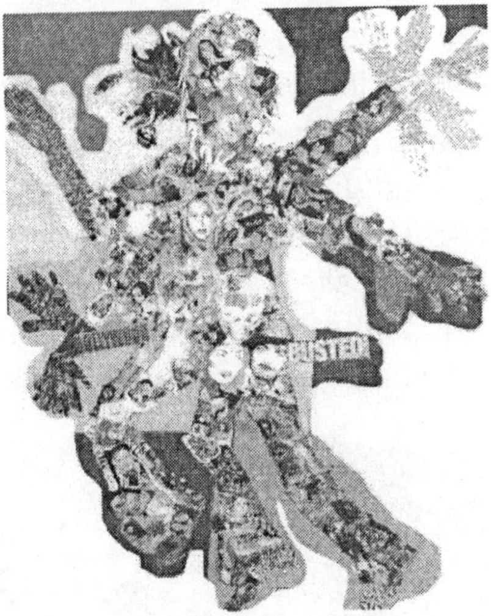

A MOMENT 2 HERSELF (COLLAGE) CHILA KUMARI BURMAN (2003)

There is an iconic quality to her mother's face that Chila has painted over a ten pound note to show the various meanings of money, of being dislocated to foreign worlds, and an awareness of being an exile.

In other works too, Chila works with techniques like Photomontage, Collages made with bindis, bras, flowers, the Hindu Iconic images, and pastiche to convey the contemporary reality of fissured and layered selves that still can't lay claim to wholeness, or assert a recognition of Self, or speak as 'I'. Both Meena and Chila's works represent a desire to figure themselves afresh, and to make up their lives in a diasporic world. Consider now, first, these words of Meena Alexander, and some images that convey a similar experience and desire in Ms. Burman's art:

"And the self that is crossed out so painfully becomes flighty, multiple, caught in the shifting strands that make up the unmoored consciousness, delighted in its fortuitous nature, free. Now of course this transition is a provisional thing, but necessary counterpart to the torment of self, part of the shift to the swelling delight in the world of the senses." [9]

Hence we see in Chila's work the sheer exuberance of the multiple figures of self-fashioning in '28 Positions in 34 Years' (1992), to a satirical comment on society and its construction of woman in a montage called 'Perfect Fit' (2001), and of course another comment on the contemporary experience of being a Punjabi living in Liverpool. In'Heaven2001Wonderland'.

28 POSITIONS IN 34 YEARS **CHILA KUMARI BURMAN (1992) 400X291**

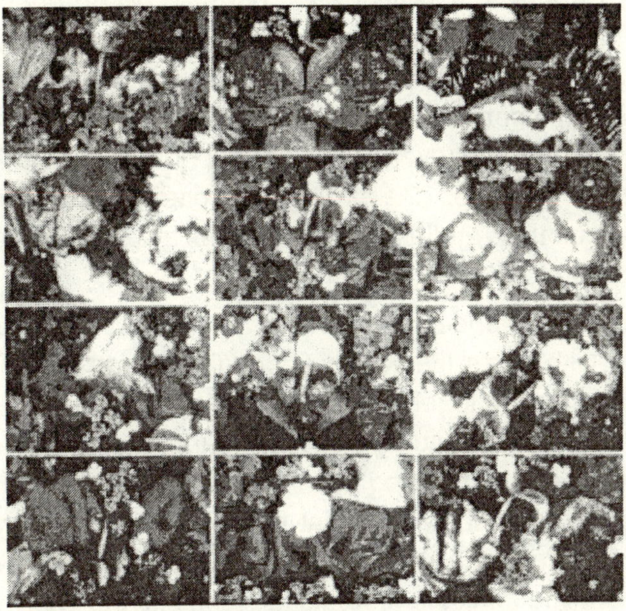

PERFECT FIT **CHILA KUMARI BURMAN (2001) 400X381**

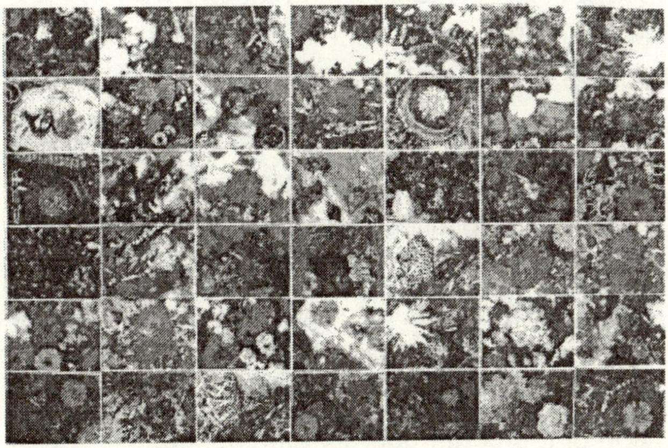

HEAVEN 2001 WONDERLAND **CHILA KUMARI BURMAN 400X255**

As Burman's work indicates, one can go on questioning what this self constitutes of. But this questioning may also lead to the 'via negativa' of our social imaginaries, neti-neti, not this, not that; I am not this or that. A quintessential being, which has no name, and is forever vanishing. Yet one that could lead to exuberant strategies, the casting off of one identity for another and yet another, and as her friend, Meena says, "fluid selves, porous boundaries."

Meena Alexander comments in this context that after all to survive with one's integrity could oddly enough mean taking apart and putting together any possible self, given a present in which one was "forced on stage with parts one had not picked to play, lines that crossed each other out, sighs, exhalations, coughs, grunts, sentences that refused translation, syntaxes that made for such a cacophonous cross hatch of memory, that merely to think them, would turn one into the equivalent of a loud poster. [9]

And Chila replies in the way of an artist, laying out the same palimpsest of self-fashioning. So that in a world without ready anchorage what one has made turns into the thread of sense, guiding one through the labyrinth of what has already been.

IV

For the woman artist who confronts the borders her body must cross, racial, political, economic, and above all, mental and sexual borders, is forced to invent a form that springs out without canonical support, a rough and ready thing, its order crude, its necessity beyond the purchase of self-invention. And in this putting together lies our most valuable and most authentic articulation of the contemporary experience.

Some of the same images used in Fault Lines surface in Alexander's poetry. "No man's land" is a particularly poignant image because it stems from growing up in a post colonial country, where boundaries and borders are blurred into a "no man's land". Here, in an excerpt from her poem "Night-Scene, the Garden," these images are very strong:

My back against barbed wire
snagged and coiled to belly height
on granite posts
glittering to the moon

No man's land
no woman's either
I stand in the middle of my life...
Out of earth's soft
and turbulent core
a drum sounds summoning ancestors

They rise
through puffs of grayish dirt
scabbed skins slit
and drop from them

They dance
atop the broken spurts
of stone

They scuff
the drum skins
with their flighty heels.[10]

References

1. Meena Alexander Remapping the Modern: Cultural and Aesthetic Transformation in Asia, Lecture at Rutgers University, March 29, 2001.

2. Meena Alexander Artist in a Time of Crisis, New York Foundation for the Arts,

Drawing Centre, SOHO, November 14, 2001.

3. Meena Alexander "Skin with Fire Inside: Indian Women Writers" The Shock of Arrival: Reflections on Postcolonial Experience. (Boston: Southend Press, 1996): 146.

4. On the internal irruption of fragments into the art space, see

   L'objet reel ... le cadre interieur du tableau, in Guillaume Apollinaire, Meditations Aesthetiques, Les Peintres Cubistes. (Paris: Hermann, 1965): 65.

5. Meena Alexander "Black River, Walled Garden" Illiterate Heart.

   (Triquarterly Books: Northwestern University Press, 2002).

6. Meena Alexander "Nomadic Memory, Rims of Place" Remapping the Modern: Cultural and Aesthetic Transformation in Asia, Rutgers University, March 29, 2001.

   (some of Alexander's observations are a part of her presentation at the panel "Artist in a Time of Crisis," New York Foundation for the Arts, Drawing Centre, SOHO, November 14, 2001).

7. Meena Alexander Post-colonial Theatre of Sense: The Art of Chila Kumari Burman

8. Chila K. Burman A Moment to Herself 2004

9. Meena Alexander Unquiet Borders. Crab Orchard Review: Special issue on Asian American Literature Spring/ Summer 1998.

10. Meena Alexander Fault Lines The Feminist Press at the City University of New York, 1993.

❑❑❑❑

6

Cultural Space and Diaspora in Gita Mehta's: A River Sutra

-Anita Sharma

Literature has often been used as a vehicle to express a country's political, cultural and emotional attitudes. Indian culture takes life as a pilgrimage and a sojourn on this planet, where diaspora and 'diasporic journey' becomes an appropriate metaphor for the human condition. Gita Mehta too reflects the Indian philosophy through the eloquent message of Naga Baba in her novel 'A River Sutra', "Don't you know the soul must travel through eighty four thousand births in order to become a man?"[1] Thus even death could be related to a 'diasporic journey' of soul. With globalization and multiculturalism migration has become an accepted reality, 'diaspora', a catchword to denote the condition of being away from the homeland. Jasbir Jain Maintains, "The narrative of the diaspora is above all a narrative of the 'self', for the very act of migration implies a 'bodily' lifting out of the familiar and relocation in the new and the unfamiliar".[2] Diaspora-be it the Biblical exodus of the Jews, or the migration of the girmit in the nineteenth century or the more recent personal decision of the professionals and the intellectuals to emigrate in search of better prospects "is a condition of uprootedness, and the dominant metaphor used to denote its co-experiences is 'transplantation'. Transplantation connotes relocation and in its turn relocation presupposes the existence of a location and dislocation therefrom."[3]

This shift from the known to the alien creates social, cultural and psychological void. This dispersal from "an original center to two or more peripheral regions, retention of collective memory of the homeland; partial alienation from the host society;"[4] aspiration to return to the homeland but inability to depart, and the urge to show solidarity to the homeland but unwillingness to threaten relations with the host country create 'Trishanku' like situation. According to Bhabha, to be "unhomed" does not mean to be homeless, ... The unhomely moment creeps up on you stealthily as your own shadow....."[5] A writer often carries his world of shadows and images of human experience into the literary creation.

Almost all Indian writers of diaspora like Anita Desai, Shashi Deshpande, Rohinton Mistry, Amitav Ghosh, Salman Rushdie, Bharti Mukherjee, Vikram Seth and so on have used their cultural identity to reinstate their subjectivity and also get away from the ambivalence of their situation. In Ruth Jhabvala's 'Heat and Dust' the protagonist is on constant move to retrieve her grandmother's life. As a quester, she moves from place to place till she resolves to stay on the mountains, probably the Himalayas. Amitav Ghosh's 'The Shadow Lines' and 'In An Antique Land' the protagonists are in search for their families diasporic identity. 'In Finding the Centre', the expatriate writer, V.S. Naipaul, tries to explain how the displaced writer goes back to locate the 'center' of his knowledge to systematize and synthesize the experiences of his travels with the demands of the fictional world. Diasporic writings are "invariably concerned with the individuals or community attachment to the centrifugal homeland,"[6] and the confusion created by the overlapping of cultures.

Gita Mehta was born in 1943 in New Delhi, India. Her parents were actively involved in Indian Freedom Movement. At the age of three, Mehta was left in a Convent in Kashmir because her traditionally educated mother had to aid her jailed husband. Gita Mehta had her university education from Cambridge in England.

She is the author of two previous books 'Karma Cola' (1979) and 'Raj' (1989) before 'A River Sutra' which came out in 1993. She has also written and filmed several television documentaries.

'Karma Cola' and 'Raj' had focused on the interactions between India and the Western World. In 'A River Sutra', Mehta explores the diversity of cultures within India. Her journey to the past both at the thematic and stylistics levels, build a bridge between the Western and the Indian discourse though the India that she creates is far away from her present day reality, it is, to use Rushdie's words "India of the mind."[7]

In 'A River Sutra', Gita Mehta presents seemingly unconnected stories about Hindu and Jain ascetics, courtesans and minstrels, diamond merchants and tea executives, Muslim clerics and music teachers, tribal folk beliefs and the anthropologists who study them. These stories are woven in a 'Sutra' by the binding force of the river Narmada and also by the narrator protagonist who is the 'sutradhar' – a retired buearocrat, in the traditional Indian mode of story telling. Gita Mehta is trying to re-define the eastern philosophy and culture for the western world, with the narrative which flows like Narmada one of the perennial and the holiest river in India. " O river born of Penance/ Named by laughter."[8] The eight hundred miles long course of the river Narmada from Amarkantak to the sea is a constant reminder to human beings that life itself is a journey where one has to make oneself helpful to others like the river. "The river is among our holiest pilgrimage sites, worshipped as the daughter of the god Shiva."[9]

The bureaucrat protagonist has joined Narmada Guest House as a manager after having "fulfilled his worldly obligations".[10] He calls himself as a vanaprasthi who is in quest of peace and tranquility in his setting life. "Bureaucrats belong too much to the world" he says and decides to immerse himself in the peaceful environment of Narmada river. "To one side of the gardens, hidden by mango trees, is a small cottage in which 'I live ..... spanning a mile from bank to bank the river has become the object of my reflections."[11] As a lively narrator he discusses the various happenings in the novel with Tariq Mia, the old Mullah of the nearby village to solve the entangled mysteries of life. The flowing water teaches him that life must go on before it unites with the eternal soul.

"Many are like myself, quite elderly persons who have completed the first stages of life prescribed by our Hindu scriptures-the infant, the student, the householder – and who have now entered the stage of vanaprasthi, to seek personal enlightenment. The purpose of the pilgrimage of life is endurance. The pilgrims generate "the heat," "the tapas" to link man to the energy of the universe like the Narmada River which is thought to link mankind to the energy of Shiva – the creator and Destroyer of Worlds."[12]

Renunciation of a Jain Monk is described in the first story of the novel. In 'The Monk's Story', Ashok is the son of a rich diamond merchant who has renounced the world like a fairly tale and is on his way to search the truth. "Whenever a jain becomes a monk, a procession and the distribution of charity mark his departure from the world."[13] During the grand initiation ceremony, Ashok realizes that it is easy to renounce the world but it is hard to follow the path. One has to be humane, devoid of ego and a staunch believer in the principle of humility and sacredness of life. "The human heart must conquer many hurdles to recapture that vision until ahimsa can become a way of life."[14] The road of the jain monk is beset with extremes where he would experience cold, hunger, heat, thirst and sickness. He will have to depend on strangers for his most basic needs.

"You will be social outcast

You will be insulted

You will be hounded."[15]

The message of the above indoctrination is a reminiscent of Jesus Christ's Rule of the Road to his disciples which do not promise nirvana but one looks for moksha that seem to be nearby, lurking on the horizon.

"You will be free from doubt

You will promote stability

You will protect life."[16]

A tragic account of a music teacher and his blind disciple is passionately told in 'The Teacher's Story'. Master Mohan is a poor and kind spirited music teacher, who takes the responsibility of Imrat – a blind and young talented boy. The mysticism in the boy's raptures lifted Mohan into a world of Charity, purity and kindness like the Sufis.

"In the very spasm of death I see Your face

O, the wonder of my submission

O, the wonder of your protection."[17]

The jealousies and hatred of the contemptuous world disguised as "The Great Sahib" award merciless death to the blind disciple of Master Mohan. Mohan held himself responsible for the cruel fate of young Imrat and so repents on the bank of Narmada. After repentance and penance, "he decided to return to his family, but he threw himself under the train .... It is only a story about the human heart."[18]

There is also a pathetic tale of unrequited love of the musician's ugly looking daughter. She eulogises the supremacy of music as a "source of mystery", a healing power and a purifying agent. The daughter gently declares, "People are always alarmed the first time they see me"[19] Gita Mehta in some of the memorable passages provide the notes of Indian music to her readers. "Each raga is related to a particular reason, a time of day, an emotion. But emotion is the key that unlocks a raga's soul."[20] Nature lends music to human beings. "Listen to the birds singing. Do you hear the half notes and microtones pouring from their throats? If I practiced for ten life times I could not reproduce that careless waterfall of sound....."[21] The veteran musician has trained his daughter like Wordsworth's Lucy in the lap of nature. "Standing under the trees we waited to hear the peacocks cry again, and when they did, my father's voice echoed them....."[22] But unfortunately, the plain looking girl becomes a quester after love and life. She comes to river Narmada to find peace and solitude.

'The Executive Story' is set in the primitive tribal ambience of Assam and later of the Narmada region, and shows the power of nature to heal sickness generated by modern society's greed, lust and aberrations. "Working at a distant tea-estate, Nitin Bose had gone from disbelief, to tranquility, to that possessiveness by which one is oneself possessed.......

At first was Death

That which did mean an utter emptiness.

And emptiness , mark thou, is Hunger's Self."[23]

Nitin Bose suffers schizophrenia born out of his lust for the magical tribal woman Rima Bose but he is restored to health by the benign touch of Narmada and the tribal rituals. The Priest of the tribals declare that only Narmada River has the power to cure him. Rationally the soothing surroundings of Narmada Guest House sublimates his lust to creativity and study. Mr. Chagla notices that Nitin was working "on something because his desk was covered with papers."[24]

The tribal ethos; the search for the tribal warrior and the tribal rituals are exotically described in 'The Courtesan's Story'. These stories are set in the salubrious atmosphere of the Narmada valley. They are the accounts of the courtesan and her daughter whom Rahul Singh, the robber abducts. Rahul Singh is "the most wanted bandit in the Vidhyas, a man the police fear, a murderer whose name is used even in Shahbag to frighten children into obedience."[25] The wanderings of Rahul Singh and his beloved of many births in the jungle are exciting. "He stretched out his arms to me. Suddenly I knew he was speaking the truth, and that night I entered my captors' embrace."[26] This journey of the lovers end in death. Rahul Singh is killed in Police firing and his beloved commits suicide for fear of social stigma.

The Protagonist in 'The Minstrel's Story' and 'The Song of the Narmada' is a traveller in search of the ultimate truth of life. For ten long years, he penanced as an ascetic popularly known as Naga Baba. Under harsh circumstances, he delved deep into the jungles and roamed near the river banks performing extreme penance. "You cannot be a Naga without overcoming human limitations," his teacher told him. "Learn to survive without water. If I find you here when I return, I will take you to our academy." [27] The Guru showed him the path of truth and enlightenment through endurance, humility and social awareness.

The Naga Baba travelled to the Himalayas and survived in freezing cold; he journeyed to the desert and faced scorching heat; he stayed in formidable caves, he went deep into the inhospitable jungles; and he even tried his moral strength by visiting a brothel. There he saved a young girl and named her Uma. "Uma means peace in the night".[28] She was taught the River-Sutra by Baba and was anointed as the wandering ministrel of Narmada. Naga Baba gave her a holy dip in Narmada announcing that "The Narmada claims all girls as hers. Tonight you became a daughter of the Narmada."[29]

Interestingly, the theory of Re-birth, transformation and renewed vision is discussed within the story. The Naga Baba disappears only to reappear as Professor Shankar, who rejects all myths associated with the river and proceeds with the excavation. Concerning the sacredness of river Narmada, Professor answers rationally, "Mere mythology! A waste of time! If anything is sacred about this river, it is the individual experiences of the human beings who have lived here."[30] Such utterances in the novel hints at East-West encounter in philosophy.

For the Professor, river is immortal and a symbol of life. He becomes the author's mouthpiece and strives to put all the myths in the rationalists' perspective. The Professor's enthusiasm for the Narmada gives the lesson of detachment through attachment. Probably the author wants to convey to her western readers the message of ecology and environment through the myths of river.

All these stories are told on the banks of Narmada and partly in the guest house. Tariq Mia and the narrator protagonist discuss each episode in the light of the Indian philosophical thought and the sum total of their discussion is that life is a journey which can be made pleasant not by renunciation but by understanding the essence of humanity across the cultures through love, fellow feeling and understanding. Naga Baba's perceptive remarks, "You have chosen a wrong place to flee the world, my friend, ... Too many lives converge on these banks," [31] declares that running away from life is not an answer to one's quest.

The river Narmada symbolizes eternity. It is the daughter of Shiva, born out of his penance.

"You remove the stains of evil.

You release the wheel of suffering.

You lift the burdens of the world,

O holy Narmada."[32]

The individual journeys of all the characters in the novel who come to the guest house or who are re-created through memory, end on the banks of the river like Chaucer's 'The Canterbury Tales'. Some have a happy positive ending while some end in tragedy, only the real seeker – the narrator remains wondering at the passing pageant. The voyage of Narmada even in the dark, with tiny lamps lit by the devotees inspires him. For him life has to go on through its long and hazardous voyage like the flowing water of Narmada. But still, there are tiny lamps radiating the path with hope; cheer and light despite the gloom of night. 'The River Sutra'' eulogizes the river thus:

"You were present at the creation
By Shiva's command you alone will remain
At the Destruction."[33]

Gita Mehta's novel reflects the complexity of India's myth and cultural diversity which stands united and immortal like river Narmada. Living in the USA, she has cast a backward glance at her homeland from the distance in time and space and has created a miniature mythological and multicultural India within her novel. In this, she seems to be a real follower of Vivekanand, who once wrote to the Raja of Khetri, "Now a days, everybody blames those who constantly look back to their Past. It is said that so much looking back to the past is the cause of India's woes. To me on the contrary, it seems that the opposite is true, so long as they forgot the past, the Hindu nation remained in a state of stupor, and as soon as they have begun to look into their past, there is on every side a fresh manifestation of life. It is out of this past that the future has to be moulded, this past will become the future."[34]

In one of her interviews, Mehta asserts to C.J.S. Wallia that her main aim was to "bring mythological time, historical time, contemporary time and narrative time" into the novel (India Star Review of Books, culled from the Internet). The exotic picture of nature, river and the faith associated with it is probably for her western readers but she too seems to be nostalgic for the familiar sights and sounds. The tribal life is recreated as she describes the scenery around the guest house. "The jungle was seething with activity. Parakeets and cuckoos, wood pigeons and mynahs shrieked and cawed as they build their nests before the heat of summer seared the forest. Even deer and wild boar were crossing the path undisturbed by any tribal women collecting firewood".[35] However, "the palpable presence of Narmada, the river, the tribal and the child like seeker, the narrator, plus the traditional narrative strategy are strong enough to make 'A River Sutra', a novel representing and re-presenting miniature India."[36]

Gita Mehta 'try to get over her isolation and ambivalent situation by creating a space away from both homeland and host country. She seems to take refuge in spirituality and mythology of river Narmada- "The Soother of Desires". Probably, the movement away from the constricting traditional culture has given her the power to discover the 'self' and the cultural spaces within diaspora.

References

- Gita Mehta, A River Sutra, (Penguin, New Delhi, India, 1993,) p. 281.
- Jasbir Jain, "The New Parochialism Homeland in the Writing of the Indian Diaspora", In Diaspora, ed., Markarand Pranjape (New Delhi: Indialog Publication, 2001), p.79.
- Usha Bande, "Cultural Space and Diaspora", Journey Metaphor in Indian Women's Writing, IIAS (Shimla, 2003), p.79.
- William Safran, "Diaspora in Modern Societies: Myths of Homeland and Return", In-Diaspora: A Journal of Transnational Studies, 1(1) 83-99.
- Homi K. bhabha, The Location of Culture (New York: Routledge, 1994), p.9.
- Victor Ramraj, National and Post Colonial Literatures: An Introduction Diasporas and Multiculturalism, ed., Bruce King (The Clarendon Press, Oxford, 1996)p. 214.
- Usha Bande, "India of the Mind – A Study of Gita Mehta's A River Sutra," ed. T.S. Anand, Modern Indian English Fiction, (New Delhi, 2002), p. 153.
- Gita Mehta, A River Sutra, (Penguin, New Delhi, India), 1993, p. 274.
- Ibid., p.2
- Ibid., p.1

- Ibid., p.3
- Ibid., p.7
- Ibid., p.5
- Ibid., p.35
- Ibid., p.57
- Ibid., p.41
- Ibid., p.87
- Ibid., p.91
- Ibid., p.195
- Ibid., p.206
- Ibid., p.203
- Ibid., p.204
- Ibid., p.123
- Ibid., p.148
- Ibid., p.171
- Ibid., p.184
- Ibid., p.239
- Ibid., p.252
- Ibid., p.254
- Ibid., p.267
- Ibid., p.57
- Ibid., p.279
- Ibid., p.277
- Beni Shankar Sharma, Swami Vivekanand: A Forgotten Chapter of His Life, (Calcutta: Oxford), p. 108-09.
- Gita Mehta, p. 259.
- Usha Bande, p. 153.

❑❑❑❑

7

THE INDIAN DIASPORA AND RAJA RAO AS A DIASPORIC WRITER

- Kiran Kamboj

The Indian Diaspora is a generic term to describe the people who migrated from territories that are currently within the borders of the Republic of India. It also refers to their descendants. The Diaspora is currently estimated to number over twenty million composed of 'NRIs" (Indian citizens not residing in India) and "PIOs" (Persons of Indian Origin who have acquired the citizenship of some other country).

It is with respect to the 'Jewish people that the word 'Diaspora' was first employed, as it suggests the idea of dispersal and fragmentation; and in much of the literature there is a presumed relationship between the Diasporic community and the land which they left and to which the possibility of return always subsists, or what we are apt to term 'motherland' or 'home'.[1] The conditions that make for a diasporic community are admittedly complex, but this presumed link between the Diasporic community and the motherland is easily questioned, nor is there any reason why we must be held hostage to any form of linguistic and epistemological tyranny. No substantive issue can be decided on the issue of 'origins'.2 It thus appears perfectly reasonable to speak of an Indian Diaspora, as it does of the Chinese Diaspora, the African Diaspora, the Palestinian Diaspora, and of course the Jewish Diaspora. If there is, then, an Indian Diaspora, we must logically inquire what makes it 'Indian'. The 'Indian ness' of Indians acquires a particular poignancy overseas, as Indians abroad are presumed to shed their regional, linguistic, and ethnic identities in reference to the more general identity of being an Indian. It is arguable that one is more easily an Indian abroad than in India; the category of 'Indian' is not contested abroad as it is in India. One can unequivocally speak of an Indian Diaspora, it is because other forces have emerged to cement the widely disparate elements from the Indian sub-continent into an 'Indian' community. One can point, for example, to Indian cinema, Hinduism, and food. Though Indians are not reputed to be a very mobile people, and despite the strictures against traveling overseas that are said to be found in the ancient shastras, the presence of Indians aboard can be attested to from the days of remote antiquity. Early Indian migration, such as to Ceylon and South-east Asia, owed its origins to the impulse of Buddhist missionaries, and the well-known Hindu kingdoms of South-east Asia in the medieval period continued to attract labor and craftsmen from India. Diverse streams of the Indian population have fed into the Indian Diaspora in the twentieth century: while a professional elite found its way to the United States, Australia, and other nations of the 'developed' West, the laboring poor were recruited to build the shattered economics of Britain, Holland and Germany in the aftermath of World War II, and another strand of this working class has been providing for some years its muscle power and much more to the Sheikdoms of the middle East.

Indian emigration has been taking place for centuries but never before in history India witnessed such massive movements of people from India to other parts of the world as in the 19th and 20th centuries. Among the immigrants of diverse nationalities, overseas Indians constitute a sizable segment.

'There were three broad patterns of overseas migration in terms of history and political economy: emigration that began in the 1830s to the British, French and Dutch colonies: emigration to the industrially developed countries during the post-World War

II period; and the recent emigration to West Asia' [3]

In India the sacred Hindu scriptures prohibited crossing the seas. There was no large scale emigration until the nineteenth century. During the second half of the eighteenth century, some Indians emigrated to Philippines, USA and Indonesia to work as agricultural laborers. It was the European imperialist expansion during the nineteenth and twentieth centuries which created conditions for emigration in large numbers. New plantations, industrial and commercial ventures in European colonies created the need for large supplies of labor. With the abolition of slavery in the British, French and Dutch colonies respectively in 1834, 1846 and 1873 there was a severe shortage of laborers working in sugar, tea, coffee, cocoa, rice and rubber plantations in the colonies and century, and India and China became the obvious alternative sources of labor. These countries also provided the entrepreneurs who settled in different colonies. Thus, by and large, there were two streams of Indian and Chinese emigrants to the colonies: unskilled laborers and small scale entrepreneurs. In countries where the two types of immigrants or their descendants co-exist, the distinction between them is a marked feature of intra-group relations in Indian community.

Emigration to Sri Lanka, Burma, Malaya, and to East Africa is different from that to the developed countries like Britain, USA, Canada, Australia and New Zealand. The first trickle of Indians to Britain occurred during the period of British Raj. However, a major influx of Indian took place only after India's independence in 1947. The number of Indians in the UK in 1987 was 12, 60,000. There was also migration to England and Netherlands of people of Indian origin from Africa and the Caribbean. In contrast to the ex-indentured populations, the Indian migrants in the industrially developed countries have been able to maintain extensive ties with India because of their comparative affluence. Marriage arrangements, kinship networks, property and religious affiliations keep many migrants well linked to their place of origin, since a large number of Indians are still first generation migrants. Another factor which has enabled overseas Indians in Britain to maintain ties with their homeland is the flow of their remittances and investments.

Indians are the largest component of peoples of South Asian origin in Canada, whose population at present is about 700,000. Majority of the Indians in Canada emigrated during the post-1947 period. As a consequence of the 1969 Immigration Policy of Canada, the flow of Indian immigrants has been highly selective. About three-fourths of the recent immigrants are educated and highly skilled. Most Indian ethno-cultural populations are from informal communities, through links between relatives and friends who share common ethnic, linguistic and religious roots. Recent emigration of the Indians to the West Asian countries is basically oriented to labor and servicing occupations on a contract basis. There were only 14,000 Indians in the Gulf in 1948 and 40,000 in 2001. Following the oil boom of the mid-1970s, the Middle East has witnessed a massive induction of the South Asian workers. The population of Indian workers, which was 154,418 in 1975, rose to 599,500 in 1981 and to 1,150,000 in 1992. Presently there are about 3.6 million Indians in the Gulf countries. Between 1975 and 1980 one million skilled workers had to be imported to manage and operate this new infrastructure. Majority of the unskilled and semi-skilled migrants from India in the Gulf is without their families and lives in communal accommodation.

The Indian Diaspora today constitutes an important, and in some respect unique, force in world culture. We can characterize Indian Diasporic community as Indian. In the United States, at least, the Indian community has occupied a place of considerable privilege. In North America and the U.K., the native Indian costume has come up for public scrutiny and discussion in an altogether different respect: Sikhs have insisted that they be exempt from the law that compels bicyclists and motorcyclists to wear helmets, for such helmets cannot be worn over turbans, and their religious faith required Sikhs to wear turbans. The religious practices of Hindus, Sikhs and Muslims in the U.S. and other overseas communities might be assisting in transforming the nature of religious faiths in India itself. Hindus all over the world are showing alarming signs of susceptibility to a resurgent and militant Hinduism; indeed it is even arguable that they seem to know the meaning of Hinduism better than do Hindus in the 'motherland'.

In spite of living in America, England, German and other countries the spirit of an Indian is always attached to its motherland. An Indian living in India is physically attached to India but Diasporic Indian is spiritually attached with it and spiritual grip is more powerful than physical. This feeling of attachment can be visualized more intensely in Diasporic literature. Diasporic writers specially 1905 to 1947 have given utterances to the hopes, desires, enthusiasm, sympathy, thrill of joy and states of pains of that time. The present paper is humble attempt of concentrate on critical examination of the presence of India in Indian Diasporic literature with special reference to the works of Raja Rao, an Indian Diasporic writer of early 20th century. It is to consider how his fiction and how far his fictional techniques, themes, motives and characters are determined by his Indian outlook. He used a technique of writing in which the familiar and ordinary aspects of life are depicted in a straightforward manner and are especially designed to reflect Indian life as it actually is. His treatment of subject matter is designed in such a way that it presents a clear and careful description of everyday Indian life, the lives of middle and lower class people of India. When we talk of Indian ness means such traits in the character of a man, in surroundings or situations which prove them to be Indian and it really means its culture the mode of the life of its people. Its social, political, religious, moral values, customs, needs, aims and aspirations all are included in it.

In spite of living in England and France, a Diasporic writer, Raja Rao's heart was always bound by the ancient India. Raja Rao spent a number of years in India in 40's and 50's and again he went to America in 1960 where he has since been teaching Indian philosophy of religion in the University of Texas at Austin. During his various visits to India Raja Rao came under the influence of Gandhi, Sri Aurobindo, Rama Maharishi and Pandit Tara Nath. The climax to his spiritual quest was his meeting with Sh. Atamnanda Guru at Trivendram in 1943. Like the true 'guru' he clarified Raja Rao's metaphysical doubts and revealed to him the path of self knowledge. Raja Rao has been visiting India regularly, almost every year to replenish his spiritual roots. Raja Rao is essentially an Indian Diasporic writer in regard to the form of his novels. They are very close to Indian Puranas and the old epics, as K.K. Sharma in Indian English Literature (p. 159) observes,

'The Puranas, which is an old Indian poem of literature, is an amalgam of history, totally of human existence, philosophical reflections on life and religion, stories, fables, legends, log poetic description of places and nature, mystical experiences observations and ideologies." [4]

India's struggle for independence is a popular theme in Indian Diasporic literature. Raja Rao's Kanthapura is a notable example. Besides being technically a good novel with a compact plot, Kanthapura is also a landmark in Indian Diasporic literature. The novel gains importance because three stands of experience-political, religious and social-are fused together as complete whole. In this novel he reveals his sensitive awareness of the forces let loose by the Gandhian revolution. During the struggle for independence of India he served the cause not as a sword man but as a penman by awakening his brothers and sisters through Kanthapura. He has pictured the struggle for freedom along with painting the condition of Satyagraha infected Indian villagers in the twenties and thirties of 20th century. That was an unforgettable epoch when the personality and the programmes of Mahatma Gandhi had thrilled and galvanized the entire Indian sub-continent. Though Gandhi never appeared personally even once in his Kanthapura, yet the whole novel from beginning to the end is overwhelmed with Gandhi's personality, philosophy and programmes through his local representative Moorthy. Political problem is the mother of all problems. Economic exploitation of the poor coolies by the white mangers is due largely to the fact that they belong to the ruling class. Hence national struggle under the charismatic leadership of Mahatma Gandhi, for the liberation of India from the foreign yoke is the very saga of noble sacrifice which calls but he is in equal measure an artiste too so he had maintained admirably the equilibrium of the artistic and purposive sides of his novel. In two other novels, he touches upon the superiority of Indian religion and the Indian culture in his unique manner. Religious mystic formula and metaphysics are also the themes that have attracted the attention of Indian Diasporic novelists. These mystic formulae may take the form of religious system of Indian philosophy like Adwitvada, which have its complex metaphysics and practices. It may also take the form of psychic communion and rapport with the beings of another world and with their help to unfold the mysteries of the world. It may also exhibit in some mysterious incarnations and supernatural powers which are supposed to be possessed by these mystic 'gurus'.

Raja Rao's religious India is a India that believes in the principle of Adwaitvada. This true interpretation of India is presented by him in the midst of materialistic West. The few Indians that are presented in the big novel, though diverse and different from one another are markedly true Indians as distinguished from Westerners. In his novel The Serpent and the Rope, the theme is religious, metaphysical and philosophical. Raja Rao has made the erudite scholar Ramaswamy and the easy-go-lucky Rama Krishna Pai, narrator of the events. So he has taken particular care to see the character and therefore the style of the narrator should be quite in keeping with the effect that he wants to produce on the reader. Raja Rao has dealt with political and social problems and with religious philosophy and metaphysics.

Raja Rao regarded the Political domination of India by the aliens as the root cause of all evils. Political problem is the mother of all problems. Economic exploitation of the poor coolies by the white managers is due largely to the fact that they belong to the ruling class. Hence national struggle under the charismatic leadership of Mahatma Gandhi, for the liberation of India from the foreign yoke is the very saga of noble sacrifice which calls for an epical treatment of the subject. Gandhian movement is not only political in character but it is economic social and religious problem also. In Kanthapura Raja Rao describes through an old woman how nobly and to a man all its inhabitants carried out Gandhian programme of Harijan uplift, Hindu Muslim unity, boycott of foreign cloth and picketing of liquor shops. This famous novel deals directly and centrally with the problem of all-comprehensive national struggle, which had permeated right through every village of India. This particular village in excitement of the thirties is a representative of Indian villages of that period. Thus in first phase of his carrier, though the novel Kanthapura (1938) and his short stories he deals with the real life of Indians which was webbed by all the social, economic and political problems of that time. In the second phase of his literary career often he suffered a deep spiritual crisis in his life, Raja Rao is inspired by the problems which were philosophical, metaphysical and religious. In this phase of his career, he comes out before us as a philosopher, novelist. Mystic philosophy of Shankracharya's 'Adwaitvada' that is the greatest contribution of India to the spiritual treasure house of the world has inspired the greatest and the most voluminous novel of Raja Rao i.e. The Serpent and the Rope. Thus in the works of Raja Rao, the reader clearly notices the various political, economical, social, philosophical and religious problems, which have influenced this novelist- philosopher.

Raja Rao's commitment to 'Vedanta', a universal religion, interpreting India to the west in the right perspective and creating international understanding has resulted in his masterpiece, The Serpent and the Rope. Raja Rao's literature is 'Sadhana' kind of spiritual discipline and growth or a sort of complete devotion to the metaphysical being of self, explaining his views, he remarks, " So the idea of literature as anything but a spiritual experience or 'Sadhana' a much better world – is outside by perspective. I really think that only through dedication to the absolute."

The ethos of ancient Indian philosophy of Shankracharya and Ramayana is perceptible i9n the works of Raja Rao. According to him one has to be a man first and a writer after wards. The writer attains his state of higher being by seeking guidance of Guru, and when he gets spiritual realization he may have an altruistic inspiration to write. In this way a true literature is created. Raja Rao's whole approach to life and literature has been outlined against the broad backdrop of Indian philosophy and tradition. He believes in the 'Advaidic' truth of 'Shivam' Shivam' (I am Shiva, an absolute truth). This realization of truth can be made possible only with the help of 'Guru'. Raja Rao realized full significance of the Vedanta Path only after he met his 'Guru'. If Kanthapura is Raja Rao's Ramayana, then The Serpent and the Rope is his Mahabharta. If Kanthapura has a recognizable epic quality, the Serpent and the Rope is more than miniature epic. It is always encyclopedic in its scope. They reflect Raja Rao's stupendous learning his mastery over a number of literature mythologies, philosophies and religious of India. Raja Rao has made an attempt to strike a balance between the extremes of unqualified acceptance and rejection of ancient India heritage. In his works he has not only treated religion philosophies but also political milieus. In Kanthapura he reveals his sensitive awareness of the forces let loose by the Gandhian revolution.

In his first novel, Kanthapura village life structured by caste-division system. With in the framework the novelist works out the destinies of his characters against a socially and politically charged background. The Serpent and the Rope however, seems to transcend many of their social concerns in its preoccupation with man's metaphysical quest. All caste considerations are simply brushed aside in the opening sentence of the novel with its pregnant truth.

"Brahmin is he who knows Brahman"[6]

The idea is carried forward in The Cat and Shakespeare. It shows that Raja Rao has moved from the 'Puranic' faith to the 'ithihasic' and from the 'ithihasic' to 'Upanishadic', there has been parallel movement too; from 'Karma' in Kanthapura to 'Jyana' in The Serpent and the Rope and on to 'Bhakthi Prapatti' in The Cat and the Shakespeare. Moorthly is a man of action and realization came to him through political action, Gandhian Satyagarh. Rama (Ramaswamy) is a scholar an intellectual. A metaphysical realization came to him only through Jyana and it is Guru that will make Rama see that the one alone remains the many merely change and pass. For him, the path of devotion (bhakthi) and the path of surrender (praptti) – one shades off into the other – is the best, following this path, one can not possibly miss one's goal. Kanthapura, The Serpent and the Rope and The Cat and Shakespeare make a trilogy and present a steady progression in Raja Rao's 'Sadhana', .which is presenting a true picture of people particularly of Indian society. In all the three novels Raja Rao has borne this important point in mind he had to deal with religious problems of life of an Indian. Being a consummate literary artist he has exercised judicious care in picking and choosing such aspects of Indian life as suited his point of view, which he wanted to convey to his readers. His point of view in each novel is circumscribed by the subject matter of that particular novel. For this purpose Raja Rao has selected one particular character person in each of his novel to narrate the incidents. The personality of the narrator as well as his or her mental emotional and religious outlook on life is in keeping with the kind effect and the atmosphere that Raja Rao aimed at creating in the novels. He properly planned what kind of atmosphere and effect he wanted to produce and what kind of style and general tone he desires to introduce in the story. He wanted to give an epical character to his novel Kanthapura. Therefore his thought is encyclopedic in its scope.

Raja Rao's attitude towards the various problems of Indian of the age is quite perceptible from his novels as the attitude of Mulk Raj Anand is. Raja Rao's hatred for foreign rule, and for evils like usury, exploitation and orthodoxy and his love and admiration for the village folk who display commendable courage are unambiguous, clear and glaring to everyone. Raja Rao reminds of the few Indian English novelists who have succeeded in achieving a synthesis between 'tradition' and the 'individual talent'.

Therefore, Indian Diasporic writers of early 20th Century have chosen all the problems prevailing in Indian life at that time and attempted to solve these problems of heterogeneous audience sometimes by choosing themes and situations that have more or less the same validity all over the country. Such recognizably Indian themes therefore are the first choice of the Indian Diasporic English writers of that time. Such themes are national and Indian in character. The curse of untouchability, social and economic exploitation of the weak and the poor evils of capitalism and industrialism, social changes resulting from the disintegration of the old hierarchical and agrarian society and the breakdown of the large joint family are some themes which have equal validity all over India. National struggle for political emancipation of India and the dynamic leadership of Mahatma Gandhi is another such all India themes, which has provided several novels not only in various state languages, but also in English. Another historic force that manifests itself in Indian in Indian English novelists is the so-called encounter between East and West. This encounter is to be found not only at the level of people, but also at the level of ideas, culture and philosophies of religion. Hence, the themes in Indian English fiction are Indian or cosmopolitan in character. Raja Rao and his contemporaries have laid the foundation of the genuine Indian English Novel. Raja Rao's metaphysical strain is organically adapted to his fables of identity exploring the spiritual core of existence. Comic, realistic or existential, the diverse approaches combine well within their respective areas of concern to project; the contemporary Indian reality and imagination. Therefore the Diasporic literature constitutes a kind of major tradition for the Indian novel in English, for taken all in all, it projects faithfully not only the identity the affiliation and continuity of India but a true image of India.

References

1. Articles in THE HINDU on 'Indian Diaspora'
2. Vinay Lal "No substantive issue can be decided on the issue of 'origins' of word Diaspora" 'Reflections on the Indian Diaspora'
3. Articles in the Business Line on Indian Diaspora
4. K.K. Sharma, Indian English Literature : A Collection of Critical Essays (Gaziabad : Vimal Parkashan Publishers, 1977)
5. S.V.V. "Face to Face" The Illustrated Weekly of India, January 5, 1964) Pp. 44-45
6. Raja Rao, The Serpent and the Rope P.2

8

Crisis of Unbelonging In Raja Rao's The Serpent And The Rope

-Alka Sharma

Writers of the Indian diaspora have been center stage in the last decade primarily because of the theoretical formulations which are now being generated by the critiquing of their work and the growing interest in cultural studies. 'Home is where your feet are, and may your heart be there'. Diasporic writing raises questions regarding the definitions of 'home'. Raja Rao (b. 1909) has spent the major part of his life in the West and from those far off places he has viewed Indian life with the nostalgia of a diaspora. When Raja Rao went to France for higher studies he looked back with nostalgia on ever changing India, and found it significant not only politically but also culturally. His long stay in France made it difficult for him either to keep in touch with day-to-day events of that fateful nationalized movement or feel as much involved in it from that distance, as he had been when he was in India. During this period Raja Rao absorbed the West fully and examined critically his attitude in so far as it was typically Indian.

Raja Rao in his magnum opus The Serpent and the Rope (1960) studies the process of marital adjustment of an Indian man and French wife in the wake of their sharply differentiated outlook and attitudes coupled with their disagreement on each other's roles, duties and responsibilities – shaped by their respective cultures. In the collapse of their marriage in the novel, Raja Rao puts forth the hypothesis of an unbridgeable gulf between the ethos of two cultures.

In the sad spectacle of disintegration and failure of the 'East-West marriage' between a South Indian Brahmin K.R.Ramaswamy and a French girl Madeleine Roussellin, Raja Rao may superficially appear to be defending Kipling's famous contention "East is East/And West is West/And twain can never meet," or Forster's pessimistic pointers to the earth and the sky as disfavoring such a union. But the fact is that Raja Rao's earth and sky would rather convey an opposite message. He does not present in this novel any personal, social, economic or political clash. Ramaswamy-Madeleine relationship becomes a vintage point for Raja Rao to bring out the racial, cultural, philosophical and metaphysical barriers to a harmonious togetherness of two spiritual worlds – East and West. He rather shows a dramatic contrast between two different, if not always opposite, ways of life and thought. Since "the good cannot know itself," it is "in evil you seek good."[1] Similarly, it is through a perception of dualities that the hero arrives at non-duality; it is in the West that he realizes what India really is. Two worlds have been brought together up to a certain distance, contrasted, but not kept perennially apart. At one place, Raja Rao writes in the novel :

The job is to build bridges-not of stone or of girders, for that would prove the permanence of the objective, but like the rope bridges in the Himalayas, you build temporary suspensions over green and gurgling space.[2]

Rama and Madeleine commute between these two worlds through the rope bridges. The crumbling of their relationship brings out the disparity between two patterns of life, modes of thinking and feeling and in the objectives that each society has set before it. The protagonists of the international marriage in the novel are conceived of by the novelist, less as vibrant human beings and more as carriers of their country's cultural and metaphysical approaches to life.

A sensitive young man born and brought up in a conservative

Brahmin family, when he went to France for higher studies, he could not adjust easily to the new social milieu. He belongs to a traditional family and a set of social values but feels isolated and alienated in a foreign land. Not that he was fascinated less by the Western culture, history and literature, but he was more inclined by nature and training to think likes a Vedantic. Therefore, the personal encounter with new reality was treated by him in the context of modern civilization, the East and the West trying to come together.

Like a true Brahmin, he had gone for knowledge, that is, with a view to earn his doctorate. It was there in France that he fell in love with Madeleine, a college teacher of history and married her. This was an experiment:

An Indian Brahmin with his sacred thread around his neck and Grammar and Brahma Sutras and the Vedas and the Upanishads and the Gita and the Tripitakas on his tongue, he could not resist the temptation of flesh and the material life of the West.[3]

Ramaswamy, to a certain extent, succeeds in crossing the gulf by the rope-bridge of marriage with a French girl, Madeleine. The marriage in this case is not a permanent bridge made of stones and girders and its fragile nature begins to be clear when under the strain of death of their first child, some of the ropes give way. Like a true Vedantic, he found death illusory as the mist in the morning but he felt obssessed with fundamental problems like death. He has a curiosity to know, to peer through the veils of life and the eternal question-mark to life that death provides:

Who is it that tells me they did not die? Who but me? .... And if they've died, I ask you, where indeed did they go? ..... Where is Sunder now? Where? ..... for I cannot understand what death means.[4]

Ramaswamy remains a 'spiritual wanderer', a 'holy vagabond,' as he calls himself:

... because my mother was dead and I had to perform her funeral ceremonies, year after year, my father having married again. So with wet cloth and an empty stomach, with devotion, and sandal paste on my forehead, I fell before the rice balls of my mother and I sobbed. I was born an orphan, and have remained one. I have wandered the world and have sobbed in hotel rooms and in trains, have looked at the cold mountains and sobbed, for I had no mother.......[5]

After having performed the funeral ceremonies of his father, when Ram returns home Villa Saint Anne at Aix, he experiences growing alienation between himself and his wife. He realizes that something vital is missing in his relationship with his French wife Madeleine, older to him by a few years. Rama does not find Madeleine at home and tells her that she has failed him. Madeleine, on the other hand, is also disappointed by the Kumkum-spoiled saree which is not a gift from Rama. Besides, his action of pushing the toe-rings on Savitri's second toes, amounts to a symbolic marriage and makes the matrimonial rope-bridge between the East and the West precarious. The process of disintegration is hastened with death of Madeleine's second child and then completed by her acceptance of Buddhism and withdrawal from the world, and the inevitable divorce.

Their marriage was doomed to be a failure from the very beginning: The gulf that separates the East and the West cannot be spanned by rope bridges of such marriages, howsoever romantic and ideal they may appear. A little strain, a natural calamity, a mischief might undo them.

The matrimonial bridges must be all-weather bridges-made of stone or steel which neither incompatibility of temperament, nor marital inconstancy might damage, reinformed as these are with stronger cultural, traditional, religious, even national bonds so that they can stand the test of time and might not give way in the roughest weather.[6]

While talking of her love for Pierre, Rama tells us :

She spoke of all the hopes she had in him. He must be tall and twenty-three; he must go to an Engineering Institute and build bridges for India when he grew up. Like all melancholic people, Madeleine loved bridges. She felt truth was always on the other side...[7]

She knows that a very long bridge would be required to go across the cultural gulfs to reach the truth on the other side. If Pierre had lived to be twenty-three, he would have constructed a bridge across these cultural gulfs – children in India, as elsewhere, do serve as strong bridges to span the gulf that separates the husband from wife. They reach out to each other through him. She tried to reach Rama through a changed religion; she could not. It was a rope bridge.

Both Rama and Madeleine are constantly interpreting their own and each other's action in terms of their national and cultural differences invariably, ending up with generalizations about 'Indian and Western' traits of character. K.R.Rao observes, "They conceive themselves as archetypes than types."[8] The two have a mutual friend, an expatriate Russian, Georges. The three of them have interminable metaphysical and mystical discussions. Madeleine responds more to Georges' emotions then to Ramaswamy's feelings. It is all at the psychic level and not at all physical, but Rama feels jealous and left out. So his love affair with Madeleine did not last long. His love for his culture and obsessive concern with himself made him live like a recluse. His father dies leaving behind his third wife of twenty-six years old and two marriageable daughters. Rama was himself entangled in the snares of married life and was not prepared to cancel his programme of higher studies. As a result he could prove useful neither to his family nor could he live happily with his French wife. Alienation and anguish were natural concomitants.

East and West are portrayed not only as geographical or historical entities but also as ideas, living traditions, cultural, racial, philosophical and metaphysical manifestations. While doing his researches, he has been exploring the possibility of constructing some rope bridges to the West by carrying India as an Idea. He writes:

> India is not a country like France is, or like England; India is an idea, a metaphysic. Why go there anyhow. I thought; I was born an exile, and I could continue to be one. My India I carried wheresoever I went. But not to see the Ganges, not to dip into her again and again ... No, the Ganges was an inner truth to me, an assurance, the origin and end of my Brahminic tradition. I would go back to India, for that India was my breath, my only sweetness, gentle and wise; she was my mother. I felt I could still love something : a river, a mountain, the name of a woman....[9]

East and West sensibilities are presented in detail and in depth by combining religion, literature, philosophy, history and by evocation of popular beliefs and myths of respective cultures and traditions. If a metaphysical view of life is seen as the central operating principle in Indian tradition, the material and intellectual slant holds the sway in the Western scheme of things. Thus India which is both a metaphysical and geographical area "has no history, for truth cannot have history."[10] Ramaswamy is too much obsessed with Indian culture, history and literature that he feels alienated in France.

The marriage encounter between Rama and Madeleine becomes a rallying point for scrutinizing the problems and prospects of establishing intimate and meaningful relationships between two culture and social groups. The novel as such becomes "a potent response to the promise or threat of a cultural collision" in its dramatic rendering of "the tension ensuing from biculturalism."[11]

Uma Parmeshwaran discovers in Rama's attraction his desire to have an intellectual equal as a life companion."[12] Madeleine feels drawn towards him partly because of his exotic nature and partly because of illusory and false notions about 'Brahmanism'. Rama claims himself to be a 'Brahamin' in true sense – One who is 'devoted to truth' and 'who knows Brahma'. He offers his assertion:

It was the Brahamin in me .... The sense that touch and untouch are so important, which she sensed; and she would let me touch her.[13]

Rama tries to understand the spirit of France and in his perception places East and West on the same level. "Paris", he says, "is a sort of Benares turned outward."[14] He starts studying Christian teachings in order to be able to better comprehend the works of Dostoevsky. Similarly Madeleine tries to come closer to her husband by identifying herself with Rama and his 'dharma'. She participates in his superstitions by offering flowers and grass to the stone image on the highland near their house at Aix, which is worshipped by Rama as Nandi, the carrier of Lord Shiva. She tries to be of utmost help to Rama by cooking his food in the Indian way. She proves a good housewife always looking for his comforts. Rama shows his gratefulness to her:

There was nothing I needed which she did not know beforehand, and bring to me: my medicine after lunch, my handkerchief when I started on a walk, my pencil, duly sharpened and laid on my notebook.[15]

Madeleine is the first to realize the artificiality of her union with Rama. She feels shocked and exasperated by his love bereft of passion and personal and emotional touch:

Your impersonal approach was strange to me, you yourself so impersonal. I loved you for it, for in touching you I smelt, as it were, some mountain air, the honey pine of the heights, the smell of incense while the mist rises. Your heart was so like a mountain stream, its tenderness so pure. I loved to bathe in it. But how cruel it can be,. How exasperating for a European. You people are sentimental about the invisible, we about the visible. And to me you were the invisible made concrete, so visible, incarnate, beside me – and my husband.[16]

The death of their first-born son is a severe trauma to Madeleine but Rama takes it passively and credits Hinduism with teaching him to see death as a continuation of life:

So sorrow is our river, sorrow our earth, but the green of our trees and the white of our mountains are the affirmation that Truth is possible; that when the cycle of birth and death is over, we can proclaim ourselves the Truth. Truth is the Himalaya, and Ganges humanity. That is why we throw the ashes of the dead to her. She delivers them to the sea, and the sun heats the waters so that, becoming clouds, they return to the Himalaya. The cycle of death and birth goes on eternally like the snows and the rivers.[17]

But this detachment and objectivity displayed by Rama strikes her as cruel and heartless. Similarly while she considers as offspring the symbol of fulfilment of mutual love, she cannot but be critical of Rama's consideration of a son as a symbol of the continuation of family name. She stresses this aspect when writing to Rama:

I bore him, your son, with such love, for he was a child of love; but you were more interested in his sonship than in his being my son. The feminine to the Indian must always be accessory, a side issue. Yet I loved my son from the time I felt him kicking inside me, for he was your son. You thought of his future : I though of the present. You told me how in India you had to have different hymns and diet according to whether you wanted the child to be a hero, a wise man, a doctor or a grammarian. I just wanted a man: my son.[18]

Her own malleability and flexibility can be seen in her consent to the cremation of their son's dead body instead of burial with Christian rites.

Consequently when he returns to France, he begins to trace in him a great change "as his Indianness has begun to weigh heavier than all other considerations."[19] As he reflects upon his return to France:

For once I felt a stranger in France.[20]

Making a confession later on, Madeleine tells him that kissing him that day "was like kissing a serpent or the body of death."[21] It was at this stage that he notices the fact of Madeleine not being an Indian. An Indian bride is:

Auspicious, so auspicious-with kumkum, coconut and cholipiece, bangles on the arm, the necklace of black beads.[22]

He dresses Madeleine in the Sari that he has brought for her as a gift from his sister, Saroja. But Madeleine shows traces of consternation and pain to learn that the gift is from her sister-in-law, and not from her husband. Little Mother has given Rama two little toe-rings of his own mother, a gesture which expresses her desire to associate Madeleine with the noble line of wives in the family and to see Madeleine carry on the tradition of an ideal wife. The hairloom, another gift is purchased out of sentimental consideration for her. But these gifts remain packed in his suitcase. M.K.Naik makes a pertinent and profoundly significant observation discussing the significance of Rama's failure to hand over those gifts to Madeleine:

All this adds up to a vague realization on Rama's part that, at least for an Indian, marriage cannot be a merely personal bond-howsoever strong-between a man and a woman, but something more; that this bond, in order to continue to remain firm and strong, must be interwoven with stronger bonds such as family traditions and loyalties, and a commonly shared spiritual and cultural ethos.[23]

The simmering awareness of differences surfaces as Rama says to Madeleine:

"Mado, something has happened." She, who was half-filling her spoon with rice, stopped, and said: "Yes, something has." I was quiet. Then she said, slowly, "To whom?" "To everything," I answered, and laid my spoon down.[24]

Ramaswamy, thus, brings into sharp focus the alteration wrought into him by Indian experience. Rama's recitals, however, do not convey the whole truth. Any detached and dispassionate probing will reveal unsuspecting dimensions of Rama's personality and character. He is married to Madeleine but he seduces Lakshmi, the wife of his friend in Bombay and develops love relationship with Savithri.

The growing rift in Madeleine-Rama relationship stands counter-balanced by developing intimacy between Rama and Savithri. Long before the marriage, Rama feels deep in his soul that the real lasting union is possible only with a Hindu woman because the wedding should be founded on deep spiritual unity. Savithri is a Hindu woman whom Rama meets in India when he goes to cremate his father. Rama analyses his relationship with her. On the one hand, they seem to be totally different persons: She is from North and he is from South; she loves London and he loves Paris; she is capable of discussing politics, and he is fond of religion. She makes friends with communists, and he with intellectuals indifferent to politics. And in general Rama "could not understand these northerness going from strict purdah to this extreme modernism with unholy haste."[25] But on the other hand, he is attracted by her. Savithri impresses Rama by the fact that she is a Hindu. Her dense oriental eyebrows, knowledge of Indian customs, ability to read Sanskrit, treasures from Agra, the fragrance of atter of roses from Lucknow – all these make Rama feel that he is in India. The mental associations, which emerge in

Rama when he thinks about Savithri, are also characteristic:

She became the awareness behind my awareness, the leap of my understanding. I lost the world and she became it. For whatever I gave her she accepted, as the Ganges receive the waters of the Himalayas, that go down to the sea and come again as white flakes of snow, then the sun comes northward again, the ice melts the waters down to the sea. So we gave love to each other.[26]

There is an internal conflict in the soul of Rama, who loves Madeleine but is attracted towards Savithri. While conversing with Madeleine each time he has to explain to her something or the other, but Savithri understands him and catches the meaning at once. Madeleine for him is purity, nobleness, and sanctity by itself, whereas Savithri personifies motherland and belief :

Savithri was there, not in me but as me-not as some one far, unreal relegated to a country in rounded space, but as light which seemed never to fade, never to know where to go.[27]

Further Rama Says :

With Madeleine everything was explanation, with Savithri it was recognition.[28]

Savithri and Rama enact a symbolic marriage in London. Rama slips the toe rings meant for Madeleine on her toes. M.K.Naik rightly finds in this ritual symbolic marriage the 'doom' of Rama-Madeleine's marriage bond.[29] However effective this wedding of the eternal lord and spouse at Rama's behest may have been, Savithri leaves for Allahabad to become Partap's wife and thus accepts house holder's 'Karmic' path to the end of her life.

Despite the accommodating nature, the barrier of her own cultural conditioning proves a stumbling block in her path. Though she 'transcends her own cultural orientation to a certain extent, 'she remains unable to acquire an inward knowledge of

Rama's Indian culture.'[30]

In her efforts to come closer to Ramaswamy and to share his religion and mythology, she erroneously embraces Buddhism considering it to be an Indian religion. But Christianity is in her blood:

> For Madeleine there is an area which is not me that she fills with Christian longings, but she won't admit it.[31]

Even in her study of Buddhism, she cannot go beyond surfaces. She is unable to realize that "dukha is the very tragedy of creation" whereas Rama with his Indian metaphysical tradition can "feel the word dukha almost with the entrails dropping into my hand."[32]

Shiv Niranjan finds behind her misery and plight, 'lack of authenticity.' The charge has basis in 'betrayal'[33] of her own catholic religion in her zeal to embrace Buddhism. In an interview with Shiv Niranjan, Raja Rao himself seems to substantiate the view:

> In trying to become a Buddhist, she was unfair to her own 'dharma' which was Catholicism. If she had been a good catholic, she might have been alright with Ramaswamy... If she had been a good catholic, it would still be different from Sankara's non-dualism. I am interested in authenticity. One should be authentic. It does not matter what you are, but you must be authentic. For example, I have seen Gandhi Ji and Maulana Azad face to face with each other at Sevagram. I have spent quite some time at Sevagram with Gandhi Ji. Gandhi was a good Hindu. Azad was a good Muslim. They talked to each other with authenticity. They had respect for each other, each was authentic. It is to those who are not authentic that misery comes.[34]

While Raja Rao demands authenticity on the part of Madeleine, it is Rama who actually needs to be authentic. Rama does talk of Hindu culture and traditions but he is not able to fulfil the norms and codes that a Hindu society puts before its inhabitants. Hindu dharama does not allow extra-marital relations. Marriage is a spiritual bond, an all weather proof bond. Rama who talks high of his Brahaminism and Hinduism, have relations with Savithri and Lakshmi. He enacts a symbolic marriage with Savithri. His Brahaminism is all sham as we do find incestuous overtones in his sister Saroja's descriptions. The incestuous feelings towards Saroja, becomes the prime cause behind his alienation from his wife Madeleine. He does not show loyalty or stability in his relationships. He cannot build permanent bridges.

Rama is not ready to come out of his Brahaminic shell to understand his wife's feelings and emotions. Madeleine tries her best to come closer to Rama and transcends her own religion into his Hindu Buddhist philosophy and religion.

Her behaviour towards Rama becomes not only casual but even cold and heartless. Aware of the meaninglessness of retaining the marriage bond, she writes:

I am sure it would also be wise to give Rama his freedom. He must marry someone younger from his own country. He will be happy with an Indian woman, I have no doubt.[35]

Separated from his wife Rama, too is haunted by the amiable memories of the past as well as the painful realization of his own isolation. He cries out in a mood of seemingly total vacancy and dejection:

There is nobody to go to now : no home, no temple, no city, no climate, no age.[36]

In treating them as "highly sensitive representatives of their countries, 'cultural and metaphysical approaches to life,"[37] their personal relationship must bear the representative burden. K.R.Rao makes a thoroughly pertinent observation:

Both Rama and Madeleine succumb to the characteristic determinisms of their individual cultures despite their endeavours to transcend them and achieve a mutual personal equation.[38]

Finally, Ramaswamy realized the cause of his doomed relatedness to Madeleine. "Had I been less of a Brahmin, I might have known more of 'love"[39].This was his tragedy : he was a Brahmin in the true sense i.e. a man devoted to higher values, but without his capacity to ignore the demands of his flesh. His is a tragedy of one who has a culture of his own and yet does not belong to it. Madeleine proposed divorce and they were separated legally.

Rama confessed:

Now, I think I know, but I must go, I must go to Travancore. I have no Benares now, no Ganga, no Jamuna; Travancore is my country, Travancore my name.[40]

All that he said in France was 'abstruse' and all that he has done in France was "mere exhibition of adolescent enthusiasm for Indian philosophy".[41] While talking about Indianism and Brahaminism, he is always talking about myths. Rama, preoccupied as he was with the ultimate problems of life, had no time to think of his mundane responsibilities. Like a "wanderer on earth", or "a holy vagabond" Rama is depicted to be passing through various situations, not ignoring them by any means but, nevertheless, using them like so many means in his endeavour to transcend the fragmented and splintered world view to arrive at an integrated one, to reach out to the absolute in order that the relative may become meaningful. It is then that he mutters to himself the metaphysical question:

Who are you and whose; whence have you come?[42]

Finally he understands that he himself needs a Guru who can show him the right path and make him understand that he needs wisdom and not knowledge; who alone can curb his ego and make him fit for the great consummation.

Ramaswamy's too much concern with his Indian background and Brahminism make him a wretched being who is not able to adjust himself either to his wife or to his family in India. He is sad to find himself an orphan in this world and so without any protection. He had lost his mother when he was a little child. And he could not love and integrate with the being of his father. It is his alienation from his present marital life with Madeleine that makes him feel a romantic, yearning for his past ancestral heritage. There he wishes to locate and be submerged in the roots which become discernible in his long line of ancestors and their metaphysical musings. We find him weeping in hotel room over the death of his protective mother, which signifies an isolated life away from his own homely environment.

Madeleine is a being who loves bridges and always remains on the look out to cross them. She finds happiness only in having her passionate love with Ramaswamy realized. But for Ramaswamy the bridge signifies only the separating gulf, which he finds himself unable to cross. The death of his mother and his continuous weeping throughout his life remind us of his lone, sad and root-less existence.

Both Ramaswamy and Madeleine find themselves in an intricate human situation where his psychological state refuses to feel the house they inhibit as his home fit for a well-knit family.

No doubt for Ramaswamy,

India represents an idea, the idea of the Absolute which makes the relative meaningful, but man must learn not to mistake the relative for the Absolute, the moment for Eternity, the particular for the Universal, the shadow for the substance, the rope for serpent. Only that knowledge is knowledge which makes for this discrimination, and space, time, the country and the world, wife, family, friends, all help if one knows they are means to an end – the end of all earthly endeavour is that knowledge of the self.[43]

First a man should know himself and only then can he be said to belong anywhere. Until then he remains a wanderer, a vagabond on the earth.

References

1. Raja Rao, "The Serpent and the Rope" (New Delhi, Oriental Paper backs, 1968), p.109.
2. Ibid., p.302.
3. R.S.Singh, "Kanthapura"(Delhi:Doaba House,1973),
4. p.7.
5. Raja Rao, op.cit., pp.5-8.
6. Ibid., pp.5-6.
7. Ramesh K. Srivastva, "Six Indian Novelists in
8. English"(Amritsar
9. Guru Nanak Dev University ,1987), p.32.
10. Raja Rao, op.cit., pp.12-13.
11. K.R Rao, "The Fiction of Raja Rao" (Aurangabad, Parimal
12. Parkashan, 1980), p.75.
13. Raja Rao, op.cit., p.376.
14. Ibid., p.102.
15. Uma Parmeswaran, "Excelsior-Raja Rao", A study of Representative Indo-English Novelists(New Delhi: Vikash Publishing House, 1975), p.1562. Quoted from Adarsh Kumar" Treatment of International Marriage in Indo-English Fiction with reference to Raja Rao's "The Serpent and the Rope", Ruth Jhabwala's "A Backward Place and Anita Desai's Bye-Bye Blackbird', An unpublished M.Phil. Dissertation (Kurukshetra: Kurukshetra University, 1987) p.24.
16. Raja Rao, op.cit., p.13.
17. Ibid., p. 52.
18. Ibid., p.77.
19. Ibid., pp. 36-37.
20. Ibid., p.35.
21. Ibid., p.36.

22. Shiv Niranjan, "Between Two Waves of the Sea", Raja Rao: Novelist as Sadhaka" (Gaziabad: Vimal Parkashan, 1985), p.76. Quoted from Adarsh Kumar, op.cit.,p.29.
23. Shiv Niranjan, op.cit., p.76.
24. Raja Rao, op.cit., p.59.
25. Ibid., p.59.
26. Ibid., p.56.
27. M.K. Naik, op.cit., p.82.
28. Raja Rao, op.cit., p.65.
29. Ibid., p.31.
30. Ibid., pp.169-70.
31. Ibid., p.242.
32. Ibid., p.340.
33. M.K. Naik, op.cit., p.82.
34. S. Krishnamoorthy Aithal and Rashmi Aithal,"Indo-English Fictiònal Experiments with inter-racial and Inter-cultural relationship", in lien Voice: "Perspective on Commonwealth Literatuire", ed. By A.K.Srivastva (Lucknow: Print House, 1981), p.95. Quoted from Adarsh Kumar, op.cit.,p.35.
35. Raja Rao, op.cit., p.80.
36. Ibid.
37. Shiv Niranjan, op.cit., p.80.
38. Quoted from Shiv Niranjan in "Between Two Waves of the Sea"' Raja Rao: Novelist as Sadhaka, p.81.
39. Raja Rao, op.cit., p.394.
40. Ibid., p. 402.
41. Shiv Niranjan, op.cit., p.77.
42. K..Rao, op.cit., pp.71-72.
43. Raja Rao, op.cit., p.400.
44. Ibid., p. 405.
45. R. S. S
46. ingh, op.cit., p.7.
47. Raja Rao, op.cit., p.402.
48. C.D. Narasimhaiah, op.cit., p.81.

9

ROHINTON MISTRY'S SUCH A LONG JOURNEY: THE PARSI FEELINGS

-Bhan Singh

It goes without saying that Rohinton Mistry, the socio-political novelist, has emerged as prominent literary figure on the world literary scene in the present times. He was born on July 3, 1952 in Bombay.He graduated in Mathematics from the University of Bombay in 1974 and eventually emigrated to Canada in 1975. He worked as a bank clerk in Toronto and studied English and Philosophy simultaneously at the University of Toronto. Mistry started his career with the publication of short-stories winning him a number of prizes. His short-story collection, Tales From Firozsha Baag was published in Canada in 1987 (later in the U.K. in 1992). He authored three novels, Such a Long Journey (1991), A Fine Balance (1996) and Family Matters (2002). The first two novels were short listed for the Booker Prize for Fiction and the third was short listed for the 2002 Man Booker Prize for Fiction.

Mistry's first novel, Such A Long Journey won Governor General's Literary Award for Fiction in Canada in 1991 and Commonwealth Writers Prize (over-all winner, Best Book) in 1992. The novel is set in Bombay against the back-drop of the Indo-Pakistan war of 1971 and the emergence of Bangladesh as a separate independent state. There are few Indian English Novels that have effectively used the back drop of the post-independent Indian political context particularly of the crucial period of the sixties and the seventies. The novelist offers commentary on the socio-political situation and raised a national debate on corruption in high places. The central character of the novel is not a conventional hero. Gustad Noble is simply a bank clerk, a family man and vulnerable figure whose world is still haunted by the war with China in 1962. The fate of his family is closely bound up with that of crises and turmoil in the Sub-continent. Mistry expertly marries the major events in India with those in the private sphere of the Noble family and the other important characters in the novel.

It is worth mentioning that the title Such A Long Journey has been taken from T.S. Eliot's famous poem "Journey of the Magi".

A cold coming we had of it,

Just the worst time of the year

For a journey,0 and such a long journey.......

Moreover, this poem leaves a deep imprint on his writing. The poem is highly symbolic in which the journey of three wise men to the birth place of Jesus Christ is not merely an ordinary physical journey. It is symbolic of man's spiritual quest in which they have to undergo numerous hardships. Later, one of the Magi gives an account of his painful journey for the benefit of a listener. He clearly reveals how he was impelled to proceed merely because of his faith. He was successful in overcoming all the hardships and hindrances that befell his way. The end of the journey was rewarding and satisfying, for he had reached his destination where he realized that the prophecy of the birth of Christ was true. The journey of the Magi is also symbolic of the re-orientation which is absolutely essential to attain higher and nobler values of life.

Gustad Noble, as his very name suggests, is noble whose character is determined to a great extent by challenges thrown up by the conspiring circumstances. He had to face many hardships and problems in his life. He had his own dreams about the future. He had plans for his eldest son, Sohrab. With the passage of time his dreams, plans and aspirations crumble down like a pack of cards. Gustad Noble's journey of life is very close to the journey of the Magi. He was keenly desirous of the fulfilment of his dreams and aspirations. At every stage of his life's journey, he had to face unprecedented obstacles and the working of inexplicable forces. But he was not the one to give in; he was like the wise man who very subtly pushed aside the hindrances of life, did not allow them to overpower him and went ahead with faith that the journey will surely end at a particular destination.

After passing through different experiences of life, Gustad Noble came to a very significant conclusion: "Luck is the spit of the Gods and Goddesses" (338). Though the novelist has made him utter this thought, yet it is totally applicable to the life of the speaker i.e. Gustad Noble. He never shunned the problems of life; nor was he in any way mortified by his experience. As he himself says, "it was his strength of spirit" which made the journey possible. He purposefully made himself tough so much so that he did not shed even a single tear on the death of his mother. But after all Gustad was a human and when his steadfastness was tested by the betrayal of Sohrab and Jimmy Bilimoria, he breaks down saying "I do not understand this world anymore........... what a world of wickedness it has become ! (142). Rohinton Mistry's ideas about fate and destiny are similar to those of Thomas Hardy, who wrote in his poem "To Life":

"O, life with the sad sacred face
I, weary, of seeing thee,
I know what thou wouldst tell
Of Death, Time, Destiny
I have known it long, and know, too well,
What it all means for me"

Hardly evidently says that man is bound to the wheel of destiny and therefore has to struggle continuously against the decrees of fate. Man should not surrender meekly. The Greeks also believed that the Malignant Power and the Immanent Will Stand firmly against the plans of the frail and feeble creature called man. William Shakespeare also express the same view in King Lear:

"As flies to wanton boys, are we to the Gods
They kill us for their sport."

The message in the novel Such A Long Journey is not that of a pessimist, rather it is that of a meliorist, who believes that man must accept what destiny has in store for him.

Gustad Noble's long journey in a cold and malevolent world in which all forms of happiness and misery are woven inseparably is the journey of an ethnic group, a community which is on the verge of extinction. Rohinton Mistry in Such A Long Journey raises certain basic issues, feelings and problems of the Parsi community to which he belongs. There are a few novelists like Rohinton Mistry whose works focus their community. He presents his community through the different narratives of his characters who invariably express their concern for their community and the changes that affect their community. Since their fate is bound up with the fate of their community, their stories tend to be the stories of their community. By centralizing their community in their narratives, they preserve and protect themselves and thus they throw light on the existing facts. The Parsi community is on a long journey to growing and knowing in Mistry's Such A Long Journey written somewhat in the manner of fiction or non-fiction. Gustad Noble's dreams and aspirations are quite modest but the circumstances conspire to deny him even these modest expectations. As the novel unfolds, he discovers that there are other forces at play, larger than him and mostly inexplicable such as loss of a dear friendship, the son's betrayal of his father's dreams, the illness of Gustad's daughter, his friend Dinshawji's death.

In this novel Dinshawji remarks: "What days those were, yaar. What fun we used to have. Parsees were the kings of banking in those days. Such respect we used to get. Now the whole atmosphere has been spoiled ever since that Indira nationalized the banks." Gustad Noble also expresses his feelings in the same way: "Nowhere in the world has nationalization worked." "What can you say to idiots?" Like Gustad, other members of the community are scared of politicians like Mrs. Gandhi whom they consider responsible for encouraging the demand for a separate Maharashtra "How much bloodshed, how much rioting she caused." (39). As a minority community, the Parsis have their little fears and anxieties. Dinshawji expresses his concern about rising communal forces:

"No future for minorities, with all these Shiv Sena Politics and Marathi language nonsense. It was going to be like the black people in America twice as good as the white men to get half as much. How could he make Sohrab understand this?" (55)

Regarding the change of the street names in Bombay, Dinshawji comments on the notion of displacement:

"Names are so important, I grew up on Lamington Road. But it has disappeared, in its place is Dadasaheb Bhadkhamar Marg. My school was on Carnac Road. Now suddenly its on Lok Manya Tilak Marg. I live at Sleater Road. Soon that will also disappear. My whole life, I have come to work at Flora Fountain. And one fine day the name changes. So what happens to the life, I have life? Was I living the wrong life, with all the wrong names? Will I get a second chance to live it all again, with these new names? Tell me what happens to my life. Rubbed out, just like that? Tell me." (74)

Major Bilimoria's reappearance on the scene of action disturbs the already precarious position of Gustad. Through the enactment of Nagarwala case, he makes an important political statement. Nagarwala received nearly sixty lakh rupees from a bank manager in Delhi, allegedly on the strength of a phone call from the P.M. which, it was said, he imitated. Nagarwala was dead after a few months. Nobody knew where the money went. Since it involved a member of Parsi Community, the Parsis were considerable perturbed and the death of Nagarwala itself raised many eyebrows. Here is a view of a Parsi about the incident:

"The Nagarwala incident, because it involved a Parsi, jolted the self image of the community no less. Having long ago lost their literature to the vandalism of Alexander the Accursed, and their dance, music, art, poetry and even their language to the process of adapting to a new home in India the Parsis have developed a particularized culture culled from a mixture of ancient myth and legend overlaid by a life sustaining sense of recent achievement. Gratified to have earned an honourable place in the country of their adoption through their contribution to every field of endeavor and proud of having retained a strong ethical tradition the Parsis were deeply anguished by the ambivalent role Nagarwala had played in the sordid story".

In Such A Long Journey, Mistry makes a 'conscious' use of the celebrated Sohrab-Rustom myth. If the confrontation between father and son in the myth ends on a tragic note. Mistry's narrative ends on a note of reconciliation. Gustad views Sohrab's rebellious gesture as a symptom of the loss of respect for tradition and values. What brings back Sohrab in the narrative is the strength of spirit demonstrated by Gustad after Tehmul's tragic death. Thus while using a Zoroastrian myth in the novel, Mistry highlights the generation gap which seems to threaten the very existence of Parsi family life.

From a purely subjective plane of self-indulgence, Gustad

Noble moves on to a much deeper and complex level to examine truths of life. His long journey is a manifestation of the universal phenomenon-the dilemma between the Good and the Evil and his survival is the victory of the Zoroastrian faith. On the whole, Such A long Journey expresses the author's feelings about his community and contributes in advancing the notion of community literature.

References

- Rohinton Mistry, Such A Long Journey (New Delhi; Rupa, 1991) p. 39.
- Ibid., p. 55.
- Ibid., p. 74
- Murial Wasi, "Putting Magic into Realism", The Hindu (Literary Review), 4 July 1993 P. 1.

□□□□

10

Oppression And Resistance In Rohintons Mistry's A Fine BAlance

-Suman Bhatia

Literally the term 'Diaspora' means the dispersion or scattering of the people of a Community. Transnational shift is the requirement of diaspora. The term also has religious meaning and can be used for a minority section living in any country. In the post colonial times it has become an umbrella term and is now used for the expatriates, the exiles, the emigrants, and the immigrants. Unlike, the other diasporic writers who share identical religious beliefs, the Indian expatriates belong to a country, which is not monolithic. So they try to relate with their original homeland, with its myth and culture.

Alienation is not a characteristic of the diasporic subject alone. Inequality and disenfranchisement related to class, gender, sexuality and ethnicity inevitably produce alienated and marginalized individuals. This normal state of thing is exacerbated during periods of acute national crisis, when the struggle between marginalised and dominant groups in society is thrown into relief. Mistry's novels focus our attention on the dynamics of internal displacements and dislocations of class, gender, caste and locality within the nation- that are, in turn, over determined by the brutality of the nation.

Rohinton Mistry emigrated to Canada in 1975. On leaving Mumbai, Mistry confesses in the literary journal (Rungh 1993) that his departure from India was partially encouraged by the expectations of his peers, especially those of his generation.

After finishing college in Mumbai or elsewhere in India, one had to go abroad for higher studies. If possible, one had to find a job after finishing a Masters or Ph. D. in the States or in England, find a job and settle in the country. That is how success is defined by Indians. So, that is why I say that coming to Canada was in some ways decided for me"(As quoted in Mehfil November 1996).

Rohinton Mistry is a writer who makes up a part of the Indian Diaspora. Moreover he is also a Zoroastrian Parṣi whose ancestors were exiled by the Islamic conquest of Iran. During India's colonized period the Parsies were favourites of the British rulers. Both parties cooperated well together. But the situation changed in 1947, after India's independence and partition. This forced many Parsies to look towards Western countries. It resulted in their migrating to England and to America, marking the western diaspora of the Parsies. Like other Parsi writers Rohinton Mistry's work is guided by this experience of double displacement. As a Parsi, Mistry finds himself at the margins of Indian society. So his writings challenge and resist absorption by the dominating and Hindu glorifying culture of India.

Though Rohinton Mistry has been amongst Canada's most successful writers over the past 20 years, he writes very little about Canada itself. Instead, he focuses almost exclusively on India, and on the state of the Parsi community within that country. Even when he writes about Canada in his short stories or novels, he often represents his adopted country as the site of a Parsi diaspora, a place where immigrant Parsies renegotiate their identities and their relationships with one of India's most endangered communities. What Mistry explores in his writings are the relationships at the heart of Parsi community, their cultural identity and the uniqueness of their community living. Misrty also seeks to shed light and embrace the syncretic nature of the diasporic Parsi experience whether that be in

North America or in India. In his short stories as well as in his novels, Mistry underlines both the heterogeneous nature of one's community's identity and its dynamism. Also, Mistry loves to take as his subject some of the most down trodden, oppressed and exploited people in Indian society. Traumatism in its inevitability brings change to the characters' lives, which Mistry zooms in. What he affirms is the power and resilience of the individual and that of the community in a world without a shread of pity.

Depending on one's perspective, the trajectory of Mistry's life and his art can be seen either as reflecting that decline or as countering it. Mistry grew up in a Parsi Baag in Mumbai. He received a bachelor's degree in Mathematics and Economics from the University of Mumbai, a compromise between more prestigious study of Engineering, medicine and law-which he did not wish to pursue- and his inclination to study literature. He left India in 1975- one month after imposition of Emergency by the then Government. In Canada while working as a Bank Teller, he followed his true inclinations, studying English and Philosophy at the University of Toronto. Soon after graduating with his second bachelor's degree, he began to be recognized as a strong voice in the developing multicultural literary landscape of Canada.

A Fine Balance is set in an unnamed Indian city situated near sea—presumably Mumbai—in 1975. It centers around the unlikely living arrangements of four characters who are forced by their strained economic circumstances to share an apartment. Dina Dalal is a widow who has spent her life trying to escape her abusive and domineering brother, in a society where independent women are, to say the least, not the norm. The apartment represents her attempts to maintain her freedom, but she cannot afford the rent on her own. She is first convinced to take in a fellow Parsi as a boarder, Maneck Kohlah, whose parents have sent him to the city from his beloved Himalayan hill country, so that he can earn a degree. Then she hires two tailors to do piece work-Ishwar Darzi and his seventeen years old nephew Omprakash. Both are dalits of the Chamar caste who have fled the caste oppression in their village. Ishwar is devoted to the task of finding his nephew a wife. Dina Dalal's brother, who is a businessman, is their employer, but she herself is struggling to preserve her fragile independence, hoping to climb into the ranks of the middle class. Maneck Kohlah, the student comes from a well-to-do family but shares the alienation of the other character in the novel. The most tragic and poignant moments in the novel are those that deal with the plight of a limbless beggar, Shanker, one of the hundreds under the supervision of the beggar master who owns them. Through these characters, Mistry presents us with a snapshot of a nation in crisis.

The novel takes a dig at political situation and oppression of downtrodden by mightier also. Om and Prakash's father grew up as 'untouchables' in a small village of India. When India obtained its independence in 1947, caste distinctions formally were abolished. The new Government of India said caste distinctions were illegal, but they continued to exist in reality. The two brothers were born into an untouchable caste that skinned animals and tanned leather. The upper caste landlords in the village beat up the untouchables in order to keep them subordinate. They were beaten when their unclean eyes met the eyes of an upper caste Brahmin, when they walked on the wrong side of a temple road and supposedly defiled it or when they went too near a prayer meeting, overhearing the sacred text.

Prakash's father dares to ask for his own election ballot, instead of just giving his fingerprints and allowing the landlord to vote for him. In response, the upper caste landlord sends his goons to whip the father, urinate on him, put burning coals on his genitals, and then stuff the coals in his mouth. The goons then go on a rampage beating up untouchables at random in their quarters. The family of Prakash's father is pursued, his two grandchildren are knifed to death, and then the house of the family is set on fire, burning up the six in it. In a nearby city, Om takes refuge where he finds assistance from a Muslim friend from the village. He comments that he has more in common with the Muslim than with the wealthy of his own religion. But soon the city is engulfed in violence between Hindus and Muslims. We get a feel of what's behind it.

Despite their backgrounds, the four characters developed into something like family, as they lean on each other in the face of financial hardships, personal troubles, and political turmoil. What unite the different characters in the novel is not only their oppression, but also their geographical and cultural displacement. Omprakash and Ishwar come to represent the thousands in search of a better life in the cities, only to live out their lives in the wretchedness of urban slums and the forced labour camps of Indira Gandhi's 'Garibi Hatao' compaign. Maneck Kohlah, on the other hand seems to stand in for the classic rural/urban dichotomy, here depicted as the relationship between the small businesses of the hill stations and the corporate capitalism of the cities in the plains. Shankar's very identity is fused with the wheeled platform that he uses to move around. Amidst these migrant and dislocated characters the one steady presence is that of Dina Dalal's home, which functions as point of reference or a center that is constantly in danger of falling apart.

And it did fall apart, when unable to cope with circumstances, Dina decided to move back to his brother's home. Om and his nephew found housing in a slum erected illegally on government land. However the web of bribery has entangled the entire government machinery. The slumlord bribes the police, water inspector and electricity officer to allow it to operate. The police damaged a taxi because the driver was late with his weekly bribe.

The novel brings us face to face with the brutalities of such supposedly welfare programs of government as Indira Gandhi's are capable and depicts what miseries they bring with. It amply demonstrates that native rule is no panacea for the ills of the third world and helps us to understand why refugees from these countries continue to seek a better life in America, long after their colonial masters have left them. Om and Ishwar get caught up in "democratic" India's family planning program of sterilization. The government decided to pay the patient to have the operation, but the money goes to the police boss of the area. Government workers are forced to produce two or three people from the village for sterilization each month, otherwise they aren't paid. So the upper caste political boss has the schoolteachers, tax collectors and food inspectors pay him a bribe. Whoever pays the most is allowed to be considered finished with the round up for sterilization that month.

Over the course of time, Om and Ishwar become beggars. We learn about the beggar master to whom the beggars pay for protection, who in turn bribes the police, and who protects the beggars against attackers and thugs. A family sells their ugly daughter to be a beggar. Numerous beggars have their deformities worsened to turn in more money.

We see a close relationship between the characters and their immediate physical environment. Ishwar's father, Dukhi, having worked with dead animals all his life, finds that his own skin became impregnated with the odor that was part of his father's smell, the leather-workers stink that would not depart even after he had washed and scrubbed in the all the cleansing river. He wondered if flaying would get rid of it. Or did it go deeper than skin? He pricked himself to smell his blood but the test was inconclusive. And what about muscles and the bone, did the stink lurk in them too? The lives of other characters including the local beggar master, a guilt ridden rent collector, a hair collector who takes his work too seriously, and even a litter of nearly feral cats-become intervened with those of the principles, providing an unusually detailed and richly textured portrait of a community of the urban poor.

A Fine Balance is a harshly realistic novel. Told almost entirely from the point of view of subaltern and petty-bourgeois characters, the novel is firmly grounded, both in its narrative voice and in its sense of time and place. This novel grimly captures the despair of these classes during this period of almost total devastation. But of this despair comes the attempt to form human connections in an inhuman world. The four key characters, which are initially strangers to one another, are thrown together by the force of circumstance and necessity. The novel traces their struggle to survive the emergence of a sense of community amongst them; and the eventual destruction of this community in the face of brutality of larger social forces. The power of A Fine Balance comes from its ability to weave together the varied histories of its characters and in its creation of a tapestry of almost five decades of Indian history.

In the novel, combinations of a brutally repressive state, crushing poverty and caste oppression overwhelm the individual act of resistance or subversion. In other words resistance in this novel is personalized, individualized and therefore necessarily short lived and ultimately doomed to failure. Opposition here gets reified into a sort of micro-resistance with organized politics and collective action as something one only hears about in terms that evoke images of unruly mobs.

The most obvious accomplishment of the novel is its realistic portrayal of the brutalities of lives lived in stifling poverty. It achieves this effect primarily by keeping any form of organized resistance on the part of the lower classes. In A Fine Balance, it is the element of subaltern activity of political agency that is constantly kept at bay. The murdered student revolutionary, the numerous anti-government protests that are mentioned in passing and the occasional newspaper articles about troublemakers and strikes alert us to the presence of organized resistance. This resistance, however hovers phantom like in the background, unseen and unheard throughout the novel. A Fine Balance thus accomplishes the task of evoking the reader's sympathy, but it remains fundamentally blind to the possibility of the agency of the subaltern classes.

This novel is notable for its ending, which is far from happy. Over the course of the novel, each character is subjected to intense physical, mental and emotional pain at the hands of sinister strangers. This culminates in the ending, where Ishwar's legs are forced to be amputated, Omprakash is castrated and his legs and body swell up greatly from the harmone changes caused by the operation, and the Maneck, overcome by how his two friends ended up, steps in front of a speeding train in the middle of a crowded train station. It is interesting to note that the characters that are able to maintain a fine balance in life are the ones that survive the ending. Mistry steers the novel around the types of balances that the characters maintain in their life and outcomes that they meet at the end.

Thus A Fine Balance reifies oppression and resistance of the oppressed and therefore presents a static view of a postcolonial society.

❑❑❑❑

11

Different Attitudes Towards West: A Study of Mistry and Lahiri

-Sarika Goyal

Today we live in the 21st century where new issues and new problems have been cropping up. One amongst these is the pressure felt by the writers of the diaspora. People from South-Asia have migrated to the western countries in the hope of greener pastures there. These countries are technologically more advanced, prosperous and also provide site to the intellect to work. For the same reason, these have been labeled to be bringing about brain drain. The inhabitants of these alien areas interact in other languages and have different cultures and religions. Thus most of the immigrants find it hard to get acclimatized with the new situation.

One undergoes identity crisis in the new atmosphere. Every human being seeks self-realization and therefore is in constant search of another person after talking to whom s/he can express her/himself. If this identity is threatened, a kind of fear-psychosis starts operating in the individual. This identity itself assumes different forms- it can be based on gender, class, religion, race, culture or economic stratification. As a result of ethnic clashes worldwide and increasing awareness about new critical theories this problem becomes acute. "At some places, identity is referred to as a conscious sense of individual uniqueness, at others, to an unconsciousness striving for continuity of experience and at yet other places as a sense of solidarity with a group's ideal" (qtd. in Pathak, Quest for Identity, 3).

Thus writers of the diaspora feel this crisis- a feeling of

otherness and try to come to terms with it but the mind, in search of answers to this crucial issue, starts narrating the experience in fiction. Most of the authors have reflected upon this rootlessness in their works. Jhabwala, Mistry, Lahiri, Seth, Rushdie, Desai and others- all have tried to voice their opinions, but with a difference- the difference of the milieu, gender, education, age, community and individual ideology. This paper is a modest attempt to study this difference in two authors viz. Mistry and Lahiri.

The writers of the diaspora inhabit different landscapes. Their minds go back to the land they have left behind. Unable to forget the past they express it in language."Writers are unable to deny the lure of the nation, its tides in our blood. Writing as mapping: the cartography of the imagination or as modern critical theory might spell it Imagi/ Nation." (Rushdie, Step Across This Line, 66).

Rushdie believes that the diasporic writers inhabit 'imaginary homelands' which they create in their fiction as most of them are unable to pay frequent visits to their motherlands and build these in their minds. Truly the writers get delocated in the new world and try to relocate themselves in the new situations- an attempt in which only a few succeed whereas most others get alienated. The outer world is one of multiculturalism, where in order to find culture one actually confronts aculturalism.

Jasbir Jain thinks that a writer living abroad lives on the margins of two societies. They act either as ambassadors or refugees in their creative works. Naturally they will be having different perspectives by which they view their individual experiences in the native land. There is no denying the fact that some of them find the new home more hospitable and favourable whereas for some others, there is always a feeling of nostalgia lurking somewhere.

A writer should not turn out to be a propagandist if s/he really wants to be acclaimed. One, on the other hand, must follow a global approach though being concerned about personal identity. " In their writings, the diaspora with its shifting boundaries and conflictual encounters between different cultures is an important locus where nationalisms and literature need to redefine themselves" (qtd in Patnayak, Diviner, 9).

The writers under study belong to the educated class and view life in the west differently. Rohinton Mistry is a Parsi, hailing from Bombay who migrated to Canada in 1975. He spent initial years of his life in India and felt ethnic clashes with the dominating group-the Hindus. Even after migration his senses bring him back to that India he had left long ago. He listens to news clips, gathers popular notions of people and amalgamates it with his own India. Being a male, he displays interest in Politics, Cricket, riddles and other stuff of the kind. Parsis consider themselves to be a part of Western Culture and therefore superior to the natives. As a result, most of his characters show a nostalgic feeling for India.

On the contrary, Jhumpa Lahiri comes from Bengal and displays subtle sensibility towards cuisine, architecture, dresses and Bengali customs. Her approach is Indian in 'Interpreter of Maladies' as far as locale and characters are concerned but she portrays adjusting nature of her protagonists in her novel. The writers thus have varying outlooks and project a significant difference. Therefore, they gain less importance in India as 'their self-definitions are rooted in their regional identities' (Rushdie, 169).

Even if we view it in another perspective, this creation of regional identity provides pleasure and satisfaction to its creater. After leaving home, one is exiled and this condition is dyspepsic or disagreeable (Edward Said qtd. In Singh, 24).

Mistry depicts ethnic consciousness in his works. Such a Long Journey, Tales from Firozsha Baag are replete with references to Parsi customs and festivals right from Behram roje to the journey upto the towers of silence. He considers himself to be one of the last witnesses of this dwindling community. He aspires to put his ethnicity on the transcultural stage. Bharucha has made an excellent study of this aspect of his fiction.

Mistry liked the western world but he found that a person feels at home only at his place of birth. Such can be the psychological pressure built on him that even his bowels refuse to function properly in an alien land. This was the plight of Sarosh Sid in the story 'Squatter' taken from Tales from Firozsha Baag. He had promised to come back if unable to become totally Canadian. After ten years he complains: "but for me life in the land of milk and honey was just a pain in the posterior" (Mistry, 167).

The nostalgia faced by Jamshed of the story 'Lend me your Light' is revolting. He writes a disgracing letter saying: "Bombay is horrible, seems dirtier than ever, and the whole trip just made me sick. I had my fill of it in just two weeks and was happy to leave" (Mistry, 181). Even Kersi was no better who had earlier defended India. He also found squalor and dirt everywhere on return. Mistry felt guilty for holding this kind of opinion and labels Kersi as the blind Tiresias, guilty of the sin of hubris, for having sought to emigrate from the land of birth. Thus the attitude is of dissatisfaction with the Indian reality, with the land that gave them refuge during the Iranian diaspora. This has been termed 'bad faith' by Chandra who believes that "Kersi waits for an epiphany. But there are no epiphanies at the quotidian level of existence"(67). He is no comparison to his brother Percy and Navjeet who are ready to lay down their lives for the upliftment of common people in India.

One thing, discernible in such a treatment is that there is a comparative study of two lands-- dirt and squalor in one area, cleanliness and orderliness in other. As long as one has no view of the other, one is satisfied with one's belongings but once 'the other' emerges into the consciousness—it holds such a hegemonic outward attraction that bonds of sentimentality get dissolved easily.

His characters that move to the west are maladjusted with the new life or to be more precise second life. Those who aspire to go there are engaged in poetic talk about the west but are disillusioned the moment they try to materialize their plans of immigration. In the novel Family Matters, Yezad has to bear racist remarks of the immigration officer. He often contrasts Bombay with his dreamland Canada. Whereas former was 'chaos personified' the latter is 'not just the land of milk and honey, also the land of deodorant and toiletry' (131).

But later on changes his opinion: "We have beggars in Bombay, they have people freezing to death on Toronto streets; instead of high and low-caste fighting, racism and police shootings; separatists in Kashmir, separatists in Quebec. Why migrate from the frying-pan into the fire?" (132).

Mistry does not throw much light on the interaction between Indians and foreigners. The works written around 1990 move back to the experience of 70's. He either moulds his dissatisfaction into the blind acceptance of things or becomes critical at times and thus stands in sharp contrast to Jhumpa Lahiri whose novel 'The Namesake' portrays complete acclimatization specially among that generation that opened its eyes in west only and hasn't undergone the trauma of diaspora in the true sense.

The story begins in 1968 when Aashima is undergoing labour pains in an American hospital. She detests the American culture where the only other occupant at such a critical time is her unborn baby. Even the neatness of the place offers her no comfort, being devoid of familial compassion. "She is terrified to raise a child in a country where she is related to no one... where life seems so tentative and spare" (6). The same culture brings about anguish of the child who is named Gogol as the hospital authorities have to register a name on the birth certificate. His namesake is a Russian, a writer of short stories his father is a fan of. Moreover the book of this writer once saved his father's life during a terrible train accident. The same culture later on permits him to change his name through a legal procedure but he has to fight for his identity upto the last.

Aashima praises America when she re-gets her lost things with the help of MBTA lost and also on getting her children's express passports as they have to leave for India due to sudden death of their parents. But she never feels contempt for India. She rebukes her son who considers Pemberton Road, Boston his home. When Gogol shows her paintings of graves, she gets upset. 'Only in America, children are taken to cemeteries in the name of art' (70).

Her husband Ashoke is a professor there. It was his third birth when he came to America. He adjusts himself to American dressing sense wearing second-hand jeans that his wife dislikes. He has delivered lectures both at Indian and American universities but passes no comment on the working of any. He strives for Bengali acquaintances in the alien land. They often invite friends to celebrate various occasions as substitute for relatives. These parties are enjoyed by adults only; children prefer to sit before television.

Their children are totally different though they try, at times, not to go against the wishes of their parents. They have melted in the 'melting pot' culture of America. One day Gogol realizes that the name on their mailbox is Gang instead of Ganguli, the work of some racist miscreants. He, at once, "is aware, in stores, of cashiers smirking at his parents' accents and of salesmen who prefer to direct their conversation to Gogol as though his parents were either incompetent or deaf" (67).

The parents eagerly await meetings with relatives and Bengali festivals whereas children are more anxious on Christmas than pujos. At the rice ceremony of Sonia, she puts a dollar into her mouth at which every one remarks: "this one is true American".

These children have adopted American culture and treat India as India and not desh whereas their cousins label them ABCD's that is America born confused deshis. From their accent, it is difficult to tell about their parentage. Moushami is "always flattered when they (her students) assume she herself is French or half- French" (253).

Gogol had relations with two American girls Ruth and Maxine before he gets married to Moushami. These girls couldn't bear his attachment with parents even at the crucial moment of his father's death. Even his mother is not willing to take anyone from them as his bride. Moushami, is of Indian origin, and thus has been selected by his parents. She had affairs with men before marriage and was to get married to Graham who broke with her because he couldn't bear the protective attitude of his in-laws during his visit to India. She even develops extra-marital relations. Similarly Sonia selects her partner herself.

The children therefore become completely westernized. Gogol considers his hand-sewn Bengali primer as toilet paper but the parents feel exotic in this land. Ultimately, Aashima decides to return to her world after the death of her husband. She was just abiding by the vows she had taken at the time of her marriage, tried to adjust to new life, worked at a public library but now there was none, who she could call her own. Her children were thoroughly American but she was still Indian, missing her culture desperately.

After the study of this novel, one fully agrees with the view-point of Harris that 'although postcolonial texts may seem to deal with racial and cultural division. Beneath the surface level, each text contains the seed of community' (qtd. In Chandramohanan, 81). The novel tries to maintain a middle class Bengali life in America. The novalist is trying to relive her past through her characters in the novel so as not to snap ties with the culture that has penetrated her soul or flows like blood in her veins.

And Gogol realizes too late, only in 2000 the importance of his name his father has been making him to. He accepts that "names die over time, that they perish just as people do". But only some great people like Nikolaivich Gogol live in memories of people.

Thus Mistry "seeks to shed light and indeed fully embrace the syncretic nature of the diasporic Parsi experience whether be in North America or in India" (Takhar, Writer from Elsewhere). On the other hand Lahiri presents a multicultural society where adjustment with the new atmosphere is necessary for a successful living. Moreover her characters admit that the decision to shift to the states was totally theirs. They have been persuaded by their parents to make fortune while living in India and the result of ignoring their advice was that they couldn't attend funeral ceremonies of their parents and add to imagine lives and death of many relatives.

Indian diasporic writing is a very vast field, describing writers' varied experiences as India is a land of diversity. Individuals also vary in their consciousness and show diverse trends in portraying human relationships. The need is to study this diversity enjoying every experience and finding out how writers perceive their lives and cope up with the new circumstances. With the emerging theories in post colonial debate concentrating on diaspora and migration, and in the wake of mass movements over the globe, many writers have put their experience into print and this leaves a vast field open for further studies.

Works Cited

- Bharucha, Nilufer E. Rohinton Mistry: Ethnic Enclosures and Transcultural Spaces.
- New Delhi: Rawat, 2003
- Chadra Subash. Bad Faith in Lend me your Light in The Fiction of Rohinton

Mistry. Ed. Jaydipsinh Dodiya. New Delhi: Prestige, 1998.

- Chandramohanan, S.R. "Ovelapping Territories": Multi cultuturalism in Postcolonial Literatures in LITTCRIT. 31.2.2005: 80-85:
- Jain, Jasbir, Introduction to Writers of the Diasopara- theory and Practice, New Delhi: Rawat, 1998
- Lahiri, Jhumpa. The Namesake. New Delhi: Harper Collins, 2004.
- Mistry, Rohinton. Family Matters. London: Faber and Faber, 2002.
- Tales from Firozshah Bag. London: Faber and Faber, 1987.
- Pathak, R.S. Ed. Quest for identity in Indian English Writing. Vol II Delhi: Bahri, 1992.
- Patnayak, Suneeta. 'Chitra Banerjee Divakaruni and her theme of female bonding'.
- Diviner.4 (2005): 8-31.
- Rushdie, Salman, Step Across This Line. London: Jonathan Cape, 2002.
- Singh, GurBhagat, Expatriate Writing and the Problematic of Centre: Edward said and Homi Bhaba in Writers of the diasopara Ed. Jasbir Jain, New Delhi. Rawat, 1998.
- Takhar, Jennifer. Rohinton Mistry: Writer from elsewhere.
- Postcolonial.web.org. 20 Sep 2004.
- <http://www.postcolonial.web.org/canada/literature/mistry/takhar1.html>

❑❑❑❑

12

RE- ROUTING SELF: DIASPORIC EXPERIENCE IN THE TIGER'S DAUGHTER BY BHARATI MUKHERJEE

-A.K. Singh

Bharati Mukherjee has received extensive accolades for her rendering of complex cultural clashes experienced by North American immigrants who find themselves strangely out of place in unfamiliar settings. Her works explore issues of identity and collision of cultures that exiles and immigrants face, familial loyalty and the question of belonging. As we are aware of the prevailing situation now, quite a few of the immigrants become rootless and get dislocated while others readjust and relocate themselves in the changed environment. This process of re-adjustment and re- location charts the many re- routings of self that lie at the heart of diasporic experience. The Tiger's Daughter is a provocative look at the tensions that exist between the real and imagined selves, the Eastern and Western worlds, and the past and the present. This novel reaffirms Mukherjee's stunning ability to depict emotionally and politically complex subject matter in powerfully expressive prose. Published in 1971, the novel was well received by the critics and the readers alike. As Mukherjee puts it in another interview: "The Tiger's Daughter was loved by everybody"[1]

The novel can be divided into four parts. The first part deals with the past of Tara, her family background, and the process of her settlement in New York. The second part deals with Tara's arrival at Bombay, her journey to Calcutta after seven year of her marriage with a foreigner and her reaction to India. The third part concentrates on Tara'a life at Calcutta with her friends.

This part portrays her new way of perception because of her diasporic status. The fourth part of the novel deals with her visit to Darjeeling with her friends to spend summers, her coming back to Calcutta, her boredom and feeling of alienation, and her victimization in a mob violence. The novel with the structure of an open ending tells about the cultural dilemma of Tara who is torn between the American and Indian activities.

When the twenty-two-year-old Tara visits India, the alien western culture, which has almost become a second self to her, is constantly in clash with the culture of her native soil. The clash is deeply felt in the psyche of Tara who finds it difficult to adjust with her friends and relatives in India; and sometimes with the traditions of her own family. The greatest irony of her return is that she feels loneliness in her own native land. Her new self is no doubt responsible for this disruption of her pleasure, but the deteriorating social conditions, and her new perspective towards the poverty and dirtiness in India aggravate her discomfort, frustration and disgust. Tara expected that her return to India would remove her displeasure of staying abroad which is described in the following lines:

> For years she had dreamed of this return to India. She had believed that all hesitations, all shadowy fears of the time abroad would be erased quite magically if she could just return home to Calcutta. But so far the return had brought only wounds. First the corrosive hours on Marine Drive, then the deformed beggar in the railway station, and now the inexorable train ride steadily undid what strength she had held in reserve. She was an embittered woman, she now thought, old and cynical at twenty-two and quick to take offence.[2]

Mukherjee managed to present the decay of Calcutta and the decadent life of its upper class with considerable skill. The city seems to be coming apart at its seams because of a number of factors: endemic violence, chronic political unrest, economic stagnation and poverty, disease, overpopulation, and class-conflicts. And yet Calcutta acted as if "the real Calcutta, the thick laughter of brutal men, open dustbins, warm and dark where carcasses were sometimes discarded, did not exist"[3]. Or if they did admit that "everything's gone down horribly", they were not ready to do anything to change the situation, having little appetite for heroic gestures. Their tendency was to talk about moving out, or to slide into inaction. A couplet from a W.H. Davies poem, quoted in the middle of a picnic arranged in Tara's honor, sums up perfectly the fin de siecle atmosphere of upper-class Calcutta evoked by Mukherjee in her novel: "What is this life, if full of care, / We have no time to stand and stare." Events such as the picnic served to assuage "their sense of panic, their racial and class fears," all allowed them to reconstruct another Calcutta, one they longed to return to, more stable, less bitter:

Temporarily their sense of panic, their racial and class fears disappeared. Delicately they reconstructed another Calcutta, one they longed to return, more subtle, less bitter. Beyond their memories of happier years, they retired indoors, the women confined to their rooms, the men to the rest of the guest house and the bar.[4]

Nostalgia or insouciance appear to be the only alternatives available to Tara's friends; after some time in the city even Tara begins to feel:

That the misery of her city was too immense and blurred to be listed and assailed on by one. That it was fatal to fight for justice; that it was better to remain passive and absorb all shocks as they came"[5]

In the course of the novel, then, Tara must come terms with the new Calcutta and must come to realize that the images of the city she had preserved in her memory in North America no longer correspond to the city scenes she was now viewing on her trip home. As she finds out:

"...except for Camac Street (where her parents lived), Calcutta had changed greatly; and even Camac Street had felt the first stirring of death."[6]

Mukherjee presents the novel through an omniscient narrator, but the reader sees things mostly from Tara's point of view; she is the third –person center-of-consciousness through whom Mukherjee registers her disenchantment with the changes that have taken place in Calcutta. Maya Manju Sharma points out:

"Tara is the alter ego of the author is clear from the autobiographical details in Days and Nights; the testings of Tara are also battles in the growth of the author's sensibility from that of the expatriate to that of the immigrant."[7]

Like Mukherjee, Tara has marked a North American novelist who prefers to stay back during his summer breaks so that he can write; like her creator, Tara was overcome by bouts of homesickness when in North America and returns to Calcutta to gauge the extent of her commitment to what was once home.

Her first stepping on the land of India at Bombay fills her with disappointment. Bombay is the same but her outlook has changed. To her Bombay railway station "was more like a hospital; there were so many sick and deformed men sitting listlessly on bundles and trunks." Her sickness at the present situation makes her think about her husband, David. The thought of her husband symbolically suggests the second self developed in her. It seems that the alien land has become more of a home to her. She repents to have come to India without her husband and she is unable to keep him off her mind. The following lines throw light on the mood of repentance in Tara.

Perhaps I was stupid to come without him, she thought, even with him rewriting his novel during the vacation. Perhaps I was too impulsive, confusing my fear of New York with homesickness. Or perhaps I was going mad.[8]

Tara's journey from Bombay to Calcutta brings an equally disgusting experience to her. In Calcutta too, she finds everything changed and deteriorated.

The seven years she has spent in the West has inevitably altered Tara's angle of vision. As she drives past Bombay's Marine Drive on her way back to Calcutta, she finds the street to be "run-down and crowded," and yet seven years earlier she had "admired" the place and found it "fashionable".

The most important cause aggravating her discomfort and unease is her marriage which hangs on her heart as a burden:

In India she felt she was not married to a person but to a foreigner, and this foreignness was a burden. It was hard for her to talk about marriage responsibilities in Camac Street; her friends were curious only about the adjustments she had made."[9]

Tara's mind is constantly at conflict with the two personalities – one of an Indian and the other of an American. During such moments she feels to go back to her husband David because she feels that she would be more at east there. Caught in this gulf between the two contrasting worlds, Tara feels that she has forgotten many of her Hindu rituals of worshipping icons which she had seen her mother performing since her childhood. The following incident throws light on this aspect:

When the sandalwood paste had been ground Tara scraped it off the slimy stone tablet with her fingers and poured it into a small silver bowl. But she could not remember the next step of the ritual. It was not a simple loss, Tara feared, this forgetting of prescribed actions; it was a little death, a hardening of the heart, a cracking of axis and center. But her mother came quickly with the relief of words.[10]

The phrase 'cracking of axis and center' symbolically points out the psyche of Tara which has come in her due to the loss of her own cultural heritage. An outcome of this loss is ironically reflected in her inability to sing bhajan which she sang in her childhood: It is the American culture that has covered Tara like an invisible spirit or 'darkness.' The use of the word 'darkness' shows that in the deepest core of her heart, Tara has an intense desire to behave like an ordinary Indian but her re-rooted self in America has made such common rituals alien to her.

When she was in North America, she could not stop thinking of home, but now in this trip of Calcutta she misses David and fears losing him continually. She remembered even now, the sense of alienation she had in New York but cannot cease ruminating in Calcutta on "the foreignness of spirit", she was experiencing in the city of her birth:

She spends a lot of time in Calcutta with her upper-class Bengali friends, recognizing that they were "shavings of her personality," and yet cannot help fearing "their tone, their omissions, their aristocratic oneness."[11]

She may react "guiltily" to her friend Pronob's comment that he would "hate to be anybody in America," but has the distinct feeling on a number of occasions in India that to at least a few of her friends and family. She is now, quite literally, an outcast because of her marriage to a White North American. On other occasions, however, she herself feels "quite cut off" from the people she grew up with. It does not take her very long to feel that depression is overcoming her, and she begins to think that it is best to return to New York.

What Tara had not known before coming to Calcutta but must discover is what is obvious to her friend Reena. As Reena puts it in her Indian-English idiom, "You've changed too much, Tara". She begins to let "little things ...upset her" and comes to realize that "of late she had been outraged by Calcutta." Even the language she had used so spontaneously once upon a time now appears strange. What surprises or shocks her in Calcutta appears to be quite routine to someone like Reena. It is because she is not a person who is a Diaspora like Tara whose multicultural consciousness has changed her vision. Her way of perception and reaction has also changed in her cross-cultural conflict. Similarly, what she considers sensible and decorous seems silly and outrageous to others.

Tara's negative reaction at the changed social situation and deterioration of Calcutta makes her friend Reena to comment about her that she has "become too self-centred and European." In spite of her European personality, the Indian pulse vibrating in Tara makes her realize that the life of Calcutta in spite of all the dark spots and drawbacks, has its own life which is found nowhere else and which her husband David would not be able to realize in spite of his vision and knowledge of Indian through books, which he constantly mentions in his letters to her.

Tara told him how much easier she thought it was to live in Calcutta. How much simpler to trust the city's police inspector and play tennis with him on Saturdays. How humane to accompany a friendly editor to watch the riots in town. New York, she confided, was a gruesome nightmare. It wasn't muggings she feared so much a rude little invasions.[12]

The attitude of her friends that they approve foreign manner, foreign etiquette, foreign fashions but they do not approve the foreign marriage ironically makes a criticism of the conservative attitude of the Indians who feel crazy for foreign things, dresses and items but they do not approve marriage with foreign people. The author ironically used the word 'racial purists' for the friends in the following lines:

They were racial purists, thought Tara desperately. They liked foreigners in movie magazines – Nat Wood and Bob Wagner in faded Photoplays. They loved English like Worthington at the British Council. But they did not approve of foreign marriage patterns. So much for the glamour of her own marriage. She had expected admiration from these friends. She had wanted them to consider her marriage an emancipated gesture. But emancipation was suspicious – it presupposed bondage.[13]

Tara finds herself a misfit everywhere she goes. With her dangling personality she tries to look Indian and adjust with her friends but there is an invisible gap between them and she feels the breakdown. She is forced to look at her inner world consisting of two cultures and the two different ideologies which are the two different ideologies which are the two worlds wide apart.

The Tiger's Daughter is designed to capture the predicament of someone returning to her homeland after a period of self-imposed exile. To such a person, home will never be home again, and life in exile, bitter draught though it often is, will be preferable to what home has become. The discovery that Tara makes at the end of the novel is that the greenery and the forests she had associated with the India of her childhood – her version of pastoral –were no longer there, something or the other hand "killed" them. In New York, she had dreamed of coming back to Calcutta, but "the return had brought only wounds".

The darkness outside the window deepened, giving Tara time for unhappy self-analysis. For years she had dreamed of this return to India. She had believed that all hesitations, all shadowy fears of the time abroad would be erased quite magically if she could just return home to Calcutta. But so far the return had brought only wounds. First the corrosive hours on Marine Drive then the deformed beggars in the railway station, and now the inexorable train ride steadily undid what strength she had held in reserve. She as an embittered woman, she now thought, old and cynical at twenty-two and quick to take offense.[14]

Particularly galling for Tara is her finding that by choosing exile she "had slipped outside" the parameters of a world in which she belonged by birthright, and that even after only seven years outside it, "recently was barred". [15] And so although the novel ends with Tara trapped in a car that is surrounded by rioters, wondering "whether she would ever get out of Calcutta, and if she didn't, whether David would ever know that she loved him fiercely" [16], Tara's mental progress in the novel leaves no doubt in the reader's mind that if she did get out of the car, it would be to take the next plane back to the United States. The novel announces a bold new voice in literature in English coming out of India to represent the pre-document of an Indian who has opted to settle in the west and must now redefine her ties to her homeland.

Although David does not take part in any of the vents described in the novel, Mukherjee uses him skilfully to comment on the problems inherent in a cross-cultural relationship. He is also the implied reader of the novel, a liberal North American who reads about Tara's experience of Calcutta with some interest but also with a measure of incomprehension. Tara often wonders about the difficulties of communicating her feelings about her city and its people to David. For instance, while imagining the indignities her Calcutta friends were having to endure then, she cannot help thinking:

How could she explain the bitterness of it to David, who would have laughed at her friends and wished them luck as refugees?[17]

How could she explain to David who was, after all, "a foreigner"[18], her mother's obsession with insurance policies? Just as she could not explain to her Calcutta friends why there were ghettos and student demonstrations in New York - they persisted in believing that "American was lovely" and that "New York was not like Calcutta"[19] - she could not explain to David, who "was hostile to genealogies and had often misunderstood her affection for the family as overdependence."[20] Because he is secure in his world of stable identities and predictable events,

Tara feels that she cannot confide in David some things about her vacation in Calcutta, for he "expected everything to have some meaning or point"[21], whereas she was experiencing so much that was chaotic or formless or incomprehensible. She knew thus that David would react to "the misery" of her city with "outrage" and a plan for quick and decisive action, but how would he understand that the problems of Calcutta were "too immense and blurred to be listed and assailed one by one" :

> It was not a toppling or sliding of identities that Tara wanted to suggest to David, but an alarming new feeling that she was an apprentice to some great thing or power. If she were pressed to tell more precisely the nature of that power, she would have to remain silent. It was so vague, so pointless, so diffuse, this trip home to India.[22]

Misunderstanding, confusion, and incomprehension, then, are inevitable in any cross-cultural encounter. Passages to and out of India, Mukherjee appears to be saying, will cause pain and bewilderment. There are limits not only to David's understanding of and tolerance for Indians, but also to India's ability to accept or comprehend someone like Tara's husband. Two memorable minor characters of The Tiger's Daughter – Washington McDowell and Antonia Whitehead – illustrate the extent of the confusion created in the contact zones between cultures. McDowell is an American student who comes to Calcutta on an exchange program and who is supposed to stay with Reena's family when in the city. They look forward to his visit with great excitement but they are shocked to discover that they would be hosting a black American. Shock gives way to dismay for Reena's mother when she begins to suspect her daughter of having an affair with an "African". But McDowell turns out to be a Black Panther who soon deserts his affluent hosts to take up the cause of Calcutta's revolutionaries.

Antonia Whitehead, a big redheaded American out on a

"mission" to save the Third World, bumbles her way through India and occasions this impassioned editorial from Tara's journalist friend Sanjay:

It has been said that she is really a blessing in disguise, that she is a missionary defrocked, that she is Deepak Ghose's special lady friend. But I say....she is dangerous. [23]

Although Tara knows that Antonia is just as she was in her first few weeks in this trip home – "impatient, menacing and equally innocent"24 - she is aware that the white American girl was destined to create much confusion during her stay in India. But because Tara has learned earlier that "it was impossible to be a bridge for anyone" since "bridges had a way of cluttering up the landscape", she lets Antonia blunder her way through India and be misconstrued by the Indians with whom she comes in contact.

By suggesting the difficulties of passages in and out of India and by pointing at bridges that cannot be built between cultures, Mukherjee is, of course, alluding to E.M. Forester's classic novel. Mukherjee has acknowledged in her interviews that she had set out in her first novel to deliberately mimic and subvert, A Passage to India. She has revealed that the swimming pool scene of her novel is based on Forster's Mau tank episode – only in The Tiger's Daughter there is no "regeneration" to be had from the swimming pool since ennui will continue to be the dominant emotion of its users. Mukherjee has also noted that her novel has "a rather British feel to it," because of her use of the omniscient point of view and irony in the manner of Jane Austen, Dickens, and Forster, Her "comic vision," she feels, puts the Tiger's Daughter in the British tradition, for "most of the characters, even when they are caught in ghastly situations, acquaint themselves in amusing ways".

In general, it can be said that Mukherjee handles the various Calcutta settings of The Tiger's Daughter dexterously. Her characters may be "fleshed out abstractions", but they express a peculiar kind of sensibility. They are explorations of the kind of sensibility which is inarticulate not because language fails but because the emotions are basically intractable to communication. Perhaps, protagonist in Tiger's Daughter is more than that for these voiceless emotions arise out of a questioning of cultural issues, and the journey which she undertakes is journey at a cultural level. Jasbir Jain opines :

> Mukherjee's novels (like those of Ruth Jhabvala), are representative of the expatriate sensibility. This alone offers an understanding of the ambivalence present not only in the psychology of the protagonists but also that of the author; this helps us understand the satiric interludes, the ironic juxtapositions, the shifting point of view and also the final disintegration.[25]

Nevertheless, Mukherjee's first novel is an impressive achievement. It announces a bold new voice in literature in English coming out of India to represent the predicament of the Indian who has opted to settle in the West and must now redefine her ties to her homeland. The Tiger's Daughter and Days and Nights in Calcutta, her next work, are the books Mukherjee had to write before she could severe her ties with the country of her birth and cast her lot with countless expatriates in North America to come to the point from where she could ultimately celebrate immigrant lives and immigration to the United States.

Notes and References

1. Michael Connell & Jessie Grearson, "An Interview with Bharati Mukherjee", Iowa Review (Spring 1990).
2. The Tiger's Daughter, p.25.
3. Ibid., p. 41.
4. Ibid., p. 98.
5. Ibid., p. 131.

6. Ibid., p. 199.
7. Maya Manju Singh, "The Inner World of Bharati Mukherjee : From Expatriate to Immigrant", Bharati Mukherjee : Critical perspectives ed. Emmanuel S. Nelson (New York : Garland Publishing, 1993), p.5.
8. See Geoff Hancock, "An Interview with Bharati Mukherjee", Canadian Fiction Magazine.
9. Op. cit., Daughter, p. 62.
10. Ibid., p. 51.
11. Ibid., p. 43.
12. Ibid., p. 69
13. Ibid., p. 86
14. Ibid., p. 25
15. See Ibid
16. Ibid., p. 110
17. Ibid., p. 45
18. See Ibid., p. 48
19. See Ibid., p. 56.
20. Ibid., p. 130
21. See Ibid., 130
22. Ibid., p. 131
23. Ibid., pp. 164-65
24. Ibid., p. 166
25. Jasbir Jain, Journal of Indian Writing in English pp. 17-18. Quoted in Modern Women Writers : A Library of Literary Criticism vol. 3.. ed. Lilian S. Robinson (Fredrick Ungar Continuum : New Work, 1996.)

❑❑❑❑

13

(Re)Membering Selves: Dislocation and Fulfilment in Chitra Banerjee Divakaruni's Arranged Marriage

-Sanjeev Kumar

Exiles or emigrants or expatriates are haunted by some sense of loss, some urge to reclaim, to look back, even at the risk of being mutated into pillars of salt. But if we do look back, we must also do so in the knowledge--which gives rise to profound uncertainties--that our physical alienation from India almost inevitably means that we will not be capable of reclaiming precisely the thing that was lost; that we will, in short, create fictions, not actual cities or villages, but invisible ones, imaginary homelands, Indias of the mind.

- Salman Rushdie, The Eye of the Beholder: Indian Writing in English, 76.

Chitra Banerjee Divakaruni is one of those Indian–American authors who have received considerable critical and commercial success in the literary world. She, along with Salman Rushdie, Rohinton Mistry, Bharti Mukherjee, Meena Alexander, and Jhumpa Lahiri, to name a few, is primarily concerned with the preoccupation of displacement, dislocation, exile, and nostalgia for India--her country of origin. Her works also deal with the sensitive issues of identity, and personal and family relationships in a world marked by deteriorating humanistic values. Arranged Marriage, a "moving and often ironic collection of stories" deals with myriad experiences of Indian women living in America and India (Columbia Companion, 2000: 38). Besides, Divakaruni gives ample space to the diasporic experiences of her characters that are caught in conflict between two value systems--one that they have inherited from India and the other that they have imbibed while living in America. It is in this perspective that the present paper attempts to study Arranged Marriage and highlight the problem that arises due to the characters' endeavour to forget their past and get involved emotionally, mentally and physiologically in the new system they have become a part of. A further attempt will be made to focus on the crisis that these characters face when they try to be a member of the new system while struggling with the issue of dislocation and, in an attempt to get fulfilment, have to suffer on different planes.

"Clothes," "one of the most lyrical of the stories in Arranged Marriage," is about a woman, who, having lived her early life in India, goes to America after getting wedlocked with Somesh, an Indian living there with his parents (Columbia Companion, 2000: 225). Sumita easily cops up with her new surroundings which she found rather interesting and exotic, and which she had imagined earlier. She would enjoy wearing unorthodox clothes she had always fancied:

> Late at night I stand in front of our bedroom mirror trying on the clothes Somesh has bought for me and smuggled in past his parents. I model each one for him, walking back and forth, clasping my hand behind my head, lips pouted, left hip thrust out just like the models on TV, while he whispers applause. I'm breathless with suppressed laughter... and my cheeks are hot with the delicious excitement of conspiracy... I'm wearing a pair of jeans now, marveling at the curves of my hips and thighs, which have always been hidden under the flowing lines of my saris. I love the color, the same pale blue as the nayantara flowers that grow in my parents' garden. The solid comforting weight. The jeans come with a close-fitting T-Shirt which outlines my breasts... The T-shirt is sunrise orange--the color I decide, of joy of my new American life (24-25).

Everything was fine until her husband was shot dead while working at night in a store in order to meet his financial needs. She did not let herself to be a dove "with cut-off wings," rebelled against Indian traditional values and decided to carry on her life in the United States, go to a college, and become a teacher (33).

The story brings before the readers the Indian cultural heritage which, in the "new dangerous land" could be ridiculous or a fancy (ibid). That a "married woman belongs to her husband, her in-laws" may look awkward to a person unaccustomed to Indian tradition. Chitra Divakaruni, however, also throws light on the superstitious nature of Indian natives who attach colours to represent "possibility" or "luck for married women;" the names of the stores piously named after gods or goddesses (20). She also engages the readers to the "wifely duty" of a traditional Indian wife who devotes herself to her husband (21). The sandalwood powder placed between the folds of the saris to protect them from "the unknown insects of America" becomes a point to ridicule the prejudiced Indian mentality. Sumita, although an Indian, starts feeling the place where the family is living in "a world so small that would make her wanting to scream" despite the fact that before coming to America she used to live with her parents (26). There is a clear indication in the story that the protagonist has been caught between two worlds—traditional Indian and the new American life. She breaks away from her hitherto orthodox Indian mentality, her sense of dislocation and paves her way to fulfill her desires in the land of unbounded opportunities. Divakaruni, it is evident, "writes to unite people, and she does this by destroying myths and stereotypes. As she breaks down these barriers, she dissolves boundaries between people of different backgrounds, communities, ages, and even different worlds" (www.chitradivakaruani.com/about/ writing)

"Silver Pavements, Golden Roofs" shows us the seamy side

of the Indians living in America. Jayanti goes to Chicago for higher studies and starts living with the family of her mother's younger sister Pratima. Her journey from "moist and weighted" Calcutta to the land of unbounded opportunities opens her hitherto dreamy eyes to the harsh reality which the Indians had to face while living in an alien land (36). They are maltreated by the racist whites and termed as "niggers" (43). Bikram uncle points out:

The Americans hate us. They are always putting us down because(Indians) are dark-skinned foreigners, Kala admi. Blaming (them) for the damn economy, for taking away their jobs (43).

He used to own a motor business which was smashed by the "trashy neighborhood" (53). This tragic and threatening incident entirely changed his perception regarding the dream which is usually held by Indians pertaining to America: "Things here aren't as perfect as people at home like to think. We all thought we'd become millionaires. But it's not so easy" (43).

The diasporic experience depicted in "Silver Pavements, Golden Roofs" is, to a large extent, tragic and demands serious attention from the Indians looking at America as a just and civilized society. The characters in the story are seen entangled between their homeland and the hostland. They are struggling people whose dreams of equality, wealth, and better and prosperous life seem to shatter as is obvious from what Bikram Uncle told Jayanti. This story, as are the other stories in Arranged Marriage, portrays Jayanti's diasporic experience who feels herself dropped suddenly at a place she did never imagine. Caught in a mood of disillusionment and doubts, the protagonist witnesses east-west encounter that, in a way, opens her eyes to harsh realities. Arranged Marriage, says Brunda Moka-Dias, is "thematically unified and explores, questions, rearticulates, and redefines the South Asian cultural construction of the feminine. That is, the characters, the imagery, the setting, and the themes deepen their significance as they recur with variation, in completely different ways, through each story, thus highlighting the reader's experience of the whole, which is greater than the sum of its parts" (Asian American Novelists, 2000: 88). While reading these stories, the readers find diversity of experiences which are of different colours but one like the fascinating rainbow—the rainbow of Indian diaspora.

In the story "The Word Love," Chitra Banerjee Divakaruni explores the mind of an Indian woman living in America. During her studies for Doctor of Philosophy, the protagonist gets involved in love with an American and starts living with him, which is unorthodox from Indian point of view. She is, however, more conscious of the disclosure of her unconventional relationship to her mother at home who is a traditional woman and would not admit it. She is caught in the labyrinth of keeping her relationships intact with her mother and, at the same time, with the boyfriend as well, This conflict arises due to her deep regard and love for both of them. We can see here how Divakaruni presents the Indian experience in America and "the conflict between the traditions of her homeland and the culture of her adopted country" (http://www.time.com/). The inevitable, however, happens and after learning the unorthodox relationship of her daughter, the mother breaks asunder her relationship with the daughter; changes her phone number, shifts to a new location and does not receive the daughter's letters. Shona, as her mother would call her, fails to bear the pangs of this apathy and anger, and, in turn, breaks off her relation with Rex and prepares herself for a new life. She "will pack (her) belongings. A few clothes, some music, a favorite book...And a word comes to (her) out of the opening sky. The word love (that she) had never understood...It is like rain...(that) washes away inessentials, leaving (her) hollow, clean, ready to begin" (71).

"The Word Love," along with other stories in Arranged Marriages, amply shows the hollowness of love and other fragile relationships that are looked upon as the forces which provide human beings solace and comfort. Divakaruni "makes us realize," maintains Rebecca Haque, "that all human relationships are in fact a gamble, a throw on the dice, a matter of chance and destiny (Indo-American Review, 2000: 208). The readers wonder how Shona and her mother reacted, which was, by and large, unconventional from the Indian point of view. She got no fulfilment and, in order to achieve that, fights with her sense of dislocation and prepares herself to be a member of the new world while deciding not to remember her past.

"A Perfect Life" presents Meera, a successful woman in America, leading a blissful life. She is satisfied with her perfect life and enjoys it, nonetheless, with some reservations. Divakaruni, however, portrays her protagonist being caught in the conflicting values of east and west. Although centered on Meera, her boyfriend Richard and Krishna--a seven-year-old waif, the story highlights the deep-rooted maternal love of Meera that she adamantly kept suppressed hitherto. Calling "The Perfect Life" a "most powerful story," Maya Yajnik opines that the story is "evocative of the mysterious tidal wave of love and maternal desire" of the protagonist (www.sawnet.org). A determined and successful professional, Meera did not want to marry and, at least, have children that are, she thinks, a real mess. Nevertheless, when she meets Krishna accidentally, she gives way to her resistance and begins caring of the orphan. She, after a few days, decides to adopt the child and, in the legal process, loses him who runs away from the house of the caretaker. The story apparently depicts the passionate episode in Meera's life but a closer look at the story reveals that the protagonist wavers between two worlds--Indian and American. In an attempt to be "a true American," Meera lets her cultural values go in the air yet, at instances, recalls her home memories (73). She fought very hard, Meera remembers, with her mother, persuaded her teachers and bosses to come to America for a better and promising career. The diasporic experience that Divakaruni has attempted to depict in the story is entirely emotional—a motherly love that Meera, until now, has controlled, but fails when she starts taking care of Krishna. She becomes attached emotionally, rather, passionately to the kid who, after flickering the maternal love, abandons her never to return. Arranged Marriage, as is evident in this story, primarily concerned about Indian immigrant women who are caught in "cultural conflict," highlights Divakaruni's preoccupation that "there is no such thing as a perfect life" (www.metroactive.com).

The world of Arranged Marriage is a large room with multiple windows that let the readers see divergent experiences of Indian Americans caught between two-dimensional conflict of 'here' and 'there.' Divakaruni, poignantly and effectively, touches upon the subtle issues of her community in the United States with the hand of a writer that thinks it to be his responsibility to give a true picture of his people in the multi-ethnic America. "Like other ethnic literatures in North America, writing by immigrants from the Indian subcontinent," maintains Craig Tapping, "is concerned with personal and communal identity, recollection of the homeland, and the active response to this "new" world. Its forms are multiple and in many traditional and some newly created genres; but an autobiographical impulse--the desire to name experience and to create identity, to emerge from the dominant language and gaze of "nonethnic" America-impels even the shortest fictions, despite frequent disclaimers by the writers (Reworldling, 1992: 35). This is applicable to Chitra Banerjee Divakaruni as well who, in one way or the other, highlights her sense of concern to the vital subjects pertaining to the immigrant Indians. Her characters are, largely, torn between home-consciousness and host-consciousness that creates diaspora.

One important aspect of Divakaruni as a literary artist is her depiction of east-west encounter involved in marital relationship. She brings effectively and with vividness the conflict that arises when two ideologies confront. In "Doors," for example, the author presents the tension that absorbs not only the mother of Preeti but the friends of Deepak also. These kiths and kins are seemingly concerned and are apprehensive whether the marriage of Deepak and Preeti would be a success or a failure. The couple, however, faces no confrontation on account of their ideology which is, by and large, amiable. Deepak, "the most enlightened man" that she knew, is considerate and gives her respect and space (184). Preeti, also, is not one of the "ABCD–American Born Confused Desis" who would make a fuss out of nothing (185). She is, nevertheless, restless when Raj, Deepak's cousin arrives from India and starts living with them. Preeti would usually lock the doors, which the newly arrived Raj could not digest. She fails to adjust herself with the kind of atmosphere created at home after the arrival of Raj. She requests her husband not to keep Raj at home but to no avail. The internal conflict in Preeti reaches its climax when she shouts at Raj when he enters the bedroom—"her last sanctuary" (200). The story closes "when the door finally clicked shut, (Preeti) did not know whether it was in the guest room or deep inside her own being" (202). Deepak and Raj are unable to understand the real problem of Preeti that leads their relationship to the verge of discord. Deepak, who is engrossed in remembering and reviving his Indian past and Raj, who fails to re-member himself in the new atmosphere, create a void in the otherwise successful life of Preeti.

Arranged Marriage successfully exhibits Divakaruni's

diasporic sensibility which she brings to fore in an unambiguous style and moving narration. She captures impressively the unsettled sensibility of Indians, women in particular, and their reality while focusing on some of the troubling doubts. "Beneath the chatty writing style peppered with clothing metaphors of saffron-colored saris and sunrise orange T-shirts," maintains Maya Yajnik, "I sensed a deep compassion for sensitive tender (Indian) women trapped in abusive relationships that undermine them and bring them down. They also capture the special pain of immigrant women trapped between different worlds and away from the safe familiarity of extended family and a traditional way of life. Also, the vast differences in cultural values strain the relationships" that are, by and large, not based on love and mutual understanding (www.sawnet.org). The readers find the characters wavering between the aura of homeland and the adopted land that creates diaspora. They become nostalgic, nay, emotionally involved in what is not and struggle for their true yet fluid identity which intensifies their diasporic experience further. The Arranged Marriage, in a way, becomes a panorama of Indian Americans looking backward from the window of their cultural background.

In a poignant and effective way, "The Ultrasound" highlights the traditional relationship between two Indian women. Anjali, although settled in America with her husband, keeps in touch with her cousin and childhood friend Runu. Both are pregnant and share their feelings through letters and, now and then, through phone calls. The story focuses on the kind of treatment that an Indian woman receives from her in-laws and how she is kept subjugated in the house. The problem, however, arises when Runu is discovered to be carrying a girl child that her family disapproves of and wants her to abort. Divakaruni gives a vivid description of this phenomenon that forces Runu leave her house and, we are told, she goes to the mother of Anjali after getting disappointment from her own mother who said that "it's not right that (Runu) should leave (her) husband's home. (Her) place is with them, for better or worse (225). At the end of the story, we find Anjali planning to bring Runu to America and help her rear up her daughter (Dayita) with her son (Anand):

Tomorrow I'll ask Sunil about sponsoring Runu, maybe getting her a student visa. I think he'll fight it at first, give me a hundred reasons why we can't do it. Why we shouldn't. But I'll fight back. Already I'm learning how. I'll use what I have to—my pregnancy, even. It's worth it—for Runu and, yes, myself. I'll get my way (230)

The author has given a true picture of traditional Indian mentality that does not accept a girl child readily. It is "not fitting that the eldest child of the Bhattacharjee household should be a female," said Runu's mother-in-law that clearly shows the orthodox mindset of the Indian mothers-in-law. "The Ultrasound" and the other stories in Arranged Marriage give an effusive expression to the east-west encounter, nostalgia for the past and India, and, at the same time, the struggle for fulfilment of the characters that are placed in diverse situations. Chitra Banerjee Divakaruni's plots whether set in India or America, "feature Indian-born women torn between old and new world values. She uses her laser-like insight and skilled use of story, plot, and lyrical description to give readers a many-layered look at her characters and their respective worlds, which are filled with fear, hope, and discovery...women learn to adapt to their new and changing culture and, as a result, discover their own sense of self amidst joy and heartbreak" (http://www.randomhouse.com/).

In Arranged Marriage, Chitra Banerjee Divakaruni addresses a variety of issues viz. interracial relationships, economic disparity, abortion, divorce, racial bigotry, etc. but her chief concern is to highlight "women on the verge of an unforgettable transformation" and the "abuse and courage" of these immigrant women (http://www.chitradivakaruni.com/). In "Affair," Abha, a traditional Indian wife is quite perturbed over her friend Meena's love affair that she comes to know from her husband Ashok. Throughout the story she remains anxious as she does not know with whom Meena has an affair (she thinks that it is with her husband). She becomes increasingly aware of her own marital relationship and thinks of making Ashok happier by doing what he likes--even love making that she has been ignoring since their marriage. Although difficult in the beginning, she steps outside the four-wall vicinity she has been living until now in order to shed her traditional Indian self and do something that her husband desires. She has been writing for The Indian Courier and now she chooses to put a cookbook about professional Indian cuisine. She concludes, when she learns that Meena is going to live with her American lover Charles: "The old rules are not always right. Not here, not even in India" (270). The story ends with Abha's positive and open thinking:

"It's better this way each of us freeing the other before it's too late...Yes, I believe it--I have to believe it. In spite of my beautiful calm kitchen which I must leave behind. In spite of the pity in the eyes of the Indian women when they hear. The gossip in India. My parents' anger. Family dishonor. In spite of Ashok, the empty ache when I remember...so we can start learning, once more, to live (271-272).

There is a clear indication that she now makes herself a member of the new environment and does not care about her dislocation. In order to get fulfilment, hitherto unseen, she begins "to pull the unraveled edges of (her) existence into a new design. One (she) cannot guess at yet" (272).

In Arranged Marriage, Divakaruni engages the readers feel sympathetic and concerned to the cause of Indian women living within the boundaries and across the Indian continent.

Nonetheless, she is criticized sometimes for not highlighting the trauma and torment of Indian Americans that are the outcome of their living in a strange alien country. She, some critics maintain, does not bring to fore the pangs of the protagonists' involvement in abusive relationships. She is also blamed for stereotyping and eroticizing Indian women and ignoring men's world. Susan Chacko, for instance, says:

The characters in the book seemed to live in a mysterious sort of time-warp--although the situations and details were contemporary, their behaviour was often what I'd associate with - an earlier generation than my own... For example, even the most conservative women I know wouldn't dream of saying 'She needs to be beaten' if they saw an Indian woman wearing a backless choli at an Indian party in the US. (beaten?!) Or the story about the high-powered skirt-wearing career woman who felt so superior to and alienated from the sari-wearing wives around her ...Indian men come off badly in the book. In all but one story, they are self-absorbed, insensitive, mean, wife-abusers, servant-rapists, or just plain unpleasant. In the single exception, the man dies. Oh yes, there is one story in which the husband is relatively pleasant to his wife -- he encourages her to build a career and so on -- but even he is blase about a woman who is being forced to undergo an abortion in India because the baby is a girl (www.sawnet.org/books).

Even if such criticism may look authentic at places yet, peeping at the deeper level, it comes out to be immature and not focused and may be, opines Brunda Moka-Dias, because the writer "explores and reveals the different experiences of women without dogmatically taking sides on women's issues" (Asian American Novelists, 2000:91). The readers get involved in the significant patterns of varied experiences of Indian-American community which are, largely, diasporic and demand a serious and positive interpretation. A conscious reader may also concentrate on the issues that Divakaruni attempts to highlight while ignoring the weaklings that sometimes creep in unintentionally. Chitra Divakaruni says in this regard:

The challenge lies in trying to bring alive, for readers from other ethnic backgrounds, the Indian--and Indian American--experience, not as something exotic and alien but as something human and shared. It lies in getting my own community to see the subject of my work (often the plight of women of Indian origin struggling within a male-dominated culture, even here in America). It is necessary and important and not, as many have complained, a betrayal of my people, an exposure of secrets that create a "bad impression" of Indians in American society. But the opportunities are more important: to be able to straddle two distinct cultures and depict both with the relatively objective hand of the outsider; to destroy stereotypes and promote understanding between different sectors of the multicultural society in which we live; to paint the complex life of the immigrant with its unique joys and sorrows, so distinct from those of people who have never left their native land. (Living in America,1995: 47).

"Meeting Mrinal," the last story in Arranged Marriage, depicts the life of an Indian-American woman who has been divorced by her husband--Mahesh. Living with her ten year son Dinesh, she ponders over fulfillment and perfection in her life and says: "What would I live on, now that I knew perfection was only a mirage" (296). After her meeting with her childhood friend and rival Mrinal, she comes to know about Mrinal's successful and glamorous, and an empty life. She attempts to commit suicide for her failures and the lie she told to Mrinal about her happy marital life. At the end of the story, however, she seems to be a promising woman that, drinking pista milk with her son, raises her glass and ponders over her life, "the glasses glitter like hope. We raise them to each other solemnly, my son and I, and drink to our precious imperfect life" (300). "Meeting Mrinal," like some of the stories in Arranged Marriage, highlights the protagonist's unfulfilled life and her decision not to remain passive, acquiescent and grief-stricken, but be a part of just and civilized America that looked a promising and fulfilling land. It is a telling story that makes "explicit an important psychological moment that many of the other characters experience—the women's lives are imperfect, but their victory lies in living" (Asian American Short Story Writers, 2003: 66). Asha, the protagonist of the story, does not feel shy of not remaining entangled in her past and its dizzy memories but takes a firm footing in order to be a part of the new world and its environment.

Looking at different stories included in Arranged Marriage (I have deliberately not taken up "Bats," "The Maid Servant's Story" and "Disappearance" into this study for the obvious reason that they are either set in India or do not throw sufficient light on the characters' diasporic experiences), the readers experience myriad layers of Indian diaspora of the characters whose mind remain in limbo—both, in their hostland and in their homeland. These characters, we have seen, try to locate their splintered selves back and, whether they succeed or fail, struggle to get fulfillment in the new world order. Quoting Divakaruni's own remarks in this connection will not be out of context when she says that she writes about the immigrant experiences of Indians because:

The underlying larger issue is of leaving home. Just about all of us have an experience of leaving home, how leaving home changes you and how when you go back, home is changed. It's never the same. And what of the home you carry with you? The sense of self. How do we deal with that as we move into a place where self means something quite different? If you repress your sense of your past and that heritage, that need comes out in other ways. It is a definite need in us, to know who we are in terms of where we come from" (San Francisco Chronicle, 2001: 79).

This is evident from Arranged Marriage where the characters jostle and find themselves fixed between remembering and re-membering in order to put their sense of dislocation under the carpet and achieve fulfilment.

References

- Benson, Heidi. "Poet, Novelist Chitra Banerjee Divakaruni." *San Francisco Chronicle*. April 29, 2001: 79.
- Davis, Rocio G. "Chitra Banerjee Divakaruni." *Asian American Short Story Writers*. Ed. Guiyou Huang. Westport: Greenwood Press, 2003.
- Divakaruni, Chitra Banerjee. *Arranged Marriage*. London: Black Swan, 1997. All the references from the book are included in the text.
- Divakaruni, Chitra Banerjee. "Chitra Banerjee Divakaruni." *Living in America: Poetry and Fiction by South Asian American Writers*. Ed.
- Roshni Rustomji-Kerns. Boulder: Westview Press, 1995.
- Gelfant, Balnchee H. ed. *The Columbia Companion to the Twentieth Century American Short Story*. New York: Columbia University Press, 2000.
- Haque, Rebecca. "Women of the South Asian Diaspora: Chitra Banerjee Divakaruni's *Arranged Marriage* and Ginu Kamanis's *Jungle Girl . The Indo American Review*. No. 9. 2000.
- Moka-Dias, Brunda. "Chitra Banerjee Divakaruni." *Asian American Novelists*. Ed. Emmanuel S. Nelson. Westport: Greenwood Press, 2000.
- Rushdie, Salman. "The Indian Writer in England." *The Eye of the Beholder: Indian Writing in English*. Ed. Maggie Butcher. London: Commonwealth Institute, 1983: 75-83.
- Tapping, Craig. "South Asia/North America: New Dwellings and the Past." *Reworldling: The Literature of the Indian Diaspora*. Ed. Emmanuel S. Nelson. New York: Greenwood Press, 1992.

Websites:

- <http://www.randomhouse.com/resources/bookgroup/divakaruni_bgc.html>
- <http://www.chitradivakruni.com/about/writing>
- <http://www.metroactive.com/papers/metro/10.03.96/books.9694.html>
- <http://www.time.com/time/daily/special/india/chitra. html>
- <http://www.sawnet.org/books/reviews.php>

14

OLD VALUES AND NEW DESIRES: EXPERIENCES OF EXPATRIATE WOMEN IN CHITRA BANEJEE'S ARRANGED MARRIAGE

-Amrit Kaur

Indian writing in English has come of age with the arrival of writers who are Non Resident Indians on the literary scene. While the major preoccupation of writers of earlier generation like R. K. Narayana, Raja Rao, Mulkraj Anand and Kamala Markandaya was sociological in terms of hunger, poverty, the new generation of writers such as Vikram Seth, Rohinton Mistry, Jhumpa Lahiri, Amit Chaudhary, Nina Abdullah, Shauna Singh Baldwin and Chitra Banerjee Divakaruni are basically concerned with deep cultural and philosophical problems that inevitably emerge in a transitional society which moves from a conservative and traditional social order to a liberal and open socio-cultural ethos.

Through this paper I attempt to explore the transformed lives of Indian women, both liberated and trapped by cultural changes on both sides of the ocean. These women struggle fiercely to carve out an identity of their own. They grow up on the edge of two often conflicting worlds. The boundaries between these worlds usually blurred, sometimes juxtaposed and often overlapped. They have one foot planted in the traditional world of their parents and grandparents within the home, the other rooted in the world outside the front door. The women who go to the US with their husbands or on study visas renegotiate their identities as women, wives and mothers. They struggle with their own sense of 'self' as they themselves adjust to a culture very different from that of their childhood and as they bring up their children in this rapidly changing and sometimes confusing world. These women have experienced immigration in various aspects of their lives. Their experiences span different generational. Religious and regional points of view: furthermore, their status as single, married or divorced women, as mothers, sisters or daughters, and as homemakers or professional women, adds additional layers to their lives as immigrants.

Immigrant women participate in American culture in all its contemporary diversity and intensity. They are very different from their parents, and the differences are evident in many ways. With respect to that very important life event, marriage, the generational differences become magnified, sometimes assuming crisis proportions. These women come from the culture in which arranged marriages have been the norm, valued for the protection and security afforded by family (not individual) selection and support systems. Marriage within same caste or group ensured that the young people shared similar cultural background and lifestyles, minimizing sources of difference between them. Extended family and caste-like group involvement in marriage network ensures stability. They also see the high divorce rate in western 'love marriage' societies and feel that arranged marriages are the better alternative.

Chitra Banerjee Divakaruni's book of short stories, *Arranged Marriage*, focuses on family arranged matches, centuries-old tradition in India. These stories about Indian Immigrant to the U.S. show how the dislocations of immigration are making this tradition problematic. The conflict between the traditions of her homeland and the culture of her and the culture of her adopted country is the focus of much of Divakaruni's writings, and it has made her acclaim and the 1996 American Book Award, constantly struggle with dual identities and values. Living in sin, indulging in an extramarital affair, the issue of personal space and the real meaning of love-the author holds up these concerns under a spotlight, concerns that have a completely different shade of meaning in an Indian context and present the interpretation in a western context. Her characters examine these concerns in the light of their evolving identities as American citizens and make choices that reveal a new emerging reality. This Calcutta born author, who shifted to the U.S. in 1976, at the age of 19, says, "what has impelled my writing so far is the desire to put women in the centre of stories, to have their voices be the voices of interpretation, their eyes the ones that we see through. There just hasn't been enough of that in the world, if you look back at literary history."

Thus, we find most of the stories in *Arranged Marriage* are about characters from the author's native region of Bengal and are told by female narrators in the first person singular point of view, often in the present tense, voice of intimacy and cinematic credibility.

There are no dramatic overtures, no startling revelations, no sudden complications. And this is precisely what makes her such an effective writer, this is exactly what gives her descriptions of women in arranged marriages a draconian element of common gloom. Let me describe some:

In 'Silver Pavements, Golden Roofs', the narrator Jayanti, comes to Chicago to stay with her aunt before beginning her graduate studies at an American University. When she last saw her aunt, Jayanti was only eight years old. The occasion was the aunt's arranged marriage in Calcutta with an Indian emigrant who, the matchmaker had assured her family, was the owner of an automobile empire in America. On arrival, Jayanti discovers that the man runs only a small auto-repair garage and the couple live in a dingy apartment in an undesirable part of the city. The aunt welcomes her warmly. Jayanti finds that her aunt stays home the whole time. At Jayanti's insistence, they both go out for a stroll in the neighborhood, which the aunt had long been forbidden to do by her husband. They are accosted by a gang of four white boys, shouting "nigger" and throwing slush at them. Badly shaken, the two women find their way home. Jayanti is so shocked and shattered that "I want to scream, or weep, or laugh, because, can't they see that I am not black at all but an Indian girl of good family? When our chauffeur Gurbans Singh drives me down the Calcutta streets in our silver-colored Fiat, people stop to whisper, 'Isn't that Jayanti Ganguli, daughter of the Bahavanipur Gangulis."

This is reminiscent of the novelist Bharati Mukharjee's statement in a published interview: "I am less shocked, less outraged and shaken to my core, by a purse snatching in New York city in which I lost all of my dowry gold....than I was by a simple question asked to in the summer of 1978 by three schoolboys on the Rosedale Subway Station platform in Toronto. Their question was, "Why don't you go back to Africa?"

Immigration to the U.S., the faraway dislocation, made this particular arranged marriage possible, without the customary verifications, between the working-class imposter and Jayanti's upper class aunt. Immigration also brought the couple into an extremely hostile social environment. Although the social environment that the Indian immigrants from the upper social classes to the U.S. come to is not overtly noxious, it exacts a poignant psychic cost-by challenging their traditional self-concept as integral parts of an extended Indian family and by pushing them instead into the American mould of autonomous, and all-too-often alienating, individualism.

This psychological struggle is visible in 'Meeting Mrinal', where Mahesh, the narrator's husband, is struggling to leave her for his red haired ex-secretary, Jassica, after a 20-year marriage (which initially had been, of course, an arranged marriage), a 17 years old son, and a plush home in Silicon valley.

"I can't take this anymore, Asha." All his life, he told me

then he'd been doing what other people wanted, being a dutiful son, then a responsible husband and father. Now he'd family found some one who made his feel alive, happy. He wanted the chance to really live his life before it was too late".

In 'Affair', two temperamentally ill matched Indo-American couples, whose marriages had been arranged on the basis of their horoscopes having matched "perfectly", divorce after many years of affluent living in Silicon valley. For two months before the split, Meena, a buoyant socialite, married to Srikant, a nerd (who gives his computer an adoring feminine name Lalita), has been having an affair with a middle-aged Euro-American man in her office. Abha, the narrator says about Meena:

"Perhaps it was because, in spite of her worldliness, Meena understood our Indian friends far less than I did. The men, for example, even the ones clustered around her, laughing at her jokes, they too would have things to say about her in the privacy of the men's room, things followed by winks and lewd, derisive laughter. For in spite of their Bill Blass suits and alligator-skin shoes and the sleek Benzes they still belonged to the villages of their fathers. Villages, where a woman caught in adultery made to ride around the market square on a donkey, her head shaved, her clothes stripped off her, while crowds jeered and pelted her with garbage."

"Clothes" is another interesting story that derives home a general point about the plight of women in arranged marriages, in a more general and distinct manner. It talks about a girl Sunita from a rural Indian town, who is married to a man, settled in the US who owns a general store. The story is again told from the perspective of the girl, but it has no elements of injustice or oppression. The husband Somesh is a good man, and he admittedly loves her and the girl's-in-laws are kind people, if somewhat strict in their demeanor. They don't even oppose her wish to teach in a school. Her husband dreams along with her about a life where they can earn enough money to live comfortably. He buys western clothes for her and she tries them at night, secretly from his parents. And then the dream world comes crashing down when one night Somesh is shot dead at his store. She is given a white saree to wear and everyone expects her to return to India. But she makes an important decision then to say back and fulfill her own and her husband's dream. She prefers a future in "a blouse and skirt the color of almonds", (bought by her husband) to a life in a white saree, bowing her veiled head like a 'Dove with cut off wings".

Because of widespread parental opposition to dating and 'love-marriages,' some times immigrant women are put into an either/or situation. They must trust their parents to arrange their marriages, or they must trust themselves. Whey they do trust themselves and act upon their own wishes, they sometimes elect to keep the marriage secret. 'The Word Love' is the story of one such girl who falls in love with an American brat soon after her arrival in the U.S. She moves into his apartment and is quite happy with him but cannot muster enough courage to disclose her live-in relationship to her widowed mother, who back home waits for her return, and plans an arranged marriage for her (for she is very competent in this job). All precautions are taken by her and her boyfriend to keep their secret but one fine morning he picks up the pone and finds her mother on the other end. The shock for the mother daughter duo is so great that their lives fall apart. Mother breaks all ties from her only daughter, even changing her will. Daughter desperately tries for reconciliation and forgiveness but fails and to her utter shock and despair finds that the mother's love was much stronger than the other one.

Thus it is the theme of immigrant conflict-old values and desires-that informs a lot of Divakaruni's work. And the challenges of writing about two distinct worlds are many. Most Indian scriptures talk of the sublimation of desire as a goal but when the author encountered a new meaning in the western model where decide is positive, charged with passion and ambition and often associated with goal-getters, it fired her to expose it in 'Arranged Marriage.' She opines, "I think desired are natural but we must examine them, see where they're leading us and manage them accordingly. It is when they control us that they lead to problems. Ultimately, as our scriptures indicate, one needs to rise above desire. For me, this means we do the things we do out of love, and not out of need."

Divakaruni places the issue of culture straddling in perspective when she talks of values. "Values are constantly in flux. I think as I grow and understand more about life, my values shift-new things become more important and the same happens to my characters". Values that empower women have become increasingly important to her. Some things are same everywhere like courage, integrity, truth, compassion. Her characters struggle with trying to hold on to them.

To conclude, Chitra Divakaruni's exquisitely wrought debut collection of short stories subtly chronicles the accommodation and the rebellion-Indian born girls and women in America undergo as they balance old treasured beliefs and surprising new desires. Every story is complete in itself, together they create a tapestry as colorful as delicate and as enduring as the finest silk sari. She leads her characters to surface into maturity, raising their heads above floods of ignorance. Her women characters are depicted as victims of changed circumstances who struggle hard to survive in the unknown society in which they find themselves-sometimes by choice and sometimes by chance.

❑❑❑❑

15

Voices of Sanity Amid Communal Frensy In Shashi Tharoor's Riot

-Jyoti Yadav and Karan Singh Yadav

Diaspora originated from the Greek word 'diaspeirein' and is defined as "the dispersion or spread of any people from their original homeland."[1] The term was initially applied to dispersal of Jews from their homeland in 6-8th centuries B.C. Indian Diaspora refers to migration of Indian to various continents in search of greener pastures. Owing to the process of globalization and other peculiar socio-economic conditions Indians constitute a respectable position in various countries of the world. Diasporic writings constitute a genre in themselves with its peculiar distinctiveness such as 'search for identity', 'East-West encounter', 'center and marginalization' etc. One dimension of the diasporic literature which has remained largely ignored by the critics is the secular character of these writings. Bred in the soil of a culture which values religion as the private affair of an individual, as well as having the added opportunity of seeing their own homeland from a distance, these writers are usually free of dogmatic influences of their religion. Their writings are full of anguish at the communal frenzy of their fellow countrymen and try to trace the way out of this labyrinth of hate and bigotry. Before evaluating this particular trait in one of the novel of Shashi Tharoor aptly named as Riot, it would be interesting to first examine communalism and its various facets.

Communalism, ethnic conflicts and their twin sister terrorism are no longer confined to the most backward, politically unstable, third world countries, their usually supposed den. For a long time these were seen as the problems of economically backward regions and got sanction or at least a nod of indulgence from the full proof security vaults of powers that be. But the ironical lesson learnt at a great cost in the post 9/11 scenario is that these monsters are no longer confined to the countries of so-called third world, but are asserting themselves with greater vehemence everywhere. The recent ethnic riots in France, confirmed the fears that our more civilized and supposedly more liberal societies are as prone to be torn apart by these disintegrating forces as their lesser developed, more conservative counterparts.

Communalism—"the sense of religious chauvinism that transforms itself into bigotry, and sometimes violence, against the followers of other faiths"[2]—has a much checkered history in the Indian Sub-Continent. There is hardly any country left in the South Asian region, which is untouched by this Frankenstein monster. Ethnic conflicts take their sustenance from the diversity in cultural, social and religious differences in the societies living in close proximities. These diverse elements instead of giving them strength make them susceptible to the vested interest in all the communities who exploit them for the sake of politics or other mercenary margins. Bipin Chandra identifies three basic elements of communalism: i. A belief that people who follow the same religion have common secular interests i.e. common political, economic, social and cultural interests ii. In a multi-religious society like India, the secular interests such as social, cultural, economic, and political of one religion are dissimilar with the followers of other religions and iii. Communalism arises when the interests of different religions are seen as mutually incompatible, antagonistic and hostile.[3]

The communalists very cleverly exploit some of the dissatisfactions and grievances of the community, some of them genuine and others imaginary to their full benefit. Asghar Ai Engineer in Islam and Muslims: A Critical Reassessment concurs: "Communalism breeds very fast in the soil of genuine grievances. If the grievances remain unattended, communalism may result in separatism. [...] The entire history of the partition of this country is proof of this, if any proof is needed."[4]

The communal elements in each society pretend to be inheritors of a glorious past to which they clamour adherence and would like to revert to that past, usually an imaginary one. For it, all courses to rational thinking are thrown to the winds and faith becomes the sole medium to prove their narrow, self-aggrandizing interests. Their Gods are false Gods of Rabindranath Tagore who 'kill for sport.' A fanatic reveres not God but Satan:

"In the temple he raises the blood-stained banner

And worships the devil in the name of God."[5]

It is ironical that while the extremists from both sides pretend to be each other's worst enemies, they actually supplement and complement each community's hatred and bitterness for each other. Hatred in the environment of mutual distrust has a cascading effect, it triggers a chain reaction in which rumour-mongers have a free hand to augment and play upon their fears. Asghar Ali Engineer notes in this connection: "When the deprived religious groups or communities express their aspirations through activated primordial consciousness, what we can term as religious fundamentalism, the privileged communities feel threatened and take recourse to the same strategy. Thus begins the nasty process of minority and majority communalisms reinforcing each other."[6] Thus clamour for 'the religion is in danger' reaches to such a pitch that soon all neighbourliness which they have shared for ages with all their common customs and distinct identities is drowned in cries of 'blood for blood' and a human being is transformed into a fiend of hate and violence. V.K.R.V. Rao in his book The Current Indian Crisis: Darkness before Dawn wonders in this connection: "One just does not understand what it is that sets of a frenzy of inter-communal killing and destruction of property on account of some incident or other involving one or more individuals of one or the other community and the swiftness with which either community as a whole gets identified with the conflict in spite of its being the handiwork of some miscreants who are to be found in both the communities."[7] The way out of this labyrinth of mutual mistrust and hatred lies in curbing this demon of sectarianism and ethnical conflicts by seeing it its true colours and identifying and segregating those elements who feed it and fighting them at all fronts-social, political, ideological and legal. Nothing less than a full-fledged war on this fiend of terror can have some chances of any success, such are the heavy odds against which all the voices of sanity are pitted against.

Shashi Tharoor presents a really grim picture of society torn by bloody riots of Hindus and Muslims in 1989 in his novel aptly entitled the 'Riot.' Written in an epistolary form the novel traces the developments leading to the death of Priscilla Hart, an American volunteer working for an NGO HELP-US in a small town of North India Zalilpur. Priscilla becomes a victim of the atmosphere of hatred and animosity between Hindus and Muslims of the city. Though she does not belong to either of the warring factions, her presence 'at the wrong place at the wrong time' becomes the apparent reason for her stabbing. There are deeper motives at play also, with writer refusing to assign a single person or reason as the cause of her death. She may have been killed by Ali, the Muslim driver whose wife was helped by Priscilla in her abortion, Makhan Singh, the father of deceased Anup who was incited by Ram Charan Gupta, or even by the disciples of Swamy, whose help Geetha solicited in her efforts to wean away her husband from Priscilla. Whoever may be the real culprit, the meanings are same, innocence and love become the first victims in this whirlpool of rapacity of mutual disbelief and animosity.

The voices of sanity in this melee of distrust and acrimony are those of Professor Sarwar, a Professor of History from Delhi University, District Magistrate, V. Laxman, Superintendent of Police Gurinder, and Gurinder's father. For Professor Sarwar Hindus and Muslims share not only composite culture but also composite religiosity. There are many saintly figures in India who are worshipped by both the communities with equal religious fervour and thus there is a need to remind people that together with all the differences in the observance of religious rites "tolerance is also a tradition in India, that communal crossovers are as common as communal clashes" (64). For it Professor Sarwar is working on the life of Ghazi Miyan, a Muslim warrior saint of 11th century. Ghazi Miyan has been canonized in popular memory of Hindus as an incarnation of Lord Krishna, as a saviour of cows from a Raja Sohal Deo. His duty as a historian, Professor Sarwar feels, is to present "nonsectarian histories of sectarian strife" (64) which can only be accomplished if people with nonpartisan outlook come together to uphold the multiculturalism of Indian society.

Prof. Sarwar dismisses those Hindu chauvinists who claim that Muslims have been responsible for the partition of India and their nationalism as such is questionable. He cites Maulana Azad's speech as the president of Indian National Congress at Ramgarh in 1940 wherein Maulana declared that he was proud of being an Indian Muslim and that Islam had as great claim to India as a religion as Hinduism. While asserting his claim to be a part of "that indivisible unity that is Indian Nationality" (108) Azad pointed out that "It was India's historic destiny that many human races and cultures and religions should flow to her, and that many a caravan should rest here....One of the last of these caravan was that of the followers of Islam. They came here and settled for good. We brought our treasures with us, and India too was full of the riches of her own precious heritage. We gave her what she needed most, the most precious of gifts from Islam's treasury, the message of human equality. Full eleven centuries have passed by since then. Islam has now as great a claim on the soil of India as Hinduism" (108). It would be pertinent to note here what Wilfred Cantwell Smith in Modern Islam in India: A Social Analysis observes about the indivisible unity of Hindus and Muslims in India. The writer grants that "deep and subtle bonds had developed between the Hindus and Muslims in India which endure today even after the partition of the country into two—bonds of language and region, of temporal and cultural values, of literature, history, and traditions. In spite of differing philosophies of religion, the Islamic doctrine of 'brotherhood of all men' and the Hindu doctrine of 'different roads to the same truth' had been subtly drawn together into an amorphous ideal of mutual tolerance and generosity that was peculiarly and characteristically Indian."[8] Professor Sarwar refutes the charges that it were Muslim who were responsible for dividing the country, he rather puts the blame on British, Muslim League and Congress equally. It is a great tragedy of this country's Muslims that instead of people like Azad who epitomized the sensibility of true Indian Muslims, people such as Jinnah triumphed and spoke for India's Muslims.

Prof. Sarwar is not ready to accept the second-class citizenship offered by Hindu radical outfits such as Visva Hindu Parishad, Bajrang dal and Shiv Sena who want to reverse whatever we have achieved throughout the ages. Affirming his very Indianness through the tastes and outlook common to the people of this country, he says: "I can eat a masala dosa at the Coffee House, chew a pan afterwards and listen to Ravi Shankar playing rag darbari, and I celebrate the Indianness in myself with each note. I hear the Muslim Dagar brothers sing Hindu devotional songs, and then I attend a qawwali performance by one of our country's greatest exponents of this Urdu musical form, who happens to be a Hindu, Shankar Shambhu, and I am transported as he chants the long list of Muslim pirs to whom he pays devotional tribute before his rendition" (113). He rightly identifies the affliction of Indian society with this canker of divisionism as "the intellectual cancer of thinking of "us" and "them." (114). For him, minority is not a mathematical concept, rather it is "a sense of powerlessness, of being out of the mainstream, of being here on sufferance" (115). To Professor Sarwar India with its multiculturalism and diverse identities is the only option available to us, if our country is to exist: "An India that denies itself to some of us could end up being denied to all of us. This would be a second partition: and a partition in the Indian soul would be as bad as a partition in the Indian soil. For my sons, the only possible idea of India is that of a nation greater than the sum of its parts. An India neither Hindu nor Muslim, but both. This is the only India that will allow them to continue to call themselves Indian" (115-116).

Professor Sarwar rightly considers Ram Janambhoomi agitation as a growing signal of bigotry and intolerance in Indian society. Refuting the claims of historians who assert that the dilapidated structure of Babri Masjid was an erstwhile temple, he speaks out with concern at the role of Hindu chauvinists in indulging in half- truths and misinformation. According to him "the bigots who spearhead it want to reinvent the past to suit their aspirations for the present. If we allow them to do it now, here, they will turn their attentions to something else, and the whole orgy of hate and violence will start again. If they get away with attacking Muslims today, they'll hit Christians tomorrow. And at a fundamental level, intolerance is the real enemy" (183).

Laxman, the district magistrate, is another voice of sanity in the atmosphere of flared up passions and bigotry. He has a deep aversion for the forces of so-called Hindu revivalism. He praises Hinduism as the "only major religion in the world that does not claim to be the only true religion" thus making him "congenial to be able to face my fellow human beings of other faiths without being burdened by the conviction that I am embarked upon a 'true path' that they have missed" (144). He understands the essentially tolerant nature of Hinduism which has been its greatest strength from centuries making it absorb as diverse influences as came its way. He is full of praise for the resilience and freedom this religion offers to him without burdening him with any kind of compulsory rituals: "As a Hindu I claim adherence to a religion without an established church, or priestly papacy, a religion whose rituals and customs I am free to reject, a religion that does not oblige me to demonstrate my faith by any visible sign, by subsuming my identity in any collectivity, not even by a specific day or time or frequency of worship [...] As a Hindu I subscribe to a creed that is free of the restrictive dogma of holy writ, that refuses to be shackled to the limitations of a single holy book" (144). That is why Laxman is ashamed when the followers of this "large, eclectic, agglomerative" Hinduism which "understands that faith is a matter of hearts and minds, not of bricks and stone" (145) show rigidity and want to destroy the worshipping places of followers of other faiths. It appears an affront to him that the essentially liberal and broadminded nature of Hinduism is being sullied by the people with vested interests who do not understand their religion. These fanatics are unable to realize that for a Hindu, religion is "an intensely personal matter, that prayer is between you and whatever image of your maker you choose to worship" (143). Laxman fully appreciates the strengths of Hinduism which have made it possible for it to survive such a long time. Hinduism has not diminished despite centuries of foreign invading and has rather become richer due to these diverse influences: "Hinduism is no monolith; its strength is found within each Hindu, not in the collectivity. As a Hindu, I take no pride in wanting to destroy othe. people's symbols, in hitting others on the head because of the cut of their beard or the cuts of their foreskins. I am proud of my Hinduism: I take pride in its diversity, in its openness, in religious freedom" (146). He openly criticizes Hindu fanatics like Mr. Gupta who claim to speak on behalf of all Hindus. These people, according to him, speak of Hinduism "as a label of identity, not a set of humane beliefs" (147).

The politics of division has created fissures and gaping sores in our society. One obvious result of it has been that "Hindu chauvinism has emerged from the competition for resources in a contentious democracy" (145). Laxman poses questions before those people who claim to be the defenders of Hinduism and advocate militant approach for the construction of temple at Ayodhya: "If the Muslims of the 1520s acted out of ignorance and fanaticism, should Hindus act the same way in the 1980s? By doing what you propose to do, you will hurt the feelings of the Muslims of today, who did not perpetrate the injustices of the past and who are in no position to inflict injustice upon you today; you will provoke violence and rage against your own kind; you will tarnish the name of the Hindu people across the world; and you will irreparably damage your own cause. Is this worth it?"(146)

Gurinder's father stops Gurinder from resigning his post on the brutal killing of his nephew in the riots of 1984. For him, as for every right thinking individual, India is a repertoire of their hopes and aspirations. Its Indianness lies in its impartiality and neutrality. Indian for the elder generation represented a land of equal opportunities for all without any discrimination on the basis of caste and creed. It was never supposed to be a theocratic state like Pakistan: "Since the days of Gandhi, we have tried to build a country that is everyone's and no one's, a country that excludes nobody, a country that no one group can claim is exclusively theirs. When Jinnah and the Muslim League wanted to create a country for Muslims, their Pakistan, did the Congress leaders say fine, w will create a country for Hindus? The whole point about India is that this is a country for everybody, and everybody has the duty, the obligation to work to keep it that way. To fight to keep it that way"(197). This forceful plea strikes favourable resonance in the heart of Gurinder who ultimately feels his responsibility towards the nation and decides to keep his job.

Thus Shashi Tharoor presents his commitment to the secular India as an amalgam of diverse cultural, social and economic influences through his characters who are liberal, rational and open-minded. These characters, and the writer seems to agree with them, voice their staunch faith in the indivisible unity of India in which every citizen has equal right to live and prosper. Communalism can be warded off only through the concerted efforts of each one of us. To flinch from our duty of protesting, when the injustice is being heaped upon our fellow human beings, would be tantamount to lending a helping hand to the crime. The sure result of this crime of passivity and neglect would be as German theologian Pastor Martin Niemoeller averred in connection with Nazi holocaust:

At first they came for the Jews, and I did not speak out, because I was not a Jew. Then they came for the communists, and I did not speak out because I was not a communist. Then they came for the trade unionists, and I did not speak out because I was not a trade unionist. Then they came for me—and there was no one left to speak out for me (184).

Diaspora, due to the spatial and temporal distance of the writer from his homeland and the experience of living in alien culture, gives him an added advantage of a neutral observer. Further, he imbibes, consciously or unconsciously, the yardsticks of the culture of his adopted land. It also leads to frequently observed complacency and superfluity as far as the depiction of complex Indian reality is concerned. These writers are charged, somewhat correctly, of adopting a morally superior tone and an elevated position. The diasporic writers bred on the alien soil and imbibing ideas put to them through the media or their brief jaunts at India see their mother land with borrowed spectacles. Their case is no different from the typical case of a migrated Indian who has been "exposed to western ideas, educational processes, and power structures. He approaches his own society and culture through western norms; he is the product of the impact of westernization on Indian life no matter how thin or superficial it may be [...] This is the problem which is shared by expatriates, immigrants and post colonials alike. They are on the periphery and their selves are divided."[9] The hackneyed pictures of diasporic writers sometimes lack verisimilitude and their forays into either idolization of mystical India or a regression into contempt and loathing are too insistent to miss. That is the reason why the outsider's view of India often tends to be either antiquated or arbitrary and deficient. This view of an outsider tends to become too insistent and is repeated with alarming frequency in novel after novel.

To point out this is not to negate the importance of diasporic location, the position of an outsider/insider who looks within his homeland and finds something amiss. Shashi Tharoor, too, adopts this position when he finds India torn by communalism destroying much that is precious to him and others like him. Secularism as a theory may be a western construct yet it has been an inalienable part of Indian sensibility since centuries and Shashi Tharoor's situation as a diasporic writer makes it easier for him to see it and appreciate it.

References

Catherine Soanes and Angus Stevenson, ed., Oxford Dictionary of English,

IInd ed. (Oxford: Oxford University Press, 2003) 481.

- [2]Shashi Tharoor, Riot (2001; New Delhi: Viking; London: Penguin Books Ltd., 2003) 44. Further references are from the same edition.
- [3]Quoted in R.C. Vermani, Colonialism and Nationalism in India (New Delhi: Gitanjali Publishing House, 2000) 304.
- [4]Asghar Ali Enginner, Islam and Muslims: A Critical Reassessment (Jaipur: Printwell Publishers, 1985) 265.
- [5]Rabindra Nath Tagore, "False Religion" Songs and Sonnets, ed. Sushil Kumar (New Delhi: Vikas Publishing House Pvt, Ltd., 1996) 12.
- [6]Asghar Ali Enginner, Islam and Muslims: A Critical Reassessment (Jaipur: Printwell Publishers, 1985) 264.
- [7]V.K.R.V. Rao, The Current Indian Crisis: Darkness before Dawn (Allahabad: Vohra Publishers and Distributors, 1984) 23.
- [8]Quoted in Rajni Kothari, Politics in India (New Delhi: Orient Longman Ltd., 1970) 62.
- [9]Jasbir Jain, ed. Writers of Indian Diaspora: Theory and Practice (Jaipur: Rawat Publications, 1998)

16

Diasporic Element of 'Liminality' in V. S. Naipaul's Early Novels and his Travelogues on India

-Sanjiv Kumar

The term 'diaspora' has varied definitions and connotations associated to it. Most of the standard dictionaries define the term as dispersion of Jews outside Israel from 6th century B.C., when they were exiled to Babylonia, and also a dispersion of people from their original homeland or the community formed by such people. It has its origin in ancient Greek implying "a scattering or sowing of seeds". The term was coined as the synonym for the 'expatriates' 'immigrants' or 'exiles' in the colonial period, when people left their homelands and settled either in some other colonies or in a colonizer country with the pursuit of better prospects and individual freedom. As a result, the native population was displaced from their home, not only physically but emotionally too; ultimately making them unhoused nomads with a persistent feeling of nostalgia, rootlessness, alienation, ambivalence and cultural insecurity. It is a journey- 'looking backward while moving forward'. An expatriate is not only the man who travels across the physical boundaries but his imagination, culture, psyche, sociology and anthropology also travel with him, causing a sort of perpetual conflict of 'fluid-identity' and 'alternative-centers'. Torn between two distinct worlds, diasporas may be termed as, according to Victor Turner 'transitional beings' or 'liminal personae', as they oscillate between one culture and another. These diasporas tend to move in an obvious circle i.e. from home culture to alien culture leading to assimilated culture which is possible only with 'cultural liminality-within the nation', according to Homi K. Bhabha. Edward W. Said adds to the definition and classification of diasporas saying-

"The person who finds his homeland sweet is still a tender beginner, he to whom every soil is as his native one is already strong, but he is perfect to whom the entire world is a foreign place" and "a survival infact is about the connection between things".

Different themes reflecting diasporic ambivalence are projected in the writings of almost all the prominent Indian Diasporic writers including Amitav Ghosh, Jhumpa Lahiri, Anita Desai, Salman Rushdie, Rohinton Mistry, Vikram Seth, Bharti Mukherjee, Vikram Seth, Chitra Banerjee Dvakaruni, Uma Parmeshwaram, Nina Abdullah, Arun Joshi, Amit Chaudhary and V.S. Naipual dealing with the common themes of rejection, anxiety, love-hate relationship with in two cultures and melancholy.

As the contention of the paper is to present the diasporic element of liminality in V. S. Naipual, an incisive analysis of his early fiction and Indian trilogy will be made. Encarta World English Dictionary defines 'liminal' as 'belonging to the point of conscious awareness below which something can not be experienced or felt,, derived from Latin 'limen' implying threshold.

Naipaul was born to the parents of Indian descent at Chaguanas in Central Trinidad, which was one of the British colonies. He could have only the second hand account about the migration of his family from India. In his essay 'Prologue to an Autobiography,' he says-

"In 1948 I won a Trinidad government scholarship.....I decided to use mine to do English at Oxford. I didn't want a degree. I wanted only to get away."

The irresistible fascination for the West and the dreams to have a sense of gratification and achievement, mixed with his apathetic attitude towards Trinidad, made him settle down among the colonizers. His strong sense of 'homelessness' and 'unhoused sensibility' turns to be extra-ordinarily intense, as he feels twice displaced i.e. firstly from the land of his ancestors and then from his own birthplace to which he never finds himself attached. It was so because, according to Lillian Feder who says that he was deprived of a national identity, enthusiasm, dignity and pride in his youth, due to the heritage of colonialism, past of slavery, indentured labour, and continual immigration. Homi K. Bhabha's concept of 'transition of culture and the obvious conflict between the East-Indian Brahmanic traditions and West-Indian aliens is the core of his early novels. The enactment of Ramayana along with other associated rites concerning marriages, last-rites, use of Hindi etc. are posed to counter the culture of Carribean island. The continual changes of the houses by his father i.e. from Chaguanas to Port of Spain in 1938, to Diego Martin in 1940, back again to Port of Spain in 1941, and ultimately to their own house in Nepaul Street in 1947, work as the addition of fuel to the fire for V. S. Naipaul in strengthening his sense of dislocation in island. Like all other diasporic writers, Naipaul's sense of identity and belongingness is at stake. His fractured-self asserts itself through his writings. For example, his masterpiece 'A House for Mr. Biswas' is derived from his father's life-long quest for finding a 'home' in the world after the migration of his family from Eastern-India as indentured labourers.

After settling there at London, his four novels were published in succession from 1955 to 1959 i.e. 'Mystic Masseur', 'Miguel Street', 'Suffrage of Elvira' and 'A House for Mr. Biswas', exhibiting the picture of the irrelevant society which he could hardly manage to escape. In The Mystic Masseur', Ganesh fails as a masseur and converts himself into a Hindu sage with a turban and loincloth. Pt. Ganesh attracts large following lured more by his airs than by his wisdom. This successful sage turns into a political figure named G. Ramsay Muir proving that status devolves from political power indicating the mimicry of the picaroon society in an era of lost identities. In the second novel 'The Suffrage of Elvira', the typical democratic system of elections is mimicked in a society, which has not so far developed the de-colonized tastes. A district election in Trinidad shows the campaigning as a carnival, a ritual of apprehensions in the guise of democracy. Elections are treated as only the rites to legitimize an indigenous order in a multi-racial post-colonial society lost in oblivion. In 'The Miguel Street', Naipaul tries to recreate the world full of violence, corruption, brutality, false dreams and a hopeless hope of bringing a sense of fulfillment in Trinidad. The street mentioned is the projection of mixture of races i.e. black, brown, Indians, Spanish, Portuguese and even whites all enveloped by ultimate despair, humiliation and aimlessness. The nostalgic feelings of the immigrants are put in parallel to the personal feelings of the writer. 'A House for Mr. Biswas,' the fourth novel of the early phase, which he considered as his closest to heart, is the autobiographical account of his father's quest for identity in a colonial society. He himself admits in his essay 'Foreward to A House for Mr. Biswas'-

"Of all my books, this is the one that is the closest to me. It is the most personal, created out of what I saw and felt as a child. It becomes the story of a man's search for a house and all that the possession of one's own house implies."

His drifted self is exposed nakedly through the novel where Mr. Biswas, the mouthpiece of writer's father undertakes a war to assert his selfhood and individuality in spite of his fractured self. The novel represents not only the trauma of its protagonist rather Mr. Biswas is a tool to symbolize the sense of alienation, homelessness and disillusioned diasporic Indian at Trinidad. The East-west encounter also comes to the front within the framework of the novel. Bruce aptly remarks-

"Biswas lives in an impoverished colonial society in which most people do not read, education is not available, English is not always used for conversations. Literary models come from abroad and are inappropriate to local society. Literature therefore, seems dead, part of the European past."

Besides, the novel presents a beautiful insight into the psyche of the protagonist who dares the feudal set up represented by Tulsi House in spite of the fact that he has not ample sources. The life-long journey to have a house of his own again shows the torn-identity of an Indian exile. His self-assertion turns destructive when he finds himself helpless and broken from inside. The objective description of Trinidadian plight for the dislocated Indians and Africans was like a reaction of a sensitive and concerned writer. Ends of the novel justifies the intention of the novelist as Mr. Biswas dies after realizing his long cherished dream of occupying a house showing the hope even for the wretched, adrift and homeless in the colonial world.

After discussing his early writings based on Trinidad, an elaborate discussion of his popular Indian travelogues will be made to defend the hypothesis. His first journey to India was not an ordinary journey rather it had an emotional background i.e. he intended to witness the much exaggerated and glorified dream-land from which his grant parents shifted to Trinidad as indentured labourers. Moreover, he was expecting that his quest for the identity and home would be over, reaching there in India. His illusion regarding his strong sense of attachment to the India of his ancestors also shattered when he undertook a journey to India in 1962. He records his experiences after feeling hurt and finding himself lost among the post-colonials of India in his book 'An Area of Darkness', the first among the three. To quote Bruce Kind-

"There is a sense of humiliation, of a personal frustration that the India of his secret imagination and longings, of his imagined origins, is another oriental third world country despite its size and ancient history. He is angry at the dirt, decay, incompetence, corruption, passivity,...by the way Gandhi has been turned into another saint...."

He feels that present India lacks an idea of its past and culture which was strong enough to rejuvenate it. His idea of homelessness so far is further defended after his observation of the hopeless picture of India. He says-

"It was only now, as my experience of India defined itself more properly against nay own homelessness, that I saw how close in the past years I had been to the total Indian negation, how much it had become the basis of thought and feeling".

He could find some comfort in his agony only when he reached Srinagar. His visit to Amarnath and Simla gave him certain sense of pleasure due to the aesthetic beauty that encircled these sites. His first visit to India brought him closer to a bold understanding of the world when he started feeling that he did not belong to India too. His emphasis o objectivity and distinct identity even among his own people perhaps, is the great hindrance in his proper understanding of India of his grandparents. He even does not allow the boy of his own family in India to ride his car in spite of IAS officer's reminding question-"Shall we take him on?" There was a response- "No, let the idler walk". His sense of apathy towards Trinidad now seemed to have reproduced for India. He himself confesses in the same book-"It was a journey that ought not to have been made; it had broken my life into two".

The second travelogue based on his voyage to India 'India: A Wounded Civilization' was written after his visit during 1975 to 1976 with a rational realization that "I can not travel only for the sights. I am at once too close and too far." It shows his dilemma regarding his emotional tie with India. During this visit, he did not seem to be sensitive or vulnerable. He observed every thing from an entirely objective perspective. His snobbish dislike of beggars and downtrodden remains intact during this visit too. He sees the inefficiency of India in parting from the conservative ideas, which is a deterrent in its way to success. He says-

"The crisis of India is not only political or economic. The larger crisis is of a wounded civilization that has at last become aware of its inadequacies and is without the intellectual means to move ahead."

He implicit support to emergency, criticism of Gandhi, description of Vinobha Bhave, visit to Bombay, Vijay Nagar, and criticism of Shiv Sena and Naxalite Movement showed that he penetrated deeper this time in the concerns of India but without any sense of loss or despair.

The last travelogue among this series 'India: A Million Mutinies Now' records varying emerging agitations even after independence. Plight of the Muslims represented by Anwar and his father who live a suppressed life, considerate attitude towards the minorities, movement of dalits, and criticism of Shiv Sena again and the operation 'blue-star' dominate this book. His defense of minorities suggests his own inner anguish he might have experienced being the member of the minority community at Trinidad. His concern for the Dalits may be witnessed in the lines-

"They had ceased to be abstractions. They had begun to do things for themselves. They had become people stressing their particularity, just as better off groups in India stressed their particularities".

These three books on India themselves show a remarkable paradigmatic shift in his attitude even towards India leading his to be more tolerant, optimistic and objective.

17

Diaspora: Vision and Image

The effervescence of diaspora gives rise to a sense of disillusionment. This sense is infect, the consciousness of exile. Such a consciousness is a reflection of crisis of a diasporic community, at being denied a central and nurturing tradition. Tradition nurtures, it offers the consistency of a bloodline, a springboard for evaluation, growth and experimentation. The diasporic community has been cut off from its own tradition and culture from osmosis and introspection, and from its own context with in it, how it deals with this trauma, and this crisis of identity is perhaps the great problem.

Diaspora raises questions regarding the definitions of 'HOME' and 'NATION'. It also shows the attachment of immigrants to the homeland. Many overseas Indians made money, but the incidence of mental breakdown is highest among this section. The following work represents the experiences of migration and question of relatedness to homeland of Indian born individuals [and also people of other nations with Indian blood] who have taken the citizenship of other countries.

The sketch 'In limine' is related to the feelings and emotions of an immigrant thinking about where is his past? Where are his roots? The bird in the background represents his present environment and the threshold shows his memories from his homeland. This memory when formulated in a certain manner, gives him a sense of distinct identity.

The work 'Amor patrie' describes that the character that is flying has deepest emotional attachment to country of his origin. The migrant from India has memories of his roots, having parted from his homeland. Holding the flag of nation or home he is focusing on relationship with his motherland. This also shows the strength of emotional ties between him and the motherland.

In 'A' la Volee' a bird, symbol of an immigrant is flying high, but not uprooted in real sense. The chain holding the root and bird shows its connectivity to originating background. It is maintaining some sort of tenuous link with the motherland. Here chain is representing 'Force of Bonding'.

The sketch 'Volia' describes the story of an immigrant who has parted from his homeland and reached upstairs and established an identity with pieces of geographical space, and sense of place. The ladder shows his progress. The connection with his homeland is shown by a rope. This rope presents that he has not been cut off from his own tradition and culture.

The drawing 'Demi Jour' shows that the diasporic community is standing in a cave. The image of figures is not clear. Here half light or subdued light presents several conceptions about the sense of identity. These immigrants entered into a new world, where their images cannot be identified. They are in search of their own identities. They know the name of the place they stay, they know their immediate surroundings, but they tend to look towards a future – tomorrow and day after tomorrow – of a better future may be.

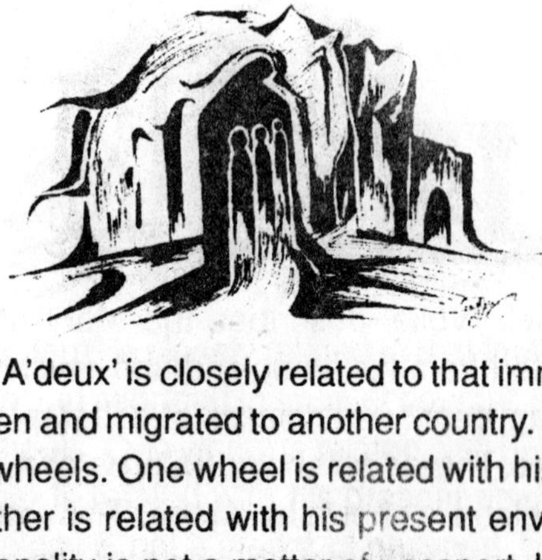

The work 'A'deux' is closely related to that immigrant who is an Indian citizen and migrated to another country. He is standing between two wheels. One wheel is related with his tradition and culture and other is related with his present environment. For him, dual nationality is not a matter of passport, but a personal identity. Recalling his roots and seeking to locate himself in new culture, he is between the two – own experience of migration and own questioning of his relatedness.

The work 'In medias res' tells that the character is surrounded with many things i.e. where is his home? Where his feet are? Where his heart is? Residing distant lands, he has succeeded spectacularly in his chosen profession by dint of his single-minded dedication and hard work. What is more, he has retained his emotional, cultural and spiritual links with the country of his origin. He is surrounded with complexity of historical and cultural dualities, conflicts, contradictions and ambivalences.

In 'Quantum mutates ab illo!' the character is looking at his own image in a mirror. The image is asking that what he was? And what he is? His image is sad in the mirror. He feels that he has lost his own identity. He has been cut off his past and his roots because he is an expatriate Indian.

The sketch ' Adsum' ' narrates the story of an immigrant who is explaining that where he is. On the one side of picture, there are empty photo frames lying in his native country. These frames show the absence of the photograph of character. On the other side, character is there and saying, 'I am here and making my presence felt. The society must feel about me, I am part of Indian Diaspora.'

In 'Impasse' the character is in difficult state. He is in turmoil. He cannot solve his own problem because on one hand he is part of India and on the other hand he is part of Diaspora and he loves both. How he deals with it, is perhaps the great problem confronting him in this situation?

'Ad referndum' shows Indian citizen moved to other places for better establishment. They struggled for getting decent jobs, and developed a feeling of restricted space. Here, open eye is germinating the feeling of nationhood for them and being recognized by others. It symbolizes the vision for further consideration.

LIST OF CONTRIBUTORS

Bhim S. Dahiya, Former Vice-Chancellor of Kurukshetra University, is a retired Professor of English from the same university. He is an eminent scholar and literature critic. He has visited abroad and lectured on different topics of literature in different conferences and seminars. He has a History of English literature and different volumes on Hemingway to his credit. He is currently Professor, Dr. Sarup Singh Chair in the Department of English, Kurukshetra University.

Tejinder Kaur, Ph.D, Professor of English, Directorate of Correspondence Courses, Panjabi University, Patiala. Punjab

Ritu Sharma, Ph.D., Dept. of English, D.A.V. College, Pundri, Haryana

Neer Kanwal Mani, Ph.D., Dept. of English, Govt. P. G. College, Faridabad, Haryana

Anita Sharma, Ph.D., Dept. of English, R. K. M.V., Simla, HImachal Pradesh

Dr Kiran Kamboj, Ph.D., ADC, O/o Higher Education Commissioner, Haryana, Chandigarh

Alka Sharma, Ph.D., Dept. of English, S. D. College, Ambala Cantt, Haryana

Bhan Singh, M. Phil, Dept. of English, D.A.V. College, Pundri, Haryana

Suman Bhatia, M. Phil, Dept. of English, Govt. College, Ambala Cantt, Haryana

Sarika Goyal, M. Phil, Dept. of English, D.A.V. College, Abohar, Punjab

A. K. Singh, Ph.D., Dept. of English, Govt. P. G. College, Faridabad, Haryana

Sanjeev Kumar, M. Phil, Dept. of English, Govt. College, Ambala Cantt, Haryana

Amrit Kaur, Ph. D., Lecturer in English, G. N. Khalsa College, Ymauna Nagar

Jyoti Yadav, M. Phil, Dept. of English, Govt. College, Ateli, Haryana

Karan Yadav, Ph. D., Dept. of English, Govt. College, Ateli, Haryana

Sanjiv Kumar, M. Phil, Govt. College, Kishan Nagar, Haryana

Gagandeep Kaur, Dept of Fine Arts, Govt. College, Ambala Cantt, Haryana

❑❑❑❑